THE IDEA
OF A UNIVERSITY

THE IDEA
OF A UNIVERSITY

by

CARDINAL JOHN HENRY NEWMAN

SAINT BENEDICT PRESS
in association with
BARONIUS PRESS
MMVI

This edition first published in 2006 by

SAINT BENEDICT PRESS

Charlotte · North Carolina · www.saintbenedictpress.com

in association with

BARONIUS PRESS LTD

London · United Kingdom · www.baroniuspress.com

© Baronius Press Limited, 2006.

10 9 8 7 6 5 4 3 2 1

ISBN (10 digit): 1-905574-19-3
ISBN (13 digit): 978-1-905574-19-3

This edition has been re-typeset using the text of the 1907 edition originally published by Longmans, Green and Co., London.

Cover Picture: An artist's impression of *St. Peter's college, Cambridge University* by William Westall.

Printed in the Czech Republic.

CONTENTS

PREFACE

No man was ever better qualified to write such a book – and the subject is more pressing today than ever before. Deriving from a series of lectures Newman was invited to deliver at the newly founded Catholic University of Ireland in 1852, *The Idea of a University* addresses some of the most important issues in the field of education and the place of religion in the public square: What is the purpose of education? What is the role of a university? What is the relationship between learning, the individual and the life of a society? And where does Catholicism fit in?

When this book was written, higher education had already set out on the road, both towards secularism and utilitarian specialisation. Newman was uniquely placed to fight his corner, both as an exemplar of the kind of culture traditional education could produce, and as a man who had already taken up the cudgels against secularism and utilitarianism in his days as a leader of the Tractarian Movement.

From the first, Newman had been concerned with the improvement of the culture and education of the Catholic laity in England:

> I want a laity, not arrogant, not rash in speech, not disputatious, but men who know their religion, who enter into it, who know just where they stand, who know what they hold and what they do not, who know their creed so well that they can give an account of it, who know so much of history that they can defend it.

In the nineteenth century, most "cradle Catholics" in England came from socially, culturally or intellectually impoverished backgrounds. Oxford and Cambridge were to remain barred to native Catholics until the close of the century, and all too often the long hostility of the Establishment bred in the average British Catholic a reactionary hatred of everything associated with the higher culture of the country – a phenomenon which has sadly persisted – though less acutely – to this day. What Newman wanted, in fact, was a laity of *gentlemen*, as he defines the term in *The Idea of a University*.

Oxford and its *ethos* provided him with a model – and a peculiarly appropriate one, for if Oxford was the bastion of traditional Anglican social values, it derived a great deal of its special character from the extent to which it had retained Catholic values after the Reformation. These included the public place of Christianity; knowledge as an end in itself; Truth as an objective standard; the formation of character; and the integration of these ideals – as a tradition, or inheritance – within a social context. Newman's Oxford experience as a teacher – as a fellow of Oriel, and as a minister of the Church of England – also stood him in good stead in this project. Running through all these issues was the defence of an objective, external order. This was constantly before Newman in his lifelong war against Liberalism – in the words of one of his editors, "the view that there was no substantive truth in religion, which was largely a matter of sentiment or feeling concerning which, therefore, one man's opinion was pretty much as good as another's." This was ultimately to be as relevant to education as it was to religion.

That provides us with a fair approach to Newman's view of secularism in society and education. A specific element in this secular revolution was – and remains – the Philistinism of utilitarian specialisation. Martin Svaglic has observed Newman's response to this approach to education:

> For Newman the "single, almost visual, image" that governs *The Idea of a University* is that "all knowledge forms one whole" or "circle," from which the various branches of learning abstract this or that segment. Liberal knowledge or what he calls "philosophy," which is the end or "idea" of a university, consists in that awareness of the bearing of each on the others by which alone the "whole" can be perceived.

And theology was one of the essential branches of learning. Newman explained that no institution professing to teach all disciplines of knowledge could be true to its mission without teaching theology; that all such disciplines, or "sciences" were ultimately interconnected and interdependent; and that theology influences a great variety of other sciences. Finally, and prophetically, he foretold the usurpation of the role of theology by other sciences in its absence.

In waging his polite war against the Philistines, Newman won the admiration and support of certain major Victorian figures unable to accept his perspective to the full, including Walter Pater and, particularly, Matthew Arnold.

Newman's plea for an integrated, "holistic" culture, and his critique of the Philistines were central to Arnold's message: *Culture and Anarchy* is full of references to, and echoes of Newman. And yet, as an agnostic, Arnold could not feel entirely at one with his mentor. In some sense, Arnold made Wordsworth's early project his own. Wordsworth encouraged men to turn to a contemplation of the forces of Nature to restore an inner wholeness. For Arnold, who did not share the younger Wordsworth's pantheistic sensibility, and who had inherited the Victorian anxiety that Nature was red in tooth and claw, such a project presented a divided prospect. Furthermore, Arnold rarely refers to Wordsworth without coupling him with Goethe, whose concerns included the full development of man's cultural and intellectual powers. Thus, for Arnold, the "calm" that was the fruit of a successful pursuit of human wholeness was, at best, a precarious and often transient achievement.

What Newman sought was indeed this wholeness: a union of the life of the intellect with the cultivation of the other human faculties and graces. But with this essential addition: the humility, piety and charity of the religious man – something Arnold's idol Goethe had left out. Newman distanced himself from Goethe, for whom "it sufficed to revel in uninterrupted solitude, and to pass from one agreeable state of existence to another, through all forms and modes of life." For Newman, the pursuit of human wholeness was, through the essential supernatural leaven, within everyman's grasp. "The whole man", as Addison had said, "must move together"; but Newman saw more of the whole than Goethe.

The issues Newman examined with incomparable insight have only become more pressing since he first published this book one hundred and fifty years ago – a book which has been recognized, even by secularists, as probably the greatest of its kind ever since. No one interested in the relationship between religion, learning, culture and politics can afford to neglect it.

Robert Asch

PREFACE TO THE ORIGINAL EDITION

The view taken of a University in these Discourses is the following:—That it is a place of *teaching* universal *knowledge*. This implies that its object is, on the one hand, intellectual, not moral; and, on the other, that it is the diffusion and extension of knowledge rather than the advancement. If its object were scientific and philosophical discovery, I do not see why a University should have students; if religious training, I do not see how it can be the seat of literature and science.

Such is a University in its *essence*, and independently of its relation to the Church. But, practically speaking, it cannot fulfil its object duly, such as I have described it, without the Church's assistance; or, to use the theological term, the Church is necessary for its *integrity*. Not that its main characters are changed by this incorporation: it still has the office of intellectual education; but the Church steadies it in the performance of that office.

Such are the main principles of the Discourses which follow; though it would be unreasonable for me to expect that I have treated so large and important a field of thought with the fulness and precision necessary to secure me from incidental misconceptions of my meaning on the part of the reader. It is true, there is nothing novel or singular in the argument which I have been pursuing, but this does not protect me from such misconceptions; for the very circumstance that the views I have been delineating are not original with me may lead to false notions as to my relations in opinion towards those from whom I happened in the first instance to learn them, and may cause me to be interpreted by the objects or sentiments of schools to which I should be simply opposed.

For instance, some persons may be tempted to complain, that I have servilely followed the English idea of a University, to the disparagement of that Knowledge which I profess to be so strenuously upholding; and they may anticipate that an academical system, formed upon my model, will result in nothing better or higher than in the production of that antiquated variety of human nature and remnant of feudalism, as they consider it, called "a gentleman."[1] Now, I have anticipated this charge in various parts of my discussion; if, however, any Catholic is found to prefer it (and to Catholics of course this Volume is primarily addressed), I would have him first of all ask himself the previous question, *what* he conceives to be the reason contemplated by the Holy See in recommending just now to the Irish Hierarchy the establishment of a Catholic University? Has the Supreme Pontiff recommended it for the sake of the Sciences, which are to be the matter, and not rather of the Students, who are to be the subjects, of its teaching? Has he any obligation or duty at all towards secular knowledge as such? Would it become his Apostolical Ministry, and his descent from the Fisherman, to have a zeal for the Baconian or other philosophy of man for its own sake? Is the Vicar of Christ bound by office or by vow to be the preacher of the theory of gravitation, or a martyr for electro-magnetism? Would he be acquitting himself of the dispensation committed to him if he were smitten with an abstract love of these matters, however true, or beautiful, or ingenious, or useful? Or rather, does he not contemplate such achievements of the intellect, as far as he contemplates them, solely and simply in their relation to the interests of Revealed Truth? Surely, what he does he does for the sake of Religion; if he looks with satisfaction on strong temporal governments, which promise perpetuity, it is for the sake of Religion; and if he encourages and patronizes art and science, it is for the sake of Religion. He rejoices in the widest and most philosophical systems of intellectual education, from an intimate conviction that Truth is his real ally, as it is his profession; and that Knowledge and Reason are sure ministers to Faith.

This being undeniable, it is plain that, when he suggests to the Irish Hierarchy the establishment of a University, his first

---

1 *Vid.* Huber's English Universities, London, 1843, vol. ii., part I., pp. 321, etc.

and chief and direct object is, not science, art, professional skill, literature, the discovery of knowledge, but some benefit or other, to accrue, by means of literature and science, to his own children; not indeed their formation on any narrow or fantastic type, as, for instance, that of an "English Gentleman" may be called, but their exercise and growth in certain habits, moral or intellectual. Nothing short of this can be his aim, if, as becomes the Successor of the Apostles, he is to be able to say with St. Paul, "Non judicavi me scire aliquid inter vos, nisi Jesum Christum, et hunc crucifixum." Just as a commander wishes to have tall and well-formed and vigorous soldiers, not from any abstract devotion to the military standard of height or age, but for the purposes of war, and no one thinks it any thing but natural and praiseworthy in him to be contemplating, not abstract qualities, but his own living and breathing men; so, in like manner, when the Church founds a University, she is not cherishing talent, genius, or knowledge, for their own sake, but for the sake of her children, with a view to their spiritual welfare and their religious influence and usefulness, with the object of training them to fill their respective posts in life better, and of making them more intelligent, capable, active members of society.

Nor can it justly be said that in thus acting she sacrifices Science, and, under a pretence of fulfilling the duties of her mission, perverts a University to ends not its own, as soon as it is taken into account that there are other institutions far more suited to act as instruments of stimulating philosophical inquiry, and extending the boundaries of our knowledge, than a University. Such, for instance, are the literary and scientific "Academies," which are so celebrated in Italy and France, and which have frequently been connected with Universities, as committees, or, as it were, congregations or delegacies subordinate to them. Thus the present Royal Society originated in Charles the Second's time, in Oxford; such just now are the Ashmolean and Architectural Societies in the same seat of learning, which have risen in our own time. Such, too, is the British Association, a migratory body, which at least at times is found in the halls of the Protestant Universities of the United Kingdom, and the faults of which lie, not in its exclusive devotion to science, but in graver matters which it is irrelevant here to enter upon. Such again is the Antiquarian Society, the Royal Academy for the Fine Arts, and others which might be mentioned. This, then, is the sort of institution, which primarily contemplates Science itself; and not students: and, in thus speaking, I am saying nothing of my own, being supported by no less an authority than Cardinal Gerdil. "Ce n'est pas," he says, "qu'il y ait aucune véritable opposition entre l'esprit des Académies et celui des Universités; ce sont seulement des vues différentes. Les Universités sont établies pour *enseigner* les sciences *aux élèves* qui veulent s'y former; les Académies se proposent *de nouvelles recherches* à faire dans la carrière des sciences. Les Universités d'Italie ont fourni des sujets qui ont fait honneur aux Académies; et celles-ci ont donné aux Universités des Professeurs, qui out rempli les chaires avec la plus grande distinction."[2]

The nature of the case and the history of philosophy combine to recommend to us this division of intellectual labour between Academies and Universities. To discover and to teach are distinct functions; they are also distinct gifts, and are not commonly found united in the same person. He, too, who spends his day in dispensing his existing knowledge to all comers is unlikely to have either leisure or energy to acquire new. The common sense of mankind has associated the search after truth with seclusion and quiet. The greatest thinkers have been too intent on their subject to admit of interruption; they have been men of absent minds and idiosyncratic habits, and have, more or less, shunned the lecture room and the public school. Pythagoras, the light of Magna Græcia, lived for a time in a cave. Thales, the light of Ionia, lived unmarried and in private, and refused the invitations of princes. Plato withdrew from Athens to the groves of Academus. Aristotle gave twenty years to a studious discipleship under him. Friar Bacon lived in his tower upon the Isis. Newton

---

2 Opere, t. iii., p. 353.

indulged in an intense severity of meditation which almost shook his reason. The great discoveries in chemistry and electricity were not made in Universities. Observatories are more frequently out of Universities than in them, and even when within their bounds need have no moral connexion with them. Porson had no classes; Elmsley lived good part of his life in the country. I do not say that there are not great examples the other way, perhaps Socrates, certainly Lord Bacon; still I think it must be allowed on the whole that, while teaching involves external engagements, the natural home for experiment and speculation is retirement.

Returning, then, to the consideration of the question, from which I may seem to have digressed, thus much I think I have made good,—that, whether or no a Catholic University should put before it, as its great object, to make its students "gentlemen," still to make them something or other is its great object, and not simply to protect the interests and advance the dominion of Science. If, then, this may be taken for granted, as I think it may, the only point which remains to be settled is, whether I have formed a probable conception of the *sort of benefit* which the Holy See has intended to confer on Catholics who speak the English tongue by recommending to the Irish Hierarchy the establishment of a University; and this I now proceed to consider.

Here, then, it is natural to ask those who are interested in the question, whether any better interpretation of the recommendation of the Holy See can be given than that which I have suggested in this Volume. Certainly it does not seem to me rash to pronounce that, whereas Protestants have great advantages of education in the Schools, Colleges, and Universities of the United Kingdom, our ecclesiastical rulers have it in purpose that Catholics should enjoy the like advantages, whatever they are, to the full. I conceive they view it as prejudicial to the interests of Religion that there should be any cultivation of mind bestowed upon Protestants which is not given to their own youth also. As they wish their schools for the poorer and middle classes to be at least on a par with those of Protestants, they contemplate the same object also as regards that higher education which is given to comparatively the few. Protestant youths, who can spare the time, continue their studies till the age of twenty-one or twenty-two; thus they employ a time of life all-important and especially favourable to mental culture. I conceive that our Prelates are impressed with the fact and its consequences, that a youth who ends his education at seventeen is no match (*cæteris paribus*) for one who ends it at twenty-two.

All classes indeed of the community are impressed with a fact so obvious as this. The consequence is, that Catholics who aspire to be on a level with Protestants in discipline and refinement of intellect have recourse to Protestant Universities to obtain what they cannot find at home. Assuming (as the Rescripts from Propaganda allow me to do) that Protestant education is inexpedient for our youth,—we see here an additional reason why those advantages, whatever they are, which Protestant communities dispense through the medium of Protestantism should be accessible to Catholics in a Catholic form.

What are these advantages? I repeat, they are in one word the culture of the intellect. Robbed, oppressed, and thrust aside, Catholics in these islands have not been in a condition for centuries to attempt the sort of education which is necessary for the man of the world, the statesman, the landholder, or the opulent gentleman. Their legitimate stations, duties, employments, have been taken from them, and the qualifications withal, social and intellectual, which are necessary both for reversing the forfeiture and for availing themselves of the reversal. The time is come when this moral disability must be removed. Our desideratum is, not the manners and habits of gentlemen;—these can be, and are, acquired in various other ways, by good society, by foreign travel, by the innate grace and dignity of the Catholic mind;—but the force, the steadiness, the comprehensiveness and the versatility of intellect, the command over our own powers, the instinctive just estimate of things as they pass before us, which sometimes indeed is a natural gift, but commonly is not gained without much effort and the exercise of years.

This is real cultivation of mind; and I do not deny that the characteristic excellences of a gentleman are included in it. Nor need we be ashamed that they should be, since the poet long ago wrote, that "Ingenuas didicisse fideliter artes Emollit mores." Certainly a liberal education does manifest itself in a courtesy, propriety, and polish of word and action, which is beautiful in itself, and acceptable to others; but it does much more. It brings the mind into form,—for the mind is like the body. Boys outgrow their shape and their strength; their limbs have to be knit together, and their constitution needs tone. Mistaking animal spirits for vigour, and overconfident in their health, ignorant what they can bear and how to manage themselves, they are immoderate and extravagant; and fall into sharp sicknesses. This is an emblem of their minds; at first they have no principles laid down within them as a foundation for the intellect to build upon; they have no discriminating convictions, and no grasp of consequences. And therefore they talk at random, if they talk much, and cannot help being flippant, or what is emphatically called "*young*." They are merely dazzled by phenomena, instead of perceiving things as they are.

It were well if none remained boys all their lives; but what more common than the sight of grown men, talking on political or moral or religious subjects, in that offhand, idle way, which we signify by the word *unreal*? "That they simply do not know what they are talking about" is the spontaneous silent remark of any man of sense who hears them. Hence such persons have no difficulty in contradicting themselves in successive sentences, without being conscious of it. Hence others, whose defect in intellectual training is more latent, have their most unfortunate crotchets, as they are called, or hobbies, which deprive them of the influence which their estimable qualities would otherwise secure. Hence others can never look straight before them, never see the point, and have no difficulties in the most difficult subjects. Others are hopelessly obstinate and prejudiced, and, after they have been driven from their opinions, return to them the next moment without even an attempt to explain why. Others are so intemperate and intractable that there is no greater calamity for a good cause than that they should get hold of it. It is very plain from the very particulars I have mentioned that, in this delineation of intellectual infirmities, I am drawing, not from Catholics, but from the world at large; I am referring to an evil which is forced upon us in every railway carriage, in every coffee-room or *table-d'hôte*, in every mixed company, an evil, however, to which Catholics are not less exposed than the rest of mankind.

When the intellect has once been properly trained and formed to have a connected view or grasp of things, it will display its powers with more or less effect according to its particular quality and capacity in the individual. In the case of most men it makes itself felt in the good sense, sobriety of thought, reasonableness, candour, self-command, and steadiness of view, which characterize it. In some it will have developed habits of business, power of influencing others, and sagacity. In others it will elicit the talent of philosophical speculation, and lead the mind forward to eminence in this or that intellectual department. In all it will be a faculty of entering with comparative ease into any subject of thought, and of taking up with aptitude any science or profession. All this it will be and will do in a measure, even when the mental formation be made after a model but partially true; for, as far as effectiveness goes, even false views of things have more influence and inspire more respect than no views at all. Men who fancy they see what is not are more energetic, and make their way better, than those who see nothing; and so the undoubting infidel, the fanatic, the heresiarch, are able to do much, while the mere hereditary Christian, who has never realized the truths which he holds, is unable to do any thing. But, if consistency of view can add so much strength even to error, what may it not be expected to furnish to the dignity, the energy, and the influence of Truth!

Some one, however, will perhaps object that I am but advocating that spurious philosophism, which shows itself in what, for want of a word, I may call "viewiness," when I speak so much of the formation, and consequent grasp, of the intellect. It may be said that the theory of University Education, which I have been delineating, if acted upon, would teach youths nothing soundly or thoroughly, and would dismiss them with nothing better than brilliant general views about all things whatever.

This indeed, if well founded, would be a most serious objection to what I have advanced in this Volume, and would demand my immediate attention, had I any reason to think that I could not remove it at once, by a simple explanation of what I consider the true *mode* of educating, were this the place to do so. But these Discourses are directed simply to the consideration of the *aims* and *principles* of Education. Suffice it, then, to say here, that I hold very strongly that the first step in intellectual training is to impress upon a boy's mind the idea of science, method, order, principle, and system; of rule and exception, of richness and harmony. This is commonly and excellently done by making him begin with Grammar; nor can too great accuracy, or minuteness and subtlety of teaching be used towards him, as his faculties expand, with this simple purpose. Hence it is that critical scholarship is so important a discipline for him when he is leaving school for the University. A second science is the Mathematics: this should follow Grammar, still with the same object, viz., to give him a conception of development and arrangement from and around a common centre. Hence it is that Chronology and Geography are so necessary for him, when he reads History, which is otherwise little better than a storybook. Hence, too, Metrical Composition, when he reads Poetry; in order to stimulate his powers into action in every practicable way, and to prevent a merely passive reception of images and ideas which in that case are likely to pass out of the mind as soon as they have entered it. Let him once gain this habit of method, of starting from fixed points, of making his ground good as he goes, of distinguishing what he knows from what he does not know, and I conceive he will be gradually initiated into the largest and truest philosophical views, and will feel nothing but impatience and disgust at the random theories and imposing sophistries and dashing paradoxes, which carry away half-formed and superficial intellects.

Such parti-coloured ingenuities are indeed one of the chief evils of the day, and men of real talent are not slow to minister to them. An intellectual man, as the world now conceives of him, is one who is full of "views" on all subjects of philosophy, on all matters of the day. It is almost thought a disgrace not to have a view at a moment's notice on any question from the Personal Advent to the Cholera or Mesmerism. This is owing in great measure to the necessities of periodical literature, now so much in request. Every quarter of a year, every month, every day, there must be a supply, for the gratification of the public, of new and luminous theories on the subjects of religion, foreign politics, home politics, civil economy, finance, trade, agriculture, emigration, and the colonies. Slavery, the gold fields, German philosophy, the French Empire, Wellington, Peel, Ireland, must all be practised on, day after day, by what are called original thinkers. As the great man's guest must produce his good stories or songs at the evening banquet, as the platform orator exhibits his telling facts at mid-day, so the journalist lies under the stern obligation of extemporizing his lucid views, leading ideas, and nutshell truths for the breakfast table. The very nature of periodical literature, broken into small wholes, and demanded punctually to an hour, involves the habit of this extempore philosophy. "Almost all the Ramblers," says Boswell of Johnson, "were written just as they were wanted for the press; he sent a certain portion of the copy of an essay, and wrote the remainder while the former part of it was printing." Few men have the gifts of Johnson, who to great vigour and resource of intellect, when it was fairly roused, united a rare common-sense and a conscientious regard for veracity, which preserved him from flippancy or extravagance in writing. Few men are Johnsons; yet how many men at this day are assailed by incessant demands on their mental powers, which only a productiveness like his could suitably supply! There is a demand for a reckless originality of thought, and a sparkling plausibility of argument, which he would have despised, even if he could have displayed; a demand for crude theory and unsound philosophy, rather than none at all. It is a sort of repetition of the "Quid novi?" of the Areopagus and it must have an answer. Men must be found who can treat, where it is necessary, like the Athenian sophist, *de omni scibili,*

> "Grammaticus, Rhetor, Geometres, Pictor, Aliptes,
> Augur, Schœnobates, Medicus, Magus, omnia novit."

I am speaking of such writers with a feeling of real sympathy for men who are under the rod of a cruel slavery. I have never indeed been in such circumstances myself nor in the temptations which they involve; but most men who have had to do with composition must know the distress which at times it occasions them to have to write—a distress sometimes so keen and so specific that it resembles nothing else than bodily pain. That pain is the token of the wear and tear of mind; and, if works done comparatively at leisure involve such mental fatigue and exhaustion, what must be the toil of those whose intellects are to be flaunted daily before the public in full dress, and that dress ever new and varied, and spun, like the silkworm's, out of themselves! Still, whatever true sympathy we may feel for the ministers of this dearly purchased luxury, and whatever sense we may have of the great intellectual power which the literature in question displays, we cannot honestly close our eyes to its direct evil.

One other remark suggests itself, which is the last I shall think it necessary to make. The authority, which in former times was lodged in Universities, now resides in very great measure in that literary world, as it is called, to which I have been referring. This is not satisfactory, if, as no one can deny, its teaching be so off-hand, so ambitious, so changeable. It increases the seriousness of the mischief, that so very large a portion of its writers are anonymous, for irresponsible power never can be any thing but a great evil; and, moreover, that, even when they are known, they can give no better guarantee for the philosophical truth of their principles than their popularity at the moment, and their happy conformity in ethical character to the age which admires them. Protestants, however, may do as they will: it is a matter for their own consideration; but at least it concerns us that our own literary tribunals and oracles of moral duty should bear a graver character. At least it is a matter of deep solicitude to Catholic Prelates that their people should be taught a wisdom, safe from the excesses and vagaries of individuals, embodied in institutions which have stood the trial and received the sanction of ages, and administered by men who have no need to be anonymous, as being supported by their consistency with their predecessors and with each other.

November 21, 1852.

I. UNIVERSITY TEACHING

CONSIDERED IN NINE DISCOURSES

Delivered to the Catholics of Dublin

DISCOURSE I

INTRODUCTORY

1.

In addressing myself, Gentlemen, to the consideration of a question which has excited so much interest, and elicited so much discussion at the present day, as that of University Education, I feel some explanation is due from me for supposing, after such high ability and wide experience have been brought to bear upon it, that any field remains for the additional labours either of a disputant or of an inquirer. If, nevertheless, I still venture to ask permission to continue the discussion, already so protracted, it is because the subject of Liberal Education, and of the principles on which it must be conducted, has ever had a hold upon my own mind; and because I have lived the greater part of my life in a place which has all that time been occupied in a series of controversies both domestic and with strangers, and of measures, experimental or definitive, bearing upon it. About fifty years since, the English University, of which I was so long a member, after a century of inactivity, at length was roused, at a time when (as I may say) it was giving no education at all to the youth committed to its keeping, to a sense of the responsibilities which its profession and its station involved, and it presents to us the singular example of an heterogeneous and an independent body of men, setting about a work of self-reformation, not from any pressure of public opinion, but because it was fitting and right to undertake it. Its initial efforts, begun and carried on amid many obstacles, were met from without, as often happens in such cases, by ungenerous and jealous criticisms, which, at the very moment that they were urged, were beginning to be unjust. Controversy did but bring out more clearly to its own apprehension the views on which its reformation was proceeding, and throw them into a philosophical form. The course of beneficial change made progress, and what was at first but the result of individual energy and an act of the academical corporation, gradually became popular, and was taken up and carried out by the separate collegiate bodies, of which the University is composed. This was the first stage of the controversy. Years passed away, and then political adversaries arose against it, and the system of education which it had established was a second time assailed; but still, since that contest was conducted for the most part through the medium, not of political acts, but of treatises and pamphlets, it happened as before that the threatened dangers, in the course of their repulse, did but afford fuller development and more exact delineation to the principles of which the University was the representative.

In the former of these two controversies the charge brought against its studies was their remoteness from the occupations and duties of life, to which they are the formal introduction, or, in other words, their *inutility;* in the latter, it was their connexion with a particular form of belief, or, in other words, their *religious exclusiveness.*

Living then so long as a witness, though hardly as an actor, in these scenes of intellectual conflict, I am able to bear witness to views of University Education, without authority indeed in themselves, but not without value to a Catholic, and less familiar to him, as I conceive, than they deserve to be. And, while an argument originating in the controversies to which I have referred, may be serviceable at this season to that great cause in which we are here so especially interested, to me personally it will afford satisfaction of a peculiar kind; for, though it has been my lot for many years to take a prominent, sometimes a presumptuous, part in theological discussions, yet the natural turn of my mind carries me off to trains of thought like those which I am now about to open, which, important though they be for Catholic objects, and admitting of a Catholic treatment, are sheltered from the extreme delicacy and peril which attach to disputations directly bearing on the subject-matter of Divine Revelation.

2.

There are several reasons why I should open the discussion with a reference to the lessons with which past years have supplied me. One reason is this: It would concern me, Gentlemen, were I supposed to have got up my opinions for the occasion. This, indeed, would have been no reflection on me personally, supposing I were persuaded of their truth, when at length addressing myself to the inquiry; but it would have destroyed, of course, the force of my testimony, and deprived such arguments, as I might adduce, of that moral persuasiveness which attends on tried and sustained conviction. It would have made me seem the advocate, rather than the cordial and deliberate maintainer and witness, of the doctrines which I was to support; and, though it might be said to evidence the faith I reposed in the practical judgment of the Church, and the intimate concurrence of my own reason with the course she had authoritatively sanctioned, and the devotion with which I could promptly put myself at her disposal, it would have cast suspicion on the validity of reasonings and conclusions which rested on no independent inquiry, and appealed to no past experience. In that case it might have been plausibly objected by opponents that I was the serviceable expedient of an emergency, and never, after all, could be more than ingenious and adroit in the management of an argument which was not my own, and which I was sure to forget again as readily as I had mastered it. But this is not so. The views to which I have referred have grown into my whole system of thought, and are, as it were, part of myself. Many changes has my mind gone through: here it has known no variation or vacillation of opinion, and though this by itself is no proof of the truth of my principles, it puts a seal upon conviction, and is a justification of earnestness and zeal. Those principles, which I am now to set forth under the sanction of the Catholic Church, were my profession at that early period of my life, when religion was to me more a matter of feeling and experience than of faith. They did but take greater hold upon me, as I was introduced to the records of Christian Antiquity, and approached in sentiment and desire to Catholicism; and my sense of their correctness has been increased with the events of every year since I have been brought within its pale.

And here I am brought to a second and more important reason for referring, on this occasion, to the conclusions at which Protestants have arrived on the subject of Liberal Education; and it is as follows: Let it be observed, then, that the principles on which I would conduct the inquiry are attainable, as I have already implied, by the mere experience of life. They do not come simply of theology; they imply no supernatural discernment; they have no special connexion with Revelation; they almost arise out of the nature of the case; they are dictated even by human prudence and wisdom, though a divine illumination be absent, and they are recognized by common sense, even where self-interest is not present to quicken it; and, therefore, though true, and just, and good in themselves, they imply nothing whatever as to the religious profession of those who maintain them. They may be held by Protestants as well as by Catholics; nay, there is reason to anticipate that in certain times and places they will be more thoroughly investigated, and better understood, and held more firmly by Protestants than by ourselves.

It is natural to expect this from the very circumstance that the philosophy of Education is founded on truths in the natural order. Where the sun shines bright, in the warm climate of the south, the natives of the place know little of safeguards against cold and wet. They have, indeed, bleak and piercing blasts; they have chill and pouring rain, but only now and then, for a day or a week; they bear the inconvenience as they best may, but they have not made it an art to repel it; it is not worth their while; the science of calefaction and ventilation is reserved for the north. It is in this way that Catholics stand relatively to Protestants in the science of Education; Protestants depending on human means mainly, are led to make the most of them: their sole resource is to use what they have; "Knowledge is" their "power" and nothing else; they are the anxious cultivators of a rugged soil. It is otherwise with us; *"funes ceciderunt mihi in præclaris."* We have a goodly inheritance. This is apt to cause us—I do not mean to rely too much on prayer, and the Divine Blessing, for that is impossible, but we sometimes forget that we shall please Him best, and get most from Him, when, according to the Fable, we "put our shoulder to the wheel," when we use what we have by nature to the utmost, at the same time that we look out for what is beyond nature in the confidence of faith and hope. However, we are sometimes tempted to let things take their course, as if they would in one way or another turn up right at last for certain; and so we go on, living from hand to mouth, getting into difficulties and getting out of them, succeeding certainly on the whole, but with failure in detail which might be avoided, and with much of imperfection or inferiority in our appointments and plans, and much disappointment, discouragement, and collision of opinion in consequence. If this be in any measure the state of the case, there is certainly so far a reason for availing ourselves of the investigations and experience of those who are not Catholics, when we have to address ourselves to the subject of Liberal Education.

Nor is there surely any thing derogatory to the position of a Catholic in such a proceeding. The Church has ever appealed and deferred to witnesses and authorities external to herself, in those matters in which she thought they had means of forming a judgment: and that on the principle, *Cuique in arte sua credendum*. She has even used unbelievers and pagans in evidence of her truth, as far as their testimony went. She avails herself of scholars, critics, and antiquarians, who are not of her communion. She has worded her theological teaching in the phraseology of Aristotle; Aquila, Symmachus, Theodotion, Origen, Eusebius, and Apollinaris, all more or less heterodox, have supplied materials for primitive exegetics. St. Cyprian called Tertullian his master; St. Augustin refers to Ticonius; Bossuet, in modern times, complimented the labours of the Anglican Bull; the Benedictine editors of the Fathers are familiar with the labours of Fell, Ussher, Pearson, and Beveridge. Pope Benedict XIV. cites according to the occasion the works of Protestants without reserve, and the late French collection of Christian Apologists contains the writings of Locke, Burnet, Tillotson, and Paley. If, then, I come forward in any degree as borrowing the views of certain Protestant schools on the point which is to be discussed, I do so, Gentlemen, as believing, first, that the Catholic Church has ever, in the plenitude of her divine illumination, made use of whatever truth or wisdom she has found in their teaching or their measures; and next, that in particular places or times her children are likely to profit from external suggestions or lessons, which have not been provided for them by herself.

3.

And here I may mention a third reason for appealing at the outset to the proceedings of Protestant bodies in regard to Liberal Education. It will serve to intimate the mode in which I propose to handle my subject altogether. Observe then, Gentlemen, I have no intention, in any thing I shall say, of bringing into the argument the authority of the Church, or any authority at all; but I shall consider the question simply on the grounds of human reason and human wisdom. I am investigating in the abstract, and am determining what is in itself right and true. For the moment I know nothing, so to say, of history. I take things as I find them; I have no concern with the past; I find myself here; I set myself to the duties I find here; I set myself to further, by every means in my power, doctrines and views, true in themselves, recognized by Catholics as such, familiar to my own mind; and to do this quite apart from the consideration of questions which have been determined without me and before me. I am here the advocate and the minister of a certain great principle; yet not merely advocate and minister, else had I not been here at all. It has been my previous keen sense and hearty reception of that principle, that has been at once the reason, as I must suppose, of my being selected for this office, and is the cause of my accepting it. I am told on authority that a principle is expedient, which I have ever felt to be true. And I argue in its behalf on its own merits, the authority, which brings me here, being my opportunity for arguing, but not the ground of my argument itself.

And a fourth reason is here suggested for consulting the history of Protestant institutions, when I am going to speak of the object and nature of University Education. It will serve to remind you, Gentlemen, that I am concerned with questions, not simply of immutable truth, but of practice and expedience. It would ill have become me to undertake a subject, on which points of dispute have arisen among persons so far above me in authority and name, in relation to a state of society, about which I have so much to learn, if it involved an appeal to sacred truths, or the determination of some imperative rule of conduct. It would have been presumptuous in me so to have acted, nor am I so acting. Even the question of the union of Theology with the secular Sciences, which is its religious side, simple as it is of solution in the abstract, has, according to difference of circumstances, been at different times differently decided. Necessity has no law, and expedience is often one form of necessity. It is no principle with sensible men, of whatever cast of opinion, to do always what is abstractedly best. Where no direct duty forbids, we may be obliged to do, as being best under circumstances, what we murmur and rise against, while we do it. We see that to attempt more is to effect less; that we must accept so much, or gain nothing; and so perforce we reconcile ourselves to what we would have far otherwise, if we could. Thus a system of what is called secular Education, in which Theology and the Sciences are taught separately, may, in a particular place or time, be the least of evils; it may be of long standing; it may be dangerous to meddle with; it may be professedly a temporary arrangement; it may be under a process of improvement; its disadvantages may be neutralized by the persons by whom, or the provisions under which, it is administered.

Hence it was, that in the early ages the Church allowed her children to attend the heathen schools for the acquisition of secular accomplishments, where, as no one can doubt, evils existed, at least as great as can attend on Mixed Education now. The gravest Fathers recommended for Christian youth the use of Pagan masters; the most saintly Bishops and most authoritative

Doctors had been sent in their adolescence by Christian parents to Pagan lecture halls.[1] And, not to take other instances, at this very time, and in this very country, as regards at least the poorer classes of the community, whose secular acquirements ever must be limited, it has seemed best to the Irish Bishops, under the circumstances, to suffer the introduction into the country of a system of Mixed Education in the schools called National. Such a state of things, however, is passing away; as regards University education at least, the highest authority has now decided that the plan, which is abstractedly best, is in this time and country also most expedient.

4.

And here I have an opportunity of recognizing once for all that higher view of approaching the subject of these Discourses, which, after this formal recognition, I mean to dispense with. Ecclesiastical authority, not argument, is the supreme rule and the appropriate guide for Catholics in matters of religion. It has always the right to interpose, and sometimes, in the conflict of parties and opinions, it is called on to exercise that right. It has lately exercised it in our own instance: it has interposed in favour of a pure University system for Catholic youth, forbidding compromise or accommodation of any kind. Of course its decision must be heartily accepted and obeyed, and that the more, because the decision proceeds, not simply from the Bishops of Ireland, great as their authority is, but the highest authority on earth, from the Chair of St. Peter.

Moreover, such a decision not only demands our submission, but has a claim upon our trust. It not only acts as a prohibition of any measures, but as an *ipso facto* confutation of any reasonings, inconsistent with it. It carries with it an earnest and an augury of its own expediency. For instance, I can fancy, Gentlemen, there may be some, among those who hear me, disposed to say that they are ready to acquit the principles of Education, which I am to advo-

---

1 *Vide* M. L'Abbé Lalanne's recent work.

cate, of all fault whatever, except that of being impracticable. I can fancy them granting to me, that those principles are most correct and most obvious, simply irresistible on paper, but maintaining, nevertheless, that after all, they are nothing more than the dreams of men who live out of the world, and who do not see the difficulty of keeping Catholicism anyhow afloat on the bosom of this wonderful nineteenth century. Proved, indeed, those principles are, to demonstration, but they will not work. Nay, it was my own admission just now, that, in a particular instance, it might easily happen, that what is only second best is best practically, because what is actually best is out of the question.

This, I hear you say to yourselves, is the state of things at present. You recount in detail the numberless impediments, great and small, formidable or only vexatious, which at every step embarrass the attempt to carry out ever so poorly a principle in itself so true and ecclesiastical. You appeal in your defence to wise and sagacious intellects, who are far from enemies to Catholicism, or to the Irish Hierarchy, and you have no hope, or rather you absolutely disbelieve, that Education can possibly be conducted, here and now, on a theological principle, or that youths of different religions can, under the circumstances of the country, be educated apart from each other. The more you think over the state of politics, the position of parties, the feelings of classes, and the experience of the past, the more chimerical does it seem to you to aim at a University, of which Catholicity is the fundamental principle. Nay, even if the attempt could accidentally succeed, would not the mischief exceed the benefit of it? How great the sacrifices, in how many ways, by which it would be preceded and followed! how many wounds, open and secret, would it inflict upon the body politic! And, if it fails, which is to be expected, then a double mischief will ensue from its recognition of evils which it has been unable to remedy. These are your deep misgivings; and, in proportion to the force with which they come to you, is the concern and anxiety which you feel, that there should be those whom you love, whom you revere, who from one cause or other refuse to enter into them.

5.

This, I repeat, is what some good Catholics will say to me, and more than this. They will express themselves better than I can speak for them in their behalf,—with more earnestness and point, with more force of argument and fulness of detail; and I will frankly and at once acknowledge, that I shall insist on the high theological view of a University without attempting to give a direct answer to their arguments against its present practicability. I do not say an answer cannot be given; on the contrary, I have a confident expectation that, in proportion as those objections are looked in the face, they will fade away. But, however this may be, it would not become me to argue the matter with those who understand the circumstances of the problem so much better than myself. What do I know of the state of things in Ireland, that I should presume to put ideas of mine, which could not be right except by accident, by the side of theirs, who speak in the country of their birth and their home? No, Gentlemen, you are natural judges of the difficulties which beset us, and they are doubtless greater than I can even fancy or forbode. Let me, for the sake of argument, admit all you say against our enterprise, and a great deal more. Your proof of its intrinsic impossibility shall be to me as cogent as my own of its theological advisableness. Why, then, should I be so rash and perverse as to involve myself in trouble not properly mine? Why go out of my own place? Why so headstrong and reckless as to lay up for myself miscarriage and disappointment, as though I were not sure to have enough of personal trial anyhow without going about to seek for it?

Reflections such as these would be decisive even with the boldest and most capable minds, but for one consideration. In the midst of our difficulties I have one ground of hope, just one stay, but, as I think, a sufficient one, which serves me in the stead of all other argument whatever, which hardens me against criticism, which supports me if I begin to despond, and to which I ever come round, when the question of the possible and the expedient is brought into discussion. It is the decision of the

Holy See; St. Peter has spoken, it is he who has enjoined that which seems to us so unpromising. He has spoken, and has a claim on us to trust him. He is no recluse, no solitary student, no dreamer about the past, no doter upon the dead and gone, no projector of the visionary. He for eighteen hundred years has lived in the world; he has seen all fortunes, he has encountered all adversaries, he has shaped himself for all emergencies. If ever there was a power on earth who had an eye for the times, who has confined himself to the practicable, and has been happy in his anticipations, whose words have been facts, and whose commands prophecies, such is he in the history of ages, who sits from generation to generation in the Chair of the Apostles, as the Vicar of Christ, and the Doctor of His Church.

6.

These are not the words of rhetoric, Gentlemen, but of history. All who take part with the Apostle, are on the winning side. He has long since given warrants for the confidence which he claims. From the first he has looked through the wide world, of which he has the burden; and, according to the need of the day, and the inspirations of his Lord, he has set himself now to one thing, now to another; but to all in season, and to nothing in vain. He came first upon an age of refinement and luxury like our own, and, in spite of the persecutor, fertile in the resources of his cruelty, he soon gathered, out of all classes of society, the slave, the soldier, the high-born lady, and the sophist, materials enough to form a people to his Master's honour. The savage hordes came down in torrents from the north, and Peter went out to meet them, and by his very eye he sobered them, and backed them in their full career. They turned aside and flooded the whole earth, but only to be more surely civilized by him, and to be made ten times more his children even than the older populations which they had overwhelmed. Lawless kings arose, sagacious as the Roman, passionate as the Hun, yet in him they found their match, and were shattered, and he lived on. The gates of the earth were opened to the east and west, and men poured out to take possession; but he went with them by his missionaries, to China, to Mexico, carried along by zeal and charity, as far as those children of men were led by enterprise, covetousness, or ambition. Has he failed in his successes up to this hour? Did he, in our fathers' day, fail in his struggle with Joseph of Germany and his confederates, with Napoleon, a greater name, and his dependent kings, that, though in another kind of fight, he should fail in ours? What grey hairs are on the head of Judah, whose youth is renewed like the eagle's, whose feet are like the feet of harts, and underneath the Everlasting arms?

In the first centuries of the Church all this practical sagacity of Holy Church was mere matter of faith, but every age, as it has come, has confirmed faith by actual sight; and shame on us, if, with the accumulated testimony of eighteen centuries, our eyes are too gross to see those victories which the Saints have ever seen by anticipation. Least of all can we, the Catholics of islands which have in the cultivation and diffusion of Knowledge heretofore been so singularly united under the auspices of the Apostolic See, least of all can we be the men to distrust its wisdom and to predict its failure, when it sends us on a similar mission now. I cannot forget that, at a time when Celt and Saxon were alike savage, it was the See of Peter that gave both of them, first faith, then civilization; and then again bound them together in one by the seal of a joint commission to convert and illuminate in their turn the pagan continent. I cannot forget how it was from Rome that the glorious St. Patrick was sent to Ireland, and did a work so great that he could not have a successor in it, the sanctity and learning and zeal and charity which followed on his death being but the result of the one impulse which he gave. I cannot forget how, in no long time, under the fostering breath of the Vicar of Christ, a country of heathen superstitions became the very wonder and asylum of all people,—the wonder by reason of its knowledge, sacred and profane, and the asylum of religion, literature and science, when chased away from the continent by the barbarian invaders. I recollect its hospitality, freely accorded to the pilgrim; its volumes munificently presented to the foreign student; and the prayers, the blessings, the holy rites, the solemn chants, which sanctified the while both giver and receiver.

Nor can I forget either, how my own England had meanwhile become the solicitude of the same unwearied eye: how Augustine was sent to us by Gregory; how he fainted in the way at the tidings of our fierceness, and, but for the Pope, would have shrunk as from an impossible expedition; how he was forced on "in weakness and in fear and in much trembling," until he had achieved the conquest of the island to Christ. Nor, again, how it came to pass that, when Augustine died and his work slackened, another Pope, unwearied still, sent three saints from Rome, to ennoble and refine the people Augustine had converted. Three holy men set out for England together, of different nations: Theodore, an Asiatic Greek, from Tarsus; Adrian, an African; Bennett alone a Saxon, for Peter knows no distinction of races in his ecumenical work. They came with theology and science in their train; with relics, with pictures, with manuscripts of the Holy Fathers and the Greek classics; and Theodore and Adrian founded schools, secular and monastic, all over England, while Bennett brought to the north the large library he had collected in foreign parts, and, with plans and ornamental work from France, erected a church of stone, under the invocation of St. Peter, after the Roman fashion, "which," says the historian,[2] "he most affected." I call to mind how St. Wilfrid, St. John of Beverley, St. Bede, and other saintly men, carried on the good work in the following generations, and how from that time forth the two islands, England and Ireland, in a dark and dreary age, were the two lights of Christendom, and had no claims on each other, and no thought of self, save in the interchange of kind offices and the rivalry of love.

7.

O memorable time, when St. Aidan and the Irish monks went up to Lindisfarne and Melrose, and taught the Saxon youth, and when a St. Cuthbert and a St. Eata repaid their charitable toil! O

---

2 Cressy.

blessed days of peace and confidence, when the Celtic Mailduf penetrated to Malmesbury in the south, which has inherited his name, and founded there the famous school which gave birth to the great St. Aldhelm! O precious seal and testimony of Gospel unity, when, as Aldhelm in turn tells us, the English went to Ireland "numerous as bees;" when the Saxon St. Egbert and St. Willibrod, preachers to the heathen Frisons, made the voyage to Ireland to prepare themselves for their work; and when from Ireland went forth to Germany the two noble Ewalds, Saxons also, to earn the crown of martyrdom! Such a period, indeed, so rich in grace, in peace, in love, and in good works, could only last for a season; but, even when the light was to pass away from them, the sister islands were destined, not to forfeit, but to transmit it together. The time came when the neighbouring continental country was in turn to hold the mission which they had exercised so long and well; and when to it they made over their honourable office, faithful to the alliance of two hundred years, they made it a joint act. Alcuin was the pupil both of the English and of the Irish schools; and when Charlemagne would revive science and letters in his own France, it was Alcuin, the representative both of the Saxon and the Celt, who was the chief of those who went forth to supply the need of the great Emperor. Such was the foundation of the School of Paris, from which, in the course of centuries, sprang the famous University, the glory of the middle ages.

The past never returns; the course of events, old in its texture, is ever new in its colouring and fashion. England and Ireland are not what they once were, but Rome is where it was, and St. Peter is the same: his zeal, his charity, his mission, his gifts are all the same. He of old made the two islands one by giving them joint work of teaching; and now surely he is giving us a like mission, and we shall become one again, while we zealously and lovingly fulfil it.

DISCOURSE II

THEOLOGY A BRANCH OF KNOWLEDGE

There were two questions, to which I drew your attention, Gentlemen, in the beginning of my first Discourse, as being of especial importance and interest at this time: first, whether it is consistent with the idea of University teaching to exclude Theology from a place among the sciences which it embraces; next, whether it is consistent with that idea to make the useful arts and sciences its direct and principal concern, to the neglect of those liberal studies and exercises of mind, in which it has heretofore been considered mainly to consist. These are the questions which will form the subject of what I have to lay before you, and I shall now enter upon the former of the two.

1.

It is the fashion just now, as you very well know, to erect so-called Universities, without making any provision in them at all for Theological chairs. Institutions of this kind exist both here and in England. Such a procedure, though defended by writers of the generation just passed with much plausible argument and not a little wit, seems to me an intellectual absurdity; and my reason for saying so runs, with whatever abruptness, into the form of a syllogism:—A University, I should lay down, by its very name professes to teach universal knowledge: Theology is surely a branch of knowledge: how then is it possible for it to profess all branches of knowledge, and yet to exclude from the subjects of its teaching one which, to say the least, is as important and as large as any of them? I do not see that either premiss of this argument is open to exception.

As to the range of University teaching, certainly the very name of University is inconsistent with restrictions of any kind. Whatever was the original reason of the adoption of that term, which is unknown,[1] I am only putting on it its popular, its recognized sense, when I say that a University should teach universal knowledge. That there is a real necessity for this universal teaching in the highest schools of intellect, I will show by-and-by; here it is sufficient to say that such universality is considered by writers on the subject to be the very characteristic of a University, as contrasted with other seats of learning. Thus Johnson, in his Dictionary, defines it to be "a school where all arts and faculties are taught;" and Mosheim, writing as an historian, says that, before the rise of the University of Paris,—for instance, at Padua, or Salamanca, or Cologne,—"the whole circle of sciences then known was not taught;" but that the school of Paris, "which exceeded all others in various respects, as well as in the number of teachers and students, was the first to embrace all the arts and sciences, and therefore first became a University."[2]

If, with other authors, we consider the word to be derived from the invitation which is held out by a University to students of every kind, the result is the same; for, if certain branches of knowledge were excluded, those students of course would be excluded also, who desired to pursue them.

Is it, then, logically consistent in a seat of learning to call itself a University, and to exclude Theology from the number of its studies? And again, is it wonderful that Catholics, even in the view of reason, putting aside faith or religious duty, should be dissatisfied with existing institutions, which profess to be Universities, and refuse to teach Theology; and that they should in consequence desire to possess seats of learning, which are, not only more Christian, but more philosophical in their construction, and larger and deeper in their provisions?

But this, of course, is to assume that Theology *is* a science, and an important one: so I will throw my argument into a more exact form. I say, then, that if a University be, from the nature of the case, a place of instruction, where universal knowledge is professed, and if in a certain University, so called, the subject of Reli-

1 In Roman law it means a Corporation. Vid. Keuffel, *de Scholis*.
2 Hist. vol. ii. p. 529. London, 1841.

gion is excluded, one of two conclusions is inevitable,—either, on the one hand, that the province of Religion is very barren of real knowledge, or, on the other hand, that in such University one special and important branch of knowledge is omitted. I say, the advocate of such an institution must say *this*, or he must say *that*; he must own, either that little or nothing is known about the Supreme Being, or that his seat of learning calls itself what it is not. This is the thesis which I lay down, and on which I shall insist as the subject of this Discourse. I repeat, such a compromise between religious parties, as is involved in the establishment of a University which makes no religious profession, implies that those parties severally consider,—not indeed that their own respective opinions are trifles in a moral and practical point of view—of course not; but certainly as much as this, that they are not knowledge. Did they in their hearts believe that their private views of religion, whatever they are, were absolutely and objectively true, it is inconceivable that they would so insult them as to consent to their omission in an Institution which is bound, from the nature of the case—from its very idea and its name—to make a profession of all sorts of knowledge whatever.

2.

I think this will be found to be no matter of words. I allow then fully, that, when men combine together for any common object, they are obliged, as a matter of course, in order to secure the advantages accruing from united action, to sacrifice many of their private opinions and wishes, and to drop the minor differences, as they are commonly called, which exist between man and man. No two persons perhaps are to be found, however intimate, however congenial in tastes and judgments, however eager to have one heart and one soul, but must deny themselves, for the sake of each other, much which they like or desire, if they are to live together happily. Compromise, in a large sense of the word, is the first principle of combination; and any one who insists on enjoying his rights to the full, and his opinions without toleration for his neighbour's, and his own way in all things, will soon have all things altogether to himself, and no one to share them with him. But most true as this confessedly is, still there is an obvious limit, on the other hand, to these compromises, however necessary they be; and this is found in the *proviso*, that the differences surrendered should be *but* "minor," or that there should be no sacrifice of the main object of the combination, in the concessions which are mutually made. Any sacrifice which compromises that object is destructive of the principle of the combination, and no one who would be consistent can be a party to it.

Thus, for instance, if men of various religious denominations join together for the dissemination of what are called "evangelical" tracts, it is under the belief, that, the object of their uniting, as recognized on all hands, being the spiritual benefit of their neighbours, no religious exhortations, whatever be their character, can essentially interfere with that benefit, which faithfully insist upon the Lutheran doctrine of Justification. If, again, they agree together in printing and circulating the Protestant Bible, it is because they, one and all, hold to the principle, that, however serious be their differences of religious sentiment, such differences fade away before the one great principle, which that circulation symbolizes—that the Bible, the whole Bible, and nothing but the Bible, is the religion of Protestants. On the contrary, if the committee of some such association inserted tracts into the copies of the said Bible which they sold, and tracts in recommendation of the Athanasian Creed or the merit of good works, I conceive any subscribing member would have a just right to complain of a proceeding, which compromised the principle of Private Judgment as the one true interpreter of Scripture. These instances are sufficient to illustrate my general position, that coalitions and comprehensions for an object, have their life in the prosecution of that object, and cease to have any meaning as soon as that object is compromised or disparaged.

When, then, a number of persons come forward, not as politicians, not as diplomatists, lawyers, traders, or speculators, but with the one object of advancing Universal Knowledge, much we may allow them to sacrifice,—ambition, reputation, leisure, comfort, party-interests, gold; one thing they may not sacrifice,—Knowledge itself. Knowledge being their object, they need not of course insist on their own private views about ancient or modern history, or national prosperity, or the balance of power; they need not of course shrink from the cooperation of those who hold the opposite views; but stipulate they must that Knowledge itself is not compromised;—and as to those views, of whatever kind, which they do allow to be dropped, it is plain they consider such to be opinions, and nothing more, however dear, however important to themselves personally; opinions ingenious, admirable, pleasurable, beneficial, expedient, but not worthy the name of Knowledge or Science. Thus no one would insist on the Malthusian teaching being a *sine quâ non* in a seat of learning, who did not think it simply ignorance not to be a Malthusian; and no one would consent to drop the Newtonian theory, who thought it to have been proved true, in the same sense as the existence of the sun and moon is true. If, then, in an Institution which professes all knowledge, nothing is professed, nothing is taught about the Supreme Being, it is fair to infer that every individual in the number of those who advocate that Institution, supposing him consistent, distinctly holds that nothing is known for certain about the Supreme Being; nothing such, as to have any claim to be regarded as a material addition to the stock of general knowledge existing in the world. If on the other hand it turns out that something considerable *is* known about the Supreme Being, whether from Reason or Revelation, then the Institution in question professes every science, and yet leaves out the foremost of them. In a word, strong as may appear the assertion, I do not see how I can avoid making it, and bear with me, Gentlemen, while I do so, viz., such an Institution cannot be what it professes, if there be a God. I do not wish to declaim; but, by the very force of the terms, it is very plain, that a Divine Being and a University so circumstanced cannot co-exist.

3.

Still, however, this may seem to many an abrupt conclusion, and will not be acquiesced in: what answer, Gentlemen, will be made to it? Perhaps this:—It will be said, that there are different kinds or spheres of Knowledge, human, divine, sensible, intellectual, and the like; and that a University certainly takes in all varieties of Knowledge in its own line, but still that it has a line of its own. It contemplates, it occupies a certain order, a certain platform, of Knowledge. I understand the remark; but I own to you, I do not understand how it can be made to apply to the matter in hand. I cannot so construct my definition of the subject-matter of University Knowledge, and so draw my boundary lines around it, as to include therein the other sciences commonly studied at Universities, and to exclude the science of Religion. For instance, are we to limit our idea of University Knowledge by the evidence of our senses? then we exclude ethics; by intuition? we exclude history; by testimony? we exclude metaphysics; by abstract reasoning? we exclude physics. Is not the being of a God reported to us by testimony, handed down by history, inferred by an inductive process, brought home to us by metaphysical necessity, urged on us by the suggestions of our conscience? It is a truth in the natural order, as well as in the supernatural. So much for its origin; and, when obtained, what is it worth? Is it a great truth or a small one? Is it a comprehensive truth? Say that no other religious idea whatever were given but it, and you have enough to fill the mind; you have at once a whole dogmatic system. The word "God" is a Theology in itself, indivisibly one, inexhaustibly various, from the vastness and the simplicity of its meaning. Admit a God, and you introduce among the subjects of your knowledge, a fact encompassing, closing in upon, absorbing, every other fact conceivable. How can we investigate any part of any order of Knowledge, and stop short of that which enters into every order? All true principles run over with it, all phenomena converge to it; it is truly the First and the Last. In word indeed, and in idea, it is easy enough to divide Knowledge into human and divine, secular and religious, and to lay down that we will address ourselves to the one without interfering with the other; but it is impossible in fact. Granting that divine truth differs in kind from human, so do human truths differ in kind one from another. If the knowledge of the Creator is in a different order from knowledge of the creature, so, in like manner, metaphysical science is in a different order from physical, physics from history, history from ethics. You will soon break up into fragments the whole circle of secular knowledge, if you begin the mutilation with divine.

I have been speaking simply of Natural Theology; my argument of course is stronger when I go on to Revelation. Let the doctrine of the Incarnation be true: is it not at once of the nature of an historical fact, and of a metaphysical? Let it be true that there are Angels: how is not this a point of knowledge in the same sense as the naturalist's asseveration, that myriads of living things might co-exist on the point of a needle? That the Earth is to be burned by fire, is, if true, as large a fact as that huge monsters once played amid its depths; that Antichrist is to come, is as categorical a heading to a chapter of history, as that Nero or Julian was Emperor of Rome; that a divine influence moves the will, is a subject of thought not more mysterious than the result of volition on our muscles, which we admit as a fact in metaphysics.

I do not see how it is possible for a philosophical mind, first, to believe these religious facts to be true; next, to consent to ignore them; and thirdly, in spite of this, to go on to profess to be teaching all the while *de omni scibili*. No; if a man thinks in his heart that these religious facts are short of truth, that they are not true in the sense in which the general fact and the law of the fall of a stone to the earth is true, I understand his excluding Religion from his University, though he professes other reasons for its exclusion. In that case the varieties of religious opinion under which he shelters his conduct, are not only his apology for publicly disowning Religion, but a cause of his privately disbelieving it. He does not think that any thing is known or can be known for certain, about the origin of the world or the end of man.

4.

This, I fear, is the conclusion to which intellects, clear, logical, and consistent, have come, or are coming, from the nature of the case; and, alas! in addition to this *primâ-facie* suspicion, there are actual tendencies in the same direction in Protestantism, viewed whether in its original idea, or again in the so-called Evangelical movement in these islands during the last century. The religious world, as it is styled, holds, generally speaking, that religion consists, not in knowledge, but in feeling or sentiment. The old Catholic notion, which still lingers in the Established Church, was, that Faith was an intellectual act, its object truth, and its result knowledge. Thus if you look into the Anglican Prayer Book, you will find definite *credenda*, as well as definite *agenda*; but in proportion as the Lutheran leaven spread, it became fashionable to say that Faith was, not an acceptance of revealed doctrine, not an act of the intellect, but a feeling, an emotion, an affection, an appetency; and, as this view of Faith obtained, so was the connexion of Faith with Truth and Knowledge more and more either forgotten or denied. At length the identity of this (so-called) spirituality of heart and the virtue of Faith was acknowledged on all hands. Some men indeed disapproved the pietism in question, others admired it; but whether they admired or disapproved, both the one party and the other found themselves in agreement on the main point, viz.—in considering that this really was in substance Religion, and nothing else; that Religion was based, not on argument, but on taste and sentiment, that nothing was objective, every thing subjective, in doctrine. I say, even those who saw through the affectation in which the religious school of which I am speaking clad itself, still came to think that Religion, as such, consisted in something short of intellectual exercises, viz., in the affections, in the imagination, in inward persuasions and consolations, in pleasurable sensations, sudden changes, and sublime fancies. They learned to believe and to take it for granted, that Religion was nothing beyond a *supply* of the wants of human nature, not an external fact and a work of God. There was, it appeared, a demand for Religion, and therefore there was a supply; human nature could not do without Religion, any more than it could do without bread; a supply was absolutely necessary, good or bad, and, as in the case of the articles of daily sustenance, an article which was really inferior was better than none at all. Thus Religion was useful, venerable, beautiful, the sanction of order, the stay of government, the curb of self-will and self-indulgence, which the laws cannot reach: but, after all, on what was it based? Why, that was a question delicate to ask, and imprudent to answer; but, if the truth must be spoken, however reluctantly, the long and the short of the matter was this, that Religion was based on custom, on prejudice, on law, on education, on habit, on loyalty, on feudalism, on enlightened expedience, on many, many things, but not at all on reason; reason was neither its warrant, nor its instrument, and science had as little connexion with it as with the fashions of the season, or the state of the weather.

You see, Gentlemen, how a theory or philosophy, which began with the religious changes of the sixteenth century, has led to conclusions, which the authors of those changes would be the first to denounce, and has been taken up by that large and influential body which goes by the name of Liberal or Latitudinarian; and how, where it prevails, it is as unreasonable of course to demand for Religion a chair in a University, as to demand one for fine feeling, sense of honour, patriotism, gratitude, maternal affection, or good companionship, proposals which would be simply unmeaning.

5.

Now, in illustration of what I have been saying, I will appeal, in the first place, to a statesman, but not merely so, to no mere politician, no trader in places, or in votes, or in the stock market, but to a philosopher, to an orator, to one whose profession, whose aim, has ever been to cultivate the fair, the noble, and the generous. I cannot forget the celebrated discourse of the celebrated man to whom I am referring; a man who is first in his peculiar walk; and who, moreover (which is much to my purpose), has had a share, as much as any one alive, in effecting the public recognition in these Islands of the principle of separating secular and religious knowledge. This brilliant thinker, during the years in which he was exerting himself in behalf of this principle, made a speech or discourse, on occasion of a public solemnity; and in reference to the bearing of general knowledge upon religious belief, he spoke as follows:

"As men," he said, "will no longer suffer themselves to be led blindfold in ignorance, so will they no more yield to the vile principle of judging and treating their fellow-creatures, not according to the intrinsic merit of their actions, but according to the accidental and involuntary coincidence of their opinions. The great truth has finally gone forth to all the ends of the earth," and he prints it in capital letters, "that man shall no more render account to man for his belief, over which he has himself no control. Henceforward, nothing shall prevail upon us to praise or to blame any one for that which he can no more change, than he can the hue of his skin or the height of his stature."[3] You see, Gentlemen, if this philosopher is to decide the matter, religious ideas are just as far from being real, or representing anything beyond themselves, are as truly peculiarities, idiosyncracies, accidents of the individual, as his having the stature of a Patagonian, or the features of a Negro.

But perhaps this was the rhetoric of an excited moment. Far from it, Gentlemen, or I should not have fastened on the words of a fertile mind, uttered so long ago. What Mr. Brougham laid down as a principle in 1825, resounds on all sides of us, with ever-growing confidence and success, in 1852. I open the Minutes of the Committee of Council on Education for the years 1848-50, presented to both Houses of Parliament by command of Her Majesty, and I find one of Her Majesty's Inspectors of Schools, at p. 467 of the second volume, dividing "the topics usually embraced in the better class of primary schools" into four:——the knowledge of *signs*, as reading and writing; of *facts*, as geography

---

3 Mr. Brougham's Glasgow Discourse.

and astronomy; of *relations and laws*, as mathematics; and lastly *sentiment*, such as poetry and music. Now, on first catching sight of this division, it occurred to me to ask myself, before ascertaining the writer's own resolution of the matter, under which of these four heads would fall Religion, or whether it fell under any of them. Did he put it aside as a thing too delicate and sacred to be enumerated with earthly studies? or did he distinctly contemplate it when he made his division? Anyhow, I could really find a place for it under the first head, or the second, or the third;—for it has to do with facts, since it tells of the Self-subsisting; it has to do with relations, for it tells of the Creator; it has to do with signs, for it tells of the due manner of speaking of Him. There was just one head of the division to which I could not refer it, viz., to *sentiment*; for, I suppose, music and poetry, which are the writer's own examples of sentiment, have not much to do with Truth, which is the main object of Religion. Judge then my surprise, Gentlemen, when I found the fourth was the very head selected by the writer of the Report in question, as the special receptacle of religious topics. "The inculcation of *sentiment*," he says, "embraces reading in its higher sense, poetry, music, together with moral and religious Education." I am far from introducing this writer for his own sake, because I have no wish to hurt the feelings of a gentleman, who is but exerting himself zealously in the discharge of anxious duties; but, taking him as an illustration of the wide-spreading school of thought to which he belongs, I ask what can more clearly prove than a candid avowal like this, that, in the view of his school, Religion is not knowledge, has nothing whatever to do with knowledge, and is excluded from a University course of instruction, not simply because the exclusion cannot be helped, from political or social obstacles, but because it has no business there at all, because it is to be considered a taste, sentiment, opinion, and nothing more?

The writer avows this conclusion himself, in the explanation into which he presently enters, in which he says: "According to the classification proposed, the *essential idea* of all religious Education will consist in the direct cultivation of the *feelings*." What we contemplate, then, what we aim at, when we give a religious Education, is, it seems, not to impart any knowledge whatever, but to satisfy anyhow desires after the Unseen which will arise in our minds in spite of ourselves, to provide the mind with a means of self-command, to impress on it the beautiful ideas which saints and sages have struck out, to embellish it with the bright hues of a celestial piety, to teach it the poetry of devotion, the music of well-ordered affections, and the luxury of doing good. As for the intellect, its exercise happens to be unavoidable, whenever moral impressions are made, from the constitution of the human mind, but it varies in the results of that exercise, in the conclusions which it draws from our impression, according to the peculiarities of the individual.

Something like this seems to be the writer's meaning, but we need not pry into its finer issues in order to gain a distinct view of its general bearing; and taking it, as I think we fairly may take it, as a specimen of the philosophy of the day, as adopted by those who are not conscious unbelievers, or open scoffers, I consider it amply explains how it comes to pass that this day's philosophy sets up a system of universal knowledge, and teaches of plants, and earths, and creeping things, and beasts, and gases, about the crust of the earth and the changes of the atmosphere, about sun, moon, and stars, about man and his doings, about the history of the world, about sensation, memory, and the passions, about duty, about cause and effect, about all things imaginable, except one—and that is, about Him that made all these things, about God. I say the reason is plain because they consider knowledge, as regards the creature, is illimitable, but impossible or hopeless as regards the being and attributes and works of the Creator.

6.

Here, however, it may be objected to me that this representation is certainly extreme, for the school in question does, in fact, lay great stress on the evidence afforded by the creation, to the Being and Attributes of the Creator. I may be referred, for instance, to the words of one of the speakers on a memorable occasion.

At the very time of laying the first stone of the University of London, I confess it, a learned person, since elevated to the Protestant See of Durham, which he still fills, opened the proceedings with prayer. He addressed the Deity, as the authoritative Report informs us, "the whole surrounding assembly standing uncovered in solemn silence." "Thou," he said, in the name of all present, "thou hast constructed the vast fabric of the universe in so wonderful a manner, so arranged its motions, and so formed its productions, that the contemplation and study of thy works exercise at once the mind in the pursuit of human science, and lead it onwards to *Divine Truth*." Here is apparently a distinct recognition that there is such a thing as Truth in the province of Religion; and, did the passage stand by itself, and were it the only means we possessed of ascertaining the sentiments of the powerful body whom this distinguished person there represented, it would, as far as it goes, be satisfactory. I admit it; and I admit also the recognition of the Being and certain Attributes of the Deity, contained in the writings of the gifted person whom I have already quoted, whose genius, versatile and multiform as it is, in nothing has been so constant, as in its devotion to the advancement of knowledge, scientific and literary. He then certainly, in his "Discourse of the objects, advantages, and pleasures of science," after variously illustrating what he terms its "gratifying treats," crowns the catalogue with mention of "the *highest* of *all* our gratifications in the contemplation of science," which he proceeds to explain thus:

"We are raised by them," says he, "to an understanding of the infinite wisdom and goodness which the Creator has displayed in all His works. Not a step can be taken in any direction," he continues, "without perceiving the most extraordinary traces of design; and the skill, every where conspicuous, is calculated in so vast a proportion of instances to promote the happiness of living creatures, and especially of ourselves, that we can feel no hesitation in concluding, that, if we knew the whole scheme of Providence, every part would be in harmony with a plan of absolute benevolence. Independent, however, of this most consoling inference, the delight is inexpressible, of being able to follow, as it were, with our eyes, the marvellous works of the Great Architect of Nature, to trace the unbounded power and exquisite skill which are exhibited in the most minute, as well as the mightiest parts of His system. The pleasure derived from this study is unceasing, and so various, that it never tires the appetite. But it is unlike the low gratifications of sense in another respect: it elevates and refines our nature, while those hurt the health, debase the understanding, and corrupt the feelings; it teaches us to look upon all earthly objects as insignificant and below our notice, except the pursuit of knowledge and the cultivation of virtue, that is to say, the strict performance of our duty in every relation of society; and it gives a dignity and importance to the enjoyment of life, which the frivolous and the grovelling cannot even comprehend."

Such are the words of this prominent champion of Mixed Education. If logical inference be, as it undoubtedly is, an instrument of truth, surely, it may be answered to me, in admitting the possibility of inferring the Divine Being and Attributes *from* the phenomena of nature, he distinctly admits a basis of truth for the doctrines of Religion.

7.

I wish, Gentlemen, to give these representations their full weight, both from the gravity of the question, and the consideration due to the persons whom I am arraigning; but, before I can feel sure I understand them, I must ask an abrupt question. When I am told, then, by the partisans of Universities without Theological teaching, that human science leads to belief in a Supreme Being, without denying the fact, nay, as a Catholic, with full conviction of it, nevertheless I am obliged to ask what the statement means in *their* mouths, what they, the speakers, understand by the word "God." Let me not be thought offensive, if I question, whether it means the same thing on the two sides of the controversy. With us Catholics, as with the first race of Protestants, as with Mahometans, and all Theists, the word contains, as I have already said, a theology in itself. At the risk of anticipating what I shall have occasion to insist upon in my next Discourse, let me say that, according to the teaching of Monotheism, God is an Individual, Self-dependent, All-perfect, Unchangeable Being; intelligent, living, personal, and present; almighty, all-seeing, all-remembering; between whom and His creatures there is an infinite gulf; who has no origin, who is all-sufficient for Himself; who created and upholds the universe; who will judge every one of us, sooner or later, according to that Law of right and wrong which He has written on our hearts. He is One who is sovereign over, operative amidst, independent of, the appointments which He has made; One in whose hands are all things, who has a purpose in every event, and a standard for every deed, and thus has relations of His own towards the subject-matter of each particular science which the book of knowledge unfolds; who has with an adorable, never-ceasing energy implicated Himself in all the history of creation, the constitution of nature, the course of the world, the origin of society, the fortunes of nations, the action of the human mind; and who thereby necessarily becomes the subject-matter of a science, far wider and more noble than any of those which are included in the circle of secular Education.

This is the doctrine which belief in a God implies in the mind of a Catholic: if it means any thing, it means all this, and cannot keep from meaning all this, and a great deal more; and, even though there were nothing in the religious tenets of the last three centuries to disparage dogmatic truth, still, even then, I should have difficulty in believing that a doctrine so mysterious, so peremptory, approved itself as a matter of course to educated men of this day, who gave their minds attentively to consider it. Rather, in a state of society such as ours, in which authority, prescription, tradition, habit, moral instinct, and the divine influences go for nothing, in which patience of thought, and depth and consistency of view, are scorned as subtle and scholastic, in which free discussion and fallible judgment are prized as the birthright of each individual, I must be excused if I exercise towards this age, as regards its belief in this doctrine, some portion of that scepticism which it exercises itself towards every received but unscrutinized assertion whatever. I cannot take it for granted, I must have it brought home to me by tangible evidence, that the spirit of the age means by the Supreme Being what Catholics mean. Nay, it would be a relief to my mind to gain some ground of assurance, that the parties influenced by that spirit had, I will not say, a true apprehension of God, but even so much as the idea of what a true apprehension is.

Nothing is easier than to use the word, and mean nothing by it. The heathens used to say, "God wills," when they meant "Fate;" "God provides," when they meant "Chance;" "God acts," when they meant "Instinct" or "Sense;" and "God is every where," when they meant "the Soul of Nature." The Almighty is something infinitely different from a principle, or a centre of action, or a quality, or a generalization of phenomena. If, then, by the word, you do but mean a Being who keeps the world in order, who acts in it, but only in the way of general Providence, who acts towards us but only through what are called laws of Nature, who is more certain not to act at all than to act independent of those laws, who is known and approached indeed, but only through the medium of those laws; such a God it is not difficult for any one to conceive, not difficult for any one to endure. If, I say, as you would revolutionize society, so you would revolutionize heaven, if you have changed the divine sovereignty into a sort of constitutional monarchy, in which the Throne has honour and ceremonial enough, but cannot issue the most ordinary command except through legal forms and precedents, and with the counter-signature of a minister, then belief in a God is no more than an acknowledgment of existing, sensible powers and phenomena, which none but an idiot can deny. If the Supreme Being is powerful or skilful, just so far forth as the telescope shows power, and the microscope shows skill, if His moral law is to be ascertained simply by the physical processes of the animal frame, or His will gathered from the immediate issues of human affairs, if His Essence is just as high and deep and broad and long as the universe, and no more; if this be the fact, then will I confess that there is no specific science about God, that theology is but a name, and a protest in its behalf an hypocrisy. Then is He but coincident with the laws of the universe; then is He but a function, or correlative, or subjective reflection and mental impression, of each phenomenon of the material or moral world, as it flits before us. Then, pious as it is to think of Him, while the pageant of experiment or abstract reasoning passes by, still, such piety is nothing more than a poetry of thought or an ornament of language, and has not even an infinitesimal influence upon philosophy or science, of which it is rather the parasitical production.

I understand, in that case, why Theology should require no specific teaching, for there is nothing to mistake about; why it is powerless against scientific anticipations, for it merely is one of them; why it is simply absurd in its denunciations of heresy, for heresy does not lie in the region of fact and experiment. I understand, in that case, how it is that the religious sense is but a "sentiment," and its exercise a "gratifying treat," for it is like the sense of the beautiful or the sublime. I understand how the contemplation of the universe "leads onwards to *divine* truth," for divine truth is not something separate from Nature, but it is Nature with a divine glow upon it. I understand the zeal expressed for Physical Theology, for this study is but a mode of looking at Physical Nature, a certain view taken of Nature, private and personal, which one man has, and another has not, which gifted minds strike out, which others see to be admirable and ingenious, and which all would be the better for adopting. It is but the theology of Nature, just as we talk of the *philosophy* or the *romance* of history, or the *poetry* of childhood, or the picturesque, or the sentimental, or the humorous, or any other abstract quality, which the genius or the caprice of the individual, or the fashion of the day, or the consent of the world, recognizes in any set of objects which are subjected to its contemplation.

8.

Such ideas of religion seem to me short of Monotheism; I do not impute them to this or that individual who belongs to the school which gives them currency; but what I read about the "gratification" of keeping pace in our scientific researches with "the Architect of Nature;" about the said gratification "giving a dignity and importance to the enjoyment of life," and teaching us that knowledge and our duties to society are the only earthly objects worth our notice, all this, I own it, Gentlemen, frightens me; nor is Dr. Maltby's address to the Deity sufficient to reassure me. I do not see much difference between avowing that there is no God, and implying that nothing definite can for certain be known about Him; and when I find Religious Education treated as the cultivation of sentiment, and Religious Belief as the accidental hue or posture of the mind, I am reluctantly but forcibly reminded of a very unpleasant page of Metaphysics, viz., of the relations between God and Nature insinuated by such philosophers as Hume. This acute, though most low-minded of speculators, in his inquiry concerning the Human Understanding, introduces, as is well known, Epicurus, that is, a teacher of atheism, delivering an harangue to the Athenian people, not indeed in defence, but in extenuation of that opinion. His object is to show that, whereas the atheistic view is nothing else than the repudiation of theory, and an accurate representation of phenomenon and fact, it cannot be dangerous, unless phenomenon and fact be dangerous. Epicurus is made to say, that the paralogism of philosophy has ever been that of arguing from Nature in behalf of something beyond Nature, greater than Nature; whereas, God, as he maintains, being known only through the visible world, our knowledge of Him is absolutely commensurate with our knowledge of it,—is nothing distinct from it,—is but a mode of viewing it. Hence it follows that, provided we admit, as we cannot help admitting, the phenomena of Nature and the world, it is only a question of words whether or not we go on to the hypothesis of a second Being, not visible but immaterial, parallel and coincident with Nature, to whom we give the name of God. "Allowing," he says, "the gods to be the authors of the existence or order of the universe, it follows that they possess that precise degree of power, intelligence, and benevolence, which appears in their workmanship; but nothing farther can be proved, except we call in the assistance of exaggeration and flattery to supply the defects of argument and reasoning. So far as the traces of any attributes, at present, appear, so far may we conclude these attributes to exist. The supposition of farther attributes is mere hypothesis; much more the supposition that, in distant periods of place and time, there has been, or will be, a more magnificent display of these attributes, and a scheme of administration more suitable to such imaginary virtues."

Here is a reasoner, who would not hesitate to deny that there is any distinct science or philosophy possible concerning the Supreme Being; since every single thing we know of Him is this or that or the other phenomenon, material or moral, which already falls under this or that natural science. In him then it would be only consistent to drop Theology in a course of University Education: but how is it consistent in any one who shrinks from his companionship? I am glad to see that the author, several times mentioned, is in opposition to Hume, in one sentence of the quotation I have made from his Discourse upon Science, deciding, as he does, that the phenomena of the material world are insufficient for the full exhibition of the Divine Attributes, and implying that they require a supplemental process to complete and harmonize their evidence. But is not this supplemental process a science? and if so, why not acknowledge its existence? If God is more than Nature, Theology claims a place among the sciences: but, on the other hand, if you are not sure of as much as this, how do you differ from Hume or Epicurus?

9.

I end then as I began: religious doctrine is knowledge. This is the important truth, little entered into at this day, which I wish that all who have honoured me with their presence here would allow me to beg them to take away with them. I am not catching at sharp arguments, but laying down grave principles. Religious doctrine is knowledge, in as full a sense as Newton's doctrine is knowledge. University Teaching without Theology is simply unphilosophical. Theology has at least as good a right to claim a place there as Astronomy.

In my next Discourse it will be my object to show that its omission from the list of recognised sciences is not only indefensible in itself, but prejudicial to all the rest.

BEARING OF THEOLOGY ON OTHER BRANCHES OF KNOWLEDGE

1.

WHEN men of great intellect, who have long and intently and exclusively given themselves to the study or investigation of some one particular branch of secular knowledge, whose mental life is concentrated and hidden in their chosen pursuit, and who have neither eyes nor ears for any thing which does not immediately bear upon it, when such men are at length made to realize that there is a clamour all around them, which must be heard, for what they have been so little accustomed to place in the category of knowledge as Religion, and that they themselves are accused of disaffection to it, they are impatient at the interruption; they call the demand tyrannical, and the requisitionists bigots or fanatics. They are tempted to say, that their only wish is to be let alone; for themselves, they are not dreaming of offending any one, or interfering with any one; they are pursuing their own particular line, they have never spoken a word against any one's religion, whoever he may be, and never mean to do so. It does not follow that they deny the existence of a God, because they are not found talking of it, when the topic would be utterly irrelevant. All they say is, that there are other beings in the world besides the Supreme Being; their business is with them. After all, the creation is not the Creator, nor things secular religious. Theology and human science are two things, not one, and have their respective provinces, contiguous it may be and cognate to each other, but not identical. When we are contemplating earth, we are not contemplating heaven; and when we are contemplating heaven, we are not contemplating earth. Separate subjects should be treated separately. As division of labour, so division of thought is the only means of successful application. "Let us go our own way," they say, "and you go yours. We do not pretend to lecture on Theology, and you have no claim to pronounce upon Science."

With this feeling they attempt a sort of compromise, between their opponents who claim for Theology a free introduction into the Schools of Science, and themselves who would exclude it altogether, and it is this: viz., that it should remain indeed excluded from the public schools, but that it should be permitted in private, wherever a sufficient number of persons is found to desire it. Such persons, they seem to say, may have it all their own way, when they are by themselves, so that they do not attempt to disturb a comprehensive system of instruction, acceptable and useful to all, by the intrusion of opinions peculiar to their own minds.

I am now going to attempt a philosophical answer to this representation, that is, to the project of teaching secular knowledge in the University Lecture Room, and remanding religious knowledge to the parish priest, the catechism, and the parlour; and in doing so, you must pardon me, Gentlemen, if my subject should oblige me to pursue a lengthy and careful course of thought, which may be wearisome to the hearer:—I begin then thus:—

2.

Truth is the object of Knowledge of whatever kind; and when we inquire what is meant by Truth, I suppose it is right to answer that Truth means facts and their relations, which stand towards each other pretty much as subjects and predicates in logic. All that exists, as contemplated by the human mind, forms one large system or complex fact, and this of course resolves itself into an indefinite number of particular facts, which, as being portions of a whole, have countless relations of every kind, one towards another. Knowledge is the apprehension of these facts, whether in themselves, or in their mutual positions and bearings. And, as all taken together form one integral subject for contemplation, so there are no natural or real limits between part and part;

one is ever running into another; all, as viewed by the mind, are combined together, and possess a correlative character one with another, from the internal mysteries of the Divine Essence down to our own sensations and consciousness, from the most solemn appointments of the Lord of all down to what may be called the accident of the hour, from the most glorious seraph down to the vilest and most noxious of reptiles.

Now, it is not wonderful that, with all its capabilities, the human mind cannot take in this whole vast fact at a single glance, or gain possession of it at once. Like a short-sighted reader, its eye pores closely, and travels slowly, over the awful volume which lies open for its inspection. Or again, as we deal with some huge structure of many parts and sides, the mind goes round about it, noting down, first one thing, then another, as it best may, and viewing it under different aspects, by way of making progress towards mastering the whole. So by degrees and by circuitous advances does it rise aloft and subject to itself a knowledge of that universe into which it has been born.

These various partial views or abstractions, by means of which the mind looks out upon its object, are called sciences, and embrace respectively larger or smaller portions of the field of knowledge; sometimes extending far and wide, but superficially, sometimes with exactness over particular departments, sometimes occupied together on one and the same portion, sometimes holding one part in common, and then ranging on this side or that in absolute divergence one from the other. Thus Optics has for its subject the whole visible creation, so far forth as it is simply visible; Mental Philosophy has a narrower province, but a richer one. Astronomy, plane and physical, each has the same subject-matter, but views it or treats it differently; lastly, Geology and Comparative Anatomy have subject-matters partly the same, partly distinct. Now these views or sciences, as being abstractions, have far more to do with the relations of things than with things themselves. They tell us what things are, only or principally by telling us their relations, or assigning predicates to subjects; and therefore they never tell us all that can be said about a thing, even when they tell something, nor do they bring it before us, as the senses do. They arrange and classify facts; they reduce separate phenomena under a common law; they trace effects to a cause. Thus they serve to transfer our knowledge from the custody of memory to the surer and more abiding protection of philosophy, thereby providing both for its spread and its advance:—for, inasmuch as sciences are forms of knowledge, they enable the intellect to master and increase it; and, inasmuch as they are instruments, to communicate it readily to others. Still after all, they proceed on the principle of a division of labour, even though that division is an abstraction, not a literal separation into parts; and, as the maker of a bridle or an epaulet has not, on that account, any idea of the science of tactics or strategy, so in a parallel way, it is not every science which equally, nor any one which fully, enlightens the mind in the knowledge of things, as they are, or brings home to it the external object on which it wishes to gaze. Thus they differ in importance; and according to their importance will be their influence, not only on the mass of knowledge to which they all converge and contribute, but on each other.

Since then sciences are the results of mental processes about one and the same subject-matter, viewed under its various aspects, and are true results, as far as they go, yet at the same time separate and partial, it follows that on the one hand they need external assistance, one by one, by reason of their incompleteness, and on the other that they are able to afford it to each other, by reason, first, of their independence in themselves, and then of their connexion in their subject-matter. Viewed altogether, they approximate to a representation or subjective reflection of the objective truth, as nearly as is possible to the human mind, which advances towards the accurate apprehension of that object, in proportion to the number of sciences which it has mastered; and which, when certain sciences are away, in such a case has but a defective apprehension, in proportion to the value of the sciences which are thus wanting, and the importance of the field on which they are employed.

3.

Let us take, for instance, man himself as our object of contemplation; then at once we shall find we can view him in a variety of relations; and according to those relations are the sciences of which he is the subject-matter, and according to our acquaintance with them is our possession of a true knowledge of him. We may view him in relation to the material elements of his body, or to his mental constitution, or to his household and family, or to the community in which he lives, or to the Being who made him; and in consequence we treat of him respectively as physiologists, or as moral philosophers, or as writers of economics, or of politics, or as theologians. When we think of him in all these relations together, or as the subject at once of all the sciences I have named, then we may be said to reach unto and rest in the idea of man as an object or external fact, similar to that which the eye takes of his outward form. On the other hand, according as we are only physiologists, or only politicians, or only moralists, so is our idea of man more or less unreal; we do not take in the whole of him, and the defect is greater or less, in proportion as the relation is, or is not, important, which is omitted, whether his relation to God, or to his king, or to his children, or to his own component parts. And if there be one relation, about which we know nothing at all except that it exists, then is our knowledge of him, confessedly and to our own consciousness, deficient and partial, and that, I repeat, in proportion to the importance of the relation.

That therefore is true of sciences in general which we are apt to think applies only to pure mathematics, though to pure mathematics it applies especially, viz., that they cannot be considered as simple representations or informants of things as they are. We are accustomed to say, and say truly, that the conclusions of pure mathematics are applied, corrected, and adapted, by mixed; but so too the conclusions of Anatomy, Chemistry, Dynamics, and other sciences, are revised and completed by each other. Those several conclusions do not represent whole and substantive things, but views, true, so far as they go; and in order to ascertain how far they do go, that is, how far they correspond to the object to which they belong, we must compare them with the views taken out of that object by other sciences. Did we proceed upon the abstract theory of forces, we should assign a much more ample range to a projectile than in fact the resistance of the air allows it to accomplish. Let, however, that resistance be made the subject of scientific analysis, and then we shall have a new science, assisting, and to a certain point completing, for the benefit of questions of fact, the science of projection. On the other hand, the science of projection itself, considered as belonging to the forces it contemplates, is not more perfect, as such, by this supplementary investigation. And in like manner, as regards the whole circle of sciences, one corrects another for purposes of fact, and one without the other cannot dogmatize, except hypothetically and upon its own abstract principles. For instance, the Newtonian philosophy requires the admission of certain metaphysical postulates, if it is to be more than a theory or an hypothesis; as, for instance, that what happened yesterday will happen tomorrow; that there is such a thing as matter, that our senses are trustworthy, that there is a logic of induction, and so on. Now to Newton metaphysicians grant all that he asks; but, if so be, they may not prove equally accommodating to another who asks something else, and then all his most logical conclusions in the science of physics would remain hopelessly on the stocks, though finished, and never could be launched into the sphere of fact.

Again, did I know nothing about the movement of bodies, except what the theory of gravitation supplies, were I simply absorbed in that theory so as to make it measure all motion on earth and in the sky, I should indeed come to many right conclusions, I should hit off many important facts, ascertain many existing relations, and correct many popular errors: I should scout and ridicule with great success the old notion, that light bodies flew up and heavy bodies fell down; but I should go on with equal confidence to deny the phenomenon of capillary attraction. Here I should be wrong, but only because I carried out my science irrespectively of other sciences. In like manner, did I simply give myself to the investigation of the external action of body upon body, I might scoff at the very idea of chemical affinities and combinations, and reject it as simply unintelligible. Were I a mere chemist, I should deny the influence of mind upon bodily health; and so on, as regards the devotees of any science, or family of sciences, to the exclusion of others; they necessarily become bigots and quacks, scorning all principles and reported facts which do not belong to their own pursuit, and thinking to effect everything without aid from any other quarter. Thus, before now, chemistry has been substituted for medicine; and again, political economy, or intellectual enlightenment, or the reading of the Scriptures, has been cried up as a panacea against vice, malevolence, and misery.

4.

Summing up, Gentlemen, what I have said, I lay it down that all knowledge forms one whole, because its subject-matter is one; for the universe in its length and breadth is so intimately knit together, that we cannot separate off portion from portion, and operation from operation, except by a mental abstraction; and then again, as to its Creator, though He of course in His own Being is infinitely separate from it, and Theology has its departments towards which human knowledge has no relations, yet He has so implicated Himself with it, and taken it into His very bosom, by His presence in it, His providence over it, His impressions upon it, and His influences through it, that we cannot truly or fully contemplate it without in some main aspects contemplating Him. Next, sciences are the results of that mental abstraction, which I have spoken of, being the logical record of this or that aspect of the whole subject-matter of knowledge. As they all belong to one and the same circle of objects, they are one and all connected together; as they are but aspects of things, they are severally incomplete in their relation to the things themselves, though complete in their own idea and for their own respective purposes; on both accounts they at once need and subserve each other. And further, the comprehension of the bearings of one science on another, and the use of each to each, and the location and limitation and adjustment and due appreciation of them all, one with another, this belongs, I conceive, to a sort of science distinct from all of them, and in some sense a science of sciences, which is my own conception of what is meant by Philosophy, in the true sense of the word, and of a philosophical habit of mind, and which in these Discourses I shall call by that name. This is what I have to say about knowledge and philosophical knowledge generally; and now I proceed to apply it to the particular science, which has led me to draw it out.

I say, then, that the systematic omission of any one science from the catalogue prejudices the accuracy and completeness of our knowledge altogether, and that, in proportion to its importance. Not even Theology itself, though it comes from heaven, though its truths were given once for all at the first, though they are more certain on account of the Giver than those of mathematics, not even Theology, so far as it is relative to us, or is the Science of Religion, do I exclude from the law to which every mental exercise is subject, viz., from that imperfection, which ever must attend the abstract, when it would determine the concrete. Nor do I speak only of Natural Religion; for even the teaching of the Catholic Church, in certain of its aspects, that is, its religious teaching, is variously influenced by the other sciences. Not to insist on the introduction of the Aristotelic philosophy into its phraseology, its explanation of dogmas is influenced by ecclesiastical acts or events; its interpretations of prophecy are directly affected by the issues of history; its comments upon Scripture by the conclusions of the astronomer and the geologist; and its casuistical decisions by the various experience, political, social, and psychological, with which times and places are ever supplying it.

What Theology gives, it has a right to take; or rather, the interests of Truth oblige it to take. If we would not be beguiled by dreams, if we would ascertain facts as they are, then, granting Theology is a real science, we cannot exclude it, and still call ourselves philosophers. I have asserted nothing as yet as to

the pre-eminent dignity of Religious Truth; I only say, if there
be Religious Truth at all, we cannot shut our eyes to it without
prejudice to truth of every kind, physical, metaphysical, historical, and moral; for it bears upon all truth. And thus I answer the
objection with which I opened this Discourse. I supposed the
question put to me by a philosopher of the day, "Why cannot
you go your way, and let us go ours?" I answer, in the name of
the Science of Religion, "When Newton can dispense with the
metaphysician, then may you dispense with us." So much at first
sight; now I am going on to claim a little more for Theology, by
classing it with branches of knowledge which may with greater
decency be compared to it.

5.

Let us see, then, how this supercilious treatment of so momentous a science, for momentous it must be, if there be a God,
runs in a somewhat parallel case. The great philosopher of antiquity, when he would enumerate the causes of the things that
take place in the world, after making mention of those which
he considered to be physical and material, adds, "and the mind
and everything which is by means of man."[1] Certainly; it would
have been a preposterous course, when he would trace the effects
he saw around him to their respective sources, had he directed
his exclusive attention upon some one class or order of originating principles, and ascribed to these everything which happened
anywhere. It would indeed have been unworthy a genius so curious, so penetrating, so fertile, so analytical as Aristotle's, to have
laid it down that everything on the face of the earth could be
accounted for by the material sciences, without the hypothesis of
moral agents. It is incredible that in the investigation of physical
results he could ignore so influential a being as man, or forget
that, not only brute force and elemental movement, but knowledge also is power. And this so much the more, inasmuch as
moral and spiritual agents belong to another, not to say a higher,

---

1 Arist. Ethic. Nicom., iii. 3.

order than physical; so that the omission supposed would not have been merely an oversight in matters of detail, but a philosophical error, and a fault in division.

However, we live in an age of the world when the career of science and literature is little affected by what was done, or would have been done, by this venerable authority; so, we will suppose, in England or Ireland, in the middle of the nineteenth century, a set of persons of name and celebrity to meet together, in spite of Aristotle, in order to adopt a line of proceeding which they conceive the circumstances of the time render imperative. We will suppose that a difficulty just now besets the enunciation and discussion of all matters of science, in consequence of the extreme sensitiveness of large classes of the community, clergy and laymen, on the subjects of necessity, responsibility, the standard of morals, and the nature of virtue. Parties run so high, that the only way of avoiding constant quarrelling in defence of this or that side of the question is, in the judgment of the persons I am supposing, to shut up the subject of anthropology altogether. This is accordingly done. Henceforth man is to be as if he were not, in the general course of Education; the moral and mental sciences are to have no professorial chairs, and the treatment of them is to be simply left as a matter of private judgment, which each individual may carry out as he will. I can just fancy such a prohibition abstractedly possible; but one thing I cannot fancy possible, viz., that the parties in question, after this sweeping act of exclusion, should forthwith send out proposals on the basis of such exclusion for publishing an Encyclopædia, or erecting a National University.

It is necessary, however, Gentlemen, for the sake of the illustration which I am setting before you, to imagine what cannot be. I say, let us imagine a project for organizing a system of scientific teaching, in which the agency of man in the material world cannot allowably be recognized, and may allowably be denied. Physical and mechanical causes are exclusively to be treated of; volition is a forbidden subject. A prospectus is put out, with a list of sciences, we will say, Astronomy, Optics, Hydrostatics, Galvanism, Pneumatics, Statics, Dynamics, Pure Mathematics, Geology, Botany, Physiology, Anatomy, and so forth; but not a word about the mind and its powers, except what is said in explanation of the omission. That explanation is to the effect that the parties concerned in the undertaking have given long and anxious thought to the subject, and have been reluctantly driven to the conclusion that it is simply impracticable to include in the list of University Lectures the Philosophy of Mind. What relieves, however, their regret is the reflection, that domestic feelings and polished manners are best cultivated in the family circle and in good society, in the observance of the sacred ties which unite father, mother, and child, in the correlative claims and duties of citizenship, in the exercise of disinterested loyalty and enlightened patriotism. With this apology, such as it is, they pass over the consideration of the human mind and its powers and works, "in solemn silence," in their scheme of University Education.

Let a charter be obtained for it; let professors be appointed, lectures given, examinations passed, degrees awarded:—what sort of exactness or trustworthiness, what philosophical largeness, will attach to views formed in an intellectual atmosphere thus deprived of some of the constituent elements of daylight? What judgment will foreign countries and future times pass on the labours of the most acute and accomplished of the philosophers who have been parties to so portentous an unreality? Here are professors gravely lecturing on medicine, or history, or political economy, who, so far from being bound to acknowledge, are free to scoff at the action of mind upon matter, or of mind upon mind, or the claims of mutual justice and charity. Common sense indeed and public opinion set bounds at first to so intolerable a licence; yet, as time goes on, an omission which was originally but a matter of expedience, commends itself to the reason; and at length a professor is found, more hardy than his brethren, still however, as he himself maintains, with sincere respect for domestic feelings and good manners, who takes on him to deny psychology *in toto*, to pronounce the influence of mind in the visible world a superstition, and to account for every effect which is found in the world by the operation of physical causes. Hitherto intelligence and volition were accounted real powers; the muscles act, and their action cannot be represented by any scientific expression; a stone flies out of the hand and the propulsive force of the muscle resides in the will; but there has been a revolution, or at least a new theory in philosophy, and our Professor, I say, after speaking with the highest admiration of the human intellect, limits its independent action to the region of speculation, and denies that it can be a motive principle, or can exercise a special interference, in the material world. He ascribes every work, every external act of man, to the innate force or soul of the physical universe. He observes that spiritual agents are so mysterious and unintelligible, so uncertain in their laws, so vague in their operation, so sheltered from experience, that a wise man will have nothing to say to them. They belong to a different order of causes, which he leaves to those whose profession it is to investigate them, and he confines himself to the tangible and sure. Human exploits, human devices, human deeds, human productions, all that comes under the scholastic terms of "genius" and "art," and the metaphysical ideas of "duty," "right," and "heroism," it is his office to contemplate all these merely in their place in the eternal system of physical cause and effect. At length he undertakes to show how the whole fabric of material civilization has arisen from the constructive powers of physical elements and physical laws. He descants upon palaces, castles, temples, exchanges, bridges, causeways, and shows that they never could have grown into the imposing dimensions which they present to us, but for the laws of gravitation and the cohesion of part with part. The pillar would come down, the loftier the more speedily, did not the centre of gravity fall within its base; and the most admired dome of Palladio or of Sir Christopher would give way, were it not for the happy principle of the arch. He surveys the complicated machinery of a single day's arrangements in a private family; our dress, our furniture, our hospitable board; what would become of them, he asks, but for the laws of physical nature? Those laws are the causes of our carpets, our furniture, our travelling, and our social intercourse. Firm stitches have a natural power, in proportion to the toughness of the material adopted, to keep together separate portions of cloth; sofas and chairs could not turn upside down, even if they would; and it is a property of caloric to relax the fibres of animal matter acting through water in one way, through oil in another, and this is the whole mystery of the most elaborate *cuisine:*—but I should be tedious if I continued the illustration.

6.

Now, Gentlemen, pray understand how it is to be here applied. I am not supposing that the principles of Theology and Psychology are the same, or arguing from the works of man to the works of God, which Paley has done, which Hume has protested against. I am not busying myself to prove the existence and attributes of God, by means of the Argument from design. I am not proving anything at all about the Supreme Being. On the contrary, I am assuming His existence, and I do but say this:—that, man existing, no University Professor, who had suppressed in physical lectures the idea of volition, who did not take volition for granted, could escape a one-sided, a radically false view of the things which he discussed; not indeed that his own definitions, principles, and laws would be wrong, or his abstract statements, but his considering his own study to be the key of everything that takes place on the face of the earth, and his passing over anthropology, this would be his error. I say, it would not be his science which was untrue, but his so-called knowledge which was unreal. He would be deciding on facts by means of theories. The various busy world, spread out before our eyes, is physical, but it is more than physical; and, in making its actual system identical with his scientific analysis, formed on a particular aspect, such a Professor as I have imagined was betraying a want of philosophical depth, and an ignorance of what an University Teaching ought to be. He was no longer a teacher of liberal knowledge, but a narrow-minded bigot. While his doctrines professed to be conclusions formed upon an hypothesis or partial truth, they were undeniable; not so if they professed to give results in facts which he could grasp and take possession of. Granting, indeed, that a man's arm is moved by a simple physical cause, then of course we may dispute about the various external influences which, when it changes its position, sway it to and fro, like a scarecrow in a garden; but to assert that the motive cause *is* physical, this is an assumption in a case, when our question is about a matter of fact, not about the logical consequences of an assumed premiss. And, in like manner, if a people prays, and the wind changes, the rain ceases, the sun shines, and the harvest is safely housed, when no one expected it, our Professor may, if he will, consult the barometer, discourse about the atmosphere, and throw what has happened into an equation, ingenious, even though it be not true; but, should he proceed to rest the phenomenon, in matter of fact, simply upon a physical cause, to the exclusion of a divine, and to say that the given case actually belongs to his science because other like cases do, I must tell him, *Ne sutor ultra crepidam:* he is making his particular craft usurp and occupy the universe. This then is the drift of my illustration. If the creature is ever setting in motion an endless series of physical causes and effects, much more is the Creator; and as our excluding volition from our range of ideas is a denial of the soul, so our ignoring Divine Agency is a virtual denial of God. Moreover, supposing man can will and act of himself in spite of physics, to shut up this great truth, though one, is to put our whole encyclopædia of knowledge out of joint; and supposing God can will and act of Himself in this world which He has made, and we deny or slur it over, then we are throwing the circle of universal science into a like, or a far worse confusion.

Worse incomparably, for the idea of God, if there be a God, is infinitely higher than the idea of man, if there be man. If to blot out man's agency is to deface the book of knowledge, on the supposition of that agency existing, what must it be, supposing it exists, to blot out the agency of God? I have hitherto been engaged in showing that all the sciences come to us as one, that they all relate to one and the same integral subject-matter, that each separately is more or less an abstraction, wholly true as an hypothesis, but not wholly trustworthy in the concrete, conversant with relations more than with facts, with principles more than with agents, needing the support and guarantee of its sister sciences, and giving in turn while it takes:—from which it follows that none can safely be omitted, if we would obtain the exactest knowledge possible of things as they are, and that the omission is more or less important, in proportion to the field which each covers, and the depth to which it penetrates, and the order to which it belongs; for its loss is a positive privation of an influence which exerts itself in the correction and completion of the rest. This is a general statement; but now as to Theology in particular, what, in matter of fact, are its pretensions, what its importance, what its influence upon other branches of knowledge, supposing there be a God, which it would not become me to set about proving? Has it vast dimensions, or does it lie in a nutshell? Will its omission be imperceptible, or will it destroy the equilibrium of the whole system of Knowledge? This is the inquiry to which I proceed.

7.

Now what is Theology? First, I will tell you what it is not. And here, in the first place (though of course I speak on the subject as a Catholic), observe that, strictly speaking, I am not assuming that Catholicism is true, while I make myself the champion of Theology. Catholicism has not formally entered into my argument hitherto, nor shall I just now assume any principle peculiar to it, for reasons which will appear in the sequel, though of course I shall use Catholic language. Neither, secondly, will I fall into the fashion of the day, of identifying Natural Theology with Physical Theology; which said Physical Theology is a most jejune study, considered as a science, and really is no science at all, for it is ordinarily nothing more than a series of pious or polemical remarks upon the physical world viewed religiously, whereas the word "Natural" properly comprehends man and society, and all that is involved therein, as the great Protestant writer, Dr.

Butler, shows us. Nor, in the third place, do I mean by Theology polemics of any kind; for instance, what are called "the Evidences of Religion," or "the Christian Evidences;" for, though these constitute a science supplemental to Theology and are necessary in their place, they are not Theology itself, unless an army is synonymous with the body politic. Nor, fourthly, do I mean by Theology that vague thing called "Christianity," or "our common Christianity," or "Christianity the law of the land," if there is any man alive who can tell what it is. I discard it, for the very reason that it cannot throw itself into a proposition. Lastly, I do not understand by Theology, acquaintance with the Scriptures; for, though no person of religious feelings can read Scripture but he will find those feelings roused, and gain much knowledge of history into the bargain, yet historical reading and religious feeling are not science. I mean none of these things by Theology, I simply mean the Science of God, or the truths we know about God put into system; just as we have a science of the stars, and call it astronomy, or of the crust of the earth, and call it geology.

For instance, I mean, for this is the main point, that, as in the human frame there is a living principle, acting upon it and through it by means of volition, so, behind the veil of the visible universe, there is an invisible, intelligent Being, acting on and through it, as and when He will. Further, I mean that this invisible Agent is in no sense a soul of the world, after the analogy of human nature, but, on the contrary, is absolutely distinct from the world, as being its Creator, Upholder, Governor, and Sovereign Lord. Here we are at once brought into the circle of doctrines which the idea of God embodies. I mean then by the Supreme Being, one who is simply self-dependent, and the only Being who is such; moreover, that He is without beginning or Eternal, and the only Eternal; that in consequence He has lived a whole eternity by Himself; and hence that He is all-sufficient, sufficient for His own blessedness, and all-blessed, and ever-blessed. Further, I mean a Being, who, having these prerogatives, has the Supreme Good, or rather is the Supreme Good, or has all the attributes of Good in infinite intenseness; all wisdom, all truth, all justice, all love, all holiness, all beautifulness; who is omnipotent, omniscient, omnipresent; ineffably one, absolutely perfect; and such, that what we do not know and cannot even imagine of Him, is far more wonderful than what we do and can. I mean One who is sovereign over His own will and actions, though always according to the eternal Rule of right and wrong, which is Himself. I mean, moreover, that He created all things out of nothing, and preserves them every moment, and could destroy them as easily as He made them; and that, in consequence, He is separated from them by an abyss, and is incommunicable in all His attributes. And further, He has stamped upon all things, in the hour of their creation, their respective natures, and has given them their work and mission and their length of days, greater or less, in their appointed place. I mean, too, that He is ever present with His works, one by one, and confronts every thing He has made by His particular and most loving Providence, and manifests Himself to each according to its needs: and has on rational beings imprinted the moral law, and given them power to obey it, imposing on them the duty of worship and service, searching and scanning them through and through with His omniscient eye, and putting before them a present trial and a judgment to come.

Such is what Theology teaches about God, a doctrine, as the very idea of its subject-matter presupposes, so mysterious as in its fulness to lie beyond any system, and in particular aspects to be simply external to nature, and to seem in parts even to be irreconcileable with itself, the imagination being unable to embrace what the reason determines. It teaches of a Being infinite, yet personal; all-blessed, yet ever operative; absolutely separate from the creature, yet in every part of the creation at every moment; above all things, yet under every thing. It teaches of a Being who, though the highest, yet in the work of creation, conservation, government, retribution, makes Himself, as it were, the minister and servant of all; who, though inhabiting eternity, allows Himself to take an interest, and to have a sympathy, in the matters of space and time. His are all beings, visible and invisible, the noblest and the vilest of them. His are the substance, and the operation, and the results of that system of physical nature into which we are born. His too are the powers and achievements of the intellectual essences, on which He has bestowed an independent action and the gift of origination. The laws of the universe, the principles of truth, the relation of one thing to another, their qualities and virtues, the order and harmony of the whole, all that exists, is from Him; and, if evil is not from Him, as assuredly it is not, this is because evil has no substance of its own, but is only the defect, excess, perversion, or corruption of that which has substance. All we see, hear, and touch, the remote sidereal firmament, as well as our own sea and land, and the elements which compose them, and the ordinances they obey, are His. The primary atoms of matter, their properties, their mutual action, their disposition and collocation, electricity, magnetism, gravitation, light, and whatever other subtle principles or operations the wit of man is detecting or shall detect, are the work of His hands. From Him has been every movement which has convulsed and re-fashioned the surface of the earth. The most insignificant or unsightly insect is from Him, and good in its kind; the ever-teeming, inexhaustible swarms of animalculæ, the myriads of living motes invisible to the naked eye, the restless ever-spreading vegetation which creeps like a garment over the whole earth, the lofty cedar, the umbrageous banana, are His. His are the tribes and families of birds and beasts, their graceful forms, their wild gestures, and their passionate cries.

And so in the intellectual, moral, social, and political world. Man, with his motives and works, his languages, his propagation, his diffusion, is from Him. Agriculture, medicine, and the arts of life, are His gifts. Society, laws, government, He is their sanction. The pageant of earthly royalty has the semblance and the benediction of the Eternal King. Peace and civilization, commerce and adventure, wars when just, conquest when humane and necessary, have His cooperation, and His blessing upon them. The course of events, the revolution of empires, the rise and fall of states, the periods and eras, the progresses and the retrogressions of the world's history, not indeed the incidental sin, over-abundant as it is, but the great outlines and the results of human affairs, are from His disposition. The elements and types and seminal principles and constructive powers of the moral world, in ruins though it be, are to be referred to Him. He "enlighteneth every man that cometh into this world." His are the dictates of the moral sense, and the retributive reproaches of conscience. To Him must be ascribed the rich endowments of the intellect, the irradiation of genius, the imagination of the poet, the sagacity of the politician, the wisdom (as Scripture calls it), which now rears and decorates the Temple, now manifests itself in proverb or in parable. The old saws of nations, the majestic precepts of philosophy, the luminous maxims of law, the oracles of individual wisdom, the traditionary rules of truth, justice, and religion, even though imbedded in the corruption, or alloyed with the pride, of the world, betoken His original agency, and His long-suffering presence. Even where there is habitual rebellion against Him, or profound far-spreading social depravity, still the undercurrent, or the heroic outburst, of natural virtue, as well as the yearnings of the heart after what it has not, and its presentiment of its true remedies, are to be ascribed to the Author of all good. Anticipations or reminiscences of His glory haunt the mind of the self-sufficient sage, and of the pagan devotee; His writing is upon the wall, whether of the Indian fane, or of the porticoes of Greece. He introduces Himself, He all but concurs, according to His good pleasure, and in His selected season, in the issues of unbelief, superstition, and false worship, and He changes the character of acts by His overruling operation. He condescends, though He gives no sanction, to the altars and shrines of imposture, and He makes His own fiat the substitute for its sorceries. He speaks amid the incantations of Balaam, raises Samuel's spirit in the witch's cavern, prophesies of the Messias by the tongue of the Sibyl, forces Python to recognize His ministers, and baptizes by the hand of the misbeliever. He is with the heathen dramatist in his denunciations of injustice and tyranny, and his auguries of divine vengeance upon crime. Even on the unseemly legends of a popular mythology He casts His shadow, and is dimly discerned in the ode or the epic, as in troubled water or in fantastic dreams. All that is good, all that is true, all that is beautiful, all that is beneficent, be it great or small, be it perfect or fragmentary, natural as well as supernatural, moral as well as material, comes from Him.

8.

If this be a sketch, accurate in substance and as far as it goes, of the doctrines proper to Theology, and especially of the doctrine of a particular Providence, which is the portion of it most on a level with human sciences, I cannot understand at all how, supposing it to be true, it can fail, considered as knowledge, to exert a powerful influence on philosophy, literature, and every intellectual creation or discovery whatever. I cannot understand how it is possible, as the phrase goes, to blink the question of its truth or falsehood. It meets us with a profession and a proffer of the highest truths of which the human mind is capable; it embraces a range of subjects the most diversified and distant from each other. What science will not find one part or other of its province traversed by its path? What results of philosophic speculation are unquestionable, if they have been gained without inquiry as to what Theology had to say to them? Does it cast no light upon history? has it no influence upon the principles of ethics? is it without any sort of bearing on physics, metaphysics, and political science? Can we drop it out of the circle of knowledge, without allowing, either that that circle is thereby mutilated, or on the other hand, that Theology is really no science?

And this dilemma is the more inevitable, because Theology is so precise and consistent in its intellectual structure. When I speak of Theism or Monotheism, I am not throwing together discordant doctrines; I am not merging belief, opinion, persuasion, of whatever kind, into a shapeless aggregate, by the help of ambiguous words, and dignifying this medley by the name of Theology. I speak of one idea unfolded in its just proportions, carried out upon an intelligible method, and issuing in necessary and immutable results; understood indeed at one time and place better than at another, held here and there with more or less of inconsistency, but still, after all, in all times and places, where it is found, the evolution, not of half-a-dozen ideas, but of one.

9.

And here I am led to another and most important point in the argument in its behalf,—I mean its wide reception. Theology, as I have described it, is no accident of particular minds, as are certain systems, for instance, of prophetical interpretation. It is not the sudden birth of a crisis, as the Lutheran or Wesleyan doctrine. It is not the splendid development of some uprising philosophy, as the Cartesian or Platonic. It is not the fashion of a season, as certain medical treatments may be considered. It has had a place, if not possession, in the intellectual world from time immemorial; it has been received by minds the most various, and in systems of religion the most hostile to each other. It has *primâ facie* claims upon us, so imposing, that it can only be rejected on the ground of those claims being nothing more than imposing, that is, being false. As to our own countries, it occupies our language, it meets us at every turn in our literature, it is the secret assumption, too axiomatic to be distinctly professed, of all our writers; nor can we help assuming it ourselves, except by the most unnatural vigilance. Whoever philosophizes, starts with it, and introduces it, when he will, without any apology. Bacon, Hooker, Taylor, Cudworth, Locke, Newton, Clarke, Berkeley, and Butler, and it would be as easy to find more, as difficult to find greater names among English authors, inculcate or comment upon it. Men the most opposed, in creed or cast of mind, Addison and Johnson, Shakespeare and Milton, Lord Herbert and Baxter, herald it forth. Nor is it an English or a Protestant notion only; you track it across the Continent, you pursue it into former ages. When was the world without it? Have the systems of Atheism or Pantheism, as sciences, prevailed in the literature of nations, or received a formation or attained a completeness such as Monotheism? We find it in old Greece, and even in Rome, as well as in Judea and the East. We find it in popular literature, in philosophy, in poetry, as a positive and settled teaching, differing not at all in the appearance it presents, whether in Protestant England, or in schismatical Russia, or in the Mahometan populations, or in the Catholic Church. If ever there was a subject of thought, which had earned by prescription to be received among the studies of a University, and which could not be rejected except on the score of convicted imposture, as astrology or alchemy; if there be a science anywhere, which at least could claim not to be ignored, but to be entertained, and either distinctly accepted or distinctly reprobated, or rather, which cannot be passed over in a scheme of universal instruction, without involving a positive denial of its truth, it is thing ancient, this far-spreading philosophy.

10.

And now, Gentlemen, I may bring a somewhat tedious discussion to a close. It will not take many words to sum up what I have been urging. I say then, if the various branches of knowledge, which are the matter of teaching in a University, so hang together, that none can be neglected without prejudice to the perfection of the rest, and if Theology be a branch of knowledge, of wide reception, of philosophical structure, of unutterable importance, and of supreme influence, to what conclusion are we brought from these two premises but this? that to withdraw Theology from the public schools is to impair the completeness and to invalidate the trustworthiness of all that is actually taught in them.

But I have been insisting simply on Natural Theology, and that, because I wished to carry along with me those who were not Catholics, and, again, as being confident, that no one can really set himself to master and to teach the doctrine of an intelligent Creator in its fulness, without going on a great deal farther than he at present dreams. I say, then, secondly:—if this Science, even as human reason may attain to it, has such claims on the regard, and enters so variously into the objects, of the Professor of Universal Knowledge, how can any Catholic imagine that it is possible for him to cultivate Philosophy and Science with due attention to their ultimate end, which is Truth, supposing that system of revealed facts and principles, which Constitutes the Catholic Faith, which goes so far beyond nature, and which he knows to be most true, be omitted from among the subjects of his teaching?

In a word, Religious Truth is not only a portion, but a condition of general knowledge. To blot it out is nothing short, if I may so speak, of unravelling the web of University Teaching. It is, according to the Greek proverb, to take the Spring from out of the year; it is to imitate the preposterous proceeding of those tragedians who represented a drama with the omission of its principal part.

BEARING OF OTHER BRANCHES OF KNOWLEDGE ON THEOLOGY

1.

Nothing is more common in the world at large than to consider the resistance, made on the part of religious men, especially Catholics, to the separation of Secular Education from Religion, as a plain token that there is some real contrariety between human science and Revelation. To the multitude who draw this inference, it matters not whether the protesting parties avow their belief in this contrariety or not; it is borne in upon the many, as if it were self-evident, that religious men would not thus be jealous and alarmed about Science, did they not feel instinctively, though they may not recognize it, that knowledge is their born enemy, and that its progress, if it is not arrested, will be certain to destroy all that they hold venerable and dear. It looks to the world like a misgiving on our part similar to that which is imputed to our refusal to educate by means of the Bible only; why should you dread the sacred text, men say, if it be not against you? And in like manner, why should you dread secular education, except that it is against you? Why impede the circulation of books which take religious views opposite to your own? Why forbid your children and scholars the free perusal of poems or tales or essays or other light literature which you fear would unsettle their minds? Why oblige them to know these persons and to shun those, if you think that your friends have reason on their side as fully as your opponents? Truth is bold and unsuspicious; want of self-reliance is the mark of falsehood.

Now, as far as this objection relates to any supposed opposition between secular science and divine, which is the subject on which I am at present engaged, I made a sufficient answer to it in my foregoing Discourse. In it I said, that, in order to have possession of truth at all, we must have the whole truth; and no one science, no two sciences, no one family of sciences, nay, not even all secular science, is the whole truth; that revealed truth enters to a very great extent into the province of science, philosophy, and literature, and that to put it on one side, in compliment to secular science, is simply, under colour of a compliment, to do science a great damage. I do not say that every science will be equally affected by the omission; pure mathematics will not suffer at all; chemistry will suffer less than politics, politics than history, ethics, or metaphysics; still, that the various branches of science are intimately connected with each other, and form one whole, which whole is impaired, and to an extent which it is difficult to limit, by any considerable omission of knowledge, of whatever kind, and that revealed knowledge is very far indeed from an inconsiderable department of knowledge, this I consider undeniable. As the written and unwritten word of God make up Revelation as a whole, and the written, taken by itself, is but a part of that whole, so in turn Revelation itself may be viewed as one of the constituent parts of human knowledge, considered as a whole, and its omission is the omission of one of those constituent parts. Revealed Religion furnishes facts to the other sciences, which those sciences, left to themselves, would never reach; and it invalidates apparent facts, which, left to themselves, they would imagine. Thus, in the science of history, the preservation of our race in Noah's ark is an historical fact, which history never would arrive at without Revelation; and, in the province of physiology and moral philosophy, our race's progress and perfectibility is a dream, because Revelation contradicts it, whatever may be plausibly argued in its behalf by scientific inquirers. It is not then that Catholics are afraid of human knowledge, but that they are proud of divine knowledge, and that they think the omission of any kind of knowledge whatever, human or divine, to be, as far as it goes, not knowledge, but ignorance.

2.

Thus I anticipated the objection in question last week: now I am going to make it the introduction to a further view of the relation of secular knowledge to divine. I observe, then, that, if you drop any science out of the circle of knowledge, you cannot keep its place vacant for it; that science is forgotten; the other sciences close up, or, in other words, they exceed their proper bounds, and intrude where they have no right. For instance, I suppose, if ethics were sent into banishment, its territory would soon disappear, under a treaty of partition, as it may be called, between law, political economy, and physiology; what, again, would become of the province of experimental science, if made over to the Antiquarian Society; or of history, if surrendered out and out to Metaphysicians? The case is the same with the subject-matter of Theology; it would be the prey of a dozen various sciences, if Theology were put out of possession; and not only so, but those sciences would be plainly exceeding their rights and their capacities in seizing upon it. They would be sure to teach wrongly, where they had no mission to teach at all. The enemies of Catholicism ought to be the last to deny this:—for they have never been blind to a like usurpation, as they have called it, on the part of theologians; those who accuse us of wishing, in accordance with Scripture language, to make the sun go round the earth, are not the men to deny that a science which exceeds its limits falls into error.

I neither then am able nor care to deny, rather I assert the fact, and today I am going on to account for it, that any secular science, cultivated exclusively, may become dangerous to Religion; and I account for it on this broad principle, that no science whatever, however comprehensive it may be, but will fall largely into error, if it be constituted the sole exponent of all things in heaven and earth, and that, for the simple reason that it is encroaching on territory not its own, and undertaking problems which it has no instruments to solve. And I set off thus:

3.

One of the first acts of the human mind is to take hold of and appropriate what meets the senses, and herein lies a chief distinction between man's and a brute's use of them. Brutes gaze on sights, they are arrested by sounds; and what they see and what they hear are mainly sights and sounds only. The intellect of man, on the contrary, energizes as well as his eye or ear, and perceives in sights and sounds something beyond them. It seizes and unites what the senses present to it; it grasps and forms what need not have been seen or heard except in its constituent parts. It discerns in lines and colours, or in tones, what is beautiful and what is not. It gives them a meaning, and invests them with an idea. It gathers up a succession of notes into the expression of a whole, and calls it a melody; it has a keen sensibility towards angles and curves, lights and shadows, tints and contours. It distinguishes between rule and exception, between accident and design. It assigns phenomena to a general law, qualities to a subject, acts to a principle, and effects to a cause. In a word, it philosophizes; for I suppose Science and Philosophy, in their elementary idea, are nothing else but this habit of *viewing*, as it may be called, the objects which sense conveys to the mind, of throwing them into system, and uniting and stamping them with one form.

This method is so natural to us, as I have said, as to be almost spontaneous; and we are impatient when we cannot exercise it, and in consequence we do not always wait to have the means of exercising it aright, but we often put up with insufficient or absurd views or interpretations of what we meet with, rather than have none at all. We refer the various matters which are brought home to us, material or moral, to causes which we happen to know of, or to such as are simply imaginary, sooner than refer them to nothing; and according to the activity of our intellect do we feel a pain and begin to fret, if we are not able to do so. Here we have an explanation of the multitude of off-hand sayings, flippant judgments, and shallow generalizations, with which the world abounds. Not from self-will only, nor from malevolence, but from the irritation which suspense occasions, is the mind forced on to pronounce, without sufficient data for pronouncing. Who does not form some view or other, for instance, of any public man, or any public event, nay, even so far in some cases as to reach the mental delineation of his appearance or of its scene?

yet how few have a right to form any view. Hence the misconceptions of character, hence the false impressions and reports of words or deeds, which are the rule, rather than the exception, in the world at large; hence the extravagances of undisciplined talent, and the narrowness of conceited ignorance; because, though it is no easy matter to view things correctly, nevertheless the busy mind will ever be viewing. We cannot do without a view, and we put up with an illusion when we cannot get a truth.

4.

Now, observe how this impatience acts in matters of research and speculation. What happens to the ignorant and hotheaded, will take place in the case of every person whose education or pursuits are contracted, whether they be merely professional, merely scientific, or of whatever other peculiar complexion. Men, whose life lies in the cultivation of one science, or the exercise of one method of thought, have no more right, though they have often more ambition, to generalize upon the basis of their own pursuit but beyond its range, than the schoolboy or the ploughman to judge of a Prime Minister. But they must have something to say on every subject; habit, fashion, the public require it of them: and, if so, they can only give sentence according to their knowledge. You might think this ought to make such a person modest in his enunciations; not so: too often it happens that, in proportion to the narrowness of his knowledge, is, not his distrust of it, but the deep hold it has upon him, his absolute conviction of his own conclusions, and his positiveness in maintaining them. He has the obstinacy of the bigot, whom he scorns, without the bigot's apology, that he has been taught, as he thinks, his doctrine from heaven. Thus he becomes, what is commonly called, a man of one idea; which properly means a man of one science, and of the view, partly true, but subordinate, partly false, which is all that can proceed out of any thing so partial. Hence it is that we have the principles of utility, of combination, of progress, of philanthropy, or, in material sciences, comparative anatomy, phrenology, electricity, exalted into leading ideas, and keys, if not of all knowledge, at least of many things more than belong to them,— principles, all of them true to a certain point, yet all degenerating into error and quackery, because they are carried to excess, viz. at the point where they require interpretation and restraint from other quarters, and because they are employed to do what is simply too much for them, inasmuch as a little science is not deep philosophy.

Lord Bacon has set down the abuse, of which I am speaking, among the impediments to the Advancement of the Sciences, when he observes that "men have used to infect their meditations, opinions, and doctrines, with some conceits which they have most admired, or *some Sciences which they have most applied*; and give all things else a *tincture* according to them *utterly untrue and improper* ... So have the alchemists made a philosophy out of a few experiments of the furnace; and Gilbertus, our countryman, hath made a philosophy out of the observations of a lodestone. So Cicero, when, reciting the several opinions of the nature of the soul, he found a musician that held the soul was but a harmony, saith pleasantly, 'hic ab arte suâ non recessit,' 'he was true to his art.' But of these conceits Aristotle speaketh seriously and wisely when he saith, 'Qui respiciunt ad pauca, de facili pronunciant,' 'they who contemplate a few things have no difficulty in deciding.'"

5.

And now I have said enough to explain the inconvenience which I conceive necessarily to result from a refusal to recognize theological truth in a course of Universal Knowledge;—it is not only the loss of Theology, it is the perversion of other sciences. What it unjustly forfeits, others unjustly seize. They have their own department, and, in going out of it, attempt to do what they really cannot do; and that the more mischievously, because they do teach what in its place is true, though when out of its place, perverted or carried to excess, it is not true. And, as every man has not the capacity of separating truth from falsehood, they persuade the world of what is false by urging upon it what is true.

Nor is it open enemies alone who encounter us here, sometimes it is friends, sometimes persons who, if not friends, at least have no wish to oppose Religion, and are not conscious they are doing so; and it will carry out my meaning more fully if I give some illustrations of it.

As to friends, I may take as an instance the cultivation of the Fine Arts, Painting, Sculpture, Architecture, to which I may add Music. These high ministers of the Beautiful and the Noble are, it is plain, special attendants and handmaids of Religion; but it is equally plain that they are apt to forget their place, and, unless restrained with a firm hand, instead of being servants, will aim at becoming principals. Here lies the advantage, in an ecclesiastical point of view, of their more rudimental state, I mean of the ancient style of architecture, of Gothic sculpture and painting, and of what is called Gregorian music, that these inchoate sciences have so little innate vigour and life in them, that they are in no danger of going out of their place, and giving the law to Religion. But the case is very different when genius has breathed upon their natural elements, and has developed them into what I may call intellectual powers. When Painting, for example, grows into the fulness of its function as a simply imitative art, it at once ceases to be a dependant on the Church. It has an end of its own, and that of earth: Nature is its pattern, and the object it pursues is the beauty of Nature, even till it becomes an ideal beauty, but a natural beauty still. It cannot imitate that beauty of Angels and Saints which it has never seen. At first, indeed, by outlines and emblems it shadowed out the Invisible, and its want of skill became the instrument of reverence and modesty; but as time went on and it attained its full dimensions as an art, it rather subjected Religion to its own ends than ministered to the ends of Religion, and in its long galleries and stately chambers, did but mingle adorable figures and sacred histories with a multitude of earthly, not to say unseemly forms, which the Art had created, borrowing withal a colouring and a character from that bad company. Not content with neutral ground for its development, it was attracted by the sublimity of divine subjects to ambitious and hazardous essays. Without my saying a word more, you will clearly understand, Gentlemen, that under these circumstances Religion was bound to exert itself, that the world might not gain an advantage over it. Put out of sight the severe teaching of Catholicism in the schools of Painting, as men now would put it aside in their philosophical studies, and in no long time you would have the hierarchy of the Church, the Anchorite and Virgin-martyr, the Confessor and the Doctor, the Angelic Hosts, the Mother of God, the Crucifix, the Eternal Trinity, supplanted by a sort of pagan mythology in the guise of sacred names, by a creation indeed of high genius, of intense, and dazzling, and soul-absorbing beauty, in which, however, there was nothing which subserved the cause of Religion, nothing on the other hand which did not directly or indirectly minister to corrupt nature and the powers of darkness.

6.

The art of Painting, however, is peculiar: Music and Architecture are more ideal, and their respective archetypes, even if not supernatural, at least are abstract and unearthly; and yet what I have been observing about Painting, holds, I think, analogously, in the marvellous development which Musical Science has undergone in the last century. Doubtless here too the highest genius may be made subservient to Religion; here too, still more simply than in the case of Painting, the Science has a field of its own, perfectly innocent, into which Religion does not and need not enter; on the other hand here also, in the case of Music as of Painting, it is certain that Religion must be alive and on the defensive, for, if its servants sleep, a potent enchantment will steal over it. Music, I suppose, though this is not the place to enlarge upon it, has an object of its own; as mathematical science also, it is the expression of ideas greater and more profound than any in the visible world, ideas, which centre indeed in Him whom Catholicism manifests, who is the seat of all beauty, order, and perfection whatever, still ideas after all which are not those on which Revelation directly and principally fixes our gaze. If then a great master in this mysterious science (if I may speak of matters which seem to lie out of my own province) throws himself on his own gift, trusts its inspirations, and absorbs himself in those thoughts which, though they come to him in the way of nature, belong to things above nature, it is obvious he will neglect everything else. Rising in his strength, he will break through the trammels of words, he will scatter human voices, even the sweetest, to the winds; he will be borne upon nothing less than the fullest flood of sounds which art has enabled him to draw from mechanical contrivances; he will go forth as a giant, as far as ever his instruments can reach, starting from their secret depths fresh and fresh elements of beauty and grandeur as he goes, and pouring them together into still more marvellous and rapturous combinations;—and well indeed and lawfully, while he keeps to that line which is his own; but, should he happen to be attracted, as he well may, by the sublimity, so congenial to him, of the Catholic doctrine and ritual, should he engage in sacred themes, should he resolve by means of his art to do honour to the Mass, or the Divine Office,—(he cannot have a more pious, a better purpose, and Religion will gracefully accept what he gracefully offers; but)—is it not certain, from the circumstances of the case, that he will be carried on rather to use Religion than to minister to it, unless Religion is strong on its own ground, and reminds him that, if he would do honour to the highest of subjects, he must make himself its scholar, must humbly follow the thoughts given him, and must aim at the glory, not of his own gift, but of the Great Giver?

7.

As to Architecture, it is a remark, if I recollect aright, both of Fénélon and Berkeley, men so different, that it carries more with it even than the names of those celebrated men, that the Gothic style is not as *simple* as befits ecclesiastical structures. I understand this to be a similar judgment to that which I have been passing on the cultivation of Painting and Music. For myself, certainly I think that that style which, whatever be its origin, is called

Gothic, is endowed with a profound and a commanding beauty, such as no other style possesses with which we are acquainted, and which probably the Church will not see surpassed till it attain to the Celestial City. No other architecture, now used for sacred purposes, seems to be the growth of an idea, whereas the Gothic style is as harmonious and as intellectual as it is graceful. But this feeling should not blind us, rather it should awaken us, to the danger lest what is really a divine gift be incautiously used as an end rather than as a means. It is surely quite within the bounds of possibility, that, as the *renaissance* three centuries ago carried away its own day, in spite of the Church, into excesses in literature and art, so that revival of an almost forgotten architecture, which is at present taking place in our own countries, in France, and in Germany, may in some way or other run away with us into this or that error, unless we keep a watch over its course. I am not speaking of Ireland; but to English Catholics at least it would be a serious evil, if it came as the emblem and advocate of a past ceremonial or an extinct nationalism. We are not living in an age of wealth and loyalty, of pomp and stateliness, of time-honoured establishments, of pilgrimage and penance, of hermitages and convents in the wild, and of fervent populations supplying the want of education by love, and apprehending in form and symbol what they cannot read in books. Our rules and our rubrics have been altered now to meet the times, and hence an obsolete discipline may be a present heresy.

8.

I have been pointing out how the Fine Arts may prejudice Religion, by laying down the law in cases where they should be subservient. The illustration is analogous rather than strictly proper to my subject, yet I think it is to the point. If then the most loyal and dutiful children of the Church must deny themselves, and do deny themselves, when they would sanctify to a heavenly purpose sciences as sublime and as divine as any which are cultivated by fallen man, it is not wonderful, when we turn to sciences of a different character, of which the object is tangible and material, and the principles belong to the Reason, not to the Imagination, that we should find their disciples, if disinclined to the Catholic Faith, acting the part of opponents to it, and that, as may often happen, even against their will and intention. Many men there are, who, devoted to one particular subject of thought, and making its principles the measure of all things, become enemies to Revealed Religion before they know it, and, only as time proceeds, are aware of their own state of mind. These, if they are writers or lecturers, while in this state of unconscious or semi-conscious unbelief, scatter infidel principles under the garb and colour of Christianity; and this, simply because they have made their own science, whatever it is, Political Economy, or Geology, or Astronomy, to the neglect of Theology, the centre of all truth, and view every part or the chief parts of knowledge as if developed from it, and to be tested and determined by its principles. Others, though conscious to themselves of their anti-christian opinions, have too much good feeling and good taste to obtrude them upon the world. They neither wish to shock people, nor to earn for themselves a confessorship which brings with it no gain. They know the strength of prejudice, and the penalty of innovation; they wish to go through life quietly; they scorn polemics; they shrink, as from a real humiliation, from being mixed up in religious controversy; they are ashamed of the very name. However, they have had occasion at some time to publish on some literary or scientific subject; they have wished to give no offence; but after all, to their great annoyance, they find when they least expect it, or when they have taken considerable pains to avoid it, that they have roused by their publication what they would style the bigoted and bitter hostility of a party. This misfortune is easily conceivable, and has befallen many a man. Before he knows where he is, a cry is raised on all sides of him; and so little does he know what we may call the *lie* of the land, that his attempts at apology perhaps only make matters worse. In other words, an exclusive line of study has led him, whether he will or no, to run counter to the principles of Religion; which principles he has never made his landmarks, and which, whatever might be their effect upon himself, at least would have warned him against practising upon the faith of others, had they been authoritatively held up before him.

9.

Instances of this kind are far from uncommon. Men who are old enough, will remember the trouble which came upon a person, eminent as a professional man in London even at that distant day, and still more eminent since, in consequence of his publishing a book in which he so treated the subject of Comparative Anatomy as to seem to deny the immateriality of the soul. I speak here neither as excusing nor reprobating sentiments about which I have not the means of forming a judgment; all indeed I have heard of him makes me mention him with interest and respect; anyhow of this I am sure, that if there be a calling which feels its position and its dignity to lie in abstaining from controversy and in cultivating kindly feelings with men of all opinions, it is the medical profession, and I cannot believe that the person in question would purposely have raised the indignation and incurred the censure of the religious public. What then must have been his fault or mistake, but that he unsuspiciously threw himself upon his own particular science, which is of a material character, and allowed it to carry him forward into a subject-matter, where it had no right to give the law, viz., that of spiritual beings, which directly belongs to the science of Theology?

Another instance occurred at a later date. A living dignitary of the Established Church wrote a History of the Jews; in which, with what I consider at least bad judgment, he took an external view of it, and hence was led to assimilate it as nearly as possible to secular history. A great sensation was the consequence among the members of his own communion, from which he still suffers. Arguing from the dislike and contempt of polemical demonstrations which that accomplished writer has ever shown, I must conclude that he was simply betrayed into a false step by the treacherous fascination of what is called the Philosophy of History, which is good in its place, but can scarcely be applied in cases where the Almighty has superseded the natural laws of society and history. From this he would have been saved, had he been a Catholic; but in the Establishment he knew of no teaching, to which he was bound to defer, which might rule that to be false which attracted him by its speciousness.

10.

I will now take an instance from another science, and will use more words about it. Political Economy is the science, I suppose, of wealth,—a science simply lawful and useful, for it is no sin to make money, any more than it is a sin to seek honour; a science at the same time dangerous and leading to occasions of sin, as is the pursuit of honour too; and in consequence, if studied by itself, and apart from the control of Revealed Truth, sure to conduct a speculator to unchristian conclusions. Holy Scripture tells us distinctly, that "covetousness," or more literally the love of money, "is the root of all evils;" and that "they that would become rich fall into temptation;" and that "hardly shall they that have riches enter into the kingdom of God;" and after drawing the picture of a wealthy and flourishing people, it adds, "They have called the people happy that hath these things; but happy is that people whose God is the Lord"—while on the other hand it says with equal distinctness, "If any will not work, neither let him eat;" and, "If any man have not care of his own, and especially of those of his house, he hath denied the faith, and is worse than an infidel." These opposite injunctions are summed up in the wise man's prayer, who says, "Give me neither beggary nor riches, give me only the necessaries of life." With this most precise view of a Christian's duty, viz., to labour indeed, but to labour for a competency for himself and his, and to be jealous of wealth, whether personal or national, the holy Fathers are, as might be expected, in simple accordance. "Judas," says St. Chrysostom, "was with Him who knew not where to lay His head, yet could not restrain himself; and how canst thou hope to escape the contagion without anxious effort?" "It is ridiculous," says St. Jerome, "to call it idolatry to offer to the creature the grains of incense that are due to God, and not to call it so, to offer the whole service of one's life to the creature." "There is not a trace of justice in that heart," says St. Leo, "in which the love of gain has made itself a dwelling." The same thing is emphatically taught us by the counsels of perfection, and by every holy monk and nun anywhere, who has ever embraced them; but it is needless to collect testimonies, when Scripture is so clear.

Now, observe, Gentlemen, my drift in setting Scripture and the Fathers over against Political Economy. Of course if there is a science of wealth, it must give rules for gaining wealth and disposing of wealth, and can do nothing more; it cannot itself declare that it is a subordinate science, that its end is not the ultimate end of all things, and that its conclusions are only hypothetical, depending on its premises, and liable to be overruled by a higher teaching. I do not then blame the Political Economist for anything which follows from the very idea of his science, from the very moment that it is recognized as a science. He must of course direct his inquiries towards his end; but then at the same time it must be recollected, that so far he is not practical, but only pursues an abstract study, and is busy himself in establishing logical conclusions from indisputable premises. Given that wealth is to be sought, this and that is the method of gaining it. This is the extent to which a Political Economist has a right to go; he has no right to determine that wealth is at any rate to be sought, or that it is the way to be virtuous and the price of happiness; I say, this is to pass the bounds of his science, independent of the question whether he be right or wrong in so determining, for he is only concerned with an hypothesis.

To take a parallel case:—a physician may tell you, that if you are to preserve your health, you must give up your employment and retire to the country. He distinctly says "if;" that is all in which he is concerned, he is no judge whether there are objects dearer to you, more urgent upon you, than the preservation of your health; he does not enter into your circumstances, your duties, your liabilities, the persons dependent on you; he knows nothing about what is advisable or what is not; he only says, "I speak *as* a physician; if you would be well, give up your profession, your trade, your office, whatever it is." However he may wish it, it would be impertinent in him to say more, unless indeed he spoke, not as a physician but as a friend; and it would be extravagant, if he asserted that bodily health was the *summum bonum*, and that no one could be virtuous whose animal system was not in good order.

11.

But now let us turn to the teaching of the actual Political Economist, in his present fashionable shape. I will take a very favourable instance of him: he shall be represented by a gentleman of high character, whose religious views are sufficiently guaranteed to us by his being the special choice, in this department of science, of a University removed more than any other Protestant body of the day from sordid or unchristian principles on the subject of money-making. I say, if there be a place where Political Economy would be kept in order, and would not be suffered to leave the high road and ride across the pastures and the gardens dedicated to other studies, it is the University of Oxford. And if a man could anywhere be found who would have too much good taste to offend the religious feeling of the place, or to say any thing which he would himself allow to be inconsistent with Revelation, I conceive it is the person whose temperate and well-considered composition, as it would be generally accounted, I am going to offer to your notice. Nor did it occasion any excitement whatever on the part of the academical or the religious public, as did the instances which I have hitherto been adducing. I am representing then the science of Political Economy, in its independent or unbridled action, to great advantage, when I select, as its specimen, the Inaugural Lecture upon it, delivered in the University in question, by its first Professor. Yet with all these circumstances in its favour, you will soon see, Gentlemen, into what extravagance, for so I must call it, a grave lawyer is led in praise of his chosen science, merely from the circumstance that he has fixed his mind upon it, till he has forgotten there are subjects of thought higher and more heavenly than it. You will find beyond mistake, that it is his object to recommend the science of wealth, by claiming for it an *ethical* quality, viz., by extolling it as the road to virtue and happiness, whatever Scripture and holy men may say to the contrary.

He begins by predicting of Political Economy, that in the course of a very few years, "it will rank in public estimation among the first of *moral* sciences in interest and in utility." Then he explains most lucidly its objects and duties, considered as "the science which teaches in what wealth consists, by what agents it is produced, and according to what laws it is distributed, and what are the institutions and customs by which production may be facilitated and distribution regulated, so as to give the largest possible amount of wealth to each individual." And he dwells upon the interest which attaches to the inquiry, "whether England has run her full career of wealth and improvement, but stands safe where she is, or whether to remain stationary is impossible." After this he notices a certain objection, which I shall set before you in his own words, as they will furnish me with the illustration I propose.

This objection, he says, is, that, "as the pursuit of wealth is one of the humblest of human occupations, far inferior to the pursuit of virtue, or of knowledge, or even of reputation, and as the possession of wealth is not necessarily joined,—perhaps it will be said, is not conducive,—to happiness, a science, of which the only subject is wealth, cannot claim to rank as the first, or nearly the first, of moral sciences."[1] Certainly, to an enthusiast in behalf of any science whatever, the temptation is great to meet an objection urged against its dignity and worth; however, from the very form of it, such an objection cannot receive a satisfactory answer by means of the science itself. It is an objection external to the science, and reminds us of the truth of Lord Bacon's remark, "No perfect discovery can be made upon a flat or a level; neither is it possible to discover the more remote and deeper

---

1   Introd. Lecture on Pol. Econ. pp. 11, 12.

parts of any science, if you stand upon the level of the science, and ascend not to a higher science."[2] The objection that Political Economy is inferior to the science of virtue, or does not conduce to happiness, is an ethical or theological objection; the question of its "rank" belongs to that Architectonic Science or Philosophy, whatever it be, which is itself the arbiter of all truth, and which disposes of the claims and arranges the places of all the departments of knowledge which man is able to master. I say, when an opponent of a particular science asserts that it does not conduce to happiness, and much more when its champion contends in reply that it certainly does conduce to virtue, as this author proceeds to contend, the obvious question which occurs to one to ask is, what does Religion, what does Revelation, say on the point? Political Economy must not be allowed to give judgment in its own favour, but must come before a higher tribunal. The objection is an appeal to the Theologian; however, the Professor does not so view the matter; he does not consider it a question for Philosophy; nor indeed on the other hand a question for Political Economy; not a question for Science at all; but for Private Judgment,—so he answers it himself, and as follows:

12.

"My answer," he says, "is, first, that the pursuit of wealth, that is, the endeavour to accumulate the means of future subsistence and enjoyment, is, to the mass of mankind, the great source of *moral* improvement." Now observe, Gentlemen, how exactly this bears out what I have been saying. It is just so far true, as to be able to instil what is false, far as the author was from any such design. I grant, then, that, ordinarily, beggary is not the means of moral improvement; and that the orderly habits which attend upon the hot pursuit of gain, not only may effect an external decency, but may at least shelter the soul from the temptations of vice. Moreover, these habits of good order guarantee regularity in a family or household, and thus are accidentally the means of good;

---

2 Advancement of Learning.

moreover, they lead to the education of its younger branches, and they thus accidentally provide the rising generation with a virtue or a truth which the present has not: but without going into these considerations, further than to allow them generally, and under circumstances, let us rather contemplate what the author's direct assertion is. He says, "the endeavour to *accumulate*," the words should be weighed, and for what? "for *enjoyment*;"—"to accumulate the means of future subsistence and enjoyment, is, to the mass of mankind, *the great* source," not merely *a* source, but *the great* source, and of what? of social and political progress?—such an answer would have been more within the limits of his art,—no, but of something individual and personal, "of *moral improvement*." The soul, in the case of "the mass of mankind," improves in moral excellence from this more than any thing else, viz., from heaping up the means of enjoying this world in time to come! I really should on every account be sorry, Gentlemen, to exaggerate, but indeed one is taken by surprise, one is startled, on meeting with so very categorical a contradiction of our Lord, St. Paul, St. Chrysostom, St. Leo, and all Saints.

"No institution," he continues, "could be more beneficial to the morals of the lower orders, that is, to at least nine-tenths of the whole body of any people, than one which should increase their power and their wish to accumulate; none more mischievous than one which should diminish their motives and means to save." No institution more beneficial than one which should increase the *wish to accumulate*! then Christianity is not one of such beneficial institutions, for it expressly says, "*Lay not up to* yourselves *treasures* on earth ... for where thy treasure is, there is thy heart also;"—no institution more mischievous than one which should diminish the *motives to save*! then Christianity is one of such mischiefs, for the inspired text proceeds, "Lay up to yourselves treasures *in heaven, where* neither the rust nor the moth doth consume, and where thieves do not dig through, nor steal."

But it is not enough that morals and happiness are made to depend on gain and accumulation; the practice of Religion is ascribed to these causes also, and in the following way. Wealth depends upon the pursuit of wealth; education depends upon wealth; knowledge depends on education; and Religion depends on knowledge; therefore Religion depends on the pursuit of wealth. He says, after speaking of a poor and savage people, "Such a population must be grossly ignorant. The desire of knowledge is one of the last results of refinement; it requires in general to have been implanted in the mind during childhood; and it is absurd to suppose that persons thus situated would have the power or the will to devote much to the education of their children. A further consequence is the *absence of all real religion*; for the religion of the grossly ignorant, if they have any, scarcely ever amounts to more than a debasing superstition."[3] The pursuit of gain then is the basis of virtue, religion, happiness; though it is all the while, as a Christian knows, the "root of all evils," and the "poor on the contrary are blessed, for theirs is the kingdom of God."

As to the argument contained in the logical *Sorites* which I have been drawing out, I anticipated just now what I should say to it in reply. I repeat, doubtless "beggary," as the wise man says, is not desirable; doubtless, if men will not work, they should not eat; there is doubtless a sense in which it may be said that mere social or political virtue tends to moral and religious excellence; but the sense needs to be defined and the statement to be kept within bounds. This is the very point on which I am all along insisting. I am not denying, I am granting, I am assuming, that there is reason and truth in the "leading ideas," as they are called, and "large views" of scientific men; I only say that, though they speak truth, they do not speak the whole truth; that they speak a narrow truth, and think it a broad truth; that their deductions must be compared with other truths, which are acknowledged to be truths, in order to verify, complete, and correct them. They say what is true, *exceptis excipiendis*; what is true, but requires guarding; true, but must not be ridden too hard, or made what is called a *hobby*; true, but not the measure of all things; true, but

3 Intr. Lect., p. 16.

if thus inordinately, extravagantly, ruinously carried out, in spite of other sciences, in spite of Theology, sure to become but a great bubble, and to burst.

13.

I am getting to the end of this Discourse, before I have noticed one tenth part of the instances with which I might illustrate the subject of it. Else I should have wished especially to have dwelt upon the not unfrequent perversion which occurs of antiquarian and historical research, to the prejudice of Theology. It is undeniable that the records of former ages are of primary importance in determining Catholic doctrine; it is undeniable also that there is a silence or a contrariety abstractedly conceivable in those records, as to an alleged portion of that doctrine, which would be sufficient to invalidate its claims on our acceptance; but it is quite as undeniable that the existing documentary testimony to Catholicism and Christianity may be so unduly valued as to be made the absolute measure of Revelation, as if no part of theological teaching were true which cannot bring its express text, as it is called, from Scripture, and authorities from the Fathers or profane writers,—whereas there are numberless facts in past times which we cannot deny, for they are indisputable, though history is silent about them. I suppose, on this score, we ought to deny that the round towers of this country had any origin, because history does not disclose it; or that any individual came from Adam who cannot produce the table of his ancestry. Yet Gibbon argues against the darkness at the Passion, from the accident that it is not mentioned by Pagan historians:—as well might he argue against the existence of Christianity itself in the first century, because Seneca, Pliny, Plutarch, the Jewish Mishna, and other authorities are silent about it. Protestants argue in a parallel way against Transubstantiation, and Arians against our Lord's Divinity, viz., on the ground that extant writings of certain Fathers do not witness those doctrines to their satisfaction:—as well might they say that Christianity was not spread by the Twelve Apostles, because we know so little of their labours. The evidence of History, I say, is invaluable in its place; but, if it assumes to be the sole means of gaining Religious Truth, it goes beyond its place. We are putting it to a larger office than it can undertake, if we countenance the usurpation; and we are turning a true guide and blessing into a source of inexplicable difficulty and interminable doubt.

And so of other sciences: just as Comparative Anatomy, Political Economy, the Philosophy of History, and the Science of Antiquities may be and are turned against Religion, by being taken by themselves, as I have been showing, so a like mistake may befall any other. Grammar, for instance, at first sight does not appear to admit of a perversion; yet Horne Tooke made it the vehicle of his peculiar scepticism. Law would seem to have enough to do with its own clients, and their affairs; and yet Mr. Bentham made a treatise on Judicial Proofs a covert attack upon the miracles of Revelation. And in like manner Physiology may deny moral evil and human responsibility; Geology may deny Moses; and Logic may deny the Holy Trinity;[4] and other sciences, now rising into notice, are or will be victims of a similar abuse.

14.

And now to sum up what I have been saying in a few words. My object, it is plain, has been—not to show that Secular Science in its various departments may take up a position hostile to Theology;—this is rather the basis of the objection with which I opened this Discourse;—but to point out the cause of an hostility to which all parties will bear witness. I have been insisting then on this, that the hostility in question, when it occurs, is coincident with an evident deflection or exorbitance of Science from its proper course; and that this exorbitance is sure to take place, almost from the necessity of the case, if Theology be not present to defend its own boundaries and to hinder the encroachment. The human mind cannot keep from speculating

---

4   Vid. Abelard, for instance.

and systematizing; and if Theology is not allowed to occupy its own territory, adjacent sciences, nay, sciences which are quite foreign to Theology, will take possession of it. And this occupation is proved to be a usurpation by this circumstance, that these foreign sciences will assume certain principles as true, and act upon them, which they neither have authority to lay down themselves, nor appeal to any other higher science to lay down for them. For example, it is a mere unwarranted assumption if the Antiquarian says, "Nothing has ever taken place but is to be found in historical documents;" or if the Philosophic Historian says, "There is nothing in Judaism different from other political institutions;" or if the Anatomist, "There is no soul beyond the brain;" or if the Political Economist, "Easy circumstances make men virtuous." These are enunciations, not of Science, but of Private Judgment; and it is Private Judgment that infects every science which it touches with a hostility to Theology, a hostility which properly attaches to no science in itself whatever.

If then, Gentlemen, I now resist such a course of acting as unphilosophical, what is this but to do as men of Science do when the interests of their own respective pursuits are at stake? If they certainly would resist the divine who determined the orbit of Jupiter by the Pentateuch, why am I to be accused of cowardice or illiberality, because I will not tolerate their attempt in turn to theologize by means of astronomy? And if experimentalists would be sure to cry out, did I attempt to install the Thomist philosophy in the schools of astronomy and medicine, why may not I, when Divine Science is ostracized, and La Place, or Buffon, or Humboldt, sits down in its chair, why may not I fairly protest against their exclusiveness, and demand the emancipation of Theology?

15.

And now I consider I have said enough in proof of the first point, which I undertook to maintain, viz., the claim of Theology to be represented among the Chairs of a University. I have shown, I think, that exclusiveness really attaches, not to those who support that claim, but to those who dispute it. I have argued in its behalf, first, from the consideration that, whereas it is the very profession of a University to teach all sciences, on this account it cannot exclude Theology without being untrue to its profession. Next, I have said that, all sciences being connected together, and having bearings one on another, it is impossible to teach them all thoroughly, unless they all are taken into account, and Theology among them. Moreover, I have insisted on the important influence, which Theology in matter of fact does and must exercise over a great variety of sciences, completing and correcting them; so that, granting it to be a real science occupied upon truth, it cannot be omitted without great prejudice to the teaching of the rest. And lastly, I have urged that, supposing Theology be not taught, its province will not simply be neglected, but will be actually usurped by other sciences, which will teach, without warrant, conclusions of their own in a subject-matter which needs its own proper principles for its due formation and disposition.

Abstract statements are always unsatisfactory; these, as I have already observed, could be illustrated at far greater length than the time allotted to me for the purpose has allowed. Let me hope that I have said enough upon the subject to suggest thoughts, which those who take an interest in it may pursue for themselves.

DISCOURSE V

KNOWLEDGE ITS OWN END

A University may be considered with reference either to its Students or to its Studies; and the principle, that all Knowledge is a whole and the separate Sciences parts of one, which I have hitherto been using in behalf of its studies, is equally important when we direct our attention to its students. Now then I turn to the students, and shall consider the education which, by virtue of this principle, a University will give them; and thus I shall be introduced, Gentlemen, to the second question, which I proposed to discuss, viz., whether and in what sense its teaching, viewed relatively to the taught, carries the attribute of Utility along with it.

1.

I have said that all branches of knowledge are connected together, because the subject-matter of knowledge is intimately united in itself, as being the acts and the work of the Creator. Hence it is that the Sciences, into which our knowledge may be said to be cast, have multiplied bearings one on another, and an internal sympathy, and admit, or rather demand, comparison and adjustment. They complete, correct, balance each other. This consideration, if well-founded, must be taken into account, not only as regards the attainment of truth, which is their common end, but as regards the influence which they exercise upon those whose education consists in the study of them. I have said already, that to give undue prominence to one is to be unjust to another; to neglect or supersede these is to divert those from their proper object. It is to unsettle the boundary lines between science and science, to disturb their action, to destroy the harmony which binds them together. Such a proceeding will have a corresponding effect when introduced into a place of education. There is no science but tells a different tale, when viewed as a portion of a whole, from what it is likely to suggest when taken by itself, without the safeguard, as I may call it, of others.

Let me make use of an illustration. In the combination of colours, very different effects are produced by a difference in their selection and juxtaposition; red, green, and white, change their shades, according to the contrast to which they are submitted. And, in like manner, the drift and meaning of a branch of knowledge varies with the company in which it is introduced to the student. If his reading is confined simply to one subject, however such division of labour may favour the advancement of a particular pursuit, a point into which I do not here enter, certainly it has a tendency to contract his mind. If it is incorporated with others, it depends on those others as to the kind of influence which it exerts upon him. Thus the Classics, which in England are the means of refining the taste, have in France subserved the spread of revolutionary and deistical doctrines. In Metaphysics, again, Butler's Analogy of Religion, which has had so much to do with the conversion to the Catholic faith of members of the University of Oxford, appeared to Pitt and others, who had received a different training, to operate only in the direction of infidelity. And so again, Watson, Bishop of Llandaff, as I think he tells us in the narrative of his life, felt the science of Mathematics to indispose the mind to religious belief, while others see in its investigations the best parallel, and thereby defence, of the Christian Mysteries. In like manner, I suppose, Arcesilas would not have handled logic as Aristotle, nor Aristotle have criticized poets as Plato; yet reasoning and poetry are subject to scientific rules.

It is a great point then to enlarge the range of studies which a University professes, even for the sake of the students; and, though they cannot pursue every subject which is open to them, they will be the gainers by living among those and under those who represent the whole circle. This I conceive to be the advantage of a seat of universal learning, considered as a place of education. An assemblage of learned men, zealous for their own sciences, and rivals of each other, are brought, by familiar inter-course and for the sake of intellectual peace, to adjust together the claims and relations of their respective subjects of investiga-tion. They learn to respect, to consult, to aid each other. Thus is created a pure and clear atmosphere of thought, which the stu-dent also breathes, though in his own case he only pursues a few sciences out of the multitude. He profits by an intellectual tradi-tion, which is independent of particular teachers, which guides him in his choice of subjects, and duly interprets for him those which he chooses. He apprehends the great outlines of knowl-edge, the principles on which it rests, the scale of its parts, its lights and its shades, its great points and its little, as he otherwise cannot apprehend them. Hence it is that his education is called "Liberal." A habit of mind is formed which lasts through life, of which the attributes are, freedom, equitableness, calmness, moderation, and wisdom; or what in a former Discourse I have ventured to call a philosophical habit. This then I would assign as the special fruit of the education furnished at a University, as contrasted with other places of teaching or modes of teaching. This is the main purpose of a University in its treatment of its students.

And now the question is asked me, What is the *use* of it? and my answer will constitute the main subject of the Discourses which are to follow.

2.

Cautious and practical thinkers, I say, will ask of me, what, after all, is the gain of this Philosophy, of which I make such account, and from which I promise so much. Even supposing it to enable us to exercise the degree of trust exactly due to every science respectively, and to estimate precisely the value of every truth which is anywhere to be found, how are we better for this master view of things, which I have been extolling? Does it not reverse the principle of the division of labour? will practical objects be obtained better or worse by its cultivation? to what then does it lead? where does it end? what does it do? how does it profit? what does it promise? Particular sciences are respectively the basis of definite arts, which carry on to results tangible and beneficial the truths which are the subjects of the knowledge attained; what is the Art of this science of sciences? what is the fruit of such a Philosophy? what are we proposing to effect, what inducements do we hold out to the Catholic community, when we set about the enterprise of founding a University?

I am asked what is the end of University Education, and of the Liberal or Philosophical Knowledge which I conceive it to impart: I answer, that what I have already said has been sufficient to show that it has a very tangible, real, and sufficient end, though the end cannot be divided from that knowledge itself. Knowledge is capable of being its own end. Such is the constitution of the human mind, that any kind of knowledge, if it be really such, is its own reward. And if this is true of all knowledge, it is true also of that special Philosophy, which I have made to consist in a comprehensive view of truth in all its branches, of the relations of science to science, of their mutual bearings, and their respective values. What the worth of such an acquirement is, compared with other objects which we seek,—wealth or power or honour or the conveniences and comforts of life, I do not profess here to discuss; but I would maintain, and mean to show, that it is an object, in its own nature so really and undeniably good, as to be the compensation of a great deal of thought in the compassing, and a great deal of trouble in the attaining.

Now, when I say that Knowledge is, not merely a means to something beyond it, or the preliminary of certain arts into which it naturally resolves, but an end sufficient to rest in and to pursue for its own sake, surely I am uttering no paradox, for I am stating what is both intelligible in itself, and has ever been the common judgment of philosophers and the ordinary feeling of mankind. I am saying what at least the public opinion of this day ought to be slow to deny, considering how much we have heard of late years, in opposition to Religion, of entertaining, curious, and various knowledge. I am but saying what whole volumes have been written to illustrate, viz., by a "selection from the records of Philosophy, Literature, and Art, in all ages and countries, of a body of examples, to show how the most unpropitious circumstances have been unable to conquer an ardent desire for the acquisition of knowledge."[1] That further advantages accrue to us and redound to others by its possession, over and above what it is in itself, I am very far indeed from denying; but, independent of these, we are satisfying a direct need of our nature in its very acquisition; and, whereas our nature, unlike that of the inferior creation, does not at once reach its perfection, but depends, in order to it, on a number of external aids and appliances, Knowledge, as one of the principal of these, is valuable for what its very presence in us does for us after the manner of a habit, even though it be turned to no further account, nor subserve any direct end.

3.

Hence it is that Cicero, in enumerating the various heads of mental excellence, lays down the pursuit of Knowledge for its own sake, as the first of them. "This pertains most of all to human nature," he says, "for we are all of us drawn to the pursuit of Knowledge; in which to excel we consider excellent, whereas to mistake, to err, to be ignorant, to be deceived, is both an evil and a disgrace."[2] And he considers Knowledge the very first object to which we are attracted, after the supply of our physical wants. After the calls and duties of our animal existence, as they may be termed, as regards ourselves, our family, and our neighbours, follows, he tells us, "the search after truth. Accordingly, as soon as we escape from the pressure of necessary cares, forthwith we desire to see, to hear, and to learn; and consider the knowledge of what is hidden or is wonderful a condition of our happiness."

This passage, though it is but one of many similar passages in a multitude of authors, I take for the very reason that it is so familiarly known to us; and I wish you to observe, Gentlemen, how distinctly it separates the pursuit of Knowledge from those

---

1 Pursuit of Knowledge under Difficulties. Introd.
2 Cicer. Offic. init.

ulterior objects to which certainly it can be made to conduce, and which are, I suppose, solely contemplated by the persons who would ask of me the use of a University or Liberal Education. So far from dreaming of the cultivation of Knowledge directly and mainly in order to our physical comfort and enjoyment, for the sake of life and person, of health, of the conjugal and family union, of the social tie and civil security, the great Orator implies, that it is only after our physical and political needs are supplied, and when we are "free from necessary duties and cares," that we are in a condition for "desiring to see, to hear, and to learn." Nor does he contemplate in the least degree the reflex or subsequent action of Knowledge, when acquired, upon those material goods which we set out by securing before we seek it; on the contrary, he expressly denies its bearing upon social life altogether, strange as such a procedure is to those who live after the rise of the Baconian philosophy, and he cautions us against such a cultivation of it as will interfere with our duties to our fellow-creatures. "All these methods," he says, "are engaged in the investigation of truth; by the pursuit of which to be carried off from public occupations is a transgression of duty. For the praise of virtue lies altogether in action; yet intermissions often occur, and then we recur to such pursuits; not to say that the incessant activity of the mind is vigorous enough to carry us on in the pursuit of knowledge, even without any exertion of our own." The idea of benefiting society by means of "the pursuit of science and knowledge" did not enter at all into the motives which he would assign for their cultivation.

This was the ground of the opposition which the elder Cato made to the introduction of Greek Philosophy among his countrymen, when Carneades and his companions, on occasion of their embassy, were charming the Roman youth with their eloquent expositions of it. The fit representative of a practical people, Cato estimated every thing by what it produced; whereas the Pursuit of Knowledge promised nothing beyond Knowledge itself. He despised that refinement or enlargement of mind of which he had no experience.

4.

Things, which can bear to be cut off from every thing else and yet persist in living, must have life in themselves; pursuits, which issue in nothing, and still maintain their ground for ages, which are regarded as admirable, though they have not as yet proved themselves to be useful, must have their sufficient end in themselves, whatever it turn out to be. And we are brought to the same conclusion by considering the force of the epithet, by which the knowledge under consideration is popularly designated. It is common to speak of "*liberal* knowledge," of the "*liberal* arts and studies," and of a "*liberal* education," as the especial characteristic or property of a University and of a gentleman; what is really meant by the word? Now, first, in its grammatical sense it is opposed to *servile*; and by "servile work" is understood, as our catechisms inform us, bodily labour, mechanical employment, and the like, in which the mind has little or no part. Parallel to such servile works are those arts, if they deserve the name, of which the poet speaks,[3] which owe their origin and their method to hazard, not to skill; as, for instance, the practice and operations of an empiric. As far as this contrast may be considered as a guide into the meaning of the word, liberal education and liberal pursuits are exercises of mind, of reason, of reflection.

But we want something more for its explanation, for there are bodily exercises which are liberal, and mental exercises which are not so. For instance, in ancient times the practitioners in medicine were commonly slaves; yet it was an art as intellectual in its nature, in spite of the pretence, fraud, and quackery with which it might then, as now, be debased, as it was heavenly in its aim. And so in like manner, we contrast a liberal education with a commercial education or a professional; yet no one can deny that commerce and the professions afford scope for the highest and most diversified powers of mind. There is then a great variety of intellectual exercises, which are not technically called "liberal;" on the other hand, I say, there are exercises of the body which

---

3 Τέχνη τύχην ἔστερξε καί τύχη τέχνην. Vid. Arist. Nic. Ethic. vi.

do receive that appellation. Such, for instance, was the palæstra, in ancient times; such the Olympic games, in which strength and dexterity of body as well as of mind gained the prize. In Xenophon we read of the young Persian nobility being taught to ride on horseback and to speak the truth; both being among the accomplishments of a gentleman. War, too, however rough a profession, has ever been accounted liberal, unless in cases when it becomes heroic, which would introduce us to another subject.

Now comparing these instances together, we shall have no difficulty in determining the principle of this apparent variation in the application of the term which I am examining. Manly games, or games of skill, or military prowess, though bodily, are, it seems, accounted liberal; on the other hand, what is merely professional, though highly intellectual, nay, though liberal in comparison of trade and manual labour, is not simply called liberal, and mercantile occupations are not liberal at all. Why this distinction? because that alone is liberal knowledge, which stands on its own pretensions, which is independent of sequel, expects no complement, refuses to be *informed* (as it is called) by any end, or absorbed into any art, in order duly to present itself to our contemplation. The most ordinary pursuits have this specific character, if they are self-sufficient and complete; the highest lose it, when they minister to something beyond them. It is absurd to balance, in point of worth and importance, a treatise on reducing fractures with a game of cricket or a fox-chase; yet of the two the bodily exercise has that quality which we call "liberal," and the intellectual has it not. And so of the learned professions altogether, considered merely as professions; although one of them be the most popularly beneficial, and another the most politically important, and the third the most intimately divine of all human pursuits, yet the very greatness of their end, the health of the body, or of the commonwealth, or of the soul, diminishes, not increases, their claim to the appellation "liberal," and that still more, if they are cut down to the strict exigencies of that end. If, for instance, Theology, instead of being cultivated as a contemplation, be limited to the purposes of the pulpit or be represented by the catechism, it loses,—not its usefulness, not its divine character, not its meritoriousness (rather it gains a claim upon these titles by such charitable condescension),—but it does lose the particular attribute which I am illustrating; just as a face worn by tears and fasting loses its beauty, or a labourer's hand loses its delicateness;—for Theology thus exercised is not simple knowledge, but rather is an art or a business making use of Theology. And thus it appears that even what is supernatural need not be liberal, nor need a hero be a gentleman, for the plain reason that one idea is not another idea. And in like manner the Baconian Philosophy, by using its physical sciences in the service of man, does thereby transfer them from the order of Liberal Pursuits to, I do not say the inferior, but the distinct class of the Useful. And, to take a different instance, hence again, as is evident, whenever personal gain is the motive, still more distinctive an effect has it upon the character of a given pursuit; thus racing, which was a liberal exercise in Greece, forfeits its rank in times like these, so far as it is made the occasion of gambling.

All that I have been now saying is summed up in a few characteristic words of the great Philosopher. "Of possessions," he says, "those rather are useful, which bear fruit; those *liberal, which tend to enjoyment*. By fruitful, I mean, which yield revenue; by enjoyable, where *nothing accrues of consequence beyond the using*."[4]

5.

Do not suppose, that in thus appealing to the ancients, I am throwing back the world two thousand years, and fettering Philosophy with the reasonings of paganism. While the world lasts, will Aristotle's doctrine on these matters last, for he is the oracle of nature and of truth. While we are men, we cannot help, to a great extent, being Aristotelians, for the great Master does but analyze the thoughts, feelings, views, and opinions of human kind. He has told us the meaning of our own words and ideas,

---

4 Aristot. Rhet. i. 5.

before we were born. In many subject-matters, to think correctly, is to think like Aristotle; and we are his disciples whether we will or no, though we may not know it. Now, as to the particular instance before us, the word "liberal" as applied to Knowledge and Education, expresses a specific idea, which ever has been, and ever will be, while the nature of man is the same, just as the idea of the Beautiful is specific, or of the Sublime, or of the Ridiculous, or of the Sordid. It is in the world now, it was in the world then; and, as in the case of the dogmas of faith, it is illustrated by a continuous historical tradition, and never was out of the world, from the time it came into it. There have indeed been differences of opinion from time to time, as to what pursuits and what arts came under that idea, but such differences are but an additional evidence of its reality. That idea must have a substance in it, which has maintained its ground amid these conflicts and changes, which has ever served as a standard to measure things withal, which has passed from mind to mind unchanged, when there was so much to colour, so much to influence any notion or thought whatever, which was not founded in our very nature. Were it a mere generalization, it would have varied with the subjects from which it was generalized; but though its subjects vary with the age, it varies not itself. The palæstra may seem a liberal exercise to Lycurgus, and illiberal to Seneca; coach-driving and prize-fighting may be recognized in Elis, and be condemned in England; music may be despicable in the eyes of certain moderns, and be in the highest place with Aristotle and Plato,—(and the case is the same in the particular application of the idea of Beauty, or of Goodness, or of Moral Virtue, there is a difference of tastes, a difference of judgments)—still these variations imply, instead of discrediting, the archetypal idea, which is but a previous hypothesis or condition, by means of which issue is joined between contending opinions, and without which there would be nothing to dispute about.

I consider, then, that I am chargeable with no paradox, when I speak of a Knowledge which is its own end, when I call it liberal knowledge, or a gentleman's knowledge, when I educate for it, and make it the scope of a University. And still less am I incurring such a charge, when I make this acquisition consist, not in Knowledge in a vague and ordinary sense, but in that Knowledge which I have especially called Philosophy or, in an extended sense of the word, Science; for whatever claims Knowledge has to be considered as a good, these it has in a higher degree when it is viewed not vaguely, not popularly, but precisely and transcendently as Philosophy. Knowledge, I say, is then especially liberal, or sufficient for itself, apart from every external and ulterior object, when and so far as it is philosophical, and this I proceed to show.

6.

Now bear with me, Gentlemen, if what I am about to say, has at first sight a fanciful appearance. Philosophy, then, or Science, is related to Knowledge in this way:—Knowledge is called by the name of Science or Philosophy, when it is acted upon, informed, or if I may use a strong figure, impregnated by Reason. Reason is the principle of that intrinsic fecundity of Knowledge, which, to those who possess it, is its especial value, and which dispenses with the necessity of their looking abroad for any end to rest upon external to itself. Knowledge, indeed, when thus exalted into a scientific form, is also power; not only is it excellent in itself, but whatever such excellence may be, it is something more, it has a result beyond itself. Doubtless; but that is a further consideration, with which I am not concerned. I only say that, prior to its being a power, it is a good; that it is, not only an instrument, but an end. I know well it may resolve itself into an art, and terminate in a mechanical process, and in tangible fruit; but it also may fall back upon that Reason which informs it, and resolve itself into Philosophy. In one case it is called Useful Knowledge, in the other Liberal. The same person may cultivate it in both ways at once; but this again is a matter foreign to my subject; here I do but say that there are two ways of using Knowledge, and in matter of fact those who use it in one way are not likely to use it in the other, or at least in a very limited measure.

You see, then, here are two methods of Education; the end of the one is to be philosophical, of the other to be mechanical; the one rises towards general ideas, the other is exhausted upon what is particular and external. Let me not be thought to deny the necessity, or to decry the benefit, of such attention to what is particular and practical, as belongs to the useful or mechanical arts; life could not go on without them; we owe our daily welfare to them; their exercise is the duty of the many, and we owe to the many a debt of gratitude for fulfilling that duty. I only say that Knowledge, in proportion as it tends more and more to be particular, ceases to be Knowledge. It is a question whether Knowledge can in any proper sense be predicated of the brute creation; without pretending to metaphysical exactness of phraseology, which would be unsuitable to an occasion like this, I say, it seems to me improper to call that passive sensation, or perception of things, which brutes seem to possess, by the name of Knowledge. When I speak of Knowledge, I mean something intellectual, something which grasps what it perceives through the senses; something which takes a view of things; which sees more than the senses convey; which reasons upon what it sees, and while it sees; which invests it with an idea. It expresses itself, not in a mere enunciation, but by an enthymeme: it is of the nature of science from the first, and in this consists its dignity. The principle of real dignity in Knowledge, its worth, its desirableness, considered irrespectively of its results, is this germ within it of a scientific or a philosophical process. This is how it comes to be an end in itself; this is why it admits of being called Liberal. Not to know the relative disposition of things is the state of slaves or children; to have mapped out the Universe is the boast, or at least the ambition, of Philosophy.

Moreover, such knowledge is not a mere extrinsic or accidental advantage, which is ours today and another's tomorrow, which may be got up from a book, and easily forgotten again, which we can command or communicate at our pleasure, which we can borrow for the occasion, carry about in our hand, and take into the market; it is an acquired illumination, it is a habit, a personal possession, and an inward endowment. And this is the reason, why it is more correct, as well as more usual, to speak of a University as a place of education, than of instruction, though, when knowledge is concerned, instruction would at first sight have seemed the more appropriate word. We are instructed, for instance, in manual exercises, in the fine and useful arts, in trades, and in ways of business; for these are methods, which have little or no effect upon the mind itself, are contained in rules committed to memory, to tradition, or to use, and bear upon an end external to themselves. But education is a higher word; it implies an action upon our mental nature, and the formation of a character; it is something individual and permanent, and is commonly spoken of in connexion with religion and virtue. When, then, we speak of the communication of Knowledge as being Education, we thereby really imply that that Knowledge is a state or condition of mind; and since cultivation of mind is surely worth seeking for its own sake, we are thus brought once more to the conclusion, which the word "Liberal" and the word "Philosophy" have already suggested, that there is a Knowledge, which is desirable, though nothing come of it, as being of itself a treasure, and a sufficient remuneration of years of labour.

7.

This, then, is the answer which I am prepared to give to the question with which I opened this Discourse. Before going on to speak of the object of the Church in taking up Philosophy, and the uses to which she puts it, I am prepared to maintain that Philosophy is its own end, and, as I conceive, I have now begun the proof of it. I am prepared to maintain that there is a knowledge worth possessing for what it is, and not merely for what it does; and what minutes remain to me today I shall devote to the removal of some portion of the indistinctness and confusion with which the subject may in some minds be surrounded.

It may be objected then, that, when we profess to seek Knowledge for some end or other beyond itself, whatever it be, we speak intelligibly; but that, whatever men may have said, however obstinately the idea may have kept its ground from age to age, still it is simply unmeaning to say that we seek Knowledge for its own sake, and for nothing else; for that it ever leads to something beyond itself, which therefore is its end, and the cause why it is desirable;—moreover, that this end is twofold, either of this world or of the next; that all knowledge is cultivated either for secular objects or for eternal; that if it is directed to secular objects, it is called Useful Knowledge, if to eternal, Religious or Christian Knowledge;—in consequence, that if, as I have allowed, this Liberal Knowledge does not benefit the body or estate, it ought to benefit the soul; but if the fact be really so, that it is neither a physical or a secular good on the one hand, nor a moral good on the other, it cannot be a good at all, and is not worth the trouble which is necessary for its acquisition.

And then I may be reminded that the professors of this Liberal or Philosophical Knowledge have themselves, in every age, recognized this exposition of the matter, and have submitted to the issue in which it terminates; for they have ever been attempting to make men virtuous; or, if not, at least have assumed that refinement of mind was virtue, and that they themselves were the virtuous portion of mankind. This they have professed on the one hand; and on the other, they have utterly failed in their professions, so as ever to make themselves a proverb among men, and a laughing-stock both to the grave and the dissipated portion of mankind, in consequence of them. Thus they have furnished against themselves both the ground and the means of their own exposure, without any trouble at all to any one else. In a word, from the time that Athens was the University of the world, what has Philosophy taught men, but to promise without practising, and to aspire without attaining? What has the deep and lofty thought of its disciples ended in but eloquent words? Nay, what has its teaching ever meditated, when it was boldest in its remedies for human ill, beyond charming us to sleep by its lessons, that we might feel nothing at all? like some melodious air, or rather like those strong and transporting perfumes, which at first spread their sweetness over every thing they touch, but in a little while do but offend in proportion as they once pleased us. Did Philosophy support Cicero under the disfavour of the fickle populace, or nerve Seneca to oppose an imperial tyrant? It abandoned Brutus, as he sorrowfully confessed, in his greatest need, and it forced Cato, as his panegyrist strangely boasts, into the false position of defying heaven. How few can be counted among its professors, who, like Polemo, were thereby converted from a profligate course, or like Anaxagoras, thought the world well lost in exchange for its possession? The philosopher in Rasselas taught a superhuman doctrine, and then succumbed without an effort to a trial of human affection.

"He discoursed," we are told, "with great energy on the government of the passions. His look was venerable, his action graceful, his pronunciation clear, and his diction elegant. He showed, with great strength of sentiment and variety of illustration, that human nature is degraded and debased, when the lower faculties predominate over the higher. He communicated the various precepts given, from time to time, for the conquest of passion, and displayed the happiness of those who had obtained the important victory, after which man is no longer the slave of fear, nor the fool of hope ... He enumerated many examples of heroes immoveable by pain or pleasure, who looked with indifference on those modes or accidents to which the vulgar give the names of good and evil."

Rasselas in a few days found the philosopher in a room half darkened, with his eyes misty, and his face pale. "Sir," said he, "you have come at a time when all human friendship is useless; what I suffer cannot be remedied, what I have lost cannot be supplied. My daughter, my only daughter, from whose tenderness I expected all the comforts of my age, died last night of a fever." "Sir," said the prince, "mortality is an event by which a wise man can never be surprised; we know that death is always near, and it should therefore always be expected." "Young man," answered the philosopher, "you speak like one who has never felt the pangs of separation." "Have you, then, forgot the precept," said Rasselas, "which you so powerfully enforced? ... consider that external things are naturally variable, but truth and reason are always the same." "What comfort," said the mourner, "can truth and reason afford me? Of what effect are they now, but to tell me that my daughter will not be restored?"

8.

Better, far better, to make no professions, you will say, than to cheat others with what we are not, and to scandalize them with what we are. The sensualist, or the man of the world, at any rate is not the victim of fine words, but pursues a reality and gains it. The Philosophy of Utility, you will say, Gentlemen, has at least done its work; and I grant it,—it aimed low, but it has fulfilled its aim. If that man of great intellect who has been its Prophet in the conduct of life played false to his own professions, he was not bound by his philosophy to be true to his friend or faithful in his trust. Moral virtue was not the line in which he undertook to instruct men; and though, as the poet calls him, he were the "meanest" of mankind, he was so in what may be called his private capacity and without any prejudice to the theory of induction. He had a right to be so, if he chose, for any thing that the Idols of the den or the theatre had to say to the contrary. His mission was the increase of physical enjoyment and social comfort;[5] and most wonderfully, most awfully has he fulfilled his conception and his design. Almost day by day have we fresh and fresh shoots, and buds, and blossoms, which are to ripen into fruit, on that magical tree of Knowledge which he planted, and to which none of us perhaps, except the very poor, but owes, if not his present life, at least his daily food, his health, and general well-being. He was the divinely provided minister of temporal benefits to all of us so great, that, whatever I am forced to think of him as a man, I have not the heart, from mere gratitude, to speak of him severely. And, in spite of the tendencies of his philosophy, which are, as we see at this day, to depreciate, or to trample on Theology, he has himself, in his writings, gone out of his way, as if with a prophetic misgiving of those tendencies, to insist on it as the

---

5 It will be seen that on the whole I agree with Lord Macaulay in his Essay on Bacon's Philosophy. I do not know whether he would agree with me.

instrument of that beneficent Father,[6] who, when He came on earth in visible form, took on Him first and most prominently the office of assuaging the bodily wounds of human nature. And truly, like the old mediciner in the tale, "he sat diligently at his work, and hummed, with cheerful countenance, a pious song;" and then in turn "went out singing into the meadows so gaily, that those who had seen him from afar might well have thought it was a youth gathering flowers for his beloved, instead of an old physician gathering healing herbs in the morning dew."[7]

Alas, that men, in the action of life or in their heart of hearts, are not what they seem to be in their moments of excitement, or in their trances or intoxications of genius,—so good, so noble, so serene! Alas, that Bacon too in his own way should after all be but the fellow of those heathen philosophers who in their disadvantages had some excuse for their inconsistency, and who surprise us rather in what they did say than in what they did not do! Alas, that he too, like Socrates or Seneca, must be stripped of his holy-day coat, which looks so fair, and should be but a mockery amid his most majestic gravity of phrase; and, for all his vast abilities, should, in the littleness of his own moral being, but typify the intellectual narrowness of his school! However, granting all this, heroism after all was not his philosophy:—I cannot deny he has abundantly achieved what he proposed. His is simply a Method whereby bodily discomforts and temporal wants are to be most effectually removed from the greatest number; and already, before it has shown any signs of exhaustion, the gifts of nature, in their most artificial shapes and luxurious profusion and diversity, from all quarters of the earth, are, it is undeniable, by its means brought even to our doors, and we rejoice in them.

---

6 De Augment. iv. 2, vid. Macaulay's Essay; vid. also "In principio operis ad Deum Patrem, Deum Verbum, Deum Spiritum, preces fundimus humillimas et ardentissimas, ut humani generis ærumnarum memores, et peregrinationis istius vitæ, in quâ dies paucos et malos terimus, *novis suis eleemosynis, per manus nostras,* familiam humanam dotare dignentur. Atque illud insuper supplices rogamus, ne *humana divinis officiant;* neve *ex reseratione viarum sensûs,* et accensione majore luminis naturalis, *aliquid incredulitatis* et noctis, animis nostris erga divina mysteria oriatur," etc. *Præf.* Instaur. Magn.

7 Fouque's Unknown Patient.

9.

Useful Knowledge then, I grant, has done its work; and Liberal Knowledge as certainly has not done its work,—that is, supposing, as the objectors assume, its direct end, like Religious Knowledge, is to make men better; but this I will not for an instant allow, and, unless I allow it, those objectors have said nothing to the purpose. I admit, rather I maintain, what they have been urging, for I consider Knowledge to have its end in itself. For all its friends, or its enemies, may say, I insist upon it, that it is as real a mistake to burden it with virtue or religion as with the mechanical arts. Its direct business is not to steel the soul against temptation or to console it in affliction, any more than to set the loom in motion, or to direct the steam carriage; be it ever so much the means or the condition of both material and moral advancement, still, taken by and in itself, it as little mends our hearts as it improves our temporal circumstances. And if its eulogists claim for it such a power, they commit the very same kind of encroachment on a province not their own as the political economist who should maintain that his science educated him for casuistry or diplomacy. Knowledge is one thing, virtue is another; good sense is not conscience, refinement is not humility, nor is largeness and justness of view faith. Philosophy, however enlightened, however profound, gives no command over the passions, no influential motives, no vivifying principles. Liberal Education makes not the Christian, not the Catholic, but the gentleman. It is well to be a gentlemen, it is well to have a cultivated intellect, a delicate taste, a candid, equitable, dispassionate mind, a noble and courteous bearing in the conduct of life;—these are the connatural qualities of a large knowledge; they are the objects of a University; I am advocating, I shall illustrate and insist upon them; but still, I repeat, they are no guarantee for sanctity or even for conscientiousness, they may attach to the man of the world, to the profligate, to the heartless,—pleasant, alas, and attractive as he shows when decked out in them. Taken by themselves, they do but seem to be what they are not; they look like virtue at a distance, but they are detected by close observers, and on the long run; and hence it is that they are popularly accused of pretence and hypocrisy, not, I repeat, from their own fault, but because their professors and their admirers persist in taking them for what they are not, and are officious in arrogating for them a praise to which they have no claim. Quarry the granite rock with razors, or moor the vessel with a thread of silk; then may you hope with such keen and delicate instruments as human knowledge and human reason to contend against those giants, the passion and the pride of man.

Surely we are not driven to theories of this kind, in order to vindicate the value and dignity of Liberal Knowledge. Surely the real grounds on which its pretensions rest are not so very subtle or abstruse, so very strange or improbable. Surely it is very intelligible to say, and that is what I say here, that Liberal Education, viewed in itself, is simply the cultivation of the intellect, as such, and its object is nothing more or less than intellectual excellence. Every thing has its own perfection, be it higher or lower in the scale of things; and the perfection of one is not the perfection of another. Things animate, inanimate, visible, invisible, all are good in their kind, and have a *best* of themselves, which is an object of pursuit. Why do you take such pains with your garden or your park? You see to your walks and turf and shrubberies; to your trees and drives; not as if you meant to make an orchard of the one, or corn or pasture land of the other, but because there is a special beauty in all that is goodly in wood, water, plain, and slope, brought all together by art into one shape, and grouped into one whole. Your cities are beautiful, your palaces, your public buildings, your territorial mansions, your churches; and their beauty leads to nothing beyond itself. There is a physical beauty and a moral: there is a beauty of person, there is a beauty of our moral being, which is natural virtue; and in like manner there is a beauty, there is a perfection, of the intellect. There is an ideal perfection in these various subject-matters, towards which individual instances are seen to rise, and which are the standards for all instances whatever. The Greek divinities and demigods, as the statuary has moulded them, with their symmetry of figure, and their high forehead and their regular features, are the perfection of physical beauty. The heroes, of whom history tells, Alexander, or Cæsar, or Scipio, or Saladin, are the representatives of that magnanimity or self-mastery which is the greatness of human nature. Christianity too has its heroes, and in the supernatural order, and we call them Saints. The artist puts before him beauty of feature and form; the poet, beauty of mind; the preacher, the beauty of grace: then intellect too, I repeat, has its beauty, and it has those who aim at it. To open the mind, to correct it, to refine it, to enable it to know, and to digest, master, rule, and use its knowledge, to give it power over its own faculties, application, flexibility, method, critical exactness, sagacity, resource, address, eloquent expression, is an object as intelligible (for here we are inquiring, not what the object of a Liberal Education is worth, nor what use the Church makes of it, but what it is in itself), I say, an object as intelligible as the cultivation of virtue, while, at the same time, it is absolutely distinct from it.

10.

This indeed is but a temporal object, and a transitory possession; but so are other things in themselves which we make much of and pursue. The moralist will tell us that man, in all his functions, is but a flower which blossoms and fades, except so far as a higher principle breathes upon him, and makes him and what he is immortal. Body and mind are carried on into an eternal state of being by the gifts of Divine Munificence; but at first they do but fail in a failing world; and if the powers of intellect decay, the powers of the body have decayed before them, and, as an Hospital or an Almshouse, though its end be ephemeral, may be sanctified to the service of religion, so surely may a University, even were it nothing more than I have as yet described it. We attain to heaven by using this world well, though it is to pass away; we perfect our nature, not by undoing it, but by adding to it what is more than nature, and directing it towards aims higher than its own.

KNOWLEDGE VIEWED IN RELATION TO LEARNING

1.

It were well if the English, like the Greek language, possessed some definite word to express, simply and generally, intellectual proficiency or perfection, such as "health," as used with reference to the animal frame, and "virtue," with reference to our moral nature. I am not able to find such a term;—talent, ability, genius, belong distinctly to the raw material, which is the subject-matter, not to that excellence which is the result of exercise and training. When we turn, indeed, to the particular kinds of intellectual perfection, words are forthcoming for our purpose, as, for instance, judgment, taste, and skill; yet even these belong, for the most part, to powers or habits bearing upon practice or upon art, and not to any perfect condition of the intellect, considered in itself. Wisdom, again, is certainly a more comprehensive word than any other, but it has a direct relation to conduct, and to human life. Knowledge, indeed, and Science express purely intellectual ideas, but still not a state or quality of the intellect; for knowledge, in its ordinary sense, is but one of its circumstances, denoting a possession or a habit; and science has been appropriated to the subject-matter of the intellect, instead of belonging in English, as it ought to do, to the intellect itself. The consequence is that, on an occasion like this, many words are necessary, in order, first, to bring out and convey what surely is no difficult idea in itself,—that of the cultivation of the intellect as an end; next, in order to recommend what surely is no unreasonable object; and lastly, to describe and make the mind realize the particular perfection in which that object consists. Every one knows practically what are the constituents of health or of virtue; and every one recognizes health and virtue as ends to be pursued; it is otherwise with intellectual excellence, and this must be my excuse, if I seem to any one to be bestowing a good deal of labour on a preliminary matter.

In default of a recognized term, I have called the perfection or virtue of the intellect by the name of philosophy, philosophical knowledge, enlargement of mind, or illumination; terms which are not uncommonly given to it by writers of this day: but, whatever name we bestow on it, it is, I believe, as a matter of history, the business of a University to make this intellectual culture its direct scope, or to employ itself in the education of the intellect,—just as the work of a Hospital lies in healing the sick or wounded, of a Riding or Fencing School, or of a Gymnasium, in exercising the limbs, of an Almshouse, in aiding and solacing the old, of an Orphanage, in protecting innocence, of a Penitentiary, in restoring the guilty. I say, a University, taken in its bare idea, and before we view it as an instrument of the Church, has this object and this mission; it contemplates neither moral impression nor mechanical production; it professes to exercise the mind neither in art nor in duty; its function is intellectual culture; here it may leave its scholars, and it has done its work when it has done as much as this. It educates the intellect to reason well in all matters, to reach out towards truth, and to grasp it.

2.

This, I said in my foregoing Discourse, was the object of a University, viewed in itself, and apart from the Catholic Church, or from the State, or from any other power which may use it; and I illustrated this in various ways. I said that the intellect must have an excellence of its own, for there was nothing which had not its specific good; that the word "educate" would not be used of intellectual culture, as it is used, had not the intellect had an end of its own; that, had it not such an end, there would be no meaning in calling certain intellectual exercises "liberal," in contrast with "useful," as is commonly done; that the very notion of a philosophical temper implied it, for it threw us back upon research and system as ends in themselves, distinct from effects and works of any kind; that a philosophical scheme of knowledge, or system of sciences, could not, from the nature of the case, issue in any one definite art or pursuit, as its end; and that, on the other hand, the discovery and contemplation of truth, to which research and systematizing led, were surely sufficient ends, though nothing beyond them were added, and that they had ever been accounted sufficient by mankind.

Here then I take up the subject; and, having determined that the cultivation of the intellect is an end distinct and sufficient in itself, and that, so far as words go it is an enlargement or illumination, I proceed to inquire what this mental breadth, or power, or light, or philosophy consists in. A Hospital heals a broken limb or cures a fever: what does an Institution effect, which professes the health, not of the body, not of the soul, but of the intellect? What is this good, which in former times, as well as our own, has been found worth the notice, the appropriation, of the Catholic Church?

I have then to investigate, in the Discourses which follow, those qualities and characteristics of the intellect in which its cultivation issues or rather consists; and, with a view of assisting myself in this undertaking, I shall recur to certain questions which have already been touched upon. These questions are three: viz. the relation of intellectual culture, first, to *mere* knowledge; secondly, to *professional* knowledge; and thirdly, to *religious* knowledge. In other words, are *acquirements* and *attainments* the scope of a University Education? or *expertness in particular arts and pursuits*? or *moral and religious proficiency*? or something besides these three? These questions I shall examine in succession, with the purpose I have mentioned; and I hope to he excused, if, in this anxious undertaking, I am led to repeat what, either in these Discourses or elsewhere, I have already put upon paper. And first, of *Mere Knowledge*, or Learning, and its connexion with intellectual illumination or Philosophy.

3.

I suppose the *primâ-facie* view which the public at large would take of a University, considering it as a place of Education, is nothing more or less than a place for acquiring a great deal of knowledge on a great many subjects. Memory is one of the first developed of the mental faculties; a boy's business when he goes to school is to learn, that is, to store up things in his memory. For some years his intellect is little more than an instrument for taking in facts, or a receptacle for storing them; he welcomes them as fast as they come to him; he lives on what is without; he has his eyes ever about him; he has a lively susceptibility of impressions; he imbibes information of every kind; and little does he make his own in a true sense of the word, living rather upon his neighbours all around him. He has opinions, religious, political, and literary, and, for a boy, is very positive in them and sure about them; but he gets them from his schoolfellows, or his masters, or his parents, as the case may be. Such as he is in his other relations, such also is he in his school exercises; his mind is observant, sharp, ready, retentive; he is almost passive in the acquisition of knowledge. I say this in no disparagement of the idea of a clever boy. Geography, chronology, history, language, natural history, he heaps up the matter of these studies as treasures for a future day. It is the seven years of plenty with him: he gathers in by handfuls, like the Egyptians, without counting; and though, as time goes on, there is exercise for his argumentative powers in the Elements of Mathematics, and for his taste in the Poets and Orators, still, while at school, or at least, till quite the last years of his time, he acquires, and little more; and when he is leaving for the University, he is mainly the creature of foreign influences and circumstances, and made up of accidents, homogeneous or not, as the case may be. Moreover, the moral habits, which are a boy's praise, encourage and assist this result; that is, diligence, assiduity, regularity, despatch, persevering application; for these are the direct conditions of acquisition, and naturally lead to it. Acquirements, again, are emphatically producible, and at a moment; they are a something to show, both for master and scholar; an audience, even though ignorant themselves of the subjects of an examination, can comprehend when questions are answered and when they are not. Here again is a reason why mental culture is in the minds of men identified with the acquisition of knowledge.

The same notion possesses the public mind, when it passes on from the thought of a school to that of a University: and with the best of reasons so far as this, that there is no true culture without acquirements, and that philosophy presupposes knowledge. It requires a great deal of reading, or a wide range of information, to warrant us in putting forth our opinions on any serious subject; and without such learning the most original mind may be able indeed to dazzle, to amuse, to refute, to perplex, but not to come to any useful result or any trustworthy conclusion. There are indeed persons who profess a different view of the matter, and even act upon it. Every now and then you will find a person of vigorous or fertile mind, who relies upon his own resources, despises all former authors, and gives the world, with the utmost fearlessness, his views upon religion, or history, or any other popular subject. And his works may sell for a while; he may get a name in his day; but this will be all. His readers are sure to find on the long run that his doctrines are mere theories, and not the expression of facts, that they are chaff instead of bread, and then his popularity drops as suddenly as it rose.

Knowledge then is the indispensable condition of expansion of mind, and the instrument of attaining to it; this cannot be denied, it is ever to be insisted on; I begin with it as a first principle; however, the very truth of it carries men too far, and confirms to them the notion that it is the whole of the matter. A narrow mind is thought to be that which contains little knowledge; and an enlarged mind, that which holds a great deal; and what seems to put the matter beyond dispute is, the fact of the great number of studies which are pursued in a University, by its very profession. Lectures are given on every kind of subject; examinations are held; prizes awarded. There are moral, metaphysical, physical Professors; Professors of languages, of history, of mathematics, of experimental science. Lists of questions are published, wonderful for their range and depth, variety and difficulty; treatises are written, which carry upon their very face the evidence of extensive reading or multifarious information; what then is wanting for mental culture to a person of large reading and scientific attainments? what is grasp of mind but acquirement? where shall philosophical repose be found, but in the consciousness and enjoyment of large intellectual possessions?

And yet this notion is, I conceive, a mistake, and my present business is to show that it is one, and that the end of a Liberal Education is not mere knowledge, or knowledge considered in its *matter*; and I shall best attain my object, by actually setting down some cases, which will be generally granted to be instances of the process of enlightenment or enlargement of mind, and others which are not, and thus, by the comparison, you will be able to judge for yourselves, Gentlemen, whether Knowledge, that is, acquirement, is after all the real principle of the enlargement, or whether that principle is not rather something beyond it.

4.

For instance,[1] let a person, whose experience has hitherto been confined to the more calm and unpretending scenery of these islands, whether here or in England, go for the first time into parts where physical nature puts on her wilder and more awful forms, whether at home or abroad, as into mountainous districts; or let one, who has ever lived in a quiet village, go for the first time to a great metropolis,—then I suppose he will have a sensation which perhaps he never had before. He has a feeling not in addition or increase of former feelings, but of something different in its nature. He will perhaps be borne forward, and find for a time that he has lost his bearings. He has made a certain progress, and he has a consciousness of mental enlargement; he does not stand where he did, he has a new centre, and a range of thoughts to which he was before a stranger.

Again, the view of the heavens which the telescope opens upon us, if allowed to fill and possess the mind, may almost

---

1　The pages which follow are taken almost verbatim from the author's 14th (Oxford) University Sermon, which, at the time of writing this Discourse, he did not expect ever to reprint.

whirl it round and make it dizzy. It brings in a flood of ideas, and is rightly called an intellectual enlargement, whatever is meant by the term.

And so again, the sight of beasts of prey and other foreign animals, their strangeness, the originality (if I may use the term) of their forms and gestures and habits and their variety and independence of each other, throw us out of ourselves into another creation, and as if under another Creator, if I may so express the temptation which may come on the mind. We seem to have new faculties, or a new exercise for our faculties, by this addition to our knowledge; like a prisoner, who, having been accustomed to wear manacles or fetters, suddenly finds his arms and legs free.

Hence Physical Science generally, in all its departments, as bringing before us the exuberant riches and resources, yet the orderly course, of the Universe, elevates and excites the student, and at first, I may say, almost takes away his breath, while in time it exercises a tranquilizing influence upon him.

Again, the study of history is said to enlarge and enlighten the mind, and why? because, as I conceive, it gives it a power of judging of passing events, and of all events, and a conscious superiority over them, which before it did not possess.

And in like manner, what is called seeing the world, entering into active life, going into society, travelling, gaining acquaintance with the various classes of the community, coming into contact with the principles and modes of thought of various parties, interests, and races, their views, aims, habits and manners, their religious creeds and forms of worship,—gaining experience how various yet how alike men are, how low-minded, how bad, how opposed, yet how confident in their opinions; all this exerts a perceptible influence upon the mind, which it is impossible to mistake, be it good or be it bad, and is popularly called its enlargement.

And then again, the first time the mind comes across the arguments and speculations of unbelievers, and feels what a novel light they cast upon what he has hitherto accounted sacred; and still more, if it gives in to them and embraces them, and throws off as so much prejudice what it has hitherto held, and, as if waking from a dream, begins to realize to its imagination that there is now no such thing as law and the transgression of law, that sin is a phantom, and punishment a bugbear, that it is free to sin, free to enjoy the world and the flesh; and still further, when it does enjoy them, and reflects that it may think and hold just what it will, that "the world is all before it where to choose," and what system to build up as its own private persuasion; when this torrent of wilful thoughts rushes over and inundates it, who will deny that the fruit of the tree of knowledge, or what the mind takes for knowledge, has made it one of the gods, with a sense of expansion and elevation,—an intoxication in reality, still, so far as the subjective state of the mind goes, an illumination? Hence the fanaticism of individuals or nations, who suddenly cast off their Maker. Their eyes are opened; and, like the judgment-stricken king in the Tragedy, they see two suns, and a magic universe, out of which they look back upon their former state of faith and innocence with a sort of contempt and indignation, as if they were then but fools, and the dupes of imposture.

On the other hand, Religion has its own enlargement, and an enlargement, not of tumult, but of peace. It is often remarked of uneducated persons, who have hitherto thought little of the unseen world, that, on their turning to God, looking into themselves, regulating their hearts, reforming their conduct, and meditating on death and judgment, heaven and hell, they seem to become, in point of intellect, different beings from what they were. Before, they took things as they came, and thought no more of one thing than another. But now every event has a meaning; they have their own estimate of whatever happens to them; they are mindful of times and seasons, and compare the present with the past; and the world, no longer dull, monotonous, unprofitable, and hopeless, is a various and complicated drama, with parts and an object, and an awful moral.

5.

Now from these instances, to which many more might be added, it is plain, first, that the communication of knowledge certainly is either a condition or the means of that sense of enlargement or enlightenment, of which at this day we hear so much in certain quarters: this cannot be denied; but next, it is equally plain, that such communication is not the whole of the process. The enlargement consists, not merely in the passive reception into the mind of a number of ideas unknown to it, but in the mind's energetic and simultaneous action upon and towards and among those new ideas, which are rushing in upon it. It is the action of a formative power, reducing to order and meaning the matter of our acquirements; it is a making the objects of our knowledge subjectively our own, or, to use a familiar word, it is a digestion of what we receive, into the substance of our previous state of thought; and without this no enlargement is said to follow. There is no enlargement, unless there be a comparison of ideas one with another, as they come before the mind, and a systematizing of them. We feel our minds to be growing and expanding *then*, when we not only learn, but refer what we learn to what we know already. It is not the mere addition to our knowledge that is the illumination; but the locomotion, the movement onwards, of that mental centre, to which both what we know, and what we are learning, the accumulating mass of our acquirements, gravitates. And therefore a truly great intellect, and recognized to be such by the common opinion of mankind, such as the intellect of Aristotle, or of St. Thomas, or of Newton, or of Goethe, (I purposely take instances within and without the Catholic pale, when I would speak of the intellect as such,) is one which takes a connected view of old and new, past and present, far and near, and which has an insight into the influence of all these one on another; without which there is no whole, and no centre. It possesses the knowledge, not only of things, but also of their mutual and true relations; knowledge, not merely considered as acquirement, but as philosophy.

Accordingly, when this analytical, distributive, harmonizing process is away, the mind experiences no enlargement, and is not reckoned as enlightened or comprehensive, whatever it may add to its knowledge. For instance, a great memory, as I have already said, does not make a philosopher, any more than a dictionary can be called a grammar. There are men who embrace in their minds a vast multitude of ideas, but with little sensibility about their real relations towards each other. These may be antiquarians, annalists, naturalists; they may be learned in the law; they may be versed in statistics; they are most useful in their own place; I should shrink from speaking disrespectfully of them; still, there is nothing in such attainments to guarantee the absence of narrowness of mind. If they are nothing more than well-read men, or men of information, they have not what specially deserves the name of culture of mind, or fulfils the type of Liberal Education.

In like manner, we sometimes fall in with persons who have seen much of the world, and of the men who, in their day, have played a conspicuous part in it, but who generalize nothing, and have no observation, in the true sense of the word. They abound in information in detail, curious and entertaining, about men and things; and, having lived under the influence of no very clear or settled principles, religious or political, they speak of every one and every thing, only as so many phenomena, which are complete in themselves, and lead to nothing, not discussing them, or teaching any truth, or instructing the hearer, but simply talking. No one would say that these persons, well informed as they are, had attained to any great culture of intellect or to philosophy.

The case is the same still more strikingly where the persons in question are beyond dispute men of inferior powers and deficient education. Perhaps they have been much in foreign countries, and they receive, in a passive, otiose, unfruitful way, the various facts which are forced upon them there. Seafaring men, for example, range from one end of the earth to the other; but the multiplicity of external objects, which they have encountered, forms no symmetrical and consistent picture upon their imagination; they see the tapestry of human life, as it were on the wrong side, and it tells no story. They sleep, and they rise up, and they find themselves, now in Europe, now in Asia; they see visions of great cities and wild regions; they are in the marts of commerce, or amid the islands of the South; they gaze on Pompey's Pillar, or on the Andes; and nothing which meets them carries them forward or backward, to any idea beyond itself. Nothing has a drift or relation; nothing has a history or a promise. Every thing stands by itself, and comes and goes in its turn, like the shifting scenes of a show, which leave the spectator where he was. Perhaps you are near such a man on a particular occasion, and expect him to be shocked or perplexed at something which occurs; but one thing is much the same to him as another, or, if he is perplexed, it is as not knowing what to say, whether it is right to admire, or to ridicule, or to disapprove, while conscious that some expression of opinion is expected from him; for in fact he has no standard of judgment at all, and no landmarks to guide him to a conclusion. Such is mere acquisition, and, I repeat, no one would dream of calling it philosophy.

6.

Instances, such as these, confirm, by the contrast, the conclusion I have already drawn from those which preceded them. That only is true enlargement of mind which is the power of viewing many things at once as one whole, of referring them severally to their true place in the universal system, of understanding their respective values, and determining their mutual dependence. Thus is that form of Universal Knowledge, of which I have on a former occasion spoken, set up in the individual intellect, and constitutes its perfection. Possessed of this real illumination, the mind never views any part of the extended subject-matter of Knowledge without recollecting that it is but a part, or without the associations which spring from this recollection. It makes every thing in some sort lead to every thing else; it would communicate the image of the whole to every separate portion, till that whole becomes in imagination like a spirit, every where pervading and penetrating its component parts, and giving them one definite meaning. Just as our bodily organs, when mentioned, recall their function in the body, as the word "creation" suggests the Creator, and "subjects" a sovereign, so, in the mind of the Philosopher, as we are abstractedly conceiving of him, the elements of the physical and moral world, sciences, arts, pursuits, ranks, offices, events, opinions, individualities, are all viewed as one, with correlative functions, and as gradually by successive combinations converging, one and all, to the true centre.

To have even a portion of this illuminative reason and true philosophy is the highest state to which nature can aspire, in the way of intellect; it puts the mind above the influences of chance and necessity, above anxiety, suspense, unsettlement, and superstition, which is the lot of the many. Men, whose minds are possessed with some one object, take exaggerated views of its importance, are feverish in the pursuit of it, make it the measure of things which are utterly foreign to it, and are startled and despond if it happens to fail them. They are ever in alarm or in transport. Those on the other hand who have no object or principle whatever to hold by, lose their way, every step they take. They are thrown out, and do not know what to think or say, at every fresh juncture; they have no view of persons, or occurrences, or facts, which come suddenly upon them, and they hang upon the opinion of others, for want of internal resources. But the intellect, which has been disciplined to the perfection of its powers, which knows, and thinks while it knows, which has learned to leaven the dense mass of facts and events with the elastic force of reason, such an intellect cannot be partial, cannot be exclusive, cannot be impetuous, cannot be at a loss, cannot but be patient, collected, and majestically calm, because it discerns the end in every beginning, the origin in every end, the law in every interruption, the limit in each delay; because it ever knows where it stands, and how its path lies from one point to another. It is the τετράγωνος of the Peripatetic, and has the "nil admirari" of the Stoic,—

> Felix qui potuit rerum cognoscere causas,
> Atque metus omnes, et inexorabile fatum
> Subjecit pedibus, strepitumque Acherontis avari.

There are men who, when in difficulties, originate at the moment vast ideas or dazzling projects; who, under the influence of excitement, are able to cast a light, almost as if from inspiration, on a subject or course of action which comes before them; who have a sudden presence of mind equal to any emergency, rising with the occasion, and an undaunted magnanimous bearing, and an energy and keenness which is but made intense by opposition. This is genius, this is heroism; it is the exhibition of a natural gift, which no culture can teach, at which no Institution can aim; here, on the contrary, we are concerned, not with mere nature, but with training and teaching. That perfection of the Intellect, which is the result of Education, and its *beau ideal*, to be imparted to individuals in their respective measures, is the clear, calm, accurate vision and comprehension of all things, as far as the finite mind can embrace them, each in its place, and with its own characteristics upon it. It is almost prophetic from its knowledge of history; it is almost heart-searching from its knowledge of human nature; it has almost supernatural charity from its freedom from littleness and prejudice; it has almost the repose of faith, because nothing can startle it; it has almost the beauty and harmony of heavenly contemplation, so intimate is it with the eternal order of things and the music of the spheres.

7.

And now, if I may take for granted that the true and adequate end of intellectual training and of a University is not Learning or Acquirement, but rather, is Thought or Reason exercised upon Knowledge, or what may be called Philosophy, I shall be in a position to explain the various mistakes which at the present day beset the subject of University Education.

I say then, if we would improve the intellect, first of all, we must ascend; we cannot gain real knowledge on a level; we must generalize, we must reduce to method, we must have a grasp of principles, and group and shape our acquisitions by means of them. It matters not whether our field of operation be wide or limited; in every case, to command it, is to mount above it. Who has not felt the irritation of mind and impatience created by a deep, rich country, visited for the first time, with winding lanes, and high hedges, and green steeps, and tangled woods, and every thing smiling indeed, but in a maze? The same feeling comes upon us in a strange city, when we have no map of its streets. Hence you hear of practised travellers, when they first come into a place, mounting some high hill or church tower, by way of reconnoitring its neighbourhood. In like manner, you must be above your knowledge, not under it, or it will oppress you; and the more you have of it, the greater will be the load. The learning of a Salmasius or a Burman, unless you are its master, will be your tyrant. "Imperat aut servit;" if you can wield it with a strong arm, it is a great weapon; otherwise,

> Vis consili expers
> Mole ruit suâ.

You will be overwhelmed, like Tarpeia, by the heavy wealth which you have exacted from tributary generations.

Instances abound; there are authors who are as pointless as they are inexhaustible in their literary resources. They measure knowledge by bulk, as it lies in the rude block, without symmetry, without design. How many commentators are there on the Classics, how many on Holy Scripture, from whom we rise up, wondering at the learning which has passed before us, and wondering why it passed! How many writers are there of Ecclesiastical History, such as Mosheim or Du Pin, who, breaking up their subject into details, destroy its life, and defraud us of the whole by their anxiety about the parts! The Sermons, again, of the English Divines in the seventeenth century, how often are they mere repertories of miscellaneous and officious learning! Of course Catholics also may read without thinking; and in their case, equally as with Protestants, it holds good, that such knowledge is unworthy of the name, knowledge which they have not thought through, and thought out. Such readers are only possessed by their knowledge, not possessed of it; nay, in matter of fact they are often even carried away by it, without any volition of their own. Recollect, the Memory can tyrannize, as well as the Imagination. Derangement, I believe, has been considered as a loss of control over the sequence of ideas. The mind, once set in motion, is henceforth deprived of the power of initiation, and becomes the victim of a train of associations, one thought suggesting another, in the way of cause and effect, as if by a mechanical process, or some physical necessity. No one, who has had experience of men of studious habits, but must recognize the existence of a parallel phenomenon in the case of those who have over-stimulated the Memory. In such persons Reason acts almost as feebly and as impotently as in the madman; once fairly started on any subject whatever, they have no power of self-control; they passively endure the succession of impulses which are evolved out of the original exciting cause; they are passed on from one idea to another and go steadily forward, plodding along one line of thought in spite of the amplest concessions of the hearer, or wandering from it in endless digression in spite of his remonstrances. Now, if, as is very certain, no one would envy the madman the glow and originality of his conceptions, why must we extol the cultivation of that intellect, which is the prey, not indeed of barren fancies but of barren facts, of random intrusions from without, though not of morbid imaginations from within? And in thus speaking, I am not denying that a strong and ready memory is in itself a real treasure; I am not disparaging a well-stored mind, though it be nothing besides, provided it be sober, any more than I would despise a bookseller's shop:—it is of great value to others, even when not so to the owner. Nor am I banishing, far from it, the possessors of deep and multifarious learning from my ideal University; they adorn it in the eyes of men; I do but say that they constitute no type of the results at which it aims; that it is no great gain to the intellect to have enlarged the memory at the expense of faculties which are indisputably higher.

8.

Nor indeed am I supposing that there is any great danger, at least in this day, of over-education; the danger is on the other side. I will tell you, Gentlemen, what has been the practical error of the last twenty years,—not to load the memory of the student with a mass of undigested knowledge, but to force upon him so much that he has rejected all. It has been the error of distracting and enfeebling the mind by an unmeaning profusion of subjects; of implying that a smattering in a dozen branches of study is not shallowness, which it really is, but enlargement, which it is not; of considering an acquaintance with the learned names of things and persons, and the possession of clever duodecimos, and attendance on eloquent lecturers, and membership with scientific institutions, and the sight of the experiments of a platform and the specimens of a museum, that all this was not dissipation of mind, but progress. All things now are to be learned at once, not first one thing, then another, not one well, but many badly. Learning is to be without exertion, without attention, without toil; without grounding, without advance, without finishing. There is to be nothing individual in it; and this, forsooth, is the wonder of the age. What the steam engine does with matter, the printing press is to do with mind; it is to act mechanically, and the population is to be passively, almost unconsciously enlightened, by the mere multiplication and dissemination of volumes. Whether it be the school boy, or the school girl, or the youth at college, or the mechanic in the town, or the politician in the senate, all have been the victims in one way or other of this most preposterous and pernicious of delusions. Wise men have lifted up their voices in vain; and at length, lest their own institutions should be outshone and should disappear in the folly of the hour, they have been obliged, as far as they could with a good conscience, to humour a spirit which they could not withstand, and make temporizing concessions at which they could not but inwardly smile.

It must not be supposed that, because I so speak, therefore I have some sort of fear of the education of the people: on the contrary, the more education they have, the better, so that it is really education. Nor am I an enemy to the cheap publication of scientific and literary works, which is now in vogue: on the contrary, I consider it a great advantage, convenience, and gain;

that is, to those to whom education has given a capacity for using them. Further, I consider such innocent recreations as science and literature are able to furnish will be a very fit occupation of the thoughts and the leisure of young persons, and may be made the means of keeping them from bad employments and bad companions. Moreover, as to that superficial acquaintance with chemistry, and geology, and astronomy, and political economy, and modern history, and biography, and other branches of knowledge, which periodical literature and occasional lectures and scientific institutions diffuse through the community, I think it a graceful accomplishment, and a suitable, nay, in this day a necessary accomplishment, in the case of educated men. Nor, lastly, am I disparaging or discouraging the thorough acquisition of any one of these studies, or denying that, as far as it goes, such thorough acquisition is a real education of the mind. All I say is, call things by their right names, and do not confuse together ideas which are essentially different. A thorough knowledge of one science and a superficial acquaintance with many, are not the same thing; a smattering of a hundred things or a memory for detail, is not a philosophical or comprehensive view. Recreations are not education; accomplishments are not education. Do not say, the people must be educated, when, after all, you only mean, amused, refreshed, soothed, put into good spirits and good humour, or kept from vicious excesses. I do not say that such amusements, such occupations of mind, are not a great gain; but they are not education. You may as well call drawing and fencing education, as a general knowledge of botany or conchology. Stuffing birds or playing stringed instruments is an elegant pastime, and a resource to the idle, but it is not education; it does not form or cultivate the intellect. Education is a high word; it is the preparation for knowledge, and it is the imparting of knowledge in proportion to that preparation. We require intellectual eyes to know withal, as bodily eyes for sight. We need both objects and organs intellectual; we cannot gain them without setting about it; we cannot gain them in our sleep, or by haphazard. The best telescope does not dispense with eyes;

the printing press or the lecture room will assist us greatly, but we must be true to ourselves, we must be parties in the work. A University is, according to the usual designation, an Alma Mater, knowing her children one by one, not a foundry, or a mint, or a treadmill.

9.

I protest to you, Gentlemen, that if I had to choose between a so-called University, which dispensed with residence and tutorial superintendence, and gave its degrees to any person who passed an examination in a wide range of subjects, and a University which had no professors or examinations at all, but merely brought a number of young men together for three or four years, and then sent them away as the University of Oxford is said to have done some sixty years since, if I were asked which of these two methods was the better discipline of the intellect,—mind, I do not say which is *morally* the better, for it is plain that compulsory study must be a good and idleness an intolerable mischief,—but if I must determine which of the two courses was the more successful in training, moulding, enlarging the mind, which sent out men the more fitted for their secular duties, which produced better public men, men of the world, men whose names would descend to posterity, I have no hesitation in giving the preference to that University which did nothing, over that which exacted of its members an acquaintance with every science under the sun. And, paradox as this may seem, still if results be the test of systems, the influence of the public schools and colleges of England, in the course of the last century, at least will bear out one side of the contrast as I have drawn it. What would come, on the other hand, of the ideal systems of education which have fascinated the imagination of this age, could they ever take effect, and whether they would not produce a generation frivolous, narrow-minded, and resourceless, intellectually considered, is a fair subject for debate; but so far is certain, that the Universities and scholastic establishments, to which I refer, and which did little more than bring together first boys and then youths in large numbers, these institutions, with miserable deformities on the side of morals, with a hollow profession of Christianity, and a heathen code of ethics,—I say, at least they can boast of a succession of heroes and statesmen, of literary men and philosophers, of men conspicuous for great natural virtues, for habits of business, for knowledge of life, for practical judgment, for cultivated tastes, for accomplishments, who have made England what it is,—able to subdue the earth, able to domineer over Catholics.

How is this to be explained? I suppose as follows: When a multitude of young men, keen, open-hearted, sympathetic, and observant, as young men are, come together and freely mix with each other, they are sure to learn one from another, even if there be no one to teach them; the conversation of all is a series of lectures to each, and they gain for themselves new ideas and views, fresh matter of thought, and distinct principles for judging and acting, day by day. An infant has to learn the meaning of the information which its senses convey to it, and this seems to be its employment. It fancies all that the eye presents to it to be close to it, till it actually learns the contrary, and thus by practice does it ascertain the relations and uses of those first elements of knowledge which are necessary for its animal existence. A parallel teaching is necessary for our social being, and it is secured by a large school or a college; and this effect may be fairly called in its own department an enlargement of mind. It is seeing the world on a small field with little trouble; for the pupils or students come from very different places, and with widely different notions, and there is much to generalize, much to adjust, much to eliminate, there are inter-relations to be defined, and conventional rules to be established, in the process, by which the whole assemblage is moulded together, and gains one tone and one character.

Let it be clearly understood, I repeat it, that I am not taking into account moral or religious considerations; I am but saying that that youthful community will constitute a whole, it will embody a specific idea, it will represent a doctrine, it will administer a code of conduct, and it will furnish principles of thought and action. It will give birth to a living teaching, which in course of time will take the shape of a self-perpetuating tradition, or a *genius loci*, as it is sometimes called; which haunts the home where it has been born, and which imbues and forms, more or less, and one by one, every individual who is successively brought under its shadow. Thus it is that, independent of direct instruction on the part of Superiors, there is a sort of self-education in the academic institutions of Protestant England; a characteristic tone of thought, a recognized standard of judgment is found in them, which, as developed in the individual who is submitted to it, becomes a twofold source of strength to him, both from the distinct stamp it impresses on his mind, and from the bond of union which it creates between him and others,—effects which are shared by the authorities of the place, for they themselves have been educated in it, and at all times are exposed to the influence of its ethical atmosphere. Here then is a real teaching, whatever be its standards and principles, true or false; and it at least tends towards cultivation of the intellect; it at least recognizes that knowledge is something more than a sort of passive reception of scraps and details; it is a something, and it does a something, which never will issue from the most strenuous efforts of a set of teachers, with no mutual sympathies and no inter-communion, of a set of examiners with no opinions which they dare profess, and with no common principles, who are teaching or questioning a set of youths who do not know them, and do not know each other, on a large number of subjects, different in kind, and connected by no wide philosophy, three times a week, or three times a year, or once in three years, in chill lecture-rooms or on a pompous anniversary.

10.

Nay, self-education in any shape, in the most restricted sense, is preferable to a system of teaching which, professing so much, really does so little for the mind. Shut your College gates against the votary of knowledge, throw him back upon the searchings and the efforts of his own mind; he will gain by being spared an entrance into your Babel. Few indeed there are who can dispense with the stimulus and support of instructors, or will do any thing at all, if left to themselves. And fewer still (though such great minds are to be found), who will not, from such unassisted attempts, contract a self-reliance and a self-esteem, which are not only moral evils, but serious hindrances to the attainment of truth. And next to none, perhaps, or none, who will not be reminded from time to time of the disadvantage under which they lie, by their imperfect grounding, by the breaks, deficiencies, and irregularities of their knowledge, by the eccentricity of opinion and the confusion of principle which they exhibit. They will be too often ignorant of what every one knows and takes for granted, of that multitude of small truths which fall upon the mind like dust, impalpable and ever accumulating; they may be unable to converse, they may argue perversely, they may pride themselves on their worst paradoxes or their grossest truisms, they may be full of their own mode of viewing things, unwilling to be put out of their way, slow to enter into the minds of others;—but, with these and whatever other liabilities upon their heads, they are likely to have more thought, more mind, more philosophy, more true enlargement, than those earnest but ill-used persons, who are forced to load their minds with a score of subjects against an examination, who have too much on their hands to indulge themselves in thinking or investigation, who devour premiss and conclusion together with indiscriminate greediness, who hold whole sciences on faith, and commit demonstrations to memory, and who too often, as might be expected, when their period of education is passed, throw up all they have learned in disgust, having gained nothing really by their anxious labours, except perhaps the habit of application.

Yet such is the better specimen of the fruit of that ambitious system which has of late years been making way among us: for its result on ordinary minds, and on the common run of students, is less satisfactory still; they leave their place of education simply dissipated and relaxed by the multiplicity of subjects, which they have never really mastered, and so shallow as not even to know their shallowness. How much better, I say, is it for the active and thoughtful intellect, where such is to be found, to eschew the College and the University altogether, than to submit to a drudgery so ignoble, a mockery so contumelious! How much more profitable for the independent mind, after the mere rudiments of education, to range through a library at random, taking down books as they meet him, and pursuing the trains of thought which his mother wit suggests! How much healthier to wander into the fields, and there with the exiled Prince to find "tongues in the trees, books in the running brooks!" How much more genuine an education is that of the poor boy in the Poem[2]—a Poem, whether in conception or in execution, one of the most touching in our language—who, not in the wide world, but ranging day by day around his widowed mother's home, "a dexterous gleaner" in a narrow field, and with only such slender outfit

> "as the village school and books a few
> Supplied,"

contrived from the beach, and the quay, and the fisher's boat, and the inn's fireside, and the tradesman's shop, and the shepherd's walk, and the smuggler's hut, and the mossy moor, and the screaming gulls, and the restless waves, to fashion for himself a philosophy and a poetry of his own!

But in a large subject, I am exceeding my necessary limits. Gentlemen, I must conclude abruptly; and postpone any summing up of my argument, should that be necessary, to another day.

---

2 Crabbe's Tales of the Hall. This Poem, let me say, I read on its first publication, above thirty years ago, with extreme delight, and have never lost my love of it; and on taking it up lately, found I was even more touched by it than heretofore. A work which can please in youth and age, seems to fulfil (in logical language) the *accidental definition* of a Classic. [A further course of twenty years has past, and I bear the same witness in favour of this Poem.]

KNOWLEDGE VIEWED IN RELATION TO PROFESSIONAL SKILL

1.

I have been insisting, in my two preceding Discourses, first, on the cultivation of the intellect, as an end which may reasonably be pursued for its own sake; and next, on the nature of that cultivation, or what that cultivation consists in. Truth of whatever kind is the proper object of the intellect; its cultivation then lies in fitting it to apprehend and contemplate truth. Now the intellect in its present state, with exceptions which need not here be specified, does not discern truth intuitively, or as a whole. We know, not by a direct and simple vision, not at a glance, but, as it were, by piecemeal and accumulation, by a mental process, by going round an object, by the comparison, the combination, the mutual correction, the continual adaptation, of many partial notions, by the employment, concentration, and joint action of many faculties and exercises of mind. Such a union and concert of the intellectual powers, such an enlargement and development, such a comprehensiveness, is necessarily a matter of training. And again, such a training is a matter of rule; it is not mere application, however exemplary, which introduces the mind to truth, nor the reading many books, nor the getting up many subjects, nor the witnessing many experiments, nor the attending many lectures. All this is short of enough; a man may have done it all, yet be lingering in the vestibule of knowledge:—he may not realize what his mouth utters; he may not see with his mental eye what confronts him; he may have no grasp of things as they are; or at least he may have no power at all of advancing one step forward of himself, in consequence of what he has already acquired, no power of discriminating between truth and falsehood, of sifting out the grains of truth from the mass, of arranging things according to their real value, and, if I may use the phrase, of building up ideas. Such a power is the result of a scientific formation of mind; it is an acquired faculty of judgment, of clear-sightedness, of sagacity, of wisdom, of philosophical reach of mind, and of intellectual self-possession and repose,—qualities which do not come of mere acquirement. The bodily eye, the organ for apprehending material objects, is provided by nature; the eye of the mind, of which the object is truth, is the work of discipline and habit.

This process of training, by which the intellect, instead of being formed or sacrificed to some particular or accidental purpose, some specific trade or profession, or study or science, is disciplined for its own sake, for the perception of its own proper object, and for its own highest culture, is called Liberal Education; and though there is no one in whom it is carried as far as is conceivable, or whose intellect would be a pattern of what intellects should be made, yet there is scarcely any one but may gain an idea of what real training is, and at least look towards it, and make its true scope and result, not something else, his standard of excellence; and numbers there are who may submit themselves to it, and secure it to themselves in good measure. And to set forth the right standard, and to train according to it, and to help forward all students towards it according to their various capacities, this I conceive to be the business of a University.

2.

Now this is what some great men are very slow to allow; they insist that Education should be confined to some particular and narrow end, and should issue in some definite work, which can be weighed and measured. They argue as if every thing, as well as every person, had its price; and that where there has been a great outlay, they have a right to expect a return in kind. This they call making Education and Instruction "useful," and "Utility" becomes their watchword. With a fundamental principle of this nature, they very naturally go on to ask, what there is to show for the expense of a University; what is the real worth in the market of the article called "a Liberal Education," on the supposition that it does not teach us definitely how to advance our manufactures, or to improve our lands, or to better our civil economy; or again, if it does not at once make this man a lawyer, that an engineer, and that a surgeon; or at least if it does not lead to discoveries in chemistry, astronomy, geology, magnetism, and science of every kind.

This question, as might have been expected, has been keenly debated in the present age, and formed one main subject of the controversy, to which I referred in the Introduction to the present Discourses, as having been sustained in the first decade of this century by a celebrated Northern Review on the one hand, and defenders of the University of Oxford on the other. Hardly had the authorities of that ancient seat of learning, waking from their long neglect, set on foot a plan for the education of the youth committed to them, than the representatives of science and literature in the city, which has sometimes been called the Northern Athens, remonstrated, with their gravest arguments and their most brilliant satire, against the direction and shape which the reform was taking. Nothing would content them, but that the University should be set to rights on the basis of the philosophy of Utility; a philosophy, as they seem to have thought, which needed but to be proclaimed in order to be embraced. In truth, they were little aware of the depth and force of the principles on which the academical authorities were proceeding, and, this being so, it was not to be expected that they would be allowed to walk at leisure over the field of controversy which they had selected. Accordingly they were encountered in behalf of the University by two men of great name and influence in their day, of very different minds, but united, as by Collegiate ties, so in the clear-sighted and large view which they took of the whole subject of Liberal Education; and the defence thus provided for the Oxford studies has kept its ground to this day.

3.

Let me be allowed to devote a few words to the memory of distinguished persons, under the shadow of whose name I once lived, and by whose doctrine I am now profiting. In the heart of Oxford there is a small plot of ground, hemmed in by public thoroughfares, which has been the possession and the home of one Society for above five hundred years. In the old time of Boniface the Eighth and John the Twenty-second, in the age of Scotus and Occam and Dante, before Wiclif or Huss had kindled those miserable fires which are still raging to the ruin of the highest interests of man, an unfortunate king of England, Edward the Second, flying from the field of Bannockburn, is said to have made a vow to the Blessed Virgin to found a religious house in her honour, if he got back in safety. Prompted and aided by his Almoner, he decided on placing this house in the city of Alfred; and the Image of our Lady, which is opposite its entrance-gate, is to this day the token of the vow and its fulfilment. King and Almoner have long been in the dust, and strangers have entered into their inheritance, and their creed has been forgotten, and their holy rites disowned; but day by day a memento is still made in the holy Sacrifice by at least one Catholic Priest, once a member of that College, for the souls of those Catholic benefactors who fed him there for so many years. The visitor, whose curiosity has been excited by its present fame, gazes perhaps with something of disappointment on a collection of buildings which have with them so few of the circumstances of dignity or wealth. Broad quadrangles, high halls and chambers, ornamented cloisters, stately walks, or umbrageous gardens, a throng of students, ample revenues, or a glorious history, none of these things were the portion of that old Catholic foundation; nothing in short which to the common eye sixty years ago would have given tokens of what it was to be. But it had at that time a spirit working within it, which enabled its inmates to do, amid its seeming insignificance, what no other body in the place could equal; not a very abstruse gift or extraordinary boast, but a rare one, the honest purpose to administer the trust committed to them in such a way as their conscience pointed out as best. So, whereas the Colleges of Oxford are self-electing bodies, the fellows in each perpetually filling up for themselves the vacancies which occur in their number, the members of this foundation determined, at a time when, either from evil custom or from ancient statute, such a thing was not known elsewhere, to throw open their fellowships to the competition of all comers, and, in the choice of associates henceforth, to cast to the winds every personal motive and feeling, family connexion, and friendship, and patronage, and political interest, and local claim, and prejudice, and party jealousy, and to elect solely on public and patriotic grounds. Nay, with a remarkable independence of mind, they resolved that even the table of honours, awarded to literary merit by the University in its new system of examination for degrees, should not fetter their judgment as electors; but that at all risks, and whatever criticism it might cause, and whatever odium they might incur, they would select the men, whoever they were, to be children of their Founder, whom they thought in their consciences to be most likely from their intellectual and moral qualities to please him, if (as they expressed it) he were still upon earth, most likely to do honour to his College, most likely to promote the objects which they believed he had at heart. Such persons did not promise to be the disciples of a low Utilitarianism; and consequently, as their collegiate reform synchronized with that reform of the Academical body, in which they bore a principal part, it was not unnatural that, when the storm broke upon the University from the North, their Alma Mater, whom they loved, should have found her first defenders within the walls of that small College, which had first put itself into a condition to be her champion.

These defenders, I have said, were two, of whom the more distinguished was the late Dr. Copleston, then a Fellow of the College, successively its Provost, and Protestant Bishop of Llandaff. In that Society, which owes so much to him, his name lives, and ever will live, for the distinction which his talents bestowed on it, for the academical importance to which he raised it, for the generosity of spirit, the liberality of sentiment, and the kindness of heart, with which he adorned it, and which even those who had least sympathy with some aspects of his mind and character could not but admire and love. Men come to their meridian at

various periods of their lives; the last years of the eminent person
I am speaking of were given to duties which, I am told, have been
the means of endearing him to numbers, but which afforded
no scope for that peculiar vigour and keenness of mind which
enabled him, when a young man, single-handed, with easy gal-
lantry, to encounter and overthrow the charge of three giants of
the North combined against him. I believe I am right in saying
that, in the progress of the controversy, the most scientific, the
most critical, and the most witty, of that literary company, all of
them now, as he himself, removed from this visible scene, Professor Playfair, Lord Jeffrey, and the Rev. Sydney Smith, threw
together their several efforts into one article of their Review, in
order to crush and pound to dust the audacious controvertist
who had come out against them in defence of his own Institutions. To have even contended with such men was a sufficient
voucher for his ability, even before we open his pamphlets, and
have actual evidence of the good sense, the spirit, the scholar-like
taste, and the purity of style, by which they are distinguished.

He was supported in the controversy, on the same general
principles, but with more of method and distinctness, and, I
will add, with greater force and beauty and perfection, both of
thought and of language, by the other distinguished writer, to
whom I have already referred, Mr. Davison; who, though not
so well known to the world in his day, has left more behind him
than the Provost of Oriel, to make his name remembered by posterity. This thoughtful man, who was the admired and intimate
friend of a very remarkable person, whom, whether he wish it or
not, numbers revere and love as the first author of the subsequent
movement in the Protestant Church towards Catholicism,[1] this
grave and philosophical writer, whose works I can never look into
without sighing that such a man was lost to the Catholic Church,
as Dr. Butler before him, by some early bias or some fault of
self-education—he, in a review of a work by Mr. Edgeworth on
Professional Education, which attracted a good deal of attention

---

1   Mr. Keble, Vicar of Hursley, late Fellow of Oriel, and Professor of Poetry in the University
of Oxford.

in its day, goes leisurely over the same ground, which had already been rapidly traversed by Dr. Copleston, and, though professedly employed upon Mr. Edgeworth, is really replying to the northern critic who had brought that writer's work into notice, and to a far greater author than either of them, who in a past age had argued on the same side.

4.

The author to whom I allude is no other than Locke. That celebrated philosopher has preceded the Edinburgh Reviewers in condemning the ordinary subjects in which boys are instructed at school, on the ground that they are not needed by them in after life; and before quoting what his disciples have said in the present century, I will refer to a few passages of the master. "'Tis matter of astonishment," he says in his work on Education, "that men of quality and parts should suffer themselves to be so far misled by custom and implicit faith. Reason, if consulted with, would advise, that their children's time should be spent in acquiring what might be *useful* to them, when they come to be men, rather than that their heads should be stuffed with a deal of trash, a great part whereof they usually never do ('tis certain they never need to) think on again as long as they live; and so much of it as does stick by them they are only the worse for."

And so again, speaking of verse-making, he says, "I know not what reason a father can have to wish his son a poet, who does not desire him to *bid defiance to all other calling and business;* which is not yet the worst of the case; for, if he proves a successful rhymer, and gets once the reputation of a wit, I desire it to be considered, what company and places he is likely to spend his time in, nay, and estate too; for it is very seldom seen that any one discovers *mines of gold or silver in Parnassus.* 'Tis a pleasant air, but a barren soil."

In another passage he distinctly limits utility in education to its bearing on the future profession or trade of the pupil, that is, he scorns the idea of any education of the intellect, simply as such. "Can there be any thing more ridiculous," he asks, "than that a father should waste his own money, and his son's time, in setting him to *learn the Roman language*, when at the same time he *designs him for a trade*, wherein he, having no use of Latin, fails not to forget that little which he brought from school, and which 'tis ten to one he abhors for the ill-usage it procured him? Could it be believed, unless we have every where amongst us examples of it, that a child should be forced to learn the rudiments of a language, which *he is never to use in the course of life that he is designed to*, and neglect all the while the writing a good hand, and casting accounts, which are of great advantage in all conditions of life, and to most trades indispensably necessary?" Nothing of course can be more absurd than to neglect in education those matters which are necessary for a boy's future calling; but the tone of Locke's remarks evidently implies more than this, and is condemnatory of any teaching which tends to the general cultivation of the mind.

Now to turn to his modern disciples. The study of the Classics had been made the basis of the Oxford education, in the reforms which I have spoken of, and the Edinburgh Reviewers protested, after the manner of Locke, that no good could come of a system which was not based upon the principle of Utility.

"Classical Literature," they said, "is the great object at Oxford. Many minds, so employed, have produced many works and much fame in that department; but if all liberal arts and sciences, *useful to human life*, had been taught there, if *some* had dedicated themselves to *chemistry, some* to *mathematics, some* to *experimental philosophy*, and if *every* attainment had been honoured in the mixt ratio of its difficulty and *utility*, the system of such a University would have been much more valuable, but the splendour of its name something less."

Utility may be made the end of education, in two respects: either as regards the individual educated, or the community at large. In which light do these writers regard it? in the latter. So far they differ from Locke, for they consider the advancement of science as the supreme and real end of a University. This is brought into view in the sentences which follow.

"When a University has been doing *useless* things for a long time, it appears at first degrading to them to be *useful*. A set of Lectures on Political Economy would be discouraged in Oxford, probably despised, probably not permitted. To discuss the inclosure of commons, and to dwell upon imports and exports, to come so near to common life, would seem to be undignified and contemptible. In the same manner, the Parr or the Bentley of the day would be scandalized, in a University, to be put on a level with the discoverer of a neutral salt; and yet, *what other measure is there of dignity in intellectual labour but usefulness*? And what ought the term University to mean, but a place where every science is taught which is liberal, and at the same time useful to mankind? Nothing would so much tend to bring classical literature within proper bounds as *a steady and invariable appeal to utility* in our appreciation of all human knowledge ... *Looking always to real utility as our guide*, we should see, with equal pleasure, a studious and inquisitive mind arranging the productions of nature, investigating the qualities of bodies, or mastering the difficulties of the learned languages. We should not care whether he was chemist, naturalist, or scholar, because we know it to be as *necessary* that matter should be studied and subdued *to the use of man*, as that taste should be gratified, and imagination inflamed."

Such then is the enunciation, as far as words go, of the theory of Utility in Education; and both on its own account, and for the sake of the able men who have advocated it, it has a claim on the attention of those whose principles I am here representing. Certainly it is specious to contend that nothing is worth pursuing but what is useful; and that life is not long enough to expend upon interesting, or curious, or brilliant trifles. Nay, in one sense, I will grant it is more than specious, it is true; but, if so, how do I propose directly to meet the objection? Why, Gentlemen, I have really met it already, viz., in laying down, that intellectual culture is its own end; for what has its *end* in itself, has its *use* in itself also. I say, if a Liberal Education consists in the culture of the intellect, and if that culture be in itself a good, here, without going further, is an answer to Locke's question; for if a healthy body is a good in itself, why is not a healthy intellect? and if a College of Physicians is a useful institution, because it contemplates bodily health, why is not an Academical Body, though it were simply and solely engaged in imparting vigour and beauty and grasp to the intellectual portion of our nature? And the Reviewers I am quoting seem to allow this in their better moments, in a passage which, putting aside the question of its justice in fact, is sound and true in the principles to which it appeals:—

"The present state of classical education," they say, "cultivates the *imagination* a great deal too much, and other *habits of mind* a great deal too little, and trains up many young men in a style of elegant imbecility, utterly unworthy of the talents with which nature has endowed them ... The matter of fact is, that a classical scholar of twenty-three or twenty-four is a man principally conversant with works of imagination. His feelings are quick, his fancy lively, and his taste good. Talents for *speculation* and *original inquiry* he has none, nor has he formed the invaluable *habit of pushing things up to their first principles*, or of collecting dry and unamusing facts as the materials for reasoning. All the solid and masculine parts of his *understanding* are left wholly without *cultivation*; he hates the pain of thinking, and suspects every man whose boldness and originality call upon him to defend his opinions and prove his assertions."

5.

Now, I am not at present concerned with the specific question of classical education; else, I might reasonably question the justice of calling an intellectual discipline, which embraces the study of Aristotle, Thucydides, and Tacitus, which involves Scholarship and Antiquities, *imaginative*; still so far I readily grant, that the cultivation of the "understanding," of a "talent for speculation and original inquiry," and of "the habit of pushing things up to their first principles," is a principal portion of a *good* or *liberal* education. If then the Reviewers consider such cultivation the characteristic of a *useful* education, as they seem to do in the foregoing passage, it follows, that what they mean by "useful" is just what I mean by "good" or "liberal:" and Locke's question becomes a verbal one. Whether youths are to be taught Latin or verse-making will depend on the *fact*, whether these studies tend to mental culture; but, however this is determined, so far is clear, that in that mental culture consists what I have called a liberal or non-professional, and what the Reviewers call a useful education.

This is the obvious answer which may be made to those who urge upon us the claims of Utility in our plans of Education; but I am not going to leave the subject here: I mean to take a wider view of it. Let us take "useful," as Locke takes it, in its proper and popular sense, and then we enter upon a large field of thought, to which I cannot do justice in one Discourse, though today's is all the space that I can give to it. I say, let us take "useful" to mean, not what is simply good, but what *tends* to good, or is the *instrument* of good; and in this sense also, Gentlemen, I will show you how a liberal education is truly and fully a useful, though it be not a professional, education. "Good" indeed means one thing, and "useful" means another; but I lay it down as a principle, which will save us a great deal of anxiety, that, though the useful is not always good, the good is always useful. Good is not only good, but reproductive of good; this is one of its attributes; nothing is excellent, beautiful, perfect, desirable for its own sake, but it overflows, and spreads the likeness of itself all around it. Good is prolific; it is not only good to the eye, but to the taste; it not only attracts us, but it communicates itself; it excites first our admiration and love, then our desire and our gratitude, and that, in proportion to its intenseness and fulness in particular instances. A great good will impart great good. If then the intellect is so excellent a portion of us, and its cultivation so excellent, it is not only beautiful, perfect, admirable, and noble in itself, but in a true and high sense it must be useful to the possessor and to all around him; not useful in any low, mechanical, mercantile sense, but as diffusing good, or as a blessing, or a gift, or power, or a treasure, first to the owner, then through him to the world. I say then, if a liberal education be good, it must necessarily be useful too.

6.

You will see what I mean by the parallel of bodily health. Health is a good in itself, though nothing came of it, and is especially worth seeking and cherishing; yet, after all, the blessings which attend its presence are so great, while they are so close to it and so redound back upon it and encircle it, that we never think of it except as useful as well as good, and praise and prize it for what it does, as well as for what it is, though at the same time we cannot point out any definite and distinct work or production which it can be said to effect. And so as regards intellectual culture, I am far from denying utility in this large sense as the end of Education, when I lay it down, that the culture of the intellect is a good in itself and its own end; I do not exclude from the idea of intellectual culture what it cannot but be, from the very nature of things; I only deny that we must be able to point out, before we have any right to call it useful, some art, or business, or profession, or trade, or work, as resulting from it, and as its real and complete end. The parallel is exact:—As the body may be sacrificed to some manual or other toil, whether moderate or oppressive, so may the intellect be devoted to some specific profession; and I do not call *this* the culture of the intellect. Again, as some member or organ of the body may be inordinately used and developed, so may memory, or imagination, or the reasoning faculty; and *this* again is not intellectual culture. On the other hand, as the body may be tended, cherished, and exercised with a simple view to its general health, so may the intellect also be generally exercised in order to its perfect state; and this *is* its cultivation.

Again, as health ought to precede labour of the body, and as a man in health can do what an unhealthy man cannot do, and as of this health the properties are strength, energy, agility, graceful carriage and action, manual dexterity, and endurance of fatigue, so in like manner general culture of mind is the best aid to professional and scientific study, and educated men can do what illiterate cannot; and the man who has learned to think and to reason and to compare and to discriminate and to analyze, who has refined his taste, and formed his judgment, and sharpened his mental vision, will not indeed at once be a lawyer, or a pleader, or an orator, or a statesman, or a physician, or a good landlord, or a man of business, or a soldier, or an engineer, or a chemist, or a geologist, or an antiquarian, but he will be placed in that state of intellect in which he can take up any one of the sciences or callings I have referred to, or any other for which he has a taste or special talent, with an ease, a grace, a versatility, and a success, to which another is a stranger. In this sense then, and as yet I have said but a very few words on a large subject, mental culture is emphatically *useful.*

If then I am arguing, and shall argue, against Professional or Scientific knowledge as the sufficient end of a University Education, let me not be supposed, Gentlemen, to be disrespectful towards particular studies, or arts, or vocations, and those who are engaged in them. In saying that Law or Medicine is not the end of a University course, I do not mean to imply that the University does not teach Law or Medicine. What indeed can it teach at all, if it does not teach something particular? It teaches *all* knowledge by teaching all *branches* of knowledge, and in no other way. I do but say that there will be this distinction as regards a Professor of Law, or of Medicine, or of Geology, or of Political Economy, in a University and out of it, that out of a University he is in danger of being absorbed and narrowed by his pursuit, and of giving Lectures which are the Lectures of nothing more than a lawyer, physician, geologist, or political economist; whereas in a University he will just know where he and his science stand, he has come to it, as it were, from a height, he has taken a survey of all knowledge, he is kept from extravagance by the very rivalry of other studies, he has gained from them a special illumination and largeness of mind and freedom and self-possession, and he treats his own in consequence with a philosophy and a resource, which belongs not to the study itself, but to his liberal education.

This then is how I should solve the fallacy, for so I must call it, by which Locke and his disciples would frighten us from cultivating the intellect, under the notion that no education is useful which does not teach us some temporal calling, or some mechanical art, or some physical secret. I say that a cultivated intellect, because it is a good in itself, brings with it a power and a grace to every work and occupation which it undertakes, and enables us to be more useful, and to a greater number. There is a duty we owe to human society as such, to the state to which we belong, to the sphere in which we move, to the individuals towards whom we are variously related, and whom we successively encounter in life; and that philosophical or liberal education, as I have called it, which is the proper function of a University, if it refuses the foremost place to professional interests, does but postpone them to the formation of the citizen, and, while it subserves the larger interests of philanthropy, prepares also for the successful prosecution of those merely personal objects, which at first sight it seems to disparage.

7.

And now, Gentlemen, I wish to be allowed to enforce in detail what I have been saying, by some extracts from the writings to which I have already alluded, and to which I am so greatly indebted.

"It is an undisputed maxim in Political Economy," says Dr. Copleston, "that the separation of professions and the division of labour tend to the perfection of every art, to the wealth of nations, to the general comfort and well-being of the community. This principle of division is in some instances pursued so far as to excite the wonder of people to whose notice it is for the first time pointed out. There is no saying to what extent it may not be carried; and the more the powers of each individual are concentrated in one employment, the greater skill and quickness will he naturally display in performing it. But, while he thus contributes more effectually to the accumulation of national wealth, he becomes himself more and more degraded as a rational being. In proportion as his sphere of action is narrowed his mental powers and habits become contracted; and he resembles a subordinate part of some powerful machinery, useful in its place, but insignificant and worthless out of it. If it be necessary, as it is beyond all question necessary, that society should be split into divisions and subdivisions, in order that its several duties may be well performed, yet we must be careful not to yield up ourselves wholly and exclusively to the guidance of this system; we must observe what its evils are, and we should modify and restrain it, by bringing into action other principles, which may serve as a check and counterpoise to the main force.

"There can be no doubt that every art is improved by confining the professor of it to that single study. But, *although the art itself is advanced by this concentration of mind in its service, the individual who is confined to it goes back.* The advantage of the community is nearly in an inverse ratio with his own.

"Society itself requires some other contribution from each individual, besides the particular duties of his profession. And, if no such liberal intercourse be established, it is the common failing of human nature, to be engrossed with petty views and interests, to underrate the importance of all in which we are not concerned, and to carry our partial notions into cases where they are inapplicable, to act, in short, as so many unconnected units, displacing and repelling one another.

"In the cultivation of literature is found that common link, which, among the higher and middling departments of life, unites the jarring sects and subdivisions into one interest, which supplies common topics, and kindles common feelings, unmixed with those narrow prejudices with which all professions are more or less infected. The knowledge, too, which is thus acquired, expands and enlarges the mind, excites its faculties, and calls those limbs and muscles into freer exercise which, by too constant use in one direction, not only acquire an illiberal air, but are apt also to lose somewhat of their native play and energy. And thus, without directly qualifying a man for any of the employ-

ments of life, it enriches and ennobles all. Without teaching him
the peculiar business of any one office or calling, it enables him
to act his part in each of them with better grace and more elevated carriage; and, if happily planned and conducted, is a main
ingredient in that complete and generous education which fits
a man 'to perform justly, skilfully, and magnanimously, all the
offices, both private and public, of peace and war.'"[2]

8.

The view of Liberal Education, advocated in these extracts, is
expanded by Mr. Davison in the Essay to which I have already
referred. He lays more stress on the "usefulness" of Liberal Education in the larger sense of the word than his predecessor in
the controversy. Instead of arguing that the Utility of knowledge
to the individual varies inversely with its Utility to the public,
he chiefly employs himself on the suggestions contained in Dr.
Copleston's last sentences. He shows, first, that a Liberal Education is something far higher, even in the scale of Utility, than
what is commonly called a Useful Education, and next, that it
is necessary or useful for the purposes even of that Professional
Education which commonly engrosses the title of Useful. The
former of these two theses he recommends to us in an argument
from which the following passages are selected:—

"It is to take a very contracted view of life," he says, "to think
with great anxiety how persons may be educated to superior skill
in their department, comparatively neglecting or excluding the
more liberal and enlarged cultivation. In his (Mr. Edgeworth's)
system, the value of every attainment is to be measured by its
subserviency to a calling. The specific duties of that calling are
exalted at the cost of those free and independent tastes and virtues which come in to sustain the common relations of society,
and raise the individual in them. In short, a man is to be usurped
by his profession. He is to be clothed in its garb from head to
foot. His virtues, his science, and his ideas are all to be put into

---

2 Vid. Milton on Education.

a gown or uniform, and the whole man to be shaped, pressed, and stiffened, in the exact mould of his technical character. Any interloping accomplishments, or a faculty which cannot be taken into public pay, if they are to be indulged in him at all, must creep along under the cloak of his more serviceable privileged merits. Such is the state of perfection to which the spirit and general tendency of this system would lead us.

"But the professional character is not the only one which a person engaged in a profession has to support. He is not always upon duty. There are services he owes, which are neither parochial, nor forensic, nor military, nor to be described by any such epithet of civil regulation, and yet are in no wise inferior to those that bear these authoritative titles; inferior neither in their intrinsic value, nor their moral import, nor their impression upon society. As a friend, as a companion, as a citizen at large; in the connections of domestic life; in the improvement and embellishment of his leisure, he has a sphere of action, revolving, if you please, within the sphere of his profession, but not clashing with it; in which if he can show none of the advantages of an improved understanding, whatever may be his skill or proficiency in the other, he is no more than an ill-educated man.

"There is a certain faculty in which all nations of any refinement are great practitioners. It is not taught at school or college as a distinct science; though it deserves that what is taught there should be made to have some reference to it; nor is it endowed at all by the public; everybody being obliged to exercise it for himself in person, which he does to the best of his skill. But in nothing is there a greater difference than in the manner of doing it. The advocates of professional learning will smile when we tell them that this same faculty which we would have encouraged, is simply that of speaking good sense in English, without fee or reward, in common conversation. They will smile when we lay some stress upon it; but in reality it is no such trifle as they imagine. Look into the huts of savages, and see, for there is nothing to listen to, the dismal blank of their stupid hours of silence; their professional avocations of war and hunting are over; and, having nothing to do, they have nothing to say. Turn to improved life, and you find conversation in all its forms the medium of something more than an idle pleasure; indeed, a very active agent in circulating and forming the opinions, tastes, and feelings of a whole people. It makes of itself a considerable affair. Its topics are the most promiscuous—all those which do not belong to any particular province. As for its power and influence, we may fairly say that it is of just the same consequence to a man's immediate society, how he talks, as how he acts. Now of all those who furnish their share to rational conversation, a mere adept in his own art is universally admitted to be the worst. The sterility and uninstructiveness of such a person's social hours are quite proverbial. Or if he escape being dull, it is only by launching into ill-tuned, learned loquacity. We do not desire of him lectures or speeches; and he has nothing else to give. Among benches he may be powerful; but seated on a chair he is quite another person. On the other hand, we may affirm, that one of the best companions is a man who, to the accuracy and research of a profession, has joined a free excursive acquaintance with various learning, and caught from it the spirit of general observation."

9.

Having thus shown that a liberal education is a real benefit to the subjects of it, as members of society, in the various duties and circumstances and accidents of life, he goes on, in the next place, to show that, over and above those direct services which might fairly be expected of it, it actually subserves the discharge of those particular functions, and the pursuit of those particular advantages, which are connected with professional exertion, and to which Professional Education is directed.

"We admit," he observes, "that when a person makes a business of one pursuit, he is in the right way to eminence in it; and that divided attention will rarely give excellence in many. But our assent will go no further. For, to think that the way to prepare a person for excelling in any one pursuit (and that is the only point in hand), is to fetter his early studies, and cramp the first development of his mind, by a reference to the exigencies of that pursuit barely, is a very different notion, and one which, we apprehend, deserves to be exploded rather than received. Possibly a few of the abstract, insulated kinds of learning might be approached in that way. The exceptions to be made are very few, and need not be recited. But for the acquisition of professional and practical ability such maxims are death to it. The main ingredients of that ability are requisite knowledge and cultivated faculties; but, of the two, the latter is by far the chief. A man of well improved faculties has the command of another's knowledge. A man without them, has not the command of his own.

"Of the intellectual powers, the judgment is that which takes the foremost lead in life. How to form it to the two habits it ought to possess, of exactness and vigour, is the problem. It would be ignorant presumption so much as to hint at any routine of method by which these qualities may with certainty be imparted to every or any understanding. Still, however, we may safely lay it down that they are not to be got 'by a gatherer of simples,' but are the combined essence and extracts of many different things, drawn from much varied reading and discipline, first, and observation afterwards. For if there be a single intelligible point on this head, it is that a man who has been trained to think upon one subject or for one subject only, will never be a good judge even in that one: whereas the enlargement of his circle gives him increased knowledge and power in a rapidly increasing ratio. So much do ideas act, not as solitary units, but by grouping and combination; and so clearly do all the things that fall within the proper province of the same faculty of the mind, intertwine with and support each other. Judgment lives as it were by comparison and discrimination. Can it be doubted, then, whether the range and extent of that assemblage of things upon which it is practised in its first essays are of use to its power?

"To open our way a little further on this matter, we will define what we mean by the power of judgment; and then try to ascertain among what kind of studies the improvement of it may be expected at all.

"Judgment does not stand here for a certain homely, useful quality of intellect, that guards a person from committing mistakes to the injury of his fortunes or common reputation; but for that master-principle of business, literature, and talent, which gives him strength in any subject he chooses to grapple with, and enables him to *seize the strong point* in it. Whether this definition be metaphysically correct or not, it comes home to the substance of our inquiry. It describes the power that every one desires to possess when he comes to act in a profession, or elsewhere; and corresponds with our best idea of a cultivated mind.

"Next, it will not be denied, that in order to do any good to the judgment, the mind must be employed upon such subjects as come within the cognizance of that faculty, and give some real exercise to its perceptions. Here we have a rule of selection by which the different parts of learning may be classed for our purpose. Those which belong to the province of the judgment are religion (in its evidences and interpretation), ethics, history, eloquence, poetry, theories of general speculation, the fine arts, and works of wit. Great as the variety of these large divisions of learning may appear, they are all held in union by two capital principles of connexion. First, they are all quarried out of one and the same great subject of man's moral, social, and feeling nature. And secondly, they are all under the control (more or less strict) of the same power of moral reason."

"If these studies," he continues, "be such as give a direct play and exercise to the faculty of the judgment, then they are the true basis of education for the active and inventive powers, whether destined for a profession or any other use. Miscellaneous as the assemblage may appear, of history, eloquence, poetry, ethics, etc., blended together, they will all conspire in an union of effect. They are necessary mutually to explain and interpret each other. The knowledge derived from them all will amalgamate, and the habits of a mind versed and practised in them by turns will join to produce a richer vein of thought and of more general and practical application than could be obtained of any single one, as the fusion of the metals into Corinthian brass gave the artist his most ductile and perfect material. Might we venture to imitate an author (whom indeed it is much safer to take as an authority than to attempt to copy), Lord Bacon, in some of his concise illustrations of the comparative utility of the different studies, we should say that history would give fulness, moral philosophy strength, and poetry elevation to the understanding. Such in reality is the natural force and tendency of the studies; but there are few minds susceptible enough to derive from them any sort of virtue adequate to those high expressions. We must be contented therefore to lower our panegyric to this, that a person cannot avoid receiving some infusion and tincture, at least, of those several qualities, from that course of diversified reading. One thing is unquestionable, that the elements of general reason are not to be found fully and truly expressed in any one kind of study; and that he who would wish to know her idiom, must read it in many books.

"If different studies are useful for aiding, they are still more useful for correcting each other; for as they have their particular merits severally, so they have their defects, and the most extensive acquaintance with one can produce only an intellect either too flashy or too jejune, or infected with some other fault of confined reading. History, for example, shows things as they are, that is, the morals and interests of men disfigured and perverted by all their imperfections of passion, folly, and ambition; philosophy strips the picture too much; poetry adorns it too much; the concentrated lights of the three correct the false peculiar colouring of each, and show us the truth. The right mode of thinking upon it is to be had from them taken all together, as every one must know who has seen their united contributions of thought and feeling expressed in the masculine sentiment of our immortal statesman, Mr. Burke, whose eloquence is inferior only to his more admirable wisdom. If any mind improved like his, is to be our instructor, we must go to the fountain head of things as he did, and study not his works but his method; by the one we may become feeble imitators, by the other arrive at some ability of our own. But, as all biography assures us, he, and every other able thinker, has been formed, not by a parsimonious admeasurement of studies to some definite future object (which is Mr. Edgeworth's maxim), but by taking a wide and liberal compass, and thinking a great deal on many subjects with no better end in view than because the exercise was one which made them more rational and intelligent beings."

10.

But I must bring these extracts to an end. Today I have confined myself to saying that that training of the intellect, which is best for the individual himself, best enables him to discharge his duties to society. The Philosopher, indeed, and the man of the world differ in their very notion, but the methods, by which they are respectively formed, are pretty much the same. The Philosopher has the same command of matters of thought, which the true citizen and gentleman has of matters of business and conduct. If then a practical end must be assigned to a University course, I say it is that of training good members of society. Its art is the art of social life, and its end is fitness for the world. It neither confines its views to particular professions on the one hand, nor creates heroes or inspires genius on the other. Works indeed of genius fall under no art; heroic minds come under no rule; a University is not a birthplace of poets or of immortal authors, of founders of schools, leaders of colonies, or conquerors of nations. It does not promise a generation of Aristotles or Newtons, of Napoleons or Washingtons, of Raphaels or Shakespeares, though such miracles of nature it has before now contained within its precincts. Nor is it content on the other hand with forming the critic or the experimentalist, the economist or the engineer, though such too it includes within its scope. But a University training is the great ordinary means to a great but ordinary end; it aims at raising the intellectual tone of society, at cultivating the public mind, at purifying the national taste, at supplying true principles to popular enthusiasm and fixed aims to popular aspiration, at giving enlargement and sobriety to the ideas of the age, at facilitating the exercise of political power, and refining the intercourse of private life. It is the education which gives a man a clear conscious view of his own opinions and judgments, a truth in developing them, an eloquence in expressing them, and a force in urging them. It teaches him to see things as they are, to go right to the point, to disentangle a skein of thought, to detect what is sophistical, and to discard what is irrelevant. It prepares him to fill any post with credit, and to master any subject with facility. It shows him how to accommodate himself to others, how to throw himself into their state of mind, how to bring before them his own, how to influence them, how to come to an understanding with them, how to bear with them. He is at home in any society, he has common ground with every class; he knows when to speak and when to be silent; he is able to converse, he is able to listen; he can ask a question pertinently, and gain a lesson seasonably, when he has nothing to impart himself; he is ever ready, yet never in the way; he is a pleasant companion, and a comrade you can depend upon; he knows when to be serious and when to trifle, and he has a sure tact which enables him to trifle with gracefulness and to be serious with effect. He has the repose of a mind which lives in itself, while it lives in the world, and which has resources for its happiness at home when it cannot go abroad. He has a gift which serves him in public, and supports him in retirement, without which good fortune is but vulgar, and with which failure and disappointment have a charm. The art which tends to make a man all this, is in the object which it pursues as useful as the art of wealth or the art of health, though it is less susceptible of method, and less tangible, less certain, less complete in its result.

KNOWLEDGE VIEWED IN RELATION TO RELIGION

1.

We shall be brought, Gentlemen, today, to the termination of the investigation which I commenced three Discourses back, and which, I was well aware, from its length, if for no other reason, would make demands upon the patience even of indulgent hearers.

First I employed myself in establishing the principle that Knowledge is its own reward; and I showed that, when considered in this light, it is called Liberal Knowledge, and is the scope of Academical Institutions.

Next, I examined what is meant by Knowledge, when it is said to be pursued for its own sake; and I showed that, in order satisfactorily to fulfil this idea, Philosophy must be its *form*; or, in other words, that its matter must not be admitted into the mind passively, as so much acquirement, but must be mastered and appropriated as a system consisting of parts, related one to the other, and interpretative of one another in the unity of a whole.

Further, I showed that such a philosophical contemplation of the field of Knowledge as a whole, leading, as it did, to an understanding of its separate departments, and an appreciation of them respectively, might in consequence be rightly called an illumination; also, it was rightly called an enlargement of mind, because it was a distinct location of things one with another, as if in space; while it was moreover its proper cultivation and its best condition, both because it secured to the intellect the sight of things as they are, or of truth, in opposition to fancy, opinion, and theory; and again, because it presupposed and involved the perfection of its various powers.

Such, I said, was that Knowledge, which deserves to be sought for its own sake, even though it promised no ulterior advantage.

But, when I had got as far as this, I went farther, and observed that, from the nature of the case, what was so good in itself could not but have a number of external uses, though it did not promise them, simply because it *was* good; and that it was necessarily the source of benefits to society, great and diversified in proportion to its own intrinsic excellence. Just as in morals, honesty is the best policy, as being profitable in a secular aspect, though such profit is not the measure of its worth, so too as regards what may be called the virtues of the Intellect, their very possession indeed is a substantial good, and is enough, yet still that substance has a shadow, inseparable from it, viz., its social and political usefulness. And this was the subject to which I devoted the preceding Discourse.

One portion of the subject remains:—this intellectual culture, which is so exalted in itself, not only has a bearing upon social and active duties, but upon Religion also. The educated mind may be said to be in a certain sense religious; that is, it has what may be considered a religion of its own, independent of Catholicism, partly co-operating with it, partly thwarting it; at once a defence yet a disturbance to the Church in Catholic countries, and in countries beyond her pale, at one time in open warfare with her, at another in defensive alliance. The history of Schools and Academies, and of Literature and Science generally, will, I think, justify me in thus speaking. Since, then, my aim in these Discourses is to ascertain the function and the action of a University, viewed in itself, and its relations to the various instruments of teaching and training which are round about it, my survey of it would not be complete unless I attempted, as I now propose to do, to exhibit its general bearings upon Religion.

2.

Right Reason, that is, Reason rightly exercised, leads the mind to the Catholic Faith, and plants it there, and teaches it in all its religious speculations to act under its guidance. But Reason, considered as a real agent in the world, and as an operative principle in man's nature, with an historical course and with definite results, is far from taking so straight and satisfactory a direction. It considers itself from first to last independent and supreme; it requires no external authority; it makes a religion for itself. Even though it accepts Catholicism, it does not go to sleep; it has an action and development of its own, as the passions have, or the moral sentiments, or the principle of self-interest. Divine grace, to use the language of Theology, does not by its presence supersede nature; nor is nature at once brought into simple concurrence and coalition with grace. Nature pursues its course, now coincident with that of grace, now parallel to it, now across, now divergent, now counter, in proportion to its own imperfection and to the attraction and influence which grace exerts over it. And what takes place as regards other principles of our nature and their developments is found also as regards the Reason. There is, we know, a Religion of enthusiasm, of superstitious ignorance, of statecraft; and each has that in it which resembles Catholicism, and that again which contradicts Catholicism. There is the Religion of a warlike people, and of a pastoral people; there is a Religion of rude times, and in like manner there is a Religion of civilized times, of the cultivated intellect, of the philosopher, scholar, and gentleman. This is that Religion of Reason, of which I speak. Viewed in itself, however near it comes to Catholicism, it is of course simply distinct from it; for Catholicism is one whole, and admits of no compromise or modification. Yet this is to view it in the abstract; in matter of fact, and in reference to individuals, we can have no difficulty in conceiving this philosophical Religion present in a Catholic country, as a spirit influencing men to a certain extent, for good or for bad or for both,—a spirit of the age, which again may be found, as among Catholics, so with still greater sway and success in a country not Catholic, yet specifically the same in such a country as it exists in a Catholic community. The problem then before us today, is to set down some portions of the outline, if we can ascertain them, of the Religion of Civilization, and to determine how they lie relatively to those principles, doctrines, and rules, which Heaven has given us in the Catholic Church.

And here again, when I speak of Revealed Truth, it is scarcely necessary to say that I am not referring to the main articles and prominent points of faith, as contained in the Creed. Had I undertaken to delineate a philosophy, which directly interfered with the Creed, I could not have spoken of it as compatible with the profession of Catholicism. The philosophy I speak of, whether it be viewed within or outside the Church, does not necessarily take cognizance of the Creed. Where the country is Catholic, the educated mind takes its articles for granted, by a sort of implicit faith; where it is not, it simply ignores them and the whole subject-matter to which they relate, as not affecting social and political interests. Truths about God's Nature, about His dealings towards the human race, about the Economy of Redemption,—in the one case it humbly accepts them, and passes on; in the other it passes them over, as matters of simple opinion, which never can be decided, and which can have no power over us to make us morally better or worse. I am not speaking then of belief in the great objects of faith, when I speak of Catholicism, but I am contemplating Catholicism chiefly as a system of pastoral instruction and moral duty; and I have to do with its doctrines mainly as they are subservient to its direction of the conscience and the conduct. I speak of it, for instance, as teaching the ruined state of man; his utter inability to gain Heaven by any thing he can do himself; the moral certainty of his losing his soul if left to himself; the simple absence of all rights and claims on the part of the creature in the presence of the Creator; the illimitable claims of the Creator on the service of the creature; the imperative and obligatory force of the voice of conscience; and the inconceivable evil of sensuality. I speak of it as teaching, that no one gains Heaven except by the free grace of God, or without a regeneration of nature; that no one can please Him without faith; that the heart is the seat both of sin and of obedience; that charity is the fulfilling of the Law; and that incorporation into the Catholic Church is the ordinary instrument of salvation. These are the lessons which distinguish Catholicism as a popular religion, and these are the subjects to which the cultivated intellect will practically be turned:— I have to compare and contrast, not the doctrinal, but the moral and social teaching of Philosophy on the one hand, and Catholicism on the other.

3.

Now, on opening the subject, we see at once a momentous benefit which the philosopher is likely to confer on the pastors of the Church. It is obvious that the first step which they have to effect in the conversion of man and the renovation of his nature, is his rescue from that fearful subjection to sense which is his ordinary state. To be able to break through the meshes of that thraldom, and to disentangle and to disengage its ten thousand holds upon the heart, is to bring it, I might almost say, half way to Heaven. Here, even divine grace, to speak of things according to their appearances, is ordinarily baffled, and retires, without expedient or resource, before this giant fascination. Religion seems too high and unearthly to be able to exert a continued influence upon us: its effort to rouse the soul, and the soul's effort to co-operate, are too violent to last. It is like holding out the arm at full length, or supporting some great weight, which we manage to do for a time, but soon are exhausted and succumb. Nothing can act beyond its own nature; when then we are called to what is supernatural, though those extraordinary aids from Heaven are given us, with which obedience becomes possible, yet even with them it is of transcendent difficulty. We are drawn down to earth every moment with the ease and certainty of a natural gravitation, and it is only by sudden impulses and, as it were, forcible plunges that we attempt to mount upwards. Religion indeed enlightens, terrifies, subdues; it gives faith, it inflicts remorse, it inspires resolutions, it draws tears, it inflames devotion, but only for the occasion. I repeat, it imparts an inward power which ought to effect more than this; I am not forgetting either the real sufficiency of its aids, nor the responsibility of those in whom they fail. I am not discussing theological questions at all, I am looking at phenomena as they lie before me, and I say that, in matter of fact, the sinful spirit repents, and protests it will never sin again, and for a while is protected by disgust and abhorrence from the malice of its foe. But that foe knows too well that such seasons of repentance are wont to have their end: he patiently waits, till nature faints with the effort of resistance, and lies passive and hopeless under the next access of temptation. What we need then is some expedient or instrument, which at least will obstruct and stave off the approach of our spiritual enemy, and which is sufficiently congenial and level with our nature to maintain as firm a hold upon us as the inducements of sensual gratification. It will be our wisdom to employ nature against itself. Thus sorrow, sickness, and care are providential antagonists to our inward disorders; they come upon us as years pass on, and generally produce their natural effects on us, in proportion as we are subjected to their influence. These, however, are God's instruments, not ours; we need a similar remedy, which we can make our own, the object of some legitimate faculty, or the aim of some natural affection, which is capable of resting on the mind, and taking up its familiar lodging with it, and engrossing it, and which thus becomes a match for the besetting power of sensuality, and a sort of homœopathic medicine for the disease. Here then I think is the important aid which intellectual cultivation furnishes to us in rescuing the victims of passion and self-will. It does not supply religious motives; it is not the cause or proper antecedent of any thing supernatural; it is not meritorious of heavenly aid or reward; but it does a work, at least *materially* good (as theologians speak), whatever be its real and formal character. It expels the excitements of sense by the introduction of those of the intellect.

This then is the *primâ facie* advantage of the pursuit of Knowledge; it is the drawing the mind off from things which will harm it to subjects which are worthy a rational being; and, though it does not raise it above nature, nor has any tendency to make us pleasing to our Maker, yet is it nothing to substitute what is in itself harmless for what is, to say the least, inexpressibly dangerous? is it a little thing to exchange a circle of ideas which are certainly sinful, for others which are certainly not so? You will say, perhaps, in the words of the Apostle, "Knowledge puffeth up:" and doubtless this mental cultivation, even when it is successful for the purpose for which I am applying it, may be from the first nothing more than the substitution of pride for sensuality. I grant it, I think I shall have something to say on this point presently; but this is not a necessary result, it is but an incidental evil, a danger which may be realized or may be averted, whereas we may in most cases predicate guilt, and guilt of a heinous kind, where the mind is suffered to run wild and indulge its thoughts without training or law of any kind; and surely to turn away a soul from mortal sin is a good and a gain so far, whatever comes of it. And therefore, if a friend in need is twice a friend, I conceive that intellectual employments, though they do no more than occupy the mind with objects naturally noble or innocent, have a special claim upon our consideration and gratitude.

4.

Nor is this all: Knowledge, the discipline by which it is gained, and the tastes which it forms, have a natural tendency to refine the mind, and to give it an indisposition, simply natural, yet real, nay, more than this, a disgust and abhorrence, towards excesses and enormities of evil, which are often or ordinarily reached at length by those who are not careful from the first to set themselves against what is vicious and criminal. It generates within the mind a fastidiousness, analogous to the delicacy or daintiness which good nurture or a sickly habit induces in respect of food; and this fastidiousness, though arguing no high principle, though no protection in the case of violent temptation, nor sure in its operation, yet will often or generally be lively enough to create an absolute loathing of certain offences, or a detestation and scorn of them as ungentlemanlike, to which ruder natures, nay, such as have far more of real religion in them, are tempted, or even betrayed. Scarcely can we exaggerate the value, in its place, of a safeguard such as this, as regards those multitudes who are thrown upon the open field of the world, or are withdrawn from its eye and from the restraint of public opinion. In many cases, where it exists, sins, familiar to those who are otherwise circumstanced, will not even occur to the mind: in others, the sense of shame and the quickened apprehension of detection will act as a sufficient obstacle to them, when they do present themselves before it. Then, again, the fastidiousness I am speaking of will create a simple hatred of that miserable tone of conversation which, obtaining as it does in the world, is a constant fuel of evil, heaped up round about the soul: moreover, it will create an irresolution and indecision in doing wrong, which will act as a *remora* till the danger is past away. And though it has no tendency, I repeat, to mend the heart, or to secure it from the dominion in other shapes of those very evils which it repels in the particular modes of approach by which they prevail over others, yet cases may occur when it gives birth, after sins have been committed, to so keen a remorse and so intense a self-hatred, as are even sufficient to cure the particular moral disorder, and to prevent its accesses ever afterwards;—as the spendthrift in the story, who, after gazing on his lost acres from the summit of an eminence, came down a miser, and remained a miser to the end of his days.

And all this holds good in a special way, in an age such as ours, when, although pain of body and mind may be rife as heretofore, yet other counteractions of evil, of a penal character, which are present at other times, are away. In rude and semi-barbarous periods, at least in a climate such as our own, it is the daily, nay, the principal business of the senses, to convey feelings of discomfort to the mind, as far as they convey feelings at all. Exposure to the elements, social disorder and lawlessness, the tyranny of the powerful, and the inroads of enemies, are a stern discipline, allowing brief intervals, or awarding a sharp penance, to sloth and sensuality. The rude food, the scanty clothing, the violent exercise, the vagrant life, the military constraint, the imperfect pharmacy, which now are the trials of only particular classes of the community, were once the lot more or less of all. In the deep woods or the wild solitudes of the medieval era, feelings of religion or superstition were naturally present to the population, which in various ways co-operated with the missionary or pastor, in retaining it in a noble simplicity of manners. But, when in the advancement of society men congregate in towns, and multiply in contracted spaces, and law gives them security, and art gives them comforts, and good government robs them of courage and manliness, and monotony of life throws them back upon themselves, who does not see that diversion or protection from evil they have none, that vice is the mere reaction of unhealthy toil, and sensual excess the holyday of resourceless ignorance? This is so well understood by the practical benevolence of the day, that it has especially busied itself in plans for supplying the masses of our town population with intellectual and honourable recreations. Cheap literature, libraries of useful and entertaining knowledge, scientific lectureships, museums, zoological collections, buildings and gardens to please the eye and to give repose to the feelings, external objects of whatever kind, which may take the mind off itself, and expand and elevate it in liberal contemplations, these are the human means, wisely suggested, and good as far as they go, for at least parrying the assaults of moral evil, and keeping at bay the enemies, not only of the individual soul, but of society at large.

Such are the instruments by which an age of advanced civilization combats those moral disorders, which Reason as well as Revelation denounces; and I have not been backward to express my sense of their serviceableness to Religion. Moreover, they are but the foremost of a series of influences, which intellectual culture exerts upon our moral nature, and all upon the type of Christianity, manifesting themselves in veracity, probity, equity, fairness, gentleness, benevolence, and amiableness; so much so, that a character more noble to look at, more beautiful, more winning, in the various relations of life and in personal duties, is hardly conceivable, than may, or might be, its result, when that culture is bestowed upon a soil naturally adapted to virtue. If you would obtain a picture for contemplation which may seem to fulfil the ideal, which the Apostle has delineated under the name of charity, in its sweetness and harmony, its generosity, its courtesy to others, and its depreciation of self, you could not have recourse to a better furnished *studio* than to that of Philosophy, with the specimens of it, which with greater or less exactness are scattered through society in a civilized age. It is enough to refer you, Gentlemen, to the various Biographies and Remains of contemporaries and others, which from time to time issue from the press, to see how striking is the action of our intellectual upon our moral nature, where the moral material is rich, and the intellectual cast is perfect. Individuals will occur to all of us, who deservedly attract our love and admiration, and whom the world almost worships as the work of its own hands. Religious principle, indeed,—that is, faith,—is, to all appearance, simply away; the work is as certainly not supernatural as it is certainly noble and beautiful. This must be insisted on, that the Intellect may have its due; but it also must be insisted on for the sake of conclusions to which I wish to conduct our investigation. The radical difference indeed of this mental refinement from genuine religion, in spite of its seeming relationship, is the very cardinal point on which my present discussion turns; yet, on the other hand, such refinement may readily be assigned to a Christian origin by hasty or distant observers, or by those who view it in a particular light. And as this is the case, I think it advisable, before proceeding with the delineation of its characteristic features, to point out to you distinctly the elementary principles on which its morality is based.

5.

You will bear in mind then, Gentlemen, that I spoke just now of the scorn and hatred which a cultivated mind feels for some kinds of vice, and the utter disgust and profound humiliation which may come over it, if it should happen in any degree to be betrayed into them. Now this feeling may have its root in faith and love, but it may not; there is nothing really religious in it, considered by itself. Conscience indeed is implanted in the breast by nature, but it inflicts upon us fear as well as shame;

when the mind is simply angry with itself and nothing more, surely the true import of the voice of nature and the depth of its intimations have been forgotten, and a false philosophy has misinterpreted emotions which ought to lead to God. Fear implies the transgression of a law, and a law implies a lawgiver and judge; but the tendency of intellectual culture is to swallow up the fear in the self-reproach, and self-reproach is directed and limited to our mere sense of what is fitting and becoming. Fear carries us out of ourselves, whereas shame may act upon us only within the round of our own thoughts. Such, I say, is the danger which awaits a civilized age; such is its besetting sin (not inevitable, God forbid! or we must abandon the use of God's own gifts), but still the ordinary sin of the Intellect; conscience tends to become what is called a moral sense; the command of duty is a sort of taste; sin is not an offence against God, but against human nature.

The less amiable specimens of this spurious religion are those which we meet not unfrequently in my own country. I can use with all my heart the poet's words,

"England, with all thy faults, I love thee still;"

but to those faults no Catholic can be blind. We find these men possessed of many virtues, but proud, bashful, fastidious, and reserved. Why is this? it is because they think and act as if there were really nothing objective in their religion; it is because conscience to them is not the word of a lawgiver, as it ought to be, but the dictate of their own minds and nothing more; it is because they do not look out of themselves, because they do not look through and beyond their own minds to their Maker, but are engrossed in notions of what is due to themselves, to their own dignity and their own consistency. Their conscience has become a mere self-respect. Instead of doing one thing and then another, as each is called for, in faith and obedience, careless of what may be called the *keeping* of deed with deed, and leaving Him who gives the command to blend the portions of their conduct into a whole, their one object, however unconscious to themselves, is to paint a smooth and perfect surface, and to be able to say to themselves that they have done their duty. When they do wrong, they feel, not contrition, of which God is the object, but remorse, and a sense of degradation. They call themselves fools, not sinners; they are angry and impatient, not humble. They shut themselves up in themselves; it is misery to them to think or to speak of their own feelings; it is misery to suppose that others see them, and their shyness and sensitiveness often become morbid. As to confession, which is so natural to the Catholic, to them it is impossible; unless indeed, in cases where they have been guilty, an apology is due to their own character, is expected of them, and will be satisfactory to look back upon. They are victims of an intense self-contemplation.

There are, however, far more pleasing and interesting forms of this moral malady than that which I have been depicting: I have spoken of the effect of intellectual culture on proud natures; but it will show to greater advantage, yet with as little approximation to religious faith, in amiable and unaffected minds. Observe, Gentlemen, the heresy, as it may be called, of which I speak, is the substitution of a moral sense or taste for conscience in the true meaning of the word; now this error may be the foundation of a character of far more elasticity and grace than ever adorned the persons whom I have been describing. It is especially congenial to men of an imaginative and poetical cast of mind, who will readily accept the notion that virtue is nothing more than the graceful in conduct. Such persons, far from tolerating fear, as a principle, in their apprehension of religious and moral truth, will not be slow to call it simply gloom and superstition. Rather a philosopher's, a gentleman's religion, is of a liberal and generous character; it is based upon honour; vice is evil, because it is unworthy, despicable, and odious. This was the quarrel of the ancient heathen with Christianity, that, instead of simply fixing the mind on the fair and the pleasant, it intermingled other ideas with them of a sad and painful nature; that it spoke of tears before joy, a cross before a crown; that it laid the foundation of heroism in penance; that it made the soul tremble with the news of Purgatory and Hell; that it insisted on views and a worship of the Deity, which to their minds was nothing else than mean, servile, and cowardly. The notion of an All-perfect, Ever-present God, in whose sight we are less than atoms, and who, while He deigns to visit us, can punish as well as bless, was abhorrent to them; they made their own minds their sanctuary, their own ideas their oracle, and conscience in morals was but parallel to genius in art, and wisdom in philosophy.

6.

Had I room for all that might be said upon the subject, I might illustrate this intellectual religion from the history of the Emperor Julian, the apostate from Christian Truth, the foe of Christian education. He, in whom every Catholic sees the shadow of the future Anti-Christ, was all but the pattern-man of philosophical virtue. Weak points in his character he had, it is true, even in a merely poetical standard; but, take him all in all, and I cannot but recognize in him a specious beauty and nobleness of moral deportment, which combines in it the rude greatness of Fabricius or Regulus with the accomplishments of Pliny or Antoninus. His simplicity of manners, his frugality, his austerity of life, his singular disdain of sensual pleasure, his military heroism, his application to business, his literary diligence, his modesty, his clemency, his accomplishments, as I view them, go to make him one of the most eminent specimens of pagan virtue which the world has ever seen.[1] Yet how shallow, how meagre, nay, how unamiable is that virtue after all, when brought upon its critical trial by his sudden summons into the presence of his Judge! His last hours form a *unique* passage in history, both as illustrating the helpless-

---

1 I do not consider I have said above any thing inconsistent with the following passage from Cardinal Gerdil, though I have enlarged on the favourable side of Julian's character. "Du génie, des connaissances, de l'habilité dans le métier de la guerre, du courage et du désintéressement dans le commandement des armées, des actions plutôt que des qualités estimables, mais le plus souvent gâtées par la vanité qui en était le principe, la superstition jointe à l'hypocrisie; un esprit fécond en ressources éclairé, mais susceptible de petitesse; des fautes essentielles dans le gouvernement; des innocens sacrifiés à la vengeance; une haîne envenimée contre le Christianisme, qu'il avait abandonné; un attachement passionné aux folies de la Théurgie; tels étaient les traits sous lesquels on nous preignait Julien." Op. t. x. p. 54.

ness of philosophy under the stern realities of our being, and as being reported to us on the evidence of an eye-witness. "Friends and fellow-soldiers," he said, to use the words of a writer, well fitted, both from his literary tastes and from his hatred of Christianity, to be his panegyrist, "the seasonable period of my departure is now arrived, and I discharge, with the cheerfulness of a ready debtor, the demands of nature ... I die without remorse, as I have lived without guilt. I am pleased to reflect on the innocence of my private life; and I can affirm with confidence that the supreme authority, that emanation of the divine Power, has been preserved in my hands pure and immaculate ... I now offer my tribute of gratitude to the Eternal Being, who has not suffered me to perish by the cruelty of a tyrant, by the secret dagger of conspiracy, or by the slow tortures of lingering disease. He has given me, in the midst of an honourable career, a splendid and glorious departure from this world, and I hold it equally absurd, equally base, to solicit, or to decline, the stroke of fate ....

"He reproved the immoderate grief of the spectators, and conjured them not to disgrace, by unmanly tears, the fate of a prince who in a few moments would be united with Heaven and with the stars. The spectators were silent; and Julian entered into a metaphysical argument with the philosophers Priscus and Maximus on the nature of the soul. The efforts which he made of mind as well as body, most probably hastened his death. His wound began to bleed with great violence; his respiration was embarrassed by the swelling of the veins; he called for a draught of cold water, and as soon as he had drank it expired without pain, about the hour of midnight."[2] Such, Gentlemen, is the final exhibition of the Religion of Reason: in the insensibility of conscience, in the ignorance of the very idea of sin, in the contemplation of his own moral consistency, in the simple absence of fear, in the cloudless self-confidence, in the serene self-possession, in the cold self-satisfaction, we recognize the mere Philosopher.

---

2 Gibbon, Hist., ch. 24.

7.

Gibbon paints with pleasure what, conformably with the senti-ments of a godless intellectualism, was an historical fulfilment of his own idea of moral perfection; Lord Shaftesbury had already drawn out that idea in a theoretical from, in his celebrated col-lection of Treatises which he has called "Characteristics of men, manners, opinions, views;" and it will be a further illustration of the subject before us, if you will allow me, Gentlemen, to make some extracts from this work.

One of his first attacks is directed against the doctrine of reward and punishment, as if it introduced a notion into religion inconsistent with the true apprehension of the beauty of virtue, and with the liberality and nobleness of spirit in which it should be pursued. "Men have not been content," he says, "to show the natural advantages of honesty and virtue. They have rather lessened these, the better, as they thought, to advance another foundation. They have made virtue so mercenary a thing, and have talked so much of its rewards, that one can hardly tell what there is in it, after all, which can be worth rewarding. For to be *bribed* only or *terrified* into an honest practice, bespeaks little of real honesty or worth." "If," he says elsewhere, insinuating what he dare not speak out, "if through hope merely of reward, or fear of punishment, the creature be inclined to do the good he hates, or restrained from doing the ill to which he is not otherwise in the least degree averse, there is in this case no virtue or goodness whatever. There is no more of rectitude, piety, or sanctity, in a creature thus reformed, than there is meekness or gentleness in a tiger strongly chained, or innocence and sobriety in a monkey under the discipline of the whip ... While the will is neither gained, nor the inclination wrought upon, but awe alone prevails and forces obedience, the obedience is servile, and all which is done through it merely servile." That is, he says that Christianity is the enemy of moral virtue, as influencing the mind by fear of God, not by love of good.

The motives then of hope and fear being, to say the least, put far into the background, and nothing being morally good but what springs simply or mainly from a love of virtue for its own sake, this love-inspiring quality in virtue is its beauty, while a bad conscience is not much more than the sort of feeling which makes us shrink from an instrument out of tune. "Some by mere nature," he says, "others by art and practice, are masters of an ear in music, an eye in painting, a fancy in the ordinary things of ornament and grace, a judgment in proportions of all kinds, and a general good taste in most of those subjects which make the amusement and delight of the ingenious people of the world. Let such gentlemen as these be as extravagant as they please, or as irregular in their morals, they must at the same time discover their *inconsistency*, live at *variance* with themselves, and in *contradiction* to that principle on which they ground their highest pleasure and entertainment. Of all other *beauties* which virtuosos pursue, poets celebrate, musicians sing, and architects or artists of whatever kind describe or form, the most delightful, the most engaging and pathetic, is that which is drawn from real life and from the passions. Nothing affects the heart like that which is purely from itself, and of its own nature: such as the beauty of sentiments, the grace of actions, the turn of characters, and the *proportions and features* of a human mind. This lesson of philosophy, even a romance, a poem, or a play may teach us ... Let poets or the men of harmony deny, if they can, this force of nature, or withstand this *moral magic* ... Every one is a virtuoso of a higher or lower degree; every one pursues a grace ... of one kind or other. The *venustum*, the *honestum*, the *decorum* of things will force its way ... The most natural beauty in the world is honesty and moral truth; for all beauty is truth."

Accordingly, virtue being only one kind of beauty, the principle which determines what is virtuous is, not conscience, but *taste*. "Could we once convince ourselves," he says, "of what is in itself so evident, viz., that in the very nature of things there must of necessity be the foundation of a right and wrong *taste*, as well in respect of inward character of features as of outward person, behaviour, and action, we should be far more ashamed of ignorance and wrong judgment in the former than in the latter of these subjects ... One who aspires to the character of a man of breeding and politeness is careful to form his judgment of arts and sciences upon right models of perfection ... He takes particular care to turn his eye from every thing which is gaudy, luscious, and of false taste. Nor is he less careful to turn his ear from every sort of music, besides that which is of the best manner and truest harmony. 'Twere to be wished we had the same regard to a *right taste in life and manners* ... If civility and humanity be a taste; if brutality, insolence, riot, be in the same manner a taste, ... who would not endeavour to force nature as well in this respect as in what relates to a taste or judgment in other arts and sciences?"

Sometimes he distinctly contrasts this taste with principle and conscience, and gives it the preference over them. "After all," he says, " *'tis not merely what we call principle*, but *a taste*, which governs men. They may think for certain, 'This is right,' or 'that wrong;' they may believe 'this is a virtue,' or 'that a sin;' 'this is punishable by man,' or 'that by God;' yet if the savour of things lies cross to honesty, if the fancy be florid, and the appetite high towards the subaltern beauties and lower orders of worldly symmetries and proportions, the conduct will infallibly turn this latter way." Thus, somewhat like a Jansenist, he makes the superior pleasure infallibly conquer, and implies that, neglecting principle, we have but to train the taste to a kind of beauty higher than sensual. He adds: "*Even conscience*, I fear, such as is owing to religious discipline, will make but a slight figure, when this taste is set amiss."

And hence the well-known doctrine of this author, that ridicule is the test of truth; for truth and virtue being beauty, and falsehood and vice deformity, and the feeling inspired by deformity being that of derision, as that inspired by beauty is admiration, it follows that vice is not a thing to weep about, but to laugh at. "Nothing is ridiculous," he says, "but what is deformed; nor is any thing proof against raillery but what is handsome and just. And therefore 'tis the hardest thing in the world to deny fair honesty the use of this weapon, which can never bear an edge against herself and bears against every thing contrary."

And hence again, conscience, which intimates a Lawgiver, being superseded by a moral taste or sentiment, which has no sanction beyond the constitution of our nature, it follows that our great rule is to contemplate ourselves, if we would gain a standard of life and morals. Thus he has entitled one of his Treatises a "Soliloquy," with the motto, "Nec te quæsiveris extra;" and he observes, "The chief interest of ambition, avarice, corruption, and every sly insinuating vice, is to prevent this interview and familiarity of discourse, which is consequent upon close retirement and inward recess. 'Tis the grand artifice of villainy and lewdness, *as well as of superstition and bigotry*, to put us upon terms of greater distance and formality with ourselves, and evade our *proving* method of soliloquy ... A passionate lover, whatever solitude he may affect, can never be truly by himself ... 'Tis the same reason which keeps the imaginary saint or mystic from being capable of this entertainment. Instead of looking narrowly into his own nature and mind, that he may be no longer a mystery to himself, he is taken up with *the contemplation of other mysterious natures*, which he never can explain or comprehend."

8.

Taking these passages as specimens of what I call the Religion of Philosophy, it is obvious to observe that there is no doctrine contained in them which is not in a certain sense true; yet, on the other hand, that almost every statement is perverted and made false, because it is not the whole truth. They are exhibitions of truth under one aspect, and therefore insufficient; conscience is most certainly a moral sense, but it is more; vice again, is a deformity, but it is worse. Lord Shaftesbury may insist, if he will, that simple and solitary fear cannot effect a moral conversion, and we are not concerned to answer him; but he will have a difficulty in proving that any real conversion follows from a doctrine which makes virtue a mere point of good taste, and vice vulgar and ungentlemanlike.

Such a doctrine is essentially superficial, and such will be its effects. It has no better measure of right and wrong than that of visible beauty and tangible fitness. Conscience indeed inflicts an acute pang, but that pang, forsooth, is irrational, and to reverence it is an illiberal superstition. But, if we will make light of what is deepest within us, nothing is left but to pay homage to what is more upon the surface. To *seem* becomes to *be*; what looks fair will be good, what causes offence will be evil; virtue will be what pleases, vice what pains. As well may we measure virtue by utility as by such a rule. Nor is this an imaginary apprehension; we all must recollect the celebrated sentiment into which a great and wise man was betrayed, in the glowing eloquence of his valediction to the spirit of chivalry. "It is gone," cries Mr. Burke; "that sensibility of principle, that chastity of honour which felt a stain like a wound; which inspired courage, while it mitigated ferocity; which ennobled whatever it touched, and under which *vice lost half its evil by losing all its grossness.*" In the last clause of this beautiful sentence we have too apt an illustration of the ethical temperament of a civilized age. It is detection, not the sin, which is the crime; private life is sacred, and inquiry into it is intolerable; and decency is virtue. Scandals, vulgarities, whatever shocks, whatever disgusts, are offences of the first order. Drinking and swearing, squalid poverty, improvidence, laziness, slovenly disorder, make up the idea of profligacy: poets may say any thing, however wicked, with impunity; works of genius may be read without danger or shame, whatever their principles; fashion, celebrity, the beautiful, the heroic, will suffice to force any evil upon the community. The splendours of a court, and the charms of good society, wit, imagination, taste, and high breeding, the *prestige* of rank, and the resources of wealth, are a screen, an instrument, and an apology for vice and irreligion. And thus at length we find, surprising as the change may be, that that very refinement of Intellectualism, which began by repelling sensuality, ends by excusing it. Under the shadow indeed of the Church, and in its due development, Philosophy does service to the cause of morality; but, when it is strong enough to have a will of its own, and is lifted up with an idea of its own importance, and attempts to form a theory, and to lay down a principle, and to

carry out a system of ethics, and undertakes the moral education of the man, then it does but abet evils to which at first it
seemed instinctively opposed. True Religion is slow in growth,
and, when once planted, is difficult of dislodgement; but its
intellectual counterfeit has no root in itself: it springs up suddenly, it suddenly withers. It appeals to what is in nature, and it
falls under the dominion of the old Adam. Then, like dethroned
princes, it keeps up a state and majesty, when it has lost the real
power. Deformity is its abhorrence; accordingly, since it cannot
dissuade men from vice, therefore in order to escape the sight of
its deformity, it embellishes it. It "skins and films the ulcerous
place," which it cannot probe or heal,

> "Whiles rank corruption, mining all within,
>   Infects unseen."

And from this shallowness of philosophical Religion it comes to
pass that its disciples seem able to fulfil certain precepts of Christianity more readily and exactly than Christians themselves. St.
Paul, as I have said, gives us a pattern of evangelical perfection;
he draws the Christian character in its most graceful form, and
its most beautiful hues. He discourses of that charity which is
patient and meek, humble and single-minded, disinterested,
contented, and persevering. He tells us to prefer each the other
before himself, to give way to each other, to abstain from rude
words and evil speech, to avoid self-conceit, to be calm and grave,
to be cheerful and happy, to observe peace with all men, truth
and justice, courtesy and gentleness, all that is modest, amiable,
virtuous, and of good repute. Such is St. Paul's exemplar of the
Christian in his external relations; and, I repeat, the school of the
world seems to send out living copies of this typical excellence
with greater success than the Church. At this day the "gentleman" is the creation, not of Christianity, but of civilization. But
the reason is obvious. The world is content with setting right
the surface of things; the Church aims at regenerating the very
depths of the heart. She ever begins with the beginning; and, as
regards the multitude of her children, is never able to get beyond

the beginning, but is continually employed in laying the foundation. She is engaged with what is essential, as previous and as introductory to the ornamental and the attractive. She is curing men and keeping them clear of mortal sin; she is "treating of justice and chastity, and the judgment to come:" she is insisting on faith and hope, and devotion, and honesty, and the elements of charity; and has so much to do with precept, that she almost leaves it to inspirations from Heaven to suggest what is of counsel and perfection. She aims at what is necessary rather than at what is desirable. She is for the many as well as for the few. She is putting souls in the way of salvation, that they may then be in a condition, if they shall be called upon, to aspire to the heroic, and to attain the full proportions, as well as the rudiments, of the beautiful.

9.

Such is the method, or the policy (so to call it), of the Church; but Philosophy looks at the matter from a very different point of view: what have Philosophers to do with the terror of judgment or the saving of the soul? Lord Shaftesbury calls the former a sort of "panic fear." Of the latter he scoffingly complains that "the saving of souls is now the heroic passion of exalted spirits." Of course he is at liberty, on his principles, to pick and choose out of Christianity what he will; he discards the theological, the mysterious, the spiritual; he makes selection of the morally or esthetically beautiful. To him it matters not at all that he begins his teaching where he should end it; it matters not that, instead of planting the tree, he merely crops its flowers for his banquet; he only aims at the present life, his philosophy dies with him; if his flowers do but last to the end of his revel, he has nothing more to seek. When night comes, the withered leaves may be mingled with his own ashes; he and they will have done their work, he and they will be no more. Certainly, it costs little to make men virtuous on conditions such as these; it is like teaching them a language or an accomplishment, to write Latin or to play on an instrument,—the profession of an artist, not the commission of an Apostle.

This embellishment of the exterior is almost the beginning and the end of philosophical morality. This is why it aims at being modest rather than humble; this is how it can be proud at the very time that it is unassuming. To humility indeed it does not even aspire; humility is one of the most difficult of virtues both to attain and to ascertain. It lies close upon the heart itself and its tests are exceedingly delicate and subtle. Its counterfeits abound; however, we are little concerned with them here, for, I repeat, it is hardly professed even by name in the code of ethics which we are reviewing. As has been often observed, ancient civilization had not the idea, and had no word to express it: or rather, it had the idea, and considered it a defect of mind, not a virtue, so that the word which denoted it conveyed a reproach. As to the modern world, you may gather its ignorance of it by its perversion of the somewhat parallel term "condescension." Humility or condescension, viewed as a virtue of conduct, may be said to consist, as in other things, so in our placing ourselves in our thoughts on a level with our inferiors; it is not only a voluntary relinquishment of the privileges of our own station, but an actual participation or assumption of the condition of those to whom we stoop. This is true humility, to feel and to behave as if we were low; not, to cherish a notion of our importance, while we affect a low position. Such was St. Paul's humility, when he called himself "the least of the saints;" such the humility of those many holy men who have considered themselves the greatest of sinners. It is an abdication, as far as their own thoughts are concerned, of those prerogatives or privileges to which others deem them entitled. Now it is not a little instructive to contrast with this idea, Gentlemen,—with this theological meaning of the word "condescension,"—its proper English sense; put them in juxtaposition, and you will at once see the difference between the world's humility and the humility of the Gospel. As the world uses the word, "condescension" is a stooping indeed of the person, but a bending forward, unattended with any the slightest effort to leave by a single inch the seat in which it is so firmly established. It is the act of a superior, who protests to himself, while he commits it, that he is superior still, and that he is doing nothing else but an act of grace towards those on whose level, in theory, he is placing himself. And this is the nearest idea which the philosopher can form of the virtue of self-abasement; to do more than this is to his mind a meanness or an hypocrisy, and at once excites his suspicion and disgust. What the world is, such it has ever been; we know the contempt which the educated pagans had for the martyrs and confessors of the Church; and it is shared by the anti-Catholic bodies of this day.

Such are the ethics of Philosophy, when faithfully represented; but an age like this, not pagan, but professedly Christian, cannot venture to reprobate humility in set terms, or to make a boast of pride. Accordingly, it looks out for some expedient by which it may blind itself to the real state of the case. Humility, with its grave and self-denying attributes, it cannot love; but what is more beautiful, what more winning, than modesty? what virtue, at first sight, simulates humility so well? though what in fact is more radically distinct from it? In truth, great as is its charm, modesty is not the deepest or the most religious of virtues. Rather it is the advanced guard or sentinel of the soul militant, and watches continually over its nascent intercourse with the world about it. It goes the round of the senses; it mounts up into the countenance; it protects the eye and ear; it reigns in the voice and gesture. Its province is the outward deportment, as other virtues have relation to matters theological, others to society, and others to the mind itself. And being more superficial than other virtues, it is more easily disjoined from their company; it admits of being associated with principles or qualities naturally foreign to it, and is often made the cloak of feelings or ends for which it was never given to us. So little is it the necessary index of humility, that it is even compatible with pride. The better for the purpose of Philosophy; humble it cannot be, so forthwith modesty becomes its humility.

Pride, under such training, instead of running to waste in the education of the mind, is turned to account; it gets a new name; it is called self-respect; and ceases to be the disagreeable,

uncompanionable quality which it is in itself. Though it be the
motive principle of the soul, it seldom comes to view; and when
it shows itself, then delicacy and gentleness are its attire, and
good sense and sense of honour direct its motions. It is no longer
a restless agent, without definite aim; it has a large field of exertion assigned to it, and it subserves those social interests which it
would naturally trouble. It is directed into the channel of industry, frugality, honesty, and obedience; and it becomes the very
staple of the religion and morality held in honour in a day like
our own. It becomes the safeguard of chastity, the guarantee of
veracity, in high and low; it is the very household god of society, as at present constituted, inspiring neatness and decency in
the servant girl, propriety of carriage and refined manners in her
mistress, uprightness, manliness, and generosity in the head of
the family. It diffuses a light over town and country; it covers the
soil with handsome edifices and smiling gardens; it tills the field,
it stocks and embellishes the shop. It is the stimulating principle
of providence on the one hand, and of free expenditure on the
other; of an honourable ambition, and of elegant enjoyment. It
breathes upon the face of the community, and the hollow sepul-
chre is forthwith beautiful to look upon.

Refined by the civilization which has brought it into activity, this self-respect infuses into the mind an intense horror of
exposure, and a keen sensitiveness of notoriety and ridicule. It
becomes the enemy of extravagances of any kind; it shrinks from
what are called scenes; it has no mercy on the mock-heroic, on
pretence or egotism, on verbosity in language, or what is called
prosiness in conversation. It detests gross adulation; not that it
tends at all to the eradication of the appetite to which the flatterer
ministers, but it sees the absurdity of indulging it, it understands
the annoyance thereby given to others, and if a tribute must be
paid to the wealthy or the powerful, it demands greater subtlety
and art in the preparation. Thus vanity is changed into a more
dangerous self-conceit, as being checked in its natural eruption.
It teaches men to suppress their feelings, and to control their
tempers, and to mitigate both the severity and the tone of their

judgments. As Lord Shaftesbury would desire, it prefers playful wit and satire in putting down what is objectionable, as a more refined and good-natured, as well as a more effectual method, than the expedient which is natural to uneducated minds. It is from this impatience of the tragic and the bombastic that it is now quietly but energetically opposing itself to the unchristian practice of duelling, which it brands as simply out of taste, and as the remnant of a barbarous age; and certainly it seems likely to effect what Religion has aimed at abolishing in vain.

10.

Hence it is that it is almost a definition of a gentleman to say he is one who never inflicts pain. This description is both refined and, as far as it goes, accurate. He is mainly occupied in merely removing the obstacles which hinder the free and unembarrassed action of those about him; and he concurs with their movements rather than takes the initiative himself. His benefits may be considered as parallel to what are called comforts or conveniences in arrangements of a personal nature: like an easy chair or a good fire, which do their part in dispelling cold and fatigue, though nature provides both means of rest and animal heat without them. The true gentleman in like manner carefully avoids whatever may cause a jar or a jolt in the minds of those with whom he is cast;—all clashing of opinion, or collision of feeling, all restraint, or suspicion, or gloom, or resentment; his great concern being to make every one at their ease and at home. He has his eyes on all his company; he is tender towards the bashful, gentle towards the distant, and merciful towards the absurd; he can recollect to whom he is speaking; he guards against unseasonable allusions, or topics which may irritate; he is seldom prominent in conversation, and never wearisome. He makes light of favours while he does them, and seems to be receiving when he is conferring. He never speaks of himself except when compelled, never defends himself by a mere retort, he has no ears for slander or gossip, is scrupulous in imputing motives to those who interfere with him, and interprets every thing for the best. He is never mean or little in his disputes, never takes unfair advantage, never mistakes personalities or sharp sayings for arguments, or insinuates evil which he dare not say out. From a long-sighted prudence, he observes the maxim of the ancient sage, that we should ever conduct ourselves towards our enemy as if he were one day to be our friend. He has too much good sense to be affronted at insults, he is too well employed to remember injuries, and too indolent to bear malice. He is patient, forbearing, and resigned, on philosophical principles; he submits to pain, because it is inevitable, to bereavement, because it is irreparable, and to death, because it is his destiny. If he engages in controversy of any kind, his disciplined intellect preserves him from the blundering discourtesy of better, perhaps, but less educated minds; who, like blunt weapons, tear and hack instead of cutting clean, who mistake the point in argument, waste their strength on trifles, misconceive their adversary, and leave the question more involved than they find it. He may be right or wrong in his opinion, but he is too clear-headed to be unjust; he is as simple as he is forcible, and as brief as he is decisive. Nowhere shall we find greater candour, consideration, indulgence: he throws himself into the minds of his opponents, he accounts for their mistakes. He knows the weakness of human reason as well as its strength, its province and its limits. If he be an unbeliever, he will be too profound and large-minded to ridicule religion or to act against it; he is too wise to be a dogmatist or fanatic in his infidelity. He respects piety and devotion; he even supports institutions as venerable, beautiful, or useful, to which he does not assent; he honours the ministers of religion, and it contents him to decline its mysteries without assailing or denouncing them. He is a friend of religious toleration, and that, not only because his philosophy has taught him to look on all forms of faith with an impartial eye, but also from the gentleness and effeminacy of feeling, which is the attendant on civilization.

Not that he may not hold a religion too, in his own way, even when he is not a Christian. In that case his religion is one of imagination and sentiment; it is the embodiment of those ideas of the sublime, majestic, and beautiful, without which there can be no large philosophy. Sometimes he acknowledges the being of God, sometimes he invests an unknown principle or quality with the attributes of perfection. And this deduction of his reason, or creation of his fancy, he makes the occasion of such excellent thoughts, and the starting-point of so varied and systematic a teaching, that he even seems like a disciple of Christianity itself. From the very accuracy and steadiness of his logical powers, he is able to see what sentiments are consistent in those who hold any religious doctrine at all, and he appears to others to feel and to hold a whole circle of theological truths, which exist in his mind no otherwise than as a number of deductions.

Such are some of the lineaments of the ethical character, which the cultivated intellect will form, apart from religious principle. They are seen within the pale of the Church and without it, in holy men, and in profligate; they form the *beau-ideal* of the world; they partly assist and partly distort the development of the Catholic. They may subserve the education of a St. Francis de Sales or a Cardinal Pole; they may be the limits of the contemplation of a Shaftesbury or a Gibbon. Basil and Julian were fellow-students at the schools of Athens; and one became the Saint and Doctor of the Church, the other her scoffing and relentless foe.

DUTIES OF THE CHURCH TOWARDS KNOWLEDGE

1.

I have to congratulate myself, Gentlemen, that at length I have accomplished, with whatever success, the difficult and anxious undertaking to which I have been immediately addressing myself. Difficult and anxious it has been in truth, though the main subject of University Teaching has been so often and so ably discussed already; for I have attempted to follow out a line of thought more familiar to Protestants just now than to Catholics, upon Catholic grounds. I declared my intention, when I opened the subject, of treating it as a philosophical and practical, rather than as a theological question, with an appeal to common sense, not to ecclesiastical rules; and for this very reason, while my argument has been less ambitious, it has been deprived of the lights and supports which another mode of handling it would have secured.

No anxiety, no effort of mind is more severe than his, who in a difficult matter has it seriously at heart to investigate without error and to instruct without obscurity; as to myself, if the past discussion has at any time tried the patience of the kind persons who have given it their attention, I can assure them that on no one can it have inflicted so great labour and fatigue as on myself. Happy they who are engaged in provinces of thought, so familiarly traversed and so thoroughly explored, that they see every where the footprints, the paths, the landmarks, and the remains of former travellers, and can never step wrong; but for myself, Gentlemen, I have felt like a navigator on a strange sea, who is out of sight of land, is surprised by night, and has to trust mainly to the rules and instruments of his science for reaching the port. The everlasting mountains, the high majestic cliffs, of the opposite coast, radiant in the sunlight, which are our ordinary guides, fail us in an excursion such as this; the lessons of antiquity, the determinations of authority, are here rather the needle, chart, and plummet, than great objects, with distinct and continuous outlines and completed details, which stand up and confront and occupy our gaze, and relieve us from the tension and suspense of our personal observation. And thus, in spite of the pains we may take to consult others and avoid mistakes, it is not till the morning comes and the shore greets us, and we see our vessel making straight for harbour, that we relax our jealous watch, and consider anxiety irrational. Such in a measure has been my feeling in the foregoing inquiry; in which indeed I have been in want neither of authoritative principles nor distinct precedents, but of treatises *in extenso* on the subject on which I have written,—the finished work of writers, who, by their acknowledged judgment and erudition, might furnish me for my private guidance with a running instruction on each point which successively came under review.

I have spoken of the arduousness of my "immediate" undertaking, because what I have been attempting has been of a preliminary nature, not contemplating the duties of the Church towards a University, nor the characteristics of a University which is Catholic, but inquiring what a University is, what is its aim, what its nature, what its bearings. I have accordingly laid down first, that all branches of knowledge are, at least implicitly, the subject-matter of its teaching; that these branches are not isolated and independent one of another, but form together a whole or system; that they run into each other, and complete each other, and that, in proportion to our view of them as a whole, is the exactness and trustworthiness of the knowledge which they separately convey; that the process of imparting knowledge to the intellect in this philosophical way is its true culture; that such culture is a good in itself; that the knowledge which is both its instrument and result is called Liberal Knowledge; that such culture, together with the knowledge which effects it, may fitly be sought for its own sake; that it is, however, in addition, of great

secular utility, as constituting the best and highest formation of
the intellect for social and political life; and lastly, that, considered in a religious aspect, it concurs with Christianity a certain
way, and then diverges from it; and consequently proves in the
event, sometimes its serviceable ally, sometimes, from its very
resemblance to it, an insidious and dangerous foe.

Though, however, these Discourses have only professed to be
preliminary, being directed to the investigation of the object and
nature of the Education which a University professes to impart,
at the same time I do not like to conclude without making some
remarks upon the duties of the Church towards it, or rather on
the ground of those duties. If the Catholic Faith is true, a University cannot exist externally to the Catholic pale, for it cannot teach Universal Knowledge if it does not teach Catholic
theology. This is certain; but still, though it had ever so many
theological Chairs, that would not suffice to make it a Catholic
University; for theology would be included in its teaching only
as a branch of knowledge, only as one out of many constituent
portions, however important a one, of what I have called Philosophy. Hence a direct and active jurisdiction of the Church
over it and in it is necessary, lest it should become the rival of the
Church with the community at large in those theological matters
which to the Church are exclusively committed,—acting as the
representative of the intellect, as the Church is the representative of the religious principle. The illustration of this proposition
shall be the subject of my concluding Discourse.

2.

I say then, that, even though the case could be so that the whole
system of Catholicism was recognized and professed, without
the direct presence of the Church, still this would not at once
make such a University a Catholic Institution, nor be sufficient
to secure the due weight of religious considerations in its philosophical studies. For it may easily happen that a particular bias or
drift may characterize an Institution, which no rules can reach,
nor officers remedy, nor professions or promises counteract. We

have an instance of such a case in the Spanish Inquisition;—here was a purely Catholic establishment, devoted to the maintenance, or rather the ascendancy of Catholicism, keenly zealous for theological truth, the stern foe of every anti-Catholic idea, and administered by Catholic theologians; yet it in no proper sense belonged to the Church. It was simply and entirely a State institution, it was an expression of that very Church-and-King spirit which has prevailed in these islands; nay, it was an instrument of the State, according to the confession of the acutest Protestant historians, in its warfare against the Holy See. Considered "*materially*," it was nothing but Catholic; but its spirit and form were earthly and secular, in spite of whatever faith and zeal and sanctity and charity were to be found in the individuals who from time to time had a share in its administration. And in like manner, it is no sufficient security for the Catholicity of a University, even that the whole of Catholic theology should be professed in it, unless the Church breathes her own pure and unearthly spirit into it, and fashions and moulds its organization, and watches over its teaching, and knits together its pupils, and superintends its action. The Spanish Inquisition came into collision with the supreme Catholic authority, and that, from the fact that its immediate end was of a secular character; and for the same reason, whereas Academical Institutions (as I have been so long engaged in showing) are in their very nature directed to social, national, temporal objects in the first instance, and since they are living and energizing bodies, if they deserve the name of University at all, and of necessity have some one formal and definite ethical character, good or bad, and do of a certainty imprint that character on the individuals who direct and who frequent them, it cannot but be that, if left to themselves, they will, in spite of their profession of Catholic Truth, work out results more or less prejudicial to its interests.

Nor is this all: such Institutions may become hostile to Revealed Truth, in consequence of the circumstances of their teaching as well as of their end. They are employed in the pursuit of Liberal Knowledge, and Liberal Knowledge has a special tendency, not necessary or rightful, but a tendency in fact, when cultivated by beings such as we are, to impress us with a mere philosophical theory of life and conduct, in the place of Revelation. I have said much on this subject already. Truth has two attributes—beauty and power; and while Useful Knowledge is the possession of truth as powerful, Liberal Knowledge is the apprehension of it as beautiful. Pursue it, either as beauty or as power, to its furthest extent and its true limit, and you are led by either road to the Eternal and Infinite, to the intimations of conscience and the announcements of the Church. Satisfy yourself with what is only visibly or intelligibly excellent, as you are likely to do, and you will make present utility and natural beauty the practical test of truth, and the sufficient object of the intellect. It is not that you will at once reject Catholicism, but you will measure and proportion it by an earthly standard. You will throw its highest and most momentous disclosures into the background, you will deny its principles, explain away its doctrines, re-arrange its precepts, and make light of its practices, even while you profess it. Knowledge, viewed as Knowledge, exerts a subtle influence in throwing us back on ourselves, and making us our own centre, and our minds the measure of all things. This then is the tendency of that Liberal Education, of which a University is the school, viz., to view Revealed Religion from an aspect of its own,—to fuse and recast it, to tune it, as it were, to a different key, and to reset its harmonies,—to circumscribe it by a circle which unwarrantably amputates here, and unduly developes there; and all under the notion, conscious or unconscious, that the human intellect, self-educated and self-supported, is more true and perfect in its ideas and judgments than that of Prophets and Apostles, to whom the sights and sounds of Heaven were immediately conveyed. A sense of propriety, order, consistency, and completeness gives birth to a rebellious stirring against miracle and mystery, against the severe and the terrible.

This Intellectualism first and chiefly comes into collision with precept, then with doctrine, then with the very principle of dogmatism;—a perception of the Beautiful becomes the substitute for faith. In a country which does not profess the faith, it at once runs, if allowed, into scepticism or infidelity; but even within the pale of the Church, and with the most unqualified profession of her Creed, it acts, if left to itself, as an element of corruption and debility. Catholicism, as it has come down to us from the first, seems to be mean and illiberal; it is a mere popular religion; it is the religion of illiterate ages or servile populations or barbarian warriors; it must be treated with discrimination and delicacy, corrected, softened, improved, if it is to satisfy an enlightened generation. It must be stereotyped as the patron of arts, or the pupil of speculation, or the protégé of science; it must play the literary academician, or the empirical philanthropist, or the political partisan; it must keep up with the age; some or other expedient it must devise, in order to explain away, or to hide, tenets under which the intellect labours and of which it is ashamed—its doctrine, for instance, of grace, its mystery of the Godhead, its preaching of the Cross, its devotion to the Queen of Saints, or its loyalty to the Apostolic See. Let this spirit be freely evolved out of that philosophical condition of mind, which in former Discourses I have so highly, so justly extolled, and it is impossible but, first indifference, then laxity of belief, then even heresy will be the successive results.

Here then are two injuries which Revelation is likely to sustain at the hands of the Masters of human reason unless the Church, as in duty bound, protects the sacred treasure which is in jeopardy. The first is a simple ignoring of Theological Truth altogether, under the pretence of not recognising differences of religious opinion;—which will only take place in countries or under governments which have abjured Catholicism. The second, which is of a more subtle character, is a recognition indeed of Catholicism, but (as if in pretended mercy to it) an adulteration of its spirit. I will now proceed to describe the dangers I speak of more distinctly, by a reference to the general subject-matter of instruction which a University undertakes.

There are three great subjects on which Human Reason employs itself:—God, Nature, and Man: and theology being put aside in the present argument, the physical and social worlds remain. These, when respectively subjected to Human Reason, form two books: the book of nature is called Science, the book of man is called Literature. Literature and Science, thus considered, nearly constitute the subject-matter of Liberal Education; and, while Science is made to subserve the former of the two injuries, which Revealed Truth sustains,—its exclusion, Literature subserves the latter,—its corruption. Let us consider the influence of each upon Religion separately.

3.

(I.) As to Physical Science, of course there can be no real collision between it and Catholicism. Nature and Grace, Reason and Revelation, come from the same Divine Author, whose works cannot contradict each other. Nevertheless, it cannot be denied that, in matter of fact, there always has been a sort of jealousy and hostility between Religion and physical philosophers. The name of Galileo reminds us of it at once. Not content with investigating and reasoning in his own province, it is said, he went out of his way directly to insult the received interpretation of Scripture; theologians repelled an attack which was wanton and arrogant; and Science, affronted in her minister, has taken its full revenge upon Theology since. A vast multitude of its teachers, I fear it must be said, have been either unbelievers or sceptics, or at least have denied to Christianity any teaching, distinctive or special, over the Religion of Nature. There have indeed been most illustrious exceptions; some men protected by their greatness of mind, some by their religious profession, some by the fear of public opinion; but I suppose the run of experimentalists, external to the Catholic Church, have more or less inherited the positive or negative unbelief of Laplace, Buffon, Franklin, Priestley, Cuvier, and Humboldt. I do not of course mean to say that there need be in every case a resentful and virulent opposition made to Religion on the part of scientific men; but their emphatic silence or phlegmatic inadvertence as to its claims have implied, more eloquently than any words, that in their opinion it had no voice at all in the subject-matter, which they had appropriated to themselves. The same antagonism shows itself in the middle ages. Friar Bacon was popularly regarded with suspicion as a dealer in unlawful arts; Pope Sylvester the Second has been accused of magic for his knowledge of natural secrets; and the geographical ideas of St. Virgil, Bishop of Saltzburg, were regarded with anxiety by the great St. Boniface, the glory of England, the Martyr-Apostle of Germany. I suppose, in matter of fact, magical superstition and physical knowledge did commonly go together in those ages: however, the hostility between experimental science and theology is far older than Christianity. Lord Bacon traces it to an era prior to Socrates; he tells us that, among the Greeks, the atheistic was the philosophy most favourable to physical discoveries, and he does not hesitate to imply that the rise of the religious schools was the ruin of science.[1]

Now, if we would investigate the reason of this opposition between Theology and Physics, I suppose we must first take into account Lord Bacon's own explanation of it. It is common in judicial inquiries to caution the parties on whom the verdict depends to put out of their minds whatever they have heard out of court on the subject to which their attention is to be directed. They are to judge by the evidence; and this is a rule which holds in other investigations as far as this, that nothing of an adventitious nature ought to be introduced into the process. In like manner, from religious investigations, as such, physics must be excluded, and from physical, as such, religion; and if we mix them, we shall spoil both. The theologian, speaking of Divine Omnipotence, for the time simply ignores the laws of nature as existing restraints upon its exercise; and the physical philosopher, on the other hand, in his experiments upon natural phenomena, is simply ascertaining those laws, putting aside the question of that Omnipotence. If the theologian, in tracing the ways of Providence, were stopped with objections grounded on the impossibility of physical miracles, he would justly protest against

---

1 Vid. Hallam's Literature of Europe, Macaulay's Essay, and the Author's Oxford University Sermons, IX.

the interruption; and were the philosopher, who was determining the motion of the heavenly bodies, to be questioned about their Final or their First Cause, he too would suffer an illogical interruption. The latter asks the cause of volcanoes, and is impatient at being told it is "the divine vengeance;" the former asks the cause of the overthrow of the guilty cities, and is preposterously referred to the volcanic action still visible in their neighbourhood. The inquiry into final causes for the moment passes over the existence of established laws; the inquiry into physical, passes over for the moment the existence of God. In other words, physical science is in a certain sense atheistic, for the very reason it is not theology.

This is Lord Bacon's justification, and an intelligible one, for considering that the fall of atheistic philosophy in ancient times was a blight upon the hopes of physical science. "Aristotle," he says, "Galen, and others frequently introduce such causes as these:—the hairs of the eyelids are for a fence to the sight; the bones for pillars whence to build the bodies of animals; the leaves of trees are to defend the fruit from the sun and wind; the clouds are designed for watering the earth. All which are properly alleged in metaphysics; but in physics, are impertinent, and as *remoras* to the ship, that hinder the sciences from holding on their course of improvement, and as introducing a neglect of searching after physical causes."[2] Here then is one reason for the prejudice of physical philosophers against Theology:—on the one hand, their deep satisfaction in the laws of nature indisposes them towards the thought of a Moral Governor, and makes them sceptical of His interposition; on the other hand, the occasional interference of religious criticism in a province not religious, has made them sore, suspicious, and resentful.

4.

Another reason of a kindred nature is to be found in the difference of method by which truths are gained in theology and in physical

---

2 In Augment., 5.

science. Induction is the instrument of Physics, and deduction only is the instrument of Theology. There the simple question is, What is revealed? all doctrinal knowledge flows from one fountain head. If we are able to enlarge our view and multiply our propositions, it must be merely by the comparison and adjustment of the original truths; if we would solve new questions, it must be by consulting old answers. The notion of doctrinal knowledge absolutely novel, and of simple addition from without, is intolerable to Catholic ears, and never was entertained by any one who was even approaching to an understanding of our creed. Revelation is all in all in doctrine; the Apostles its sole depository, the inferential method its sole instrument, and ecclesiastical authority its sole sanction. The Divine Voice has spoken once for all, and the only question is about its meaning. Now this process, as far as it was reasoning, was the very mode of reasoning which, as regards physical knowledge, the school of Bacon has superseded by the inductive method:—no wonder, then, that that school should be irritated and indignant to find that a subject-matter remains still, in which their favourite instrument has no office; no wonder that they rise up against this memorial of an antiquated system, as an eyesore and an insult; and no wonder that the very force and dazzling success of their own method in its own departments should sway or bias unduly the religious sentiments of any persons who come under its influence. They assert that no new truth can be gained by deduction; Catholics assent, but add that, as regards religious truth, they have not to seek at all, for they have it already. Christian Truth is purely of revelation; that revelation we can but explain, we cannot increase, except relatively to our own apprehensions; without it we should have known nothing of its contents, with it we know just as much as its contents, and nothing more. And, as it was given by a divine act independent of man, so will it remain in spite of man. Niebuhr may revolutionize history, Lavoisier chemistry, Newton astronomy; but God Himself is the author as well as the subject of theology. When Truth can change, its Revelation can change; when human reason can outreason the Omniscient, then may it supersede His work.

Avowals such as these fall strange upon the ear of men whose first principle is the search after truth, and whose starting-points of search are things material and sensible. They scorn any process of inquiry not founded on experiment; the Mathematics indeed they endure, because that science deals with ideas, not with facts, and leads to conclusions hypothetical rather than real; "Metaphysics" they even use as a by-word of reproach; and Ethics they admit only on condition that it gives up conscience as its scientific ground, and bases itself on tangible utility: but as to Theology, they cannot deal with it, they cannot master it, and so they simply outlaw it and ignore it. Catholicism, forsooth, "confines the intellect," because it holds that God's intellect is greater than theirs, and that what He has done, man cannot improve. And what in some sort justifies them to themselves in this extravagance is the circumstance that there is a religion close at their doors which, discarding so severe a tone, has actually adopted their own principle of inquiry. Protestantism treats Scripture just as they deal with Nature; it takes the sacred text as a large collection of phenomena, from which, by an inductive process, each individual Christian may arrive at just those religious conclusions which approve themselves to his own judgment. It considers faith a mere modification of reason, as being an acquiescence in certain probable conclusions till better are found. Sympathy, then, if no other reason, throws experimental philosophers into alliance with the enemies of Catholicism.

5.

I have another consideration to add, not less important than any I have hitherto adduced. The physical sciences, Astronomy, Chemistry, and the rest, are doubtless engaged upon divine works, and cannot issue in untrue religious conclusions. But at the same time it must be recollected that Revelation has reference to circumstances which did not arise till after the heavens and the earth were made. They were made before the introduction of moral evil into the world: whereas the Catholic Church is the instrument of a remedial dispensation to meet that introduction. No wonder then that her teaching is simply distinct, though not divergent, from the theology which Physical Science suggests to its followers. She sets before us a number of attributes and acts on the part of the Divine Being, for which the material and animal creation gives no scope; power, wisdom, goodness are the burden of the physical world, but it does not and could not speak of mercy, long-suffering, and the economy of human redemption, and but partially of the moral law and moral goodness. "Sacred Theology," says Lord Bacon, "must be drawn from the words and the oracles of God: not from the light of nature or the dictates of reason. It is written, that 'the Heavens declare the glory of God;' but we nowhere find it that the Heavens declare the will of God; which is pronounced a law and a testimony, that men should do according to it. Nor does this hold only in the great mysteries of the Godhead, of the creation, of the redemption ... We cannot doubt that a large part of the moral law is too sublime to be attained by the light of nature; though it is still certain that men, even with the light and law of nature, have some notions of virtue, vice, justice, wrong, good, and evil."[3] That the new and further manifestations of the Almighty, made by Revelation, are in perfect harmony with the teaching of the natural world, forms indeed one subject of the profound work of the Anglican Bishop Butler; but they cannot in any sense be gathered from nature, and the silence of nature concerning them may easily seduce the imagination, though it has no force to persuade the reason, to revolt from doctrines which have not been authenticated by facts, but are enforced by authority. In a scientific age, then, there will naturally be a parade of what is called Natural Theology, a widespread profession of the Unitarian creed, an impatience of mystery, and a scepticism about miracles.

And to all this must be added the ample opportunity which physical science gives to the indulgence of those sentiments of beauty, order, and congruity, of which I have said so much, as the ensigns and colours (as they may be called) of a civilized age in its warfare against Catholicism.

---

3   De Augm., § 28.

It being considered, then, that Catholicism differs from physical science, in drift, in method of proof, and in subject-matter, how can it fail to meet with unfair usage from the philosophers of any Institution in which there is no one to take its part? That Physical Science itself will be ultimately the loser by such ill treatment of Theology, I have insisted on at great length in some preceding Discourses; for to depress unduly, to encroach upon any science, and much more on an important one, is to do an injury to all. However, this is not the concern of the Church; the Church has no call to watch over and protect Science: but towards Theology she has a distinct duty: it is one of the special trusts committed to her keeping. Where Theology is, there she must be; and if a University cannot fulfil its name and office without the recognition of Revealed Truth, she must be there to see that it is a *bonâ fide* recognition, sincerely made and consistently acted on.

6.

(II.) And if the interposition of the Church is necessary in the Schools of Science, still more imperatively is it demanded in the other main constituent portion of the subject-matter of Liberal Education,—Literature. Literature stands related to Man as Science stands to Nature; it is his history. Man is composed of body and soul; he thinks and he acts; he has appetites, passions, affections, motives, designs; he has within him the lifelong struggle of duty with inclination; he has an intellect fertile and capacious; he is formed for society, and society multiplies and diversifies in endless combinations his personal characteristics, moral and intellectual. All this constitutes his life; of all this Literature is the expression; so that Literature is to man in some sort what autobiography is to the individual; it is his Life and Remains. Moreover, he is this sentient, intelligent, creative, and operative being, quite independent of any extraordinary aid from Heaven, or any definite religious belief; and *as such*, as he is in himself, does Literature represent him; it is the Life and Remains of the *natural* man, innocent or guilty. I do not mean to say that it is impossible in its very notion that Literature should be tinctured by a religious spirit; Hebrew Literature, as far as it can be called Literature, certainly is simply theological, and has a character imprinted on it which is above nature; but I am speaking of what is to be expected without any extraordinary dispensation; and I say that, in matter of fact, as Science is the reflection of Nature, so is Literature also—the one, of Nature physical, the other, of Nature moral and social. Circumstances, such as locality, period, language, seem to make little or no difference in the character of Literature, as such; on the whole, all Literatures are one; they are the voices of the natural man.

I wish this were all that had to be said to the disadvantage of Literature; but while Nature physical remains fixed in its laws, Nature moral and social has a will of its own, is self-governed, and never remains any long while in that state from which it started into action. Man will never continue in a mere state of innocence; he is sure to sin, and his literature will be the expression of his sin, and this whether he be heathen or Christian. Christianity has thrown gleams of light on him and his literature; but as it has not converted him, but only certain choice specimens of him, so it has not changed the characters of his mind or of his history; his literature is either what it was, or worse than what it was, in proportion as there has been an abuse of knowledge granted and a rejection of truth. On the whole, then, I think it will be found, and ever found, as a matter of course, that Literature, as such, no matter of what nation, is the science or history, partly and at best of the natural man, partly of man in rebellion.

7.

Here then, I say, you are involved in a difficulty greater than that which besets the cultivation of Science; for, if Physical Science be dangerous, as I have said, it is dangerous, because it necessarily ignores the idea of moral evil; but Literature is open to the more grievous imputation of recognizing and understanding it too well. Some one will say to me perhaps: "Our youth shall not be corrupted. We will dispense with all general or national Literature whatever, if it be so exceptionable; we will have a Christian Literature of our own, as pure, as true, as the Jewish." You cannot have it:—I do not say you cannot form a select literature for the young, nay, even for the middle or lower classes; this is another matter altogether: I am speaking of University Education, which implies an extended range of reading, which has to deal with standard works of genius, or what are called the *classics* of a language: and I say, from the nature of the case, if Literature is to be made a study of human nature, you cannot have a Christian Literature. It is a contradiction in terms to attempt a sinless Literature of sinful man. You may gather together something very great and high, something higher than any Literature ever was; and when you have done so, you will find that it is not Literature at all. You will have simply left the delineation of man, as such, and have substituted for it, as far as you have had any thing to substitute, that of man, as he is or might be, under certain special advantages. Give up the study of man, as such, if so it must be; but say you do so. Do not say you are studying him, his history, his mind and his heart, when you are studying something else. Man is a being of genius, passion, intellect, conscience, power. He exercises these various gifts in various ways, in great deeds, in great thoughts, in heroic acts, in hateful crimes. He founds states, he fights battles, he builds cities, he ploughs the forest, he subdues the elements, he rules his kind. He creates vast ideas, and influences many generations. He takes a thousand shapes, and undergoes a thousand fortunes. Literature records them all to the life,

> Quicquid agunt homines, votum, timor, ira, voluptas,
> Gaudia, discursus.

He pours out his fervid soul in poetry; he sways to and fro, he soars, he dives, in his restless speculations; his lips drop eloquence; he touches the canvas, and it glows with beauty; he sweeps the strings, and they thrill with an ecstatic meaning. He looks back into himself, and he reads his own thoughts, and notes them down; he looks out into the universe, and tells over and celebrates the elements and principles of which it is the product.

Such is man: put him aside, keep him before you; but, whatever you do, do not take him for what he is not, for something more divine and sacred, for man regenerate. Nay, beware of showing God's grace and its work at such disadvantage as to make the few whom it has thoroughly influenced compete in intellect with the vast multitude who either have it not, or use it ill. The elect are few to choose out of, and the world is inexhaustible. From the first, Jabel and Tubalcain, Nimrod "the stout hunter," the learning of the Pharaohs, and the wisdom of the East country, are of the world. Every now and then they are rivalled by a Solomon or a Beseleel, but the *habitat* of natural gifts is the natural man. The Church may use them, she cannot at her will originate them. Not till the whole human race is made new will its literature be pure and true. Possible of course it is in idea, for nature, inspired by heavenly grace, to exhibit itself on a large scale, in an originality of thought or action, even far beyond what the world's literature has recorded or exemplified; but, if you would in fact have a literature of saints, first of all have a nation of them.

What is a clearer proof of the truth of all this than the structure of the Inspired Word itself? It is undeniably *not* the reflection or picture of the many, but of the few; it is no picture of life, but an anticipation of death and judgment. Human literature is about all things, grave or gay, painful or pleasant; but the Inspired Word views them only in one aspect, and as they tend to one scope. It gives us little insight into the fertile developments of mind; it has no terms in its vocabulary to express with exactness the intellect and its separate faculties: it knows nothing of genius, fancy, wit, invention, presence of mind, resource. It does not discourse of empire, commerce, enterprise, learning, philosophy, or the fine arts. Slightly too does it touch on the more simple and innocent courses of nature and their reward. Little does it say[4] of those temporal blessings which rest upon our worldly occupations, and make them easy; of the blessings

---

4 *Vid.* the Author's Parochial Sermons, vol. i. 25.

which we derive from the sunshine day and the serene night, from the succession of the seasons, and the produce of the earth. Little about our recreations and our daily domestic comforts; little about the ordinary occasions of festivity and mirth, which sweeten human life; and nothing at all about various pursuits or amusements, which it would be going too much into detail to mention. We read indeed of the feast when Isaac was weaned, and of Jacob's courtship, and of the religious merry-makings of holy Job; but exceptions, such as these, do but remind us what might be in Scripture, and is not. If then by Literature is meant the manifestation of human nature in human language, you will seek for it in vain except in the world. Put up with it, as it is, or do not pretend to cultivate it; take things as they are, not as you could wish them.

8.

Nay, I am obliged to go further still; even if we could, still we should be shrinking from our plain duty, Gentlemen, did we leave out Literature from Education. For why do we educate, except to prepare for the world? Why do we cultivate the intellect of the many beyond the first elements of knowledge, except for this world? Will it be much matter in the world to come whether our bodily health or whether our intellectual strength was more or less, except of course as this world is in all its circumstances a trial for the next? If then a University is a direct preparation for this world, let it be what it professes. It is not a Convent, it is not a Seminary; it is a place to fit men of the world for the world. We cannot possibly keep them from plunging into the world, with all its ways and principles and maxims, when their time comes; but we can prepare them against what is inevitable; and it is not the way to learn to swim in troubled waters, never to have gone into them. Proscribe (I do not merely say particular authors, particular works, particular passages) but Secular Literature as such; cut out from your class books all broad manifestations of the natural man; and those manifestations are waiting for your pupil's benefit at the very doors of your lecture room in living and breathing substance. They will meet him there in all the charm of novelty, and all the fascination of genius or of amiableness. Today a pupil, tomorrow a member of the great world: today confined to the Lives of the Saints, tomorrow thrown upon Babel;—thrown on Babel, without the honest indulgence of wit and humour and imagination having ever been permitted to him, without any fastidiousness of taste wrought into him, without any rule given him for discriminating "the precious from the vile," beauty from sin, the truth from the sophistry of nature, what is innocent from what is poison. You have refused him the masters of human thought, who would in some sense have educated him, because of their incidental corruption: you have shut up from him those whose thoughts strike home to our hearts, whose words are proverbs, whose names are indigenous to all the world, who are the standard of their mother tongue, and the pride and boast of their countrymen, Homer, Ariosto, Cervantes, Shakespeare, because the old Adam smelt rank in them; and for what have you reserved him? You have given him "a liberty unto" the multitudinous blasphemy of his day; you have made him free of its newspapers, its reviews, its magazines, its novels, its controversial pamphlets, of its Parliamentary debates, its law proceedings, its platform speeches, its songs, its drama, its theatre, of its enveloping, stifling atmosphere of death. You have succeeded but in this,—in making the world his University.

Difficult then as the question may be, and much as it may try the judgments and even divide the opinions of zealous and religious Catholics, I cannot feel any doubt myself, Gentlemen, that the Church's true policy is not to aim at the exclusion of Literature from Secular Schools, but at her own admission into them. Let her do for Literature in one way what she does for Science in another; each has its imperfection, and she has her remedy for each. She fears no knowledge, but she purifies all; she represses no element of our nature, but cultivates the whole. Science is grave, methodical, logical; with Science then she argues, and opposes reason to reason. Literature does not argue, but declaims and insinuates; it is multiform and versatile: it persuades instead of convincing, it seduces, it carries captive; it appeals to the sense of honour, or to the imagination, or to the stimulus of curiosity; it makes its way by means of gaiety, satire, romance, the beautiful, the pleasurable. Is it wonderful that with an agent like this the Church should claim to deal with a vigour corresponding to its restlessness, to interfere in its proceedings with a higher hand, and to wield an authority in the choice of its studies and of its books which would be tyrannical, if reason and fact were the only instruments of its conclusions? But, any how, her principle is one and the same throughout: not to prohibit truth of any kind, but to see that no doctrines pass under the name of Truth but those which claim it rightfully.

9.

Such at least is the lesson which I am taught by all the thought which I have been able to bestow upon the subject; such is the lesson which I have gained from the history of my own special Father and Patron, St. Philip Neri. He lived in an age as traitorous to the interests of Catholicism as any that preceded it, or can follow it. He lived at a time when pride mounted high, and the senses held rule; a time when kings and nobles never had more of state and homage, and never less of personal responsibility and peril; when medieval winter was receding, and the summer sun of civilization was bringing into leaf and flower a thousand forms of luxurious enjoyment; when a new world of thought and beauty had opened upon the human mind, in the discovery of the treasures of classic literature and art. He saw the great and the gifted, dazzled by the Enchantress, and drinking in the magic of her song; he saw the high and the wise, the student and the artist, painting, and poetry, and sculpture, and music, and architecture, drawn within her range, and circling round the abyss: he saw heathen forms mounting thence, and forming in the thick air:—all this he saw, and he perceived that the mischief was to be met, not with argument, not with science, not with protests and warnings, not by the recluse or the preacher, but by means of the great counter-fascination of purity and truth. He was raised up to do a work almost peculiar in the Church,—not to be a Jerome Savonarola, though Philip had a true devotion towards him and a tender memory of his Florentine house; not to be a St. Charles, though in his beaming countenance Philip had recognized the aureole of a saint; not to be a St. Ignatius, wrestling with the foe, though Philip was termed the Society's bell of call, so many subjects did he send to it; not to be a St. Francis Xavier, though Philip had longed to shed his blood for Christ in India with him; not to be a St. Caietan, or hunter, of souls, for Philip preferred, as he expressed it, tranquilly to cast in his net to gain them; he preferred to yield to the stream, and direct the current, which he could not stop, of science, literature, art, and fashion, and to sweeten and to sanctify what God had made very good and man had spoilt.

And so he contemplated as the idea of his mission, not the propagation of the faith, nor the exposition of doctrine, nor the catechetical schools; whatever was exact and systematic pleased him not; he put from him monastic rule and authoritative speech, as David refused the armour of his king. No; he would be but an ordinary individual priest as others: and his weapons should be but unaffected humility and unpretending love. All He did was to be done by the light, and fervour, and convincing eloquence of his personal character and his easy conversation. He came to the Eternal City and he sat himself down there, and his home and his family gradually grew up around him, by the spontaneous accession of materials from without. He did not so much seek his own as draw them to him. He sat in his small room, and they in their gay worldly dresses, the rich and the wellborn, as well as the simple and the illiterate, crowded into it. In the mid-heats of summer, in the frosts of winter, still was he in that low and narrow cell at San Girolamo, reading the hearts of those who came to him, and curing their souls' maladies by the very touch of his hand. It was a vision of the Magi worshipping the infant Saviour, so pure and innocent, so sweet and beautiful was he; and so loyal and so dear to the gracious Virgin Mother. And they who came remained gazing and listening, till at length, first one and then another threw off their bravery, and took his poor cassock and girdle instead: or, if they kept it, it was to put haircloth under it, or to take on them a rule of life, while to the world they looked as before.

In the words of his biographer, "he was all things to all men. He suited himself to noble and ignoble, young and old, subjects and prelates, learned and ignorant; and received those who were strangers to him with singular benignity, and embraced them with as much love and charity as if he had been a long while expecting them. When he was called upon to be merry he was so; if there was a demand upon his sympathy he was equally ready. He gave the same welcome to all: caressing the poor equally with the rich, and wearying himself to assist all to the utmost limits of his power. In consequence of his being so accessible and willing to receive all comers, many went to him every day, and some continued for the space of thirty, nay forty years, to visit him very often both morning and evening, so that his room went by the agreeable nickname of the Home of Christian mirth. Nay, people came to him, not only from all parts of Italy, but from France, Spain, Germany, and all Christendom; and even the infidels and Jews, who had ever any communication with him, revered him as a holy man."[5] The first families of Rome, the Massimi, the Aldobrandini, the Colonnas, the Altieri, the Vitelleschi, were his friends and his penitents. Nobles of Poland, Grandees of Spain, Knights of Malta, could not leave Rome without coming to him. Cardinals, Archbishops, and Bishops were his intimates; Federigo Borromeo haunted his room and got the name of "Father Philip's soul." The Cardinal-Archbishops of Verona and Bologna wrote books in his honour. Pope Pius the Fourth died in his arms. Lawyers, painters, musicians, physicians, it was the same too with them. Baronius, Zazzara, and Ricci, left the law at his bidding, and joined his congregation, to do its work, to write the annals of the Church, and to die in the odour of sanctity. Palestrina had Father Philip's ministrations in his last moments. Animuccia hung about him during life, sent him a message after

---

5   Bacci, vol. i., p. 192, ii., p. 98.

death, and was conducted by him through Purgatory to Heaven. And who was he, I say, all the while, but an humble priest, a stranger in Rome, with no distinction of family or letters, no claim of station or of office, great simply in the attraction with which a Divine Power had gifted him? and yet thus humble, thus unennobled, thus empty-handed, he has achieved the glorious title of Apostle of Rome.

10.

Well were it for his clients and children, Gentlemen, it they could promise themselves the very shadow of his special power, or could hope to do a miserable fraction of the sort of work in which he was pre-eminently skilled. But so far at least they may attempt,— to take his position, and to use his method, and to cultivate the arts of which he was so bright a pattern. For me, if it be God's blessed will that in the years now coming I am to have a share in the great undertaking, which has been the occasion and the subject of these Discourses, so far I can say for certain that, whether or not I can do any thing at all in St. Philip's way, at least I can do nothing in any other. Neither by my habits of life, nor by vigour of age, am I fitted for the task of authority, or of rule, or of initiation. I do but aspire, if strength is given me, to be your minister in a work which must employ younger minds and stronger lives than mine. I am but fit to bear my witness, to proffer my suggestions, to express my sentiments, as has in fact been my occupation in these discussions; to throw such light upon general questions, upon the choice of objects, upon the import of principles, upon the tendency of measures, as past reflection and experience enable me to contribute. I shall have to make appeals to your consideration, your friendliness, your confidence, of which I have had so many instances, on which I so tranquilly repose; and after all, neither you nor I must ever be surprised, should it so happen that the Hand of Him, with whom are the springs of life and death, weighs heavy on me, and makes me unequal to anticipations in which you have been too kind, and to hopes in which I may have been too sanguine.

I. UNIVERSITY SUBJECTS

DISCUSSED IN OCCASIONAL LECTURES AND ESSAYS

Addressed to the members of the Catholic University

My Dear Monsell,

I seem to have some claim for asking leave of you to prefix your name to the following small volume, since it is a memorial of work done in a country which you so dearly love, and in behalf of an undertaking in which you feel so deep an interest.

Nor do I venture on the step without some hope that it is worthy of your acceptance, at least on account of those portions of it which have already received the approbation of the learned men to whom they were addressed, and which have been printed at their desire.

But, even though there were nothing to recommend it except that it came from me, I know well that you would kindly welcome it as a token of the truth and constancy with which I am,

My Dear Monsell,

Yours very affectionately,

November, 1858.

AUTHOR'S NOTE

It has been the fortune of the author through life, that the volumes which he has published have grown for the most part out of the duties which lay upon him, or out of the circumstances of the moment. Rarely has he been master of his own studies.

The present collection of lectures and essays, written by him while Rector of the Catholic University of Ireland, is certainly not an exception to this remark. Rather, it requires the above consideration to be kept in view, as an apology for the want of keeping which is apparent between its separate portions, some of them being written for public delivery, others with the privileged freedom of anonymous compositions.

However, whatever be the inconvenience which such varieties in tone and character may involve, the author cannot affect any compunction for having pursued the illustration of one and the same important subject matter, with which he had been put in charge, by such methods, graver or lighter, so that they were lawful, as successively came to his hand.

November, 1858.

---

1 Now Lord Emly.

I.

CHRISTIANITY AND LETTERS

A LECTURE IN THE SCHOOL OF PHILOSOPHY AND LETTERS

1.

It seems but natural, Gentlemen, now that we are opening the School of Philosophy and Letters, or, as it was formerly called, of Arts, in this new University, that we should direct our attention to the question, what are the subjects generally included under that name, and what place they hold, and how they come to hold that place, in a University, and in the education which a University provides. This would be natural on such an occasion, even though the Faculty of Arts held but a secondary place in the academical system; but it seems to be even imperative on us, considering that the studies which that Faculty embraces are almost the direct subject-matter and the staple of the mental exercises proper to a University.

It is indeed not a little remarkable that, in spite of the special historical connexion of University Institutions with the Sciences of Theology, Law, and Medicine, a University, after all, should be formally based (as it really is), and should emphatically live in, the Faculty of Arts; but such is the deliberate decision of those who have most deeply and impartially considered the subject.[1] Arts existed before other Faculties; the Masters of Arts were the ruling and directing body; the success and popularity of the Faculties of Law and Medicine were considered to be in no slight measure an encroachment and a usurpation, and were met with jealousy and resistance. When Colleges arose and became the medium and instrument of University action, they did but con-

---

1 *Vid.* Huber.

firm the ascendency of the Faculty of Arts; and thus, even down to this day, in those academical corporations which have more than others retained the traces of their medieval origin,—I mean the Universities of Oxford and Cambridge,—we hear little of Theology, Medicine, or Law, and almost exclusively of Arts.

Now, considering the reasonable association, to which I have already referred, which exists in our minds between Universities and the three learned professions, here is a phenomenon which has to be contemplated for its own sake and accounted for, as well as a circumstance enhancing the significance and importance of the act in which we have been for some weeks engaged; and I consider that I shall not be employing our time unprofitably, if I am able to make a suggestion, which, while it illustrates the fact, is able to explain the difficulty.

2.

Here I must go back, Gentlemen, a very great way, and ask you to review the course of Civilization since the beginning of history. When we survey the stream of human affairs for the last three thousand years, we find it to run thus:—At first sight there is so much fluctuation, agitation, ebbing and flowing, that we may despair to discern any law in its movements, taking the earth as its bed, and mankind as its contents; but, on looking more closely and attentively, we shall discern, in spite of the heterogeneous materials and the various histories and fortunes which are found in the race of man during the long period I have mentioned, a certain formation amid the chaos,—one and one only,—and extending, though not over the whole earth, yet through a very considerable portion of it. Man is a social being and can hardly exist without society, and in matter of fact societies have ever existed all over the habitable earth. The greater part of these associations have been political or religious, and have been comparatively limited in extent, and temporary. They have been formed and dissolved by the force of accidents or by inevitable circumstances; and, when we have enumerated them one by one, we have made of them all that can be made. But there is one remarkable association which attracts the attention of the philosopher, not political nor religious, or at least only partially and not essentially such, which began in the earliest times and grew with each succeeding age, till it reached its complete development, and then continued on, vigorous and unwearied, and which still remains as definite and as firm as ever it was. Its bond is a common civilization; and, though there are other civilizations in the world, as there are other societies, yet this civilization, together with the society which is its creation and its home, is so distinctive and luminous in its character, so imperial in its extent, so imposing in its duration, and so utterly without rival upon the face of the earth, that the association may fitly assume to itself the title of "Human Society," and its civilization the abstract term "Civilization."

There are indeed great outlying portions of mankind which are not, perhaps never have been, included in this Human Society; still they are outlying portions and nothing else, fragmentary, unsociable, solitary, and unmeaning, protesting and revolting against the grand central formation of which I am speaking, but not uniting with each other into a second whole. I am not denying of course the civilization of the Chinese, for instance, though it be not our civilization; but it is a huge, stationary, unattractive, morose civilization. Nor do I deny a civilization to the Hindoos, nor to the ancient Mexicans, nor to the Saracens, nor (in a certain sense) to the Turks; but each of these races has its own civilization, as separate from one another as from ours. I do not see how they can be all brought under one idea. Each stands by itself, as if the other were not; each is local; many of them are temporary; none of them will bear a comparison with the Society and the Civilization which I have described as alone having a claim to those names, and on which I am going to dwell.

Gentlemen, let me here observe that I am not entering upon the question of races, or upon their history. I have nothing to do with ethnology. I take things as I find them on the surface of history, and am but classing phenomena. Looking, then, at the countries which surround the Mediterranean Sea as a whole, I see them to be, from time immemorial, the seat of an association of intellect and mind, such as to deserve to be called the Intellect and the Mind of the Human Kind. Starting as it does and advancing from certain centres, till their respective influences intersect and conflict, and then at length intermingle and combine, a common Thought has been generated, and a common Civilization defined and established. Egypt is one such starting point, Syria another, Greece a third, Italy a fourth, and North Africa a fifth,—afterwards France and Spain. As time goes on, and as colonization and conquest work their changes, we see a great association of nations formed, of which the Roman empire is the maturity and the most intelligible expression; an association, however, not political, but mental, based on the same intellectual ideas, and advancing by common intellectual methods. And this association or social commonwealth, with whatever reverses, changes, and momentary dissolutions, continues down to this day; not, indeed, precisely on the same territory, but with such only partial and local disturbances, and on the other hand, with so combined and harmonious a movement, and such a visible continuity, that it would be utterly unreasonable to deny that it is throughout all that interval but one and the same.

In its earliest age it included far more of the eastern world than it has since; in these later times it has taken into its compass a new hemisphere; in the middle ages it lost Africa, Egypt, and Syria, and extended itself to Germany, Scandinavia, and the British Isles. At one time its territory was flooded by strange and barbarous races, but the existing civilization was vigorous enough to vivify what threatened to stifle it, and to assimilate to the old social forms what came to expel them; and thus the civilization of modern times remains what it was of old, not Chinese, or Hindoo, or Mexican, or Saracenic, or of any new description hitherto unknown, but the lineal descendant, or rather the continuation, *mutatis mutandis*, of the civilization which began in Palestine and Greece.

Considering, then, the characteristics of this great civilized Society, which I have already insisted on, I think it has a claim to be considered as the representative Society and Civilization of the human race, as its perfect result and limit, in fact;—those portions of the race which do not coalesce with it being left to stand by themselves as anomalies, unaccountable indeed, but for that very reason not interfering with what on the contrary has been turned to account and has grown into a whole. I call then this commonwealth pre-eminently and emphatically Human Society, and its intellect the Human Mind, and its decisions the sense of mankind, and its disciplined and cultivated state Civilization in the abstract, and the territory on which it lies the *orbis terrarum*, or the World. For, unless the illustration be fanciful, the object which I am contemplating is like the impression of a seal upon the wax; which rounds off and gives form to the greater portion of the soft material, and presents something definite to the eye, and preoccupies the space against any second figure, so that we overlook and leave out of our thoughts the jagged outline or unmeaning lumps outside of it, intent upon the harmonious circle which fills the imagination within it.

3.

Now, before going on to speak of the education, and the standards of education, which the Civilized World, as I may now call it, has enjoined and requires, I wish to draw your attention, Gentlemen, to the circumstance that this same *orbis terrarum*, which has been the seat of Civilization, will be found, on the whole, to be the seat also of that supernatural society and system which our Maker has given us directly from Himself, the Christian Polity. The natural and divine associations are not indeed exactly coincident, nor ever have been. As the territory of Civilization has varied with itself in different ages, while on the whole it has been the same, so, in like manner, Christianity has fallen partly outside Civilization, and Civilization partly outside Christianity; but, on the whole, the two have occupied one and the same *orbis terrarum*. Often indeed they have even moved *pari passu*, and at all times there has been found the most intimate connexion between them. Christianity waited till the *orbis terrarum* attained its most perfect form before it appeared; and it soon coalesced, and has ever since co-operated, and often seemed identical, with the Civilization which is its companion.

There are certain analogies, too, which hold between Civilization and Christianity. As Civilization does not cover the whole earth, neither does Christianity; but there is nothing else like the one, and nothing else like the other. Each is the only thing of its kind. Again, there are, as I have already said, large outlying portions of the world in a certain sense cultivated and educated, which, if they could exist together in one, would go far to constitute a second *orbis terrarum*, the home of a second distinct civilization; but every one of these is civilized on its own principle and idea, or at least they are separated from each other, and have not run together, while the Civilization and Society which I have been describing is one organized whole. And, in like manner, Christianity coalesces into one vast body, based upon common ideas; yet there are large outlying organizations of religion independent of each other and of it. Moreover, Christianity, as is the case in the parallel instance of Civilization, continues on in the world without interruption from the date of its rise, while other religious bodies, huge, local, and isolated, are rising and falling, or are helplessly stationary, from age to age, on all sides of it.

There is another remarkable analogy between Christianity and Civilization, and the mention of it will introduce my proper subject, to which what I have hitherto said is merely a preparation. We know that Christianity is built upon definite ideas, principles, doctrines, and writings, which were given at the time of its first introduction, and have never been superseded, and admit of no addition. I am not going to parallel any thing which is the work of man, and in the natural order, with what is from heaven, and in consequence infallible, and irreversible, and obligatory; but, after making this reserve, lest I should possibly be misunderstood, still I would remark that, in matter of fact, looking at the state of the case historically, Civilization too has its common principles, and views, and teaching, and especially its books, which have more or less been given from the earliest times, and are, in fact, in equal esteem and respect, in equal use now, as they were when they were received in the beginning. In a word, the Classics, and the subjects of thought and the studies to which they give rise, or, to use the term most to our present purpose, the Arts, have ever, on the whole, been the instruments of education which the civilized *orbis terrarum* has adopted; just as inspired works, and the lives of saints, and the articles of faith, and the catechism, have ever been the instrument of education in the case of Christianity. And this consideration, you see, Gentlemen (to drop down at once upon the subject proper to the occasion which has brought us together), invests the opening of the School in Arts with a solemnity and moment of a peculiar kind, for we are but reiterating an old tradition, and carrying on those august methods of enlarging the mind, and cultivating the intellect, and refining the feelings, in which the process of Civilization has ever consisted.

4.

In the country which has been the fountain head of intellectual gifts, in the age which preceded or introduced the first formations of Human Society, in an era scarcely historical, we may dimly discern an almost mythical personage, who, putting out of consideration the actors in Old Testament history, may be called the first Apostle of Civilization. Like an Apostle in a higher order of things, he was poor and a wanderer, and feeble in the flesh, though he was to do such great things, and to live in the mouths of a hundred generations and a thousand tribes. A blind old man; whose wanderings were such that, when he became famous, his birth-place could not be ascertained, so that it was said,—

> "Seven famous towns contend for Homer dead,
> Through which the living Homer begged his bread."

Yet he had a name in his day; and, little guessing in what vast measures his wish would be answered, he supplicated, with a tender human sentiment, as he wandered over the islands of the Ægean and the Asian coasts, that those who had known and loved him would cherish his memory when he was away. Unlike the proud boast of the Roman poet, if he spoke it in earnest, "Exegi monumentum ære perennius," he did but indulge the hope that one, whose coming had been expected with pleasure, might excite regret when he had departed, and be rewarded by the sympathy and praise of his friends even in the presence of other minstrels. A set of verses remains, which is ascribed to him, in which he addresses the Delian women in the tone of feeling which I have described. "Farewell to you all," he says, "and remember me in time to come, and when any one of men on earth, a stranger from far, shall inquire of you, O maidens, who is the sweetest of minstrels here about, and in whom do you most delight? then make answer modestly, It is a blind man, and he lives in steep Chios."

The great poet remained unknown for some centuries,—that is, unknown to what we call fame. His verses were cherished by his countrymen, they might be the secret delight of thousands, but they were not collected into a volume, nor viewed as a whole, nor made a subject of criticism. At length an Athenian Prince took upon him the task of gathering together the scattered fragments of a genius which had not aspired to immortality, of reducing them to writing, and of fitting them to be the text-book of ancient education. Henceforth the vagrant ballad-singer, as he might be thought, was submitted, to his surprise, to a sort of literary canonization, and was invested with the office of forming the young mind of Greece to noble thoughts and bold deeds. To be read in Homer soon became the education of a gentleman; and a rule, recognized in her free age, remained as a tradition even in the times of her degradation. Xenophon introduces to us a youth who knew both Iliad and Odyssey by heart; Dio witnesses that they were some of the first books put into the hands of boys; and Horace decided that they taught the science of life better than Stoic or Academic. Alexander the Great nourished his imagination by the scenes of the Iliad. As time went on, other poets were associated with Homer in the work of education, such as Hesiod and the Tragedians. The majestic lessons concerning duty and religion, justice and providence, which occur in Æschylus and Sophocles, belong to a higher school than that of Homer; and the verses of Euripides, even in his lifetime, were so familiar to Athenian lips and so dear to foreign ears, that, as is reported, the captives of Syracuse gained their freedom at the price of reciting them to their conquerors.

Such poetry may be considered oratory also, since it has so great a power of persuasion; and the alliance between these two gifts had existed from the time that the verses of Orpheus had, according to the fable, made woods and streams and wild animals to follow him about. Soon, however, Oratory became the subject of a separate art, which was called Rhetoric, and of which the Sophists were the chief masters. Moreover, as Rhetoric was especially political in its nature, it presupposed or introduced the cultivation of History; and thus the pages of Thucydides became one of the special studies by which Demosthenes rose to be the first orator of Greece.

But it is needless to trace out further the formation of the course of liberal education; it is sufficient to have given some specimens in illustration of it. The studies, which it was found to involve, were four principal ones, Grammar, Rhetoric, Logic, and Mathematics; and the science of Mathematics, again, was divided into four, Geometry, Arithmetic, Astronomy, and Music; making in all seven, which are known by the name of the Seven Liberal Arts. And thus a definite school of intellect was formed, founded on ideas and methods of a distinctive character, and (as we may say) of the highest and truest character, as far as they went, and which gradually associated in one, and assimilated, and took possession of, that multitude of nations which I have considered to represent mankind, and to possess the *orbis terrarum.*

When we pass from Greece to Rome, we are met with the common remark, that Rome produced little that was original, but borrowed from Greece. It is true; Terence copied from

Menander, Virgil from Homer, Hesiod, and Theocritus; and
Cicero professed merely to reproduce the philosophy of Greece.
But, granting its truth ever so far, I do but take it as a proof of the
sort of instinct which has guided the course of Civilization. The
world was to have certain intellectual teachers, and no others;
Homer and Aristotle, with the poets and philosophers who circle
round them, were to be the schoolmasters of all generations, and
therefore the Latins, falling into the law on which the world's
education was to be carried on, so added to the classical library
as not to reverse or interfere with what had already been determined. And there was the more meaning in this arrangement,
when it is considered that Greek was to be forgotten during
many centuries, and the tradition of intellectual training to be
conveyed through Latin; for thus the world was secured against
the consequences of a loss which would have changed the character of its civilization. I think it very remarkable, too, how soon
the Latin writers became text-books in the boys' schools. Even to
this day Shakespeare and Milton are not studied in our course
of education; but the poems of Virgil and Horace, as those of
Homer and the Greek authors in an earlier age, were in school-
boys' satchels not much more than a hundred years after they
were written.

I need not go on to show at length that they have preserved
their place in the system of education in the *orbis terrarum*, and
the Greek writers with them or through them, down to this day.
The induction of centuries has often been made. Even in the
lowest state of learning the tradition was kept up. St. Gregory the
Great, whose era, not to say whose influence, is often considered
especially unfavourable to the old literature, was himself well
versed in it, encouraged purity of Latinity in his court, and is
said figuratively by the contemporary historian of his life to have
supported the hall of the Apostolic See upon the columns of the
Seven Liberal Arts. In the ninth century, when the dark age was
close at hand, we still hear of the cultivation, with whatever success (according of course to the opportunities of the times, but I
am speaking of the nature of the studies, not of the proficiency

of the students), the cultivation of Music, Dialectics, Rhetoric, Grammar, Mathematics, Astronomy, Physics, and Geometry; of the supremacy of Horace in the schools, "and the great Virgil, Sallust, and Statius." In the thirteenth or following centuries, of "Virgil, Lucian, Statius, Ovid, Livy, Sallust, Cicero, and Quintilian;" and after the revival of literature in the commencement of the modern era, we find St. Carlo Borromeo enjoining the use of works of Cicero, Ovid, Virgil, and Horace.[2]

5.

I pass thus cursorily over the series of informations which history gives us on the subject, merely with a view of recalling to your memory, Gentlemen, and impressing upon you the fact, that the literature of Greece, continued into, and enriched by, the literature of Rome, together with the studies which it involves, has been the instrument of education, and the food of civilization, from the first times of the world down to this day;—and now we are in a condition to answer the question which thereupon arises, when we turn to consider, by way of contrast, the teaching which is characteristic of Universities. How has it come to pass that, although the genius of Universities is so different from that of the schools which preceded them, nevertheless the course of study pursued in those schools was not superseded in the middle ages by those more brilliant sciences which Universities introduced? It might have seemed as if Scholastic Theology, Law, and Medicine would have thrown the Seven Liberal Arts into the shade, but in the event they failed to do so. I consider the reason to be, that the authority and function of the monastic and secular schools, as supplying to the young the means of education, lay deeper than in any appointment of Charlemagne, who was their nominal founder, and were based in the special character of that civilization which is so intimately associated with Christianity, that it may even be called the soil out of which Christianity grew. The medieval sciences, great as is their dignity and utility, were never

2 *Vid.* the treatises of P. Daniel and Mgr. Landriot, referred to in Historical Sketches, vol. ii., p. 460, note.

intended to supersede that more real and proper cultivation of the mind which is effected by the study of the liberal Arts; and, when certain of these sciences did in fact go out of their province and did attempt to prejudice the traditional course of education, the encroachment was in matter of fact resisted. There were those in the middle age, as John of Salisbury, who vigorously protested against the extravagances and usurpations which ever attend the introduction of any great good whatever, and which attended the rise of the peculiar sciences of which Universities were the seat; and, though there were times when the old traditions seemed to be on the point of failing, somehow it has happened that they have never failed; for the instinct of Civilization and the common sense of Society prevailed, and the danger passed away, and the studies which seemed to be going out gained their ancient place, and were acknowledged, as before, to be the best instruments of mental cultivation, and the best guarantees for intellectual progress.

And this experience of the past we may apply to the circumstances in which we find ourselves at present; for, as there was a movement against the Classics in the middle age, so has there been now. The truth of the Baconian method for the purposes for which it was created, and its inestimable services and inexhaustible applications in the interests of our material well-being, have dazzled the imaginations of men, somewhat in the same way as certain new sciences carried them away in the age of Abelard; and since that method does such wonders in its own province, it is not unfrequently supposed that it can do as much in any other province also. Now, Bacon himself never would have so argued; he would not have needed to be reminded that to advance the useful arts is one thing, and to cultivate the mind another. The simple question to be considered is, how best to strengthen, refine, and enrich the intellectual powers; the perusal of the poets, historians, and philosophers of Greece and Rome will accomplish this purpose, as long experience has shown; but that the study of the experimental sciences will do the like, is proved to us as yet by no experience whatever.

Far indeed am I from denying the extreme attractiveness, as well as the practical benefit to the world at large, of the sciences of Chemistry, Electricity, and Geology; but the question is not what department of study contains the more wonderful facts, or promises the more brilliant discoveries, and which is in the higher and which in an inferior rank; but simply which out of all provides the most robust and invigorating discipline for the unformed mind. And I conceive it is as little disrespectful to Lord Bacon to prefer the Classics in this point of view to the sciences which have grown out of his philosophy as it would be disrespectful to St. Thomas in the middle ages to have hindered the study of the Summa from doing prejudice to the Faculty of Arts. Accordingly, I anticipate that, as in the middle ages both the teaching and the government of the University remained in the Faculty of Arts, in spite of the genius which created or illus-trated Theology and Law, so now too, whatever be the splendour of the modern philosophy, the marvellousness of its disclosures, the utility of its acquisitions, and the talent of its masters, still it will not avail in the event, to detrude classical literature and the studies connected with it from the place which they have held in all ages in education.

Such, then, is the course of reflection obviously suggested by the act in which we have been lately engaged, and which we are now celebrating. In the nineteenth century, in a country which looks out upon a new world, and anticipates a coming age, we have been engaged in opening the Schools dedicated to the stud-ies of polite literature and liberal science, or what are called the Arts, as a first step towards the establishment on Catholic ground of a Catholic University. And while we thus recur to Greece and Athens with pleasure and affection, and recognize in that famous land the source and the school of intellectual culture, it would be strange indeed if we forgot to look further south also, and there to bow before a more glorious luminary, and a more sacred oracle of truth, and the source of another sort of knowledge, high and supernatural, which is seated in Palestine. Jerusalem is the fountain-head of religious knowledge, as Athens is of secular.

In the ancient world we see two centres of illumination, acting independently of each other, each with its own movement, and at first apparently without any promise of convergence. Greek civilization spreads over the East, conquering in the conquests of Alexander, and, when carried captive into the West, subdues the conquerors who brought it thither. Religion, on the other hand, is driven from its own aboriginal home to the North and West by reason of the sins of the people who were in charge of it, in a long course of judgments and plagues and persecutions. Each by itself pursues its career and fulfils its mission; neither of them recognizes, nor is recognized by the other. At length the Temple of Jerusalem is rooted up by the armies of Titus, and the effete schools of Athens are stifled by the edict of Justinian. So pass away the ancient Voices of religion and learning; but they are silenced only to revive more gloriously and perfectly elsewhere. Hitherto they came from separate sources, and performed separate works. Each leaves an heir and successor in the West, and that heir and successor is one and the same. The grace stored in Jerusalem, and the gifts which radiate from Athens, are made over and concentrated in Rome. This is true as a matter of history. Rome has inherited both sacred and profane learning; she has perpetuated and dispensed the traditions of Moses and David in the supernatural order, and of Homer and Aristotle in the natural. To separate those distinct teachings, human and divine, which meet in Rome, is to retrograde; it is to rebuild the Jewish Temple and to plant anew the groves of Academus.

6.

On this large subject, however, on which I might say much, time does not allow me to enter. To show how sacred learning and profane are dependent on each other, correlative and mutually complementary, how faith operates by means of reason, and reason is directed and corrected by faith, is really the subject of a distinct lecture. I would conclude, then, with merely congratulating you, Gentlemen, on the great undertaking which we have so auspiciously commenced. Whatever be its fortunes, whatever its difficulties, whatever its delays, I cannot doubt at all that the encouragement which it has already received, and the measure of success which it has been allotted, are but a presage and an anticipation of a gradual advance towards its completion, in such times and such manner as Providence shall appoint. For myself, I have never had any misgiving about it, because I had never known anything of it before the time when the Holy See had definitely decided upon its prosecution. It is my happiness to have no cognizance of the anxieties and perplexities of venerable and holy prelates, or the discussions of experienced and prudent men, which preceded its definitive recognition on the part of the highest ecclesiastical authority. It is my happiness to have no experience of the time when good Catholics despaired of its success, distrusted its expediency, or even felt an obligation to oppose it. It has been my happiness that I have never been in controversy with persons in this country external to the Catholic Church, nor have been forced into any direct collision with institutions or measures which rest on a foundation hostile to Catholicism. No one can accuse me of any disrespect towards those whose principles or whose policy I disapprove; nor am I conscious of any other aim than that of working in my own place, without going out of my way to offend others. If I have taken part in the undertaking which has now brought us together, it has been because I believed it was a great work, great in its conception, great in its promise, and great in the authority from which it proceeds. I felt it to be so great that I did not dare to incur the responsibility of refusing to take part in it.

How far indeed, and how long, I am to be connected with it, is another matter altogether. It is enough for one man to lay only one stone of so noble and grand an edifice; it is enough, more than enough for me, if I do so much as merely begin, what others may more hopefully continue. One only among the sons of men has carried out a perfect work, and satisfied and exhausted the mission on which He came. One alone has with His last breath said "Consummatum est." But all who set about their duties in faith and hope and love, with a resolute heart and a devoted will, are able, weak though they be, to do what, though incomplete, is imperishable. Even their failures become successes, as being necessary steps in a course, and as terms (so to say) in a long series, which will at length fulfil the object which they propose. And they will unite themselves in spirit, in their humble degree, with those real heroes of Holy Writ and ecclesiastical history, Moses, Elias, and David, Basil, Athanasius, and Chrysostom, Gregory the Seventh, St. Thomas of Canterbury, and many others, who did most when they fancied themselves least prosperous, and died without being permitted to see the fruit of their labours.

II.

LITERATURE

1.

Wishing to address you, Gentlemen, at the commencement of a
new Session, I tried to find a subject for discussion, which might
be at once suitable to the occasion, yet neither too large for your
time, nor too minute or abstruse for your attention. I think I
see one for my purpose in the very title of your Faculty. It is the
Faculty of Philosophy and Letters. Now the question may arise
as to what is meant by "Philosophy," and what is meant by "Letters." As to the other Faculties, the subject-matter which they
profess is intelligible, as soon as named, and beyond all dispute.
We know what Science is, what Medicine, what Law, and what
Theology; but we have not so much ease in determining what
is meant by Philosophy and Letters. Each department of that
twofold province needs explanation: it will be sufficient, on an
occasion like this, to investigate one of them. Accordingly I shall
select for remark the latter of the two, and attempt to determine
what we are to understand by Letters or Literature, in what Literature consists, and how it stands relatively to Science. We speak,
for instance, of ancient and modern literature, the literature of
the day, sacred literature, light literature; and our lectures in this
place are devoted to classical literature and English literature. Are
Letters, then, synonymous with books? This cannot be, or they
would include in their range Philosophy, Law, and, in short, the
teaching of all the other Faculties. Far from confusing these various studies, we view the works of Plato or Cicero sometimes as
philosophy, sometimes as literature; on the other hand, no one
would ever be tempted to speak of Euclid as literature, or of

Matthiæ's Greek Grammar. Is, then, literature synonymous with composition? with books written with an attention to style? is literature fine writing? again, is it studied and artificial writing?

There are excellent persons who seem to adopt this last account of Literature as their own idea of it. They depreciate it, as if it were the result of a mere art or trick of words. Professedly indeed, they are aiming at the Greek and Roman classics, but their criticisms have quite as great force against all literature as against any. I think I shall be best able to bring out what I have to say on the subject by examining the statements which they make in defence of their own view of it. They contend then, 1. that fine writing, as exemplified in the Classics, is mainly a matter of conceits, fancies, and prettinesses, decked out in choice words; 2. that this is the proof of it, that the classics will not bear translating;—(and this is why I have said that the real attack is upon literature altogether, not the classical only; for, to speak generally, all literature, modern as well as ancient, lies under this disadvantage. This, however, they will not allow; for they maintain,) 3. that Holy Scripture presents a remarkable contrast to secular writings on this very point, viz., in that Scripture does easily admit of translation, though it is the most sublime and beautiful of all writings.

2.

Now I will begin by stating these three positions in the words of a writer, who is cited by the estimable Catholics in question as a witness, or rather as an advocate, in their behalf, though he is far from being able in his own person to challenge the respect which is inspired by themselves.

"There are two sorts of eloquence," says this writer, "the one indeed scarce deserves the name of it, which consists chiefly in laboured and polished periods, an over-curious and artificial arrangement of figures, tinselled over with a gaudy embellishment of words, which glitter, but convey little or no light to the understanding. This kind of writing is for the most part much affected and admired by the people of weak judgment and vicious taste;

but it is a piece of affectation and formality the sacred writers are utter strangers to. It is a vain and boyish eloquence; and, as it has always been esteemed below the great geniuses of all ages, so much more so with respect to those writers who were actuated by the spirit of Infinite Wisdom, and therefore wrote with that force and majesty with which never man writ. The other sort of eloquence is quite the reverse to this, and which may be said to be the true characteristic of the Holy Scriptures; where the excellence does not arise from a laboured and far-fetched elocution, but from a surprising mixture of simplicity and majesty, which is a double character, so difficult to be united that it is seldom to be met with in compositions merely human. We see nothing in Holy Writ of affectation and superfluous ornament ... Now, it is observable that the most excellent profane authors, whether Greek or Latin, lose most of their graces whenever we find them literally translated. Homer's famed representation of Jupiter—his cried-up description of a tempest, his relation of Neptune's shaking the earth and opening it to its centre, his description of Pallas's horses, with numbers of other long-since admired passages, flag, and almost vanish away, in the vulgar Latin translation.

"Let any one but take the pains to read the common Latin interpretations of Virgil, Theocritus, or even of Pindar, and one may venture to affirm he will be able to trace out but few remains of the graces which charmed him so much in the original. The natural conclusion from hence is, that in the classical authors, the expression, the sweetness of the numbers, occasioned by a musical placing of words, constitute a great part of their beauties; whereas, in the sacred writings, they consist more in the greatness of the things themselves than in the words and expressions. The ideas and conceptions are so great and lofty in their own nature that they necessarily appear magnificent in the most artless dress. Look but into the Bible, and we see them shine through the most simple and literal translations. That glorious description which Moses gives of the creation of the heavens and the earth, which Longinus ... was so greatly taken with, has not lost the least whit of its intrinsic worth, and though it has undergone so many translations, yet triumphs over all, and breaks forth with as much force and vehemence as in the original … In the history of Joseph, where Joseph makes himself known, and weeps aloud upon the neck of his dear brother Benjamin, that all the house of Pharaoh heard him, at that instant none of his brethren are introduced as uttering aught, either to express their present joy or palliate their former injuries to him. On all sides there immediately ensues a deep and solemn silence; a silence infinitely more eloquent and expressive than anything else that could have been substituted in its place. Had Thucydides, Herodotus, Livy, or any of the celebrated classical historians, been employed in writing this history, when they came to this point they would doubtless have exhausted all their fund of eloquence in furnishing Joseph's brethren with laboured and studied harangues, which, however fine they might have been in themselves, would nevertheless have been unnatural, and altogether improper on the occasion."[1]

This is eloquently written, but it contains, I consider, a mixture of truth and falsehood, which it will be my business to discriminate from each other. Far be it from me to deny the unapproachable grandeur and simplicity of Holy Scripture; but I shall maintain that the classics are, as human compositions, simple and majestic and natural too. I grant that Scripture is concerned with things, but I will not grant that classical literature is simply concerned with words. I grant that human literature is often elaborate, but I will maintain that elaborate composition is not unknown to the writers of Scripture. I grant that human literature cannot easily be translated out of the particular language to which it belongs; but it is not at all the rule that Scripture can easily be translated either;—and now I address myself to my task:—

3.

Here, then, in the first place, I observe, Gentlemen, that Literature, from the derivation of the word, implies writing, not speaking; this, however, arises from the circumstance of the copi-

---

1   Sterne, Sermon xlii.

ousness, variety, and public circulation of the matters of which it consists. What is spoken cannot outrun the range of the speaker's voice, and perishes in the uttering. When words are in demand to express a long course of thought, when they have to be conveyed to the ends of the earth, or perpetuated for the benefit of posterity, they must be written down, that is, reduced to the shape of literature; still, properly speaking, the terms, by which we denote this characteristic gift of man, belong to its exhibition by means of the voice, not of handwriting. It addresses itself in its primary idea, to the ear, not to the eye. We call it the power of speech, we call it language, that is, the use of the tongue; and, even when we write, we still keep in mind what was its original instrument, for we use freely such terms in our books as "saying," "speaking," "telling," "talking," "calling;" we use the terms "phraseology" and "diction;" as if we were still addressing ourselves to the ear.

Now I insist on this, because it shows that speech, and therefore literature, which is its permanent record, is essentially a personal work, it is not some production or result, attained by the partnership of several persons, or by machinery, or by any natural process, but in its very idea it proceeds, and must proceed, from some one given individual. Two persons cannot be the authors of the sounds which strike our ear; and, as they cannot be speaking one and the same speech, neither can they be writing one and the same lecture or discourse,—which must certainly belong to some one person or other, and is the expression of that one person's ideas and feelings,—ideas and feelings personal to himself, though others may have parallel and similar ones,—proper to himself in the same sense as his voice, his air, his countenance, his carriage, and his action, are personal. In other words, Literature expresses, not objective truth, as it is called, but subjective; not things, but thoughts.

Now this doctrine will become clearer by considering another use of words, which does relate to objective truth, or to things; which relates to matters, not personal, not subjective to the individual, but which, even were there no individual man in the whole world to know them or to talk about them, would exist still. Such objects become the matter of Science, and words indeed are used to express them, but such words are rather symbols than language, and however many we use, and however we may perpetuate them by writing, we never could make any kind of literature out of them, or call them by that name. Such, for instance, would be Euclid's Elements; they relate to truths universal and eternal; they are not mere thoughts, but things: they exist in themselves, not by virtue of our understanding them, not in dependence upon our will, but in what is called the *nature* of things, or at least on conditions external to us. The words, then, in which they are set forth are not language, speech, literature, but rather, as I have said, symbols. And, as a proof of it, you will recollect that it is possible, nay usual, to set forth the propositions of Euclid in algebraical notation, which, as all would admit, has nothing to do with literature. What is true of mathematics is true also of every study, so far forth as it is scientific; it makes use of words as the mere vehicle of things, and is thereby withdrawn from the province of literature. Thus metaphysics, ethics, law, political economy, chemistry, theology, cease to be literature in the same degree as they are capable of a severe scientific treatment. And hence it is that Aristotle's works on the one hand, though at first sight literature, approach in character, at least a great number of them, to mere science; for even though the things which he treats of and exhibits may not always be real and true, yet he treats them as if they were, not as if they were the thoughts of his own mind; that is, he treats them scientifically. On the other hand, Law or Natural History has before now been treated by an author with so much of colouring derived from his own mind as to become a sort of literature; this is especially seen in the instance of Theology, when it takes the shape of Pulpit Eloquence. It is seen too in historical composition, which becomes a mere specimen of chronology, or a chronicle, when divested of the philosophy, the skill, or the party and personal feelings of the particular writer. Science, then, has to do with things, literature with thoughts; science is universal, literature is personal; science uses words merely as symbols, but literature uses language in its full compass, as including phraseology, idiom, style, composition, rhythm, eloquence, and whatever other properties are included in it.

Let us then put aside the scientific use of words, when we are to speak of language and literature. Literature is the personal use or exercise of language. That this is so is further proved from the fact that one author uses it so differently from another. Language itself in its very origination would seem to be traceable to individuals. Their peculiarities have given it its character. We are often able in fact to trace particular phrases or idioms to individuals; we know the history of their rise. Slang surely, as it is called, comes of, and breathes of the personal. The connection between the force of words in particular languages and the habits and sentiments of the nations speaking them has often been pointed out. And, while the many use language as they find it, the man of genius uses it indeed, but subjects it withal to his own purposes, and moulds it according to his own peculiarities. The throng and succession of ideas, thoughts, feelings, imaginations, aspirations, which pass within him, the abstractions, the juxtapositions, the comparisons, the discriminations, the conceptions, which are so original in him, his views of external things, his judgments upon life, manners, and history, the exercises of his wit, of his humour, of his depth, of his sagacity, all these innumerable and incessant creations, the very pulsation and throbbing of his intellect, does he image forth, to all does he give utterance, in a corresponding language, which is as multiform as this inward mental action itself and analogous to it, the faithful expression of his intense personality, attending on his own inward world of thought as its very shadow: so that we might as well say that one man's shadow is another's as that the style of a really gifted mind can belong to any but himself. It follows him about *as* a shadow. His thought and feeling are personal, and so his language is personal.

4.

Thought and speech are inseparable from each other. Matter and expression are parts of one: style is a thinking out into language.

This is what I have been laying down, and this is literature; not *things*, not the verbal symbols of things; not on the other hand mere *words*; but thoughts expressed in language. Call to mind, Gentlemen, the meaning of the Greek word which expresses this special prerogative of man over the feeble intelligence of the inferior animals. It is called Logos: what does Logos mean? it stands both for *reason* and for *speech*, and it is difficult to say which it means more properly. It means both at once: why? because really they cannot be divided,—because they are in a true sense one. When we can separate light and illumination, life and motion, the convex and the concave of a curve, then will it be possible for thought to tread speech under foot, and to hope to do without it—then will it be conceivable that the vigorous and fertile intellect should renounce its own double, its instrument of expression, and the channel of its speculations and emotions.

Critics should consider this view of the subject before they lay down such canons of taste as the writer whose pages I have quoted. Such men as he is consider fine writing to be an *addition from without* to the matter treated of,—a sort of ornament superinduced, or a luxury indulged in, by those who have time and inclination for such vanities. They speak as if *one* man could do the thought, and *another* the style. We read in Persian travels of the way in which young gentlemen go to work in the East, when they would engage in correspondence with those who inspire them with hope or fear. They cannot write one sentence themselves; so they betake themselves to the professional letter-writer. They confide to him the object they have in view. They have a point to gain from a superior, a favour to ask, an evil to deprecate; they have to approach a man in power, or to make court to some beautiful lady. The professional man manufactures words for them, as they are wanted, as a stationer sells them paper, or a schoolmaster might cut their pens. Thought and word are, in their conception, two things, and thus there is a division of labour. The man of thought comes to the man of words; and the man of words, duly instructed in the thought, dips the pen of desire into the ink of devotedness, and proceeds to spread it over the page of desolation. Then the nightingale of affection is heard to warble to the rose of loveliness, while the breeze of anxiety plays around the brow of expectation. This is what the Easterns are said to consider fine writing; and it seems pretty much the idea of the school of critics to whom I have been referring.

We have an instance in literary history of this very proceeding nearer home, in a great University, in the latter years of the last century. I have referred to it before now in a public lecture else-where;[2] but it is too much in point here to be omitted. A learned Arabic scholar had to deliver a set of lectures before its doctors and professors on an historical subject in which his reading had lain. A linguist is conversant with science rather than with litera-ture; but this gentleman felt that his lectures must not be without a style. Being of the opinion of the Orientals, with whose writ-ings he was familiar, he determined to buy a style. He took the step of engaging a person, at a price, to turn the matter which he had got together into ornamental English. Observe, he did not wish for mere grammatical English, but for an elaborate, preten-tious style. An artist was found in the person of a country curate, and the job was carried out. His lectures remain to this day, in their own place in the protracted series of annual Discourses to which they belong, distinguished amid a number of heavyish compositions by the rhetorical and ambitious diction for which he went into the market. This learned divine, indeed, and the author I have quoted, differ from each other in the estimate they respectively form of literary composition; but they agree together in this,—in considering such composition a trick and a trade; they cut it on a par with the gold plate and the flowers and the music of a banquet, which do not make the viands better, but the entertainment more pleasurable; as if language were the hired servant, the mere mistress of the reason, and not the lawful wife in her own house.

But can they really think that Homer, or Pindar, or Shake-speare, or Dryden, or Walter Scott, were accustomed to aim at

---

2 "Position of Catholics in England," pp. 101-2.

diction for its own sake, instead of being inspired with their subject, and pouring forth beautiful words because they had beautiful thoughts? this is surely too great a paradox to be borne. Rather, it is the fire within the author's breast which overflows in the torrent of his burning, irresistible eloquence; it is the poetry of his inner soul, which relieves itself in the Ode or the Elegy; and his mental attitude and bearing, the beauty of his moral countenance, the force and keenness of his logic, are imaged in the tenderness, or energy, or richness of his language. Nay, according to the well-known line, "facit indignatio *versus*;" not the words alone, but even the rhythm, the metre, the verse, will be the contemporaneous offspring of the emotion or imagination which possesses him. "Poeta nascitur, non fit," says the proverb; and this is in numerous instances true of his poems, as well as of himself. They are born, not framed; they are a strain rather than a composition; and their perfection is the monument, not so much of his skill as of his power. And this is true of prose as well as of verse in its degree: who will not recognize in the vision of Mirza a delicacy and beauty of style which is very difficult to describe, but which is felt to be in exact correspondence to the ideas of which it is the expression?

5.

And, since the thoughts and reasonings of an author have, as I have said, a personal character, no wonder that his style is not only the image of his subject, but of his mind. That pomp of language, that full and tuneful diction, that felicitousness in the choice and exquisiteness in the collocation of words, which to prosaic writers seems artificial, is nothing else but the mere habit and way of a lofty intellect. Aristotle, in his sketch of the magnanimous man, tells us that his voice is deep, his motions slow, and his stature commanding. In like manner, the elocution of a great intellect is great. His language expresses, not only his great thoughts, but his great self. Certainly he might use fewer words than he uses; but he fertilizes his simplest ideas, and germinates into a multitude of details, and prolongs the march of his sentences, and sweeps round to the full diapason of his harmony, as if κύδεϊ γαίων, rejoicing in his own vigour and richness of resource. I say, a narrow critic will call it verbiage, when really it is a sort of fulness of heart, parallel to that which makes the merry boy whistle as he walks, or the strong man, like the smith in the novel, flourish his club when there is no one to fight with.

Shakespeare furnishes us with frequent instances of this peculiarity, and all so beautiful, that it is difficult to select for quotation. For instance, in Macbeth:—

> "Canst thou not minister to a mind diseased,
>   Pluck from the memory a rooted sorrow,
>   Raze out the written troubles of the brain,
>   And, with some sweet oblivious antidote,
>   Cleanse the foul bosom of that perilous stuff,
>   Which weighs upon the heart?"

Here a simple idea, by a process which belongs to the orator rather than to the poet, but still comes from the native vigour of genius, is expanded into a many-membered period.

The following from Hamlet is of the same kind:—

> "'Tis not alone my inky cloak, good mother,
>   Nor customary suits of solemn black,
>   Nor windy suspiration of forced breath,
>   No, nor the fruitful river in the eye,
>   Nor the dejected haviour of the visage,
>   Together with all forms, modes, shows of grief,
>   That can denote me truly."

Now, if such declamation, for declamation it is, however noble, be allowable in a poet, whose genius is so far removed from pompousness or pretence, much more is it allowable in an orator, whose very province it is to put forth words to the best advantage he can. Cicero has nothing more redundant in any part of his writings than these passages from Shakespeare. No lover then at least of Shakespeare may fairly accuse Cicero of gorgeousness of phraseology or diffuseness of style. Nor will any sound critic be tempted to do so. As a certain unaffected neatness and propriety and grace of diction may be required of any author who lays claim to be a classic, for the same reason that a certain attention to dress is expected of every gentleman, so to Cicero may be allowed the privilege of the "os magna sonaturum," of which the ancient critic speaks. His copious, majestic, musical flow of language, even if sometimes beyond what the subject-matter demands, is never out of keeping with the occasion or with the speaker. It is the expression of lofty sentiments in lofty sentences, the "mens magna in corpore magno." It is the development of the inner man. Cicero vividly realised the *status* of a Roman senator and statesman, and the "pride of place" of Rome, in all the grace and grandeur which attached to her; and he imbibed, and became what he admired. As the exploits of Scipio or Pompey are the expression of this greatness in deed, so the language of Cicero is the expression of it in word. And, as the acts of the Roman ruler or soldier represent to us, in a manner special to themselves, the characteristic magnanimity of the lords of the earth, so do the speeches or treatises of her accomplished orator bring it home to our imaginations as no other writing could do. Neither Livy, nor Tacitus, nor Terence, nor Seneca, nor Pliny, nor Quintilian, is an adequate spokesman for the Imperial City. They write Latin; Cicero writes Roman.

6.

You will say that Cicero's language is undeniably studied, but that Shakespeare's is as undeniably natural and spontaneous; and that this is what is meant, when the Classics are accused of being mere artists of words. Here we are introduced to a further large question, which gives me the opportunity of anticipating a misapprehension of my meaning. I observe, then, that, not only is that lavish richness of style, which I have noticed in Shakespeare, justifiable on the principles which I have been laying down, but, what is less easy to receive, even elaborateness in composition is no mark of trick or artifice in an author. Undoubtedly the works of the Classics, particularly the Latin, *are* elaborate; they have cost a great deal of time, care, and trouble. They have had many rough copies; I grant it. I grant also that there are writers of name, ancient and modern, who really are guilty of the absurdity of making sentences, as the very end of their literary labour. Such was Isocrates; such were some of the sophists; they were set on words, to the neglect of thoughts or things; I cannot defend them. If I must give an English instance of this fault, much as I love and revere the personal character and intellectual vigour of Dr. Johnson, I cannot deny that his style often outruns the sense and the occasion, and is wanting in that simplicity which is the attribute of genius. Still, granting all this, I cannot grant, notwithstanding, that genius never need take pains,—that genius may not improve by practice,—that it never incurs failures, and succeeds the second time,—that it never finishes off at leisure what it has thrown off in the outline at a stroke.

Take the instance of the painter or the sculptor; he has a conception in his mind which he wishes to represent in the medium of his art;—the Madonna and Child, or Innocence, or Fortitude, or some historical character or event. Do you mean to say he does not study his subject? does he not make sketches? does he not even call them "studies"? does he not call his workroom a *studio?* is he not ever designing, rejecting, adopting, correcting, perfecting? Are not the first attempts of Michael Angelo and Raffaelle extant, in the case of some of their most celebrated compositions? Will any one say that the Apollo Belvidere is not a conception patiently elaborated into its proper perfection? These departments of taste are, according to the received notions of the world, the very province of genius, and yet we call them *arts*; they are the "Fine Arts." Why may not that be true of literary composition which is true of painting, sculpture, architecture, and music? Why may not language be wrought as well as the clay of the modeller? why may not words be worked up as well as colours? why should not skill in diction be simply subservient and instrumental to the great prototypal ideas which are the contemplation of a Plato or a Virgil? Our greatest poet tells us,

"The poet's eye, in a fine frenzy rolling,
  Doth glance from heaven to earth, from earth to heaven,
  And, as imagination bodies forth
  The forms of things unknown, the poet's pen
  Turns them to shapes, and gives to airy nothing
  A local habitation and a name."

Now, is it wonderful that that pen of his should sometimes be at fault for a while,—that it should pause, write, erase, re-write, amend, complete, before he satisfies himself that his language has done justice to the conceptions which his mind's eye contemplated?

In this point of view, doubtless, many or most writers are elaborate; and those certainly not the least whose style is furthest removed from ornament, being simple and natural, or vehement, or severely business-like and practical. Who so energetic and manly as Demosthenes? Yet he is said to have transcribed Thucydides many times over in the formation of his style. Who so gracefully natural as Herodotus? yet his very dialect is not his own, but chosen for the sake of the perfection of his narrative. Who exhibits such happy negligence as our own Addison? yet artistic fastidiousness was so notorious in his instance that the report has got abroad, truly or not, that he was too late in his issue of an important state-paper, from his habit of revision and re-composition. Such great authors were working by a model which was before the eyes of their intellect, and they were labouring to say what they had to say, in such a way as would most exactly and suitably express it. It is not wonderful that other authors, whose style is not simple, should be instances of a similar literary diligence. Virgil wished his Æneid to be burned, elaborate as is its composition, because he felt it needed more labour still, in order to make it perfect. The historian Gibbon in the last century is another instance in point. You must not suppose I am going to recommend his style for imitation, any more than his principles; but I refer to him as the example of a writer feeling the task which lay before him, feeling that he had to bring out into words for the comprehension of his readers a great and complicated scene, and wishing that those words should be adequate to his undertaking. I think he wrote the first chapter of his History three times over; it was not that he corrected or improved the first copy; but he put his first essay, and then his second, aside—he recast his matter, till he had hit the precise exhibition of it which he thought demanded by his subject.

Now in all these instances, I wish you to observe, that what I have admitted about literary workmanship differs from the doctrine which I am opposing in this,—that the mere dealer in words cares little or nothing for the subject which he is embellishing, but can paint and gild anything whatever to order; whereas the artist, whom I am acknowledging, has his great or rich visions before him, and his only aim is to bring out what he thinks or what he feels in a way adequate to the thing spoken of, and appropriate to the speaker.

7.

The illustration which I have been borrowing from the Fine Arts will enable me to go a step further. I have been showing the connection of the thought with the language in literary composition; and in doing so I have exposed the unphilosophical notion, that the language was an extra which could be dispensed with, and provided to order according to the demand. But I have not yet brought out, what immediately follows from this, and which was the second point which I had to show, viz., that to be capable of easy translation is no test of the excellence of a composition. If I must say what I think, I should lay down, with little hesitation, that the truth was almost the reverse of this doctrine. Nor are many words required to show it. Such a doctrine, as is contained in the passage of the author whom I quoted when I began, goes upon the assumption that one language is just like another language,—that every language has all the ideas, turns of thought, delicacies of expression, figures, associations, abstractions, points of view, which every other language has. Now, as far as regards Science, it is true that all languages are pretty much alike for the purposes of Science; but even in this respect some are more suitable than others, which have to coin words, or to borrow them, in order to express scientific ideas. But if languages are not all equally adapted even to furnish symbols for those universal and eternal truths in which Science consists, how can they reasonably be expected to be all equally rich, equally forcible, equally musical, equally exact, equally happy in expressing the idiosyncratic peculiarities of thought of some original and fertile mind, who has availed himself of one of them? A great author takes his native language, masters it, partly throws himself into it, partly moulds and adapts it, and pours out his multitude of ideas through the variously ramified and delicately minute channels of expression which he has found or framed:—does it follow that this his personal presence (as it may be called) can forthwith be transferred to every other language under the sun? Then may we reasonably maintain that Beethoven's *piano* music is not really beautiful, because it cannot be played on the hurdy-gurdy. Were not this astonishing doctrine maintained by persons far superior to the writer whom I have selected for animadversion, I should find it difficult to be patient under a gratuitous extravagance. It seems that a really great author must admit of translation, and that we have a test of his excellence when he reads to advantage in a foreign language as well as in his own. Then Shakespeare *is* a genius because he can be translated into German, and *not* a genius because he cannot be translated into French. Then the multiplication-table is the most gifted of all conceivable compositions, because it loses nothing by translation, and can hardly be said to belong to any one language whatever. Whereas I should rather have conceived that, in proportion as ideas are novel and recondite, they would be difficult to put into words, and that the very fact of their having insinuated themselves into one language would diminish the chance of that happy accident being repeated in another. In the language of savages you can hardly express any idea or act of the intellect at all: is the tongue of the Hottentot or Esquimaux to be made the measure of the genius of Plato, Pindar, Tacitus, St. Jerome, Dante, or Cervantes?

Let us recur, I say, to the illustration of the Fine Arts. I suppose you can express ideas in painting which you cannot express in sculpture; and the more an artist is of a painter, the less he is likely to be of a sculptor. The more he commits his genius to the methods and conditions of his own art, the less he will be able to throw himself into the circumstances of another. Is the genius of Fra Angelico, of Francia, or of Raffaelle disparaged by the fact that he was able to do that in colours which no man that ever lived, which no Angel, could achieve in wood? Each of the Fine Arts has its own subject-matter; from the nature of the case you can do in one what you cannot do in another; you can do in painting what you cannot do in carving; you can do in oils what you cannot do in fresco; you can do in marble what you cannot do in ivory; you can do in wax what you cannot do in bronze. Then, I repeat, applying this to the case of languages, why should not genius be able to do in Greek what it cannot do in Latin? and why are its Greek and Latin works defective because they will not turn into English? That genius, of which we are speaking, did not make English; it did not make all languages, present, past, and future; it did not make the laws of *any* language: why is it to be judged of by that in which it had no part, over which it has no control?

8.

And now we are naturally brought on to our third point, which is on the characteristics of Holy Scripture as compared with profane literature. Hitherto we have been concerned with the doctrine of these writers, viz., that style is an *extra*, that it is a mere artifice, and that hence it cannot be translated; now we come to their fact, viz., that Scripture has no such artificial style, and that Scripture can easily be translated. Surely their fact is as untenable as their doctrine.

Scripture easy of translation! then why have there been so few good translators? why is it that there has been such great difficulty in combining the two necessary qualities, fidelity to the original and purity in the adopted vernacular? why is it that the authorized versions of the Church are often so inferior to the original as compositions, except that the Church is bound above all things to see that the version is doctrinally correct, and in a difficult problem is obliged to put up with defects in what is of secondary importance, provided she secure what is of first? If it were so easy to transfer the beauty of the original to the copy, she would not have been content with her received version in various languages which could be named.

And then in the next place, Scripture not elaborate! Scripture not ornamented in diction, and musical in cadence! Why, consider the Epistle to the Hebrews—where is there in the classics any composition more carefully, more artificially written? Consider the book of Job—is it not a sacred drama, as artistic, as perfect, as any Greek tragedy of Sophocles or Euripides? Consider the Psalter—are there no ornaments, no rhythm, no studied cadences, no responsive members, in that divinely beautiful book? And is it not hard to understand? are not the Prophets hard to understand? is not St. Paul hard to understand? Who can say that these are popular compositions? who can say that they are level at first reading with the understandings of the multitude?

That there are portions indeed of the inspired volume more simple both in style and in meaning, and that these are the more sacred and sublime passages, as, for instance, parts of the Gospels, I grant at once; but this does not militate against the doctrine I have been laying down. Recollect, Gentlemen, my distinction when I began. I have said Literature is one thing, and that Science is another; that Literature has to do with ideas, and Science with realities; that Literature is of a personal character, that Science treats of what is universal and eternal. In proportion, then, as Scripture excludes the personal colouring of its writers, and rises into the region of pure and mere inspiration, when it ceases in any sense to be the writing of man, of St. Paul or St. John, of Moses or Isaias, then it comes to belong to Science, not Literature. Then it conveys the things of heaven, unseen verities, divine manifestations, and them alone—not the ideas, the feelings, the aspirations, of its human instruments, who, for all that they were inspired and infallible, did not cease to be men. St.

Paul's epistles, then, I consider to be literature in a real and true sense, as personal, as rich in reflection and emotion, as Demosthenes or Euripides; and, without ceasing to be revelations of objective truth, they are expressions of the subjective notwithstanding. On the other hand, portions of the Gospels, of the book of Genesis, and other passages of the Sacred Volume, are of the nature of Science. Such is the beginning of St. John's Gospel, which we read at the end of Mass. Such is the Creed. I mean, passages such as these are the mere enunciation of eternal things, without (so to say) the medium of any human mind transmitting them to us. The words used have the grandeur, the majesty, the calm, unimpassioned beauty of Science; they are in no sense Literature, they are in no sense personal; and therefore they are easy to apprehend, and easy to translate.

Did time admit I could show you parallel instances of what I am speaking of in the Classics, inferior to the inspired word in proportion as the subject-matter of the classical authors is immensely inferior to the subjects treated of in Scripture—but parallel, inasmuch as the classical author or speaker ceases for the moment to have to do with Literature, as speaking of things objectively, and rises to the serene sublimity of Science. But I should be carried too far if I began.

9.

I shall then merely sum up what I have said, and come to a conclusion. Reverting, then, to my original question, what is the meaning of Letters, as contained, Gentlemen, in the designation of your Faculty, I have answered, that by Letters or Literature is meant the expression of thought in language, where by "thought" I mean the ideas, feelings, views, reasonings, and other operations of the human mind. And the Art of Letters is the method by which a speaker or writer brings out in words, worthy of his subject, and sufficient for his audience or readers, the thoughts which impress him. Literature, then, is of a personal character; it consists in the enunciations and teachings of those who have a right to speak as representatives of their kind, and in whose

words their brethren find an interpretation of their own sentiments, a record of their own experience, and a suggestion for
their own judgments. A great author, Gentlemen, is not one who
merely has a *copia verborum*, whether in prose or verse, and can,
as it were, turn on at his will any number of splendid phrases and
swelling sentences; but he is one who has something to say and
knows how to say it. I do not claim for him, as such, any great
depth of thought, or breadth of view, or philosophy, or sagacity, or knowledge of human nature, or experience of human life,
though these additional gifts he may have, and the more he has
of them the greater he is; but I ascribe to him, as his characteristic gift, in a large sense the faculty of Expression. He is master
of the two-fold Logos, the thought and the word, distinct, but
inseparable from each other. He may, if so be, elaborate his compositions, or he may pour out his improvisations, but in either
case he has but one aim, which he keeps steadily before him, and
is conscientious and single-minded in fulfilling. That aim is to
give forth what he has within him; and from his very earnestness
it comes to pass that, whatever be the splendour of his diction
or the harmony of his periods, he has with him the charm of
an incommunicable simplicity. Whatever be his subject, high or
low, he treats it suitably and for its own sake. If he is a poet, "nil
molitur *ineptè*" If he is an orator, then too he speaks, not only
"distinctè" and "splendidè," but also *"aptè."* His page is the lucid
mirror of his mind and life—

> "Quo fit, ut omnis
> Votivâ pateat veluti descripta tabellâ
> Vita senis."

He writes passionately, because he feels keenly; forcibly, because
he conceives vividly; he sees too clearly to be vague; he is too serious to be otiose; he can analyze his subject, and therefore he is
rich; he embraces it as a whole and in its parts, and therefore he is
consistent; he has a firm hold of it, and therefore he is luminous.
When his imagination wells up, it overflows in ornament; when
his heart is touched, it thrills along his verse. He always has the

right word for the right idea, and never a word too much. If he is brief, it is because few words suffice; when he is lavish of them, still each word has its mark, and aids, not embarrasses, the vigorous march of his elocution. He expresses what all feel, but all cannot say; and his sayings pass into proverbs among his people, and his phrases become household words and idioms of their daily speech, which is tesselated with the rich fragments of his language, as we see in foreign lands the marbles of Roman grandeur worked into the walls and pavements of modern palaces.

Such pre-eminently is Shakespeare among ourselves; such pre-eminently Virgil among the Latins; such in their degree are all those writers who in every nation go by the name of Classics. To particular nations they are necessarily attached from the circumstance of the variety of tongues, and the peculiarities of each; but so far they have a catholic and ecumenical character, that what they express is common to the whole race of man, and they alone are able to express it.

10.

If then the power of speech is a gift as great as any that can be named,—if the origin of language is by many philosophers even considered to be nothing short of divine,—if by means of words the secrets of the heart are brought to light, pain of soul is relieved, hidden grief is carried off, sympathy conveyed, counsel imparted, experience recorded, and wisdom perpetuated,—if by great authors the many are drawn up into unity, national character is fixed, a people speaks, the past and the future, the East and the West are brought into communication with each other,—if such men are, in a word, the spokesmen and prophets of the human family,—it will not answer to make light of Literature or to neglect its study; rather we may be sure that, in proportion as we master it in whatever language, and imbibe its spirit, we shall ourselves become in our own measure the ministers of like benefits to others, be they many or few, be they in the obscurer or the more distinguished walks of life,—who are united to us by social ties, and are within the sphere of our personal influence.

III.

ENGLISH CATHOLIC LITERATURE

One of the special objects which a Catholic University would promote is that of the formation of a Catholic Literature in the English language. It is an object, however, which must be understood before it can be suitably prosecuted; and which will not be understood without some discussion and investigation. First ideas on the subject must almost necessarily be crude. The real state of the case, what is desirable, what is possible, has to be ascertained; and then what has to be done, and what is to be expected. We have seen in public matters, for half a year past,[1] to what mistakes, and to what disappointments, the country has been exposed, from not having been able distinctly to put before it what was to be aimed at by its fleets and armies, what was practicable, what was probable, in operations of war: and so, too, in the field of literature, we are sure of falling into a parallel perplexity and dissatisfaction, if we start with a vague notion of doing something or other important by means of a Catholic University, without having the caution to examine what is feasible, and what is unnecessary or hopeless. Accordingly, it is natural I should wish to direct attention to this subject, even though it be too difficult to handle in any exact or complete way, and though my attempt must be left for others to bring into a more perfect shape, who are more fitted for the task.

Here I shall chiefly employ myself in investigating what the object is *not*.

§ 1. In its relation to Religious Literature

When a "Catholic Literature in the English tongue" is spoken of as a *desideratum*, no reasonable person will mean by "Catholic

---

1 August, 1854.

works" much more than the "works of Catholics." The phrase does not mean a *religious* literature. "Religious Literature" indeed would mean much more than "the Literature of religious men;" it means over and above this, that the subject-matter of the Literature is religious; but by "Catholic Literature" is not to be understood a literature which treats exclusively or primarily of Catholic matters, of Catholic doctrine, controversy, history, persons, or politics; but it includes all subjects of literature whatever, treated as a Catholic would treat them, and as he only can treat them. Why it is important to have them treated by Catholics hardly need be explained here, though something will be incidentally said on the point as we proceed: meanwhile I am drawing attention to the distinction between the two phrases in order to avoid a serious misapprehension. For it is evident that, if by a Catholic Literature were meant nothing more or less than a religious literature, its writers would be mainly ecclesiastics; just as writers on Law are mainly lawyers, and writers on Medicine are mainly physicians or surgeons. And if this be so, a Catholic Literature is no object special to a University, unless a University is to be considered identical with a Seminary or a Theological School.

I am not denying that a University might prove of the greatest benefit even to our religious literature; doubtless it would, and in various ways; still it is concerned with Theology only as one great subject of thought, as the greatest indeed which can occupy the human mind, yet not as the adequate or direct scope of its institution. Yet I suppose it is not impossible for a literary layman to wince at the idea, and to shrink from the proposal, of taking part in a scheme for the formation of a Catholic Literature, under the apprehension that in some way or another he will be entangling himself in a semi-clerical occupation. It is not uncommon, on expressing an anticipation that the Professors of a Catholic University will promote a Catholic Literature, to have to encounter a vague notion that a lecturer or writer so employed must have something polemical about him, must moralize or preach, must (in Protestant language) *improve the occasion*, though his subject is not at all a religious one; in short, that he must do something else besides fairly and boldly go right on, and be a Catholic speaking as a Catholic spontaneously will speak, on the Classics, or Fine Arts, or Poetry, or whatever he has taken in hand. Men think that he cannot give a lecture on Comparative Anatomy without being bound to digress into the Argument from Final Causes; that he cannot recount the present geological theories without forcing them into an interpretation *seriatim* of the first two chapters of Genesis. Many, indeed, seem to go further still, and actually pronounce that, since our own University has been recommended by the Holy See, and is established by the Hierarchy, it cannot but be engaged in teaching religion and nothing else, and must and will have the discipline of a Seminary; which is about as sensible and logical a view of the matter as it would be to maintain that the Prime Minister *ipso facto* holds an ecclesiastical office, since he is always a Protestant; or that the members of the House of Commons must necessarily have been occupied in clerical duties, as long as they took an oath about Transubstantiation. Catholic Literature is not synonymous with Theology, nor does it supersede or interfere with the work of catechists, divines, preachers, or schoolmen.

§ 2. In its relation to Science

1.

And next, it must be borne in mind, that when we aim at providing a Catholic Literature for Catholics, in place of an existing literature which is of a marked Protestant character, we do not, strictly speaking, include the pure sciences in our *desideratum*. Not that we should not feel pleased and proud to find Catholics distinguish themselves in publications on abstract or experimental philosophy, on account of the honour it does to our religion in the eyes of the world;—not that we are insensible to the congruity and respectability of depending in these matters on ourselves, and not on others, at least as regards our text-books;—not that we do not confidently anticipate that Catholics of these countries will in time to come be able to point to authorities and discoverers in science of their own, equal to those of Protestant England, Germany, or Sweden;—but because, as regards mathematics, chemistry, astronomy, and similar subjects, one man will not, on the score of his religion, treat of them better than another, and because the works of even an unbeliever or idolator, while he kept within the strict range of such studies, might be safely admitted into Catholic lecture-rooms, and put without scruple into the hands of Catholic youths. There is no crying demand, no imperative necessity, for our acquisition of a Catholic Euclid or a Catholic Newton. The object of all science is truth;—the pure sciences proceed to their enunciations from principles which the intellect discerns by a natural light, and by a process recognized by natural reason; and the experimental sciences investigate facts by methods of analysis or by ingenious expedients, ultimately resolvable into instruments of thought equally native to the human mind. If then we may assume that there is an objective truth, and that the constitution of the human mind is in correspondence with it, and acts truly when it acts according to its own laws; if we may assume that God made us, and that what He made is good, and that no action from and according to nature can in itself be evil; it will follow that, so long as it is man who is the geometrician, or natural philosopher, or mechanic, or critic, no matter what man he be, Hindoo, Mahometan, or infidel, his conclusions within his own science, according to the laws of that science, are unquestionable, and not to be suspected by Catholics, unless Catholics may legitimately be jealous of fact and truth, of divine principles and divine creations.

I have been speaking of the scientific treatises or investigations of those who are not Catholics, to which the subject of Literature leads me; but I might even go on to speak of them in their persons as well as in their books. Were it not for the scandal which they would create; were it not for the example they would set; were it not for the certain tendency of the human mind involuntarily to outleap the strict boundaries of an abstract science, and to teach it upon extraneous principles, to embody

it in concrete examples, and to carry it on to practical conclusions; above all, were it not for the indirect influence, and living energetic presence, and collateral duties, which accompany a
Professor in a great school of learning, I do not see (abstracting
from him, I repeat, in hypothesis, what never could possibly be
abstracted from him in fact), why the chair of Astronomy in a
Catholic University should not be filled by a La Place, or that of
Physics by a Humboldt. Whatever they might wish to say, still,
while they kept to their own science, they would be unable, like
the heathen Prophet in Scripture, to "go beyond the word of the
Lord, to utter any thing of their own head."

2.

So far the arguments hold good of certain celebrated writers in a
Northern Review, who, in their hostility to the principle of dogmatic teaching, seem obliged to maintain, because subject-matters are distinct, that living opinions are distinct too, and that
men are abstractions as well as their respective sciences. "On the
morning of the thirteenth of August, in the year 1704," says a
justly celebrated author, in illustration and defence of the anti-
dogmatic principle in political and social matters, "two great
captains, equal in authority, united by close private and public
ties, but of different creeds, prepared for battle, on the event of
which were staked the liberties of Europe ... Marlborough gave
orders for public prayers; the English chaplains read the service at the head of the English regiments; the Calvinistic chaplains of the Dutch army, with heads on which hand of Bishop
had never been laid, poured forth their supplications in front
of their countrymen. In the meantime the Danes might listen
to the Lutheran ministers; and Capuchins might encourage the
Austrian squadrons, and pray to the Virgin for a blessing on the
arms of the holy Roman Empire. The battle commences; these
men of various religions all act like members of one body: the
Catholic and the Protestant generals exert themselves to assist
and to surpass each other; before sunset the Empire is saved;
France has lost in a day the fruits of eight years of intrigue and of

victory; and the allies, after conquering together, return thanks to God separately, each after his own form of worship."[2]

The writer of this lively passage would be doubtless unwilling himself to carry out the principle which it insinuates to those extreme conclusions to which it is often pushed by others, in matters of education. Viewed in itself, viewed in the abstract, that principle is simply, undeniably true; and is only sophistical when it is carried out in practical matters at all. A religious opinion, though not formally recognized, cannot fail of influencing *in fact* the school, or society, or polity in which it is found; though in the abstract that opinion is one thing, and the school, society, or polity, another. Here were Episcopalians, Lutherans, Calvinists, and Catholics found all fighting on one side, it is true, without any prejudice to their respective religious tenets: and, certainly, I never heard that in a battle soldiers did do any thing else but fight. I did not know they had time for going beyond the matter in hand; yet, even as regards this very illustration which he has chosen, if we were bound to decide by it the controversy, it does so happen that that danger of interference and collision between opposite religionists actually does occur upon a campaign, which could not be incurred in a battle: and at this very time some jealousy or disgust has been shown in English popular publications, when they have had to record that our ally, the Emperor of the French, has sent his troops, who are serving with the British against the Russians, to attend High Mass, or has presented his sailors with a picture of the Madonna.

If, then, we could have Professors who were mere abstractions and phantoms, marrowless in their bones, and without speculation in their eyes; or if they could only open their mouths on their own special subject, and in their scientific pedantry were dead to the world; if they resembled the well known character in the Romance, who was so imprisoned or fossilized in his erudition, that, though "he stirred the fire with some address," nevertheless, on attempting to snuff the candles, he "was unsuc-

_____

2 Macaulay's Essays.

cessful, and relinquished that ambitious post of courtesy, after having twice reduced the parlour to total darkness," then indeed Voltaire himself might be admitted, not without scandal, but without risk, to lecture on astronomy or galvanism in Catholic, or Protestant, or Presbyterian Colleges, or in all of them at once; and we should have no practical controversy with philosophers who, after the fashion of the author I have been quoting, are so smart in proving that we, who differ from them, must needs be so bigotted and puzzle-headed.

And in strict conformity with these obvious distinctions, it will be found that, so far as we are able to reduce scientific men of anti-Catholic opinions to the type of the imaginary book-worm to whom I have been alluding, we do actually use them in our schools. We allow our Catholic student to use them, so far as he can surprise them (if I may use the expression), in their formal treatises, and can keep them close prisoners there.

> Vix defessa senem passus componere membra,
> Cum clamore ruit magno, manicisque jacentem
> Occupat.

The fisherman, in the Arabian tale, took no harm from the genius, till he let him out from the brass bottle in which he was confined. "He examined the vessel and shook it, to see if what was within made any noise, but he heard nothing." All was safe till he had succeeded in opening it, and "then came out a very thick smoke, which, ascending to the clouds and extending itself along the sea shore in a thick mist, astonished him very much. After a time the smoke collected, and was converted into a genius of enormous height. At the sight of this monster, whose head appeared to reach the clouds, the fisherman trembled with fear." Such is the difference between an unbelieving or heretical philosopher in person, and in the mere disquisitions proper to his science. Porson was no edifying companion for young men of eighteen, nor are his letters on the text of the Three Heavenly Witnesses to be recommended; but that does not hinder his being admitted into Catholic schools, while he is confined within the limits of his Preface to the Hecuba. Franklin certainly would have been intolerable in person, if he began to talk freely, and throw out, as I think he did in private, that each solar system had its own god; but such extravagances of so able a man do not interfere with the honour we justly pay his name in the history of experimental science. Nay, the great Newton himself would have been silenced in a Catholic University, when he got upon the Apocalypse; yet is that any reason why we should not study his Principia, or avail ourselves of the wonderful analysis which he, Protestant as he was, originated, and which French infidels have developed? We are glad, for their own sakes, that anti-Catholic writers should, in their posthumous influence, do as much real service to the human race as ever they can, and we have no wish to interfere with it.

3.

Returning, then, to the point from which we set out, I observe that, this being the state of the case as regards abstract science, viz., that we have no quarrel with its anti-Catholic commentators, till they thrust their persons into our Chairs, or their popular writings into our reading-rooms, it follows that, when we contemplate the formation of a Catholic Literature, we do not consider scientific works as among our most prominent desiderata. They are to be looked for, not so much for their own sake, as because they are indications that we have able scientific men in our communion; for if we have such, they will be certain to write, and in proportion as they increase in number will there be the chance of really profound, original, and standard books issuing from our Lecture-rooms and Libraries. But, after all, there is no reason why these should be better than those which we have already received from Protestants; though it is at once more becoming and more agreeable to our feelings to use books of our own, instead of being indebted to the books of others.

Literature, then, is not synonymous with Science; nor does Catholic education imply the exclusion of works of abstract reasoning, or of physical experiment, or the like, though written by persons of another or of no communion.

There is another consideration in point here, or rather prior to what I have been saying; and that is, that, considering certain scientific works, those on Criticism, for instance, are so often written in a technical phraseology, and since others, as mathematical, deal so largely in signs, symbols, and figures, which belong to all languages, these abstract studies cannot properly be said to fall under English *Literature* at all;—for by Literature I understand Thought, conveyed under the forms of some particular language. And this brings me to speak of Literature in its highest and most genuine sense, viz., as an historical and national fact; and I fear, in this sense of the word also, it is altogether beside or beyond any object which a Catholic University can reasonably contemplate, at least in any moderate term of years; but so large a subject here opens upon us that I must postpone it to another Section.

§ 3. In its relation to Classical Literature

1.

I HAVE been directing the reader's attention, first to what we do not, and next to what we need not contemplate, when we turn our thoughts to the formation of an English Catholic Literature. I said that our object was neither a library of theological nor of scientific knowledge, though theology in its literary aspect, and abstract science as an exercise of intellect, have both of course a place in the Catholic encyclopædia. One undertaking, however, there is, which not merely does not, and need not, but unhappily cannot, come into the reasonable contemplation of any set of persons, whether members of a University or not, who are desirous of Catholicizing the English language, as is very evident; and that is simply the creation of an *English Classical Literature*, for that has been done long ago, and would be a work beyond the powers of any body of men, even if it had still to be done. If I insist on this point here, no one must suppose I do not consider it to be self-evident; for I shall not be aiming at proving it, so much as at bringing it home distinctly to the mind, that we may, one and all, have a clearer perception of the state of things with which we have to deal. There is many an undeniable truth which is not practically felt and appreciated; and, unless we master our position in the matter before us, we may be led off into various wild imaginations or impossible schemes, which will, as a matter of course, end in disappointment.

Were the Catholic Church acknowledged from this moment through the length and breadth of these islands, and the English tongue henceforth baptized into the Catholic faith, and sealed and consecrated to Catholic objects, and were the present intellectual activity of the nation to continue, as of course it would continue, we should at once have an abundance of Catholic works, which would be English, and purely English, literature and high literature; but still all these would not constitute "English Literature," as the words are commonly understood, nor even then could we say that the "English Literature" was Catholic. Much less can we ever aspire to affirm it, while we are but a portion of the vast English-speaking world-wide race, and are but striving to create a current in the direction of Catholic truth, when the waters are rapidly flowing the other way. In no case can we, strictly speaking, form an English Literature; for by the Literature of a Nation is meant its Classics, and its Classics have been given to England, and have been recognized as such, long since.

2.

A Literature, when it is formed, is a national and historical fact; it is a matter of the past and the present, and can be as little ignored as the present, as little undone as the past. We can deny, supersede, or change it, then only, when we can do the same towards the race or language which it represents. Every great people has a character of its own, which it manifests and perpetuates in a variety of ways. It developes into a monarchy or republic;—by means of commerce or in war, in agriculture or in manufactures, or in all of these at once; in its cities, its public edifices and works, bridges, canals, and harbours; in its laws, traditions, customs, and manners; in its songs and its proverbs; in its religion; in its line of policy, its bearing, its action towards foreign nations; in its alliances, fortunes, and the whole course of its history. All these are peculiar, and parts of a whole, and betoken the national character, and savour of each other; and the case is the same with the national language and literature. They are what they are, and cannot be any thing else, whether they be good or bad or of a mixed nature; before they are formed, we cannot prescribe them, and afterwards, we cannot reverse them. We may feel great repugnance to Milton or Gibbon as men; we may most seriously protest against the spirit which ever lives, and the tendency which ever operates, in every page of their writings; but there they are, an integral portion of English Literature; we cannot extinguish them; we cannot deny their power; we cannot write a new Milton or a new Gibbon; we cannot expurgate what needs to be exorcised. They are great English authors, each breathing hatred to the Catholic Church in his own way, each a proud and rebellious creature of God, each gifted with incomparable gifts.

We must take things as they are, if we take them at all. We may refuse to say a word to English literature, if we will; we may have recourse to French or to Italian instead, if we think either of these less exceptionable than our own; we may fall back upon the Classics of Greece and Rome; we may have nothing whatever to do with literature, as such, of any kind, and confine ourselves to purely amorphous or monstrous specimens of language; but if we do once profess in our Universities the English language and literature, if we think it allowable to know the state of things we live in, and that national character which we share, if we think it desirable to have a chance of writing what may be read after our day, and praiseworthy to aim at providing for Catholics who speak English a Catholic Literature then—I do not say that we must at once throw open every sort of book to the young, the weak, or the untrained,—I do not say that we may dispense with our ecclesiastical indexes and emendations, but—we must not fancy ourselves creating what is already created in spite of us, and which never could at a moment be created by means of us, and we must recognize that historical literature, which is in occupation of the language, both as a fact, nay, and as a standard for ourselves.

There is surely nothing either "temerarious" or paradoxical in a statement like this. The growth of a nation is like that of an individual; its tone of voice and subjects for speech vary with its age. Each age has its own propriety and charm; as a boy's beauty is not a man's, and the sweetness of a treble differs from the richness of a bass, so it is with a whole people. The same period does not produce its most popular poet, its most effective orator, and its most philosophic historian. Language changes with the progress of thought and the events of history, and style changes with it; and while in successive generations it passes through a series of separate excellences, the respective deficiencies of all are supplied alternately by each. Thus language and literature may be considered as dependent on a process of nature, and admitting of subjection to her laws. Father Hardouin indeed, who maintained that, with the exception of Pliny, Cicero, Virgil's Georgics, and Horace's Satires and Epistles, Latin literature was the work of the medieval monks, had the conception of a literature neither national nor historical; but the rest of the world will be apt to consider time and place as necessary conditions in its formation, and will be unable to conceive of classical authors, except as either the elaboration of centuries, or the rare and fitful accident of genius.

First-rate excellence in literature, as in other matters, is either an accident or the outcome of a process; and in either case demands a course of years to secure. We cannot reckon on a Plato, we cannot force an Aristotle, any more than we can command a fine harvest, or create a coal field. If a literature be, as I have said, the voice of a particular nation, it requires a territory and a period, as large as that nation's extent and history, to mature in. It is broader and deeper than the capacity of any body of men, however gifted, or any system of teaching, however true. It is the exponent, not of truth, but of nature, which is true only in its elements. It is the result of the mutual action of a hundred simultaneous influences and operations, and the issue of a hundred strange accidents in independent places and times; it is the scanty compensating produce of the wild discipline of the world and of life, so fruitful in failures; and it is the concentration of those rare manifestations of intellectual power, which no one can account for. It is made up, in the particular language here under consideration, of human beings as heterogeneous as Burns and Bunyan, De Foe and Johnson, Goldsmith and Cowper, Law and Fielding, Scott and Byron. The remark has been made that the history of an author is the history of his works; it is far more exact to say that, at least in the case of great writers, the history of their works is the history of their fortunes or their times. Each is, in his turn, the man of his age, the type of a generation, or the interpreter of a crisis. He is made for his day, and his day for him. Hooker would not have been, but for the existence of Catholics and Puritans, the defeat of the former and the rise of the latter; Clarendon would not have been without the Great Rebellion; Hobbes is the prophet of the reaction to scoffing infidelity; and Addison is the child of the Revolution and its attendant changes. If there be any of our classical authors, who might at first sight have been pronounced a University man, with the exception of Johnson, Addison is he; yet even Addison, the son and brother of clergymen, the fellow of an Oxford Society, the resident of a College which still points to the walk which he planted, must be something more, in order to take his place among the Classics of the language, and owed the variety of his matter to his experience of life, and to the call made on his resources by the exigencies of his day. The world he lived in made him and used him. While his writings educated his own generation, they have delineated it for all posterity after him.

3.

I have been speaking of the authors of a literature, in their relation to the people and course of events to which they belong; but a prior consideration, at which I have already glanced, is their connection with the language itself, which has been their organ. If they are in great measure the creatures of their times, they are on the other hand in a far higher sense the creators of their language. It is indeed commonly called their mother tongue, but virtually it did not exist till they gave it life and form. All greater matters are carried on and perfected by a succession of individual minds; what is true in the history of thought and of action is true of language also. Certain masters of composition, as Shakespeare, Milton, and Pope, the writers of the Protestant Bible and Prayer Book, Hooker and Addison, Swift, Hume, and Goldsmith, have been the making of the English language; and as that language is a fact, so is the literature a fact, by which it is formed, and in which it lives. Men of great ability have taken it in hand, each in his own day, and have done for it what the master of a gymnasium does for the bodily frame. They have formed its limbs, and developed its strength; they have endowed it with vigour, exercised it in suppleness and dexterity, and taught it grace. They have made it rich, harmonious, various, and precise. They have furnished it with a variety of styles, which from their individuality may almost be called dialects, and are monuments both of the powers of the language and the genius of its cultivators.

How real a creation, how *sui generis*, is the style of Shakespeare, or of the Protestant Bible and Prayer Book, or of Swift, or of Pope, or of Gibbon, or of Johnson! Even were the subject-matter without meaning, though in truth the style cannot really be abstracted from the sense, still the style would, on that supposition, remain as perfect and original a work as Euclid's elements or a symphony of Beethoven. And, like music, it has seized upon the public mind; and the literature of England is no longer a mere letter, printed in books, and shut up in libraries, but it is a living voice, which has gone forth in its expressions and its sentiments into the world of men, which daily thrills upon our ears and syllables our thoughts, which speaks to us through our correspondents, and dictates when we put pen to paper. Whether we will or no, the phraseology and diction of Shakespeare, of the Protestant formularies, of Milton, of Pope, of Johnson's Tabletalk, and of Walter Scott, have become a portion of the vernacular tongue, the household words, of which perhaps we little guess the origin, and the very idioms of our familiar conversation. The man in the comedy spoke prose without knowing it; and we Catholics, without consciousness and without offence, are ever repeating the half sentences of dissolute playwrights and heretical partizans and preachers. So tyrannous is the literature of a nation; it is too much for us. We cannot destroy or reverse it; we may confront and encounter it, but we cannot make it over again. It is a great work of man, when it is no work of God's.

I repeat, then, whatever we be able or unable to effect in the great problem which lies before us, any how we cannot undo the past. English Literature will ever *have been* Protestant. Swift and Addison, the most native and natural of our writers, Hooker and Milton, the most elaborate, never can become our co-religionists; and, though this is but the enunciation of a truism, it is not on that account an unprofitable enunciation.

4.

I trust we are not the men to give up an undertaking because it is perplexed or arduous; and to do nothing because we cannot do everything. Much may be attempted, much attained, even granting English Literature is not Catholic. Something indeed may be said even in alleviation of the misfortune itself, on which I have been insisting; and with two remarks bearing upon this latter point I will bring this Section to an end.

1. First, then, it is to be considered that, whether we look to countries Christian or heathen, we find the state of literature there as little satisfactory as it is in these islands; so that, whatever are our difficulties here, they are not worse than those of Catholics all over the world. I would not indeed say a word to extenuate the calamity, under which we lie, of having a literature formed in Protestantism; still, other literatures have disadvantages of their own; and, though in such matters comparisons are impossible, I doubt whether we should be better pleased if our English Classics were tainted with licentiousness, or defaced by infidelity or scepticism. I conceive we should not much mend matters if we were to exchange literatures with the French, Ital-

ians, or Germans. About Germany, however, I will not speak; as to France, it has great and religious authors; its classical drama, even in comedy, compared with that of other literatures, is singularly unexceptionable; but who is there that holds a place among its writers so historical and important, who is so copious, so versatile, so brilliant, as that Voltaire who is an open scoffer at every thing sacred, venerable, or high-minded? Nor can Rousseau, though he has not the pretensions of Voltaire, be excluded from the classical writers of France. Again, the gifted Pascal, in the work on which his literary fame is mainly founded, does not approve himself to a Catholic judgment; and Descartes, the first of French philosophers, was too independent in his inquiries to be always correct in his conclusions. The witty Rabelais is said, by a recent critic,[3] to show covertly in his former publications, and openly in his latter, his "dislike to the Church of Rome." La Fontaine was with difficulty brought, on his death-bed, to make public satisfaction for the scandal which he had done to religion by his immoral *Contes*, though at length he threw into the fire a piece which he had just finished for the stage. Montaigne, whose Essays "make an epoch in literature," by "their influence upon the tastes and opinions of Europe;" whose "school embraces a large proportion of French and English literature;" and of whose "brightness and felicity of genius there can be but one opinion," is disgraced, as the same writer tells us, by "a sceptical bias and great indifference of temperament;" and "has led the way" as an habitual offender, "to the indecency too characteristic of French literature."

Nor does Italy present a more encouraging picture. Ariosto, one of the few names, ancient or modern, who is allowed on all hands to occupy the first rank of Literature, is, I suppose, rightly arraigned by the author I have above quoted, of "coarse sensuality." Pulci, "by his sceptical insinuations, seems clearly to display an intention of exposing religion to contempt." Boccaccio, the first of Italian prose-writers, had in his old age touchingly to

---

3 Hallam.

lament the corrupting tendency of his popular compositions; and Bellarmine has to vindicate him, Dante, and Petrarch, from the charge of virulent abuse of the Holy See. Dante certainly does not scruple to place in his *Inferno* a Pope, whom the Church has since canonized, and his work on *Monarchia* is on the Index. Another great Florentine, Macchiavel, is on the Index also; and Giannone, as great in political history at Naples as Macchiavel at Florence, is notorious for his disaffection to the interests of the Roman Pontiff.

These are but specimens of the general character of secular literature, whatever be the people to whom it belongs. One literature may be better than another, but bad will be the best, when weighed in the balance of truth and morality. It cannot be otherwise; human nature is in all ages and all countries the same; and its literature, therefore, will ever and everywhere be one and the same also. Man's work will savour of man; in his elements and powers excellent and admirable, but prone to disorder and excess, to error and to sin. Such too will be his literature; it will have the beauty and the fierceness, the sweetness and the rankness, of the natural man, and, with all its richness and greatness, will necessarily offend the senses of those who, in the Apostle's words, are really "exercised to discern between good and evil." "It is said of the holy Sturme," says an Oxford writer, "that, in passing a horde of unconverted Germans, as they were bathing and gambolling in the stream, he was so overpowered by the intolerable scent which arose from them that he nearly fainted away." National Literature is, in a parallel way, the untutored movements of the reason, imagination, passions, and affections of the natural man, the leapings and the friskings, the plungings and the snortings, the sportings and the buffoonings, the clumsy play and the aimless toil, of the noble, lawless savage of God's intellectual creation.

It is well that we should clearly apprehend a truth so simple and elementary as this, and not expect from the nature of man, or the literature of the world, what they never held out to us. Certainly, I did not know that the world was to be regarded as favourable to Christian faith or practice, or that it would be breaking any engagement with us, if it took a line divergent from our own. I have never fancied that we should have reasonable ground for surprise or complaint, though man's intellect *puris naturalibus* did prefer, of the two, liberty to truth, or though his heart cherished a leaning towards licence of thought and speech in comparison with restraint.

5.

2. If we do but resign ourselves to facts, we shall soon be led on to the second reflection which I have promised—viz., that, not only are things not better abroad, but they might be worse at home. We have, it is true, a Protestant literature; but then it is neither atheistical nor immoral; and, in the case of at least half a dozen of its highest and most influential departments, and of the most popular of its authors, it comes to us with very considerable alleviations. For instance, there surely is a call on us for thankfulness that the most illustrious amongst English writers has so little of a Protestant about him that Catholics have been able, without extravagance, to claim him as their own, and that enemies to our creed have allowed that he is only not a Catholic, because, and as far as, his times forbade it. It is an additional satisfaction to be able to boast that he offends in neither of those two respects, which reflect so seriously upon the reputation of great authors abroad. Whatever passages may be gleaned from his dramas disrespectful to ecclesiastical authority, still these are but passages; on the other hand, there is in Shakespeare neither contempt of religion nor scepticism, and he upholds the broad laws of moral and divine truth with the consistency and severity of an Æschylus, Sophocles, or Pindar. There is no mistaking in his works on which side lies the right; Satan is not made a hero, nor Cain a victim, but pride is pride, and vice is vice, and, whatever indulgence he may allow himself in light thoughts or unseemly words, yet his admiration is reserved for sanctity and truth. From the second chief fault of Literature, as indeed my last words imply, he is not so free; but, often as he may offend against modesty, he

is clear of a worse charge, sensuality, and hardly a passage can be instanced in all that he has written to seduce the imagination or to excite the passions.

A rival to Shakespeare, if not in genius, at least in copiousness and variety, is found in Pope; and he was actually a Catholic, though personally an unsatisfactory one. His freedom indeed from Protestantism is but a poor compensation for a false theory of religion in one of his poems; but taking his works as a whole, we may surely acquit them of being dangerous to the reader, whether on the score of morals or of faith.

Again, the special title of moralist in English Literature is accorded by the public voice to Johnson, whose bias towards Catholicity is well known.

If we were to ask for a report of our philosophers, the investigation would not be so agreeable; for we have three of evil, and one of unsatisfactory repute. Locke is scarcely an honour to us in the standard of truth, grave and manly as he is; and Hobbes, Hume, and Bentham, in spite of their abilities, are simply a disgrace. Yet, even in this department, we find some compensation in the names of Clarke, Berkeley, Butler, and Reid, and in a name more famous than them all. Bacon was too intellectually great to hate or to contemn the Catholic faith; and he deserves by his writings to be called the most orthodox of Protestant philosophers.

§ 4. In its relation to the Literature of the Day

1.

THE past cannot be undone. That our English Classical Literature is not Catholic is a plain fact, which we cannot deny, to which we must reconcile ourselves, as best we may, and which, as I have shown above, has after all its compensations. When, then, I speak of the desirableness of forming a Catholic Literature, I am contemplating no such vain enterprise as that of reversing history; no, nor of redeeming the past by the future. I have no dream of Catholic Classics as still reserved for the English language. In truth, classical authors not only are national, but belong to a particular age of a nation's life; and I should not wonder if, as regards ourselves, that age is passing away. Moreover, they perform a particular office towards its language, which is not likely to be called for beyond a definite time. And further, though analogies or parallels cannot be taken to decide a question of this nature, such is the fact, that the series of our classical writers has already extended through a longer period than was granted to the Classical Literature either of Greece or of Rome; and thus the English language also may have a long course of literature still to come through many centuries, without that Literature being classical.

Latin, for instance, was a living language for many hundred years after the date of the writers who brought it to its perfection; and then it continued for a second long period to be the medium of European correspondence. Greek was a living language to a date not very far short of that of the taking of Constantinople, ten centuries after the date of St. Basil, and seventeen hundred years after the period commonly called classical. And thus, as the year has its spring and summer, so even for those celebrated languages there was but a season of splendour, and, compared with the whole course of their duration, but a brief season. Since, then, English has had its great writers for a term of about three hundred years,—as long, that is, as the period from Sappho to Demosthenes, or from Pisistratus to Arcesilas, or from Æschylus and Pindar to Carneades, or from Ennius to Pliny,—we should have no right to be disappointed if the classical period be close upon its termination.

By the Classics of a national Literature I mean those authors who have the foremost place in exemplifying the powers and conducting the development of its language. The language of a nation is at first rude and clumsy; and it demands a succession of skilful artists to make it malleable and ductile, and to work it up to its proper perfection. It improves by use, but it is not every one who can use it while as yet it is unformed. To do this is an effort of genius; and so men of a peculiar talent arise, one after another, according to the circumstances of the times, and accomplish it.

One gives it flexibility, that is, shows how it can be used without difficulty to express adequately a variety of thoughts and feelings in their nicety or intricacy; another makes it perspicuous or forcible; a third adds to its vocabulary; and a fourth gives it grace and harmony. The style of each of such eminent masters becomes henceforth in some sort a property of the language itself; words, phrases, collocations, and structure, which hitherto did not exist, gradually passing into the conversation and the composition of the educated classes.

2.

Now I will attempt to show how this process of improvement is effected, and what is its limit. I conceive then that these gifted writers act upon the spoken and written language by means of the particular schools which form about them respectively. Their style, using the word in a large sense, forcibly arrests the reader, and draws him on to imitate it, by virtue of what is excellent in it, in spite of such defects as, in common with all human works, it may contain. I suppose all of us will recognize this fascination. For myself when I was fourteen or fifteen, I imitated Addison; when I was seventeen, I wrote in the style of Johnson; about the same time I fell in with the twelfth volume of Gibbon, and my ears rang with the cadence of his sentences, and I dreamed of it for a night or two. Then I began to make an analysis of Thucydides in Gibbon's style. In like manner, most Oxford undergraduates, forty years ago, when they would write poetry, adopted the versification of Pope Darwin, and the Pleasures of Hope, which had been made popular by Heber and Milman. The literary schools, indeed, which I am speaking of, as resulting from the attractions of some original, or at least novel artist, consist for the most part of mannerists, none of whom rise much above mediocrity; but they are not the less serviceable as channels, by means of which the achievements of genius may be incorporated into the language itself, or become the common property of the nation. Henceforth, the most ordinary composer, the very student in the lecture-room, is able to write with a precision, a grace, or a copiousness, as the case may be, unknown before the date of the authors whom he imitates, and he wonders at, if he does not rather pride himself on, his

> novas frondes, et non sua poma.

If there is any one who illustrates this remark, it is Gibbon; I seem to trace his vigorous condensation and peculiar rhythm at every turn in the literature of the present day. Pope, again, is said to have tuned our versification. Since his time, any one, who has an ear and turn for poetry, can with little pains throw off a copy of verses equal or superior to the poet's own, and with far less of study and patient correction than would have been demanded of the poet himself for their production. Compare the choruses of the Samson Agonistes with any stanza taken at random in Thalaba: how much had the language gained in the interval between them! Without denying the high merits of Southey's beautiful romance, we surely shall not be wrong in saying, that in its unembarrassed eloquent flow, it is the language of the nineteenth century that speaks, as much as the author himself.

I will give an instance of what I mean: let us take the beginning of the first chorus in the Samson:—

> Just are the ways of God,
> And justifiable to men;
> Unless there be who think not God at all;
> If any be, they walk obscure,
> For of such doctrine never was there school,
> But the heart of the fool,
> And no man therein doctor but himself.
> But men there be, who doubt His ways not just,
> As to His own edicts found contradicting,
> Then give the reins to wandering thought,
> Regardless of His glory's diminution;
> Till, by their own perplexities involved,
> They ravel more, still less resolved,
> But never find self-satisfying solution.

And now take the opening stanza of Thalaba:—

> How beautiful is night!
> A dewy freshness fills the silent air;
> No mist obscures, nor cloud, nor speck, nor stain,
> Breaks the serene of heaven.
> In full-orb'd glory yonder Moon divine
> Rolls through the dark blue depths.
> Beneath her steady ray
> The desert circle spreads,
> Like the round ocean girdled with the sky.
> How beautiful is night!

Does not Southey show to advantage here? yet the voice of the world proclaims Milton pre-eminently a poet; and no one can affect a doubt of the delicacy and exactness of his ear. Yet, much as he did for the language in verse and in prose, he left much for other artists to do after him, which they have successfully accomplished. We see the fruit of the literary labours of Pope, Thomson, Gray, Goldsmith, and other poets of the eighteenth century, in the musical eloquence of Southey.

3.

So much for the process; now for its termination. I think it is brought about in some such way as the following:—

The influence of a great classic upon the nation which he represents is twofold; on the one hand he advances his native language towards its perfection; but on the other hand he discourages in some measure any advance beyond his own. Thus, in the parallel case of science, it is commonly said on the continent, that the very marvellousness of Newton's powers was the bane of English mathematics: inasmuch as those who succeeded him were content with his discoveries, bigoted to his methods of investigation, and averse to those new instruments which have carried on the French to such brilliant and successful results. In Literature, also, there is something oppressive in the authority of a great writer, and something of tyranny in the use to which his admirers put his name. The school which he forms would fain monopolize the language, draws up canons of criticism from his writings, and is intolerant of innovation. Those who come under its influence are dissuaded or deterred from striking out a path of their own. Thus Virgil's transcendent excellence fixed the character of the hexameter in subsequent poetry, and took away the chances, if not of improvement, at least of variety. Even Juvenal has much of Virgil in the structure of his verse. I have known those who prefer the rhythm of Catullus.

However, so summary a result is not of necessary occurrence. The splendour of an author may excite a generous emulation, or the tyrannous formalism of his followers a re-action; and thus other authors and other schools arise. We read of Thucydides, on hearing Herodotus read his history at Olympia, being incited to attempt a similar work, though of an entirely different and of an original structure. Gibbon, in like manner, writing of Hume and Robertson, says: "The perfect composition, the nervous language, the well-turned periods of Dr. Robertson, inflamed me to the ambitious hope that I might one day tread in his footsteps; the calm philosophy, the careless inimitable beauties of his friend and rival, often forced me to close the volume with a mixed sensation of delight and despair."[4]

As to re-actions, I suppose there has been something of the kind against the supremacy of Pope, since the time that his successors, Campbell especially, have developed his peculiarities and even defects into extravagance. Crabbe, for instance, turned back to a versification having much more of Dryden in it; and Byron, in spite of his high opinion of Pope, threw into his lines the rhythm of blank verse. Still, on the whole, the influence of a Classic acts in the way of discouraging any thing new, rather than in that of exciting rivalry or provoking reaction.

And another consideration is to be taken into account. When a language has been cultivated in any particular department of thought, and so far as it has been generally perfected, an existing

---

4 Misc. Works, p. 55.

want has been supplied, and there is no need for further work-men. In its earlier times, while it is yet unformed, to write in it at all is almost a work of genius. It is like crossing a country before roads are made communicating between place and place. The authors of that age deserve to be Classics, both because of what they do and because they can do it. It requires the courage or the force of great talent to compose in the language at all; and the composition, when effected, makes a permanent impression on it. In those early times, too, the licence of speech unfettered by precedents, the novelty of the work, the state of society, and the absence of criticism, enable an author to write with spirit and freshness. But, as centuries pass on, this stimulus is taken away; the language by this time has become manageable for its various purposes, and is ready at command. Ideas have found their cor-responding expressions; and one word will often convey what once required half a dozen. Roots have been expanded, deriva-tions multiplied, terms invented or adopted. A variety of phrases has been provided, which form a sort of compound words. Sepa-rate professions, pursuits, and provinces of literature have gained their conventional terminology. There is an historical, political, social, commercial style. The ear of the nation has become accus-tomed to useful expressions or combinations of words, which otherwise would sound harsh. Strange metaphors have been nat-uralized in the ordinary prose, yet cannot be taken as precedents for a similar liberty. Criticism has become an art, and exercises a continual and jealous watch over the free genius of new writers. It is difficult for them to be original in the use of their mother tongue without being singular.

Thus the language has become in a great measure stereotype; as in the case of the human frame, it has expanded to the loss of its elasticity, and can expand no more. Then the general style of educated men, formed by the accumulated improvements of centuries, is far superior perhaps in perfectness to that of any one of those national Classics, who have taught their countrymen to write more clearly, or more elegantly, or more forcibly than them-selves. And literary men submit themselves to what they find so well provided for them; or, if impatient of conventionalities, and resolved to shake off a yoke which tames them down to the loss of individuality, they adopt no half measures, but indulge in novelties which offend against the genius of the language, and the true canons of taste. Political causes may co-operate in a revolt of this kind; and, as a nation declines in patriotism, so does its language in purity. It seems to me as if the sententious, epigrammatic style of writing, which set in with Seneca, and is seen at least as late as in the writings of St. Ambrose, is an attempt to escape from the simplicity of Cæsar and the majestic elocution of Cicero; while Tertullian, with more of genius than good sense, relieves himself in the harsh originality of his provincial Latin.

There is another impediment, as time goes on, to the rise of fresh classics in any nation; and that is the effect which foreigners, or foreign literature, will exert upon it. It may happen that a certain language, like Greek, is adopted and used familiarly by educated men in other countries; or again, that educated men, to whom it is native, may abandon it for some other language, as the Romans of the second and third centuries wrote in Greek instead of Latin. The consequence will be, that the language in question will tend to lose its nationality—that is, its distinctive character; it will cease to be idiomatic in the sense in which it once was so; and whatever grace or propriety it may retain, it will be comparatively tame and spiritless; or, on the other hand, it will be corrupted by the admixture of foreign elements.

4.

Such, as I consider, being the fortunes of Classical Literature, viewed generally, I should never be surprised to find that, as regards this hemisphere, for I can prophesy nothing of America, we have well nigh seen the end of English Classics. Certainly, it is in no expectation of Catholics continuing the series here that I speak of the duty and necessity of their cultivating English literature. When I speak of the formation of a Catholic school of writers, I have respect principally to the matter of what is written, and to composition only so far forth as style is necessary to convey and to recommend the matter. I mean a literature which resembles the literature of the day. This is not a day for great writers, but for good writing, and a great deal of it. There never was a time when men wrote so much and so well, and that, without being of any great account themselves. While our literature in this day, especially the periodical, is rich and various, its language is elaborated to a perfection far beyond that of our Classics, by the jealous rivalry, the incessant practice, the mutual influence, of its many writers. In point of mere style, I suppose, many an article in the *Times* newspaper, or Edinburgh Review, is superior to a preface of Dryden's, or a Spectator, or a pamphlet of Swift's, or one of South's sermons.

Our writers write so well that there is little to choose between them. What they lack is that individuality, that earnestness, most personal yet most unconscious of self, which is the greatest charm of an author. The very form of the compositions of the day suggests to us their main deficiency. They are anonymous. So was it not in the literature of those nations which we consider the special standard of classical writing; so is it not with our own Classics. The Epic was sung by the voice of the living, present poet. The drama, in its very idea, is poetry in persons. Historians begin, "Herodotus, of Halicarnassus, publishes his researches;" or, "Thucydides, the Athenian, has composed an account of the war." Pindar is all through his odes a speaker. Plato, Xenophon, and Cicero, throw their philosophical dissertations into the form of a dialogue. Orators and preachers are by their very profession known persons, and the personal is laid down by the Philosopher of antiquity as the source of their greatest persuasiveness. Virgil and Horace are ever bringing into their poetry their own characters and tastes. Dante's poems furnish a series of events for the chronology of his times. Milton is frequent in allusions to his own history and circumstances. Even when Addison writes anonymously, he writes under a professed character, and that in a great measure his own; he writes in the first person. The "I", of the Spectator, and the "we" of the modern Review or Newspaper, are the respective symbols of the two ages in our literature.

Catholics must do as their neighbours; they must be content to serve their generation, to promote the interests of religion, to recommend truth, and to edify their brethren today, though their names are to have little weight, and their works are not to last much beyond themselves.

5.

And now having shown what it is that a Catholic University does not think of doing, what it need not do, and what it cannot do, I might go on to trace out in detail what it is that it really might and will encourage and create. But, as such an investigation would neither be difficult to pursue, nor easy to terminate, I prefer to leave the subject at the preliminary point to which I have brought it.

IV.

ELEMENTARY STUDIES

It has often been observed that, when the eyes of the infant first open upon the world, the reflected rays of light which strike them from the myriad of surrounding objects present to him no image, but a medley of colours and shadows. They do not form into a whole; they do not rise into foregrounds and melt into distances; they do not divide into groups; they do not coalesce into unities; they do not combine into persons; but each particular hue and tint stands by itself, wedged in amid a thousand others upon the vast and flat mosaic, having no intelligence, and conveying no story, any more than the wrong side of some rich tapestry. The little babe stretches out his arms and fingers, as if to grasp or to fathom the many-coloured vision; and thus he gradually learns the connexion of part with part, separates what moves from what is stationary, watches the coming and going of figures, masters the idea of shape and of perspective, calls in the information conveyed through the other senses to assist him in his mental process, and thus gradually converts a calidoscope into a picture. The first view was the more splendid, the second the more real; the former more poetical, the latter more philosophical. Alas! what are we doing all through life, both as a necessity and as a duty, but unlearning the world's poetry, and attaining to its prose! This is our education, as boys and as men, in the action of life, and in the closet or library; in our affections, in our aims, in our hopes, and in our memories. And in like manner it is the education of our intellect; I say, that one main portion of intellectual education, of the labours of both school and university, is to remove the original dimness of the mind's eye; to strengthen and perfect its vision; to enable it to look out into the world right forward, steadily and truly; to give the mind clearness, accuracy, precision; to enable it to use words aright, to understand what it says, to conceive justly what it thinks about, to abstract, compare, analyze, divide, define, and reason, correctly. There is a particular science which takes these matters in hand, and it is called logic; but it is not by logic, certainly not by logic alone, that the faculty I speak of is acquired. The infant does not learn to spell and read the hues upon his retina by any scientific rule; nor does the student learn accuracy of thought by any manual or treatise. The instruction given him, of whatever kind, if it be really instruction, is mainly, or at least pre-eminently, this,—a discipline in accuracy of mind.

Boys are always more or less inaccurate, and too many, or rather the majority, remain boys all their lives. When, for instance, I hear speakers at public meetings declaiming about "large and enlightened views," or about "freedom of conscience," or about "the Gospel," or any other popular subject of the day, I am far from denying that some among them know what they are talking about; but it would be satisfactory, in a particular case, to be sure of the fact; for it seems to me that those household words may stand in a man's mind for a something or other, very glorious indeed, but very misty, pretty much like the idea of "civilization" which floats before the mental vision of a Turk,—that is, if, when he interrupts his smoking to utter the word, he condescends to reflect whether it has any meaning at all. Again, a critic in a periodical dashes off, perhaps, his praises of a new work, as "talented, original, replete with intense interest, irresistible in argument, and, in the best sense of the word, a very readable book;"—can we really believe that he cares to attach any definite sense to the words of which he is so lavish? nay, that, if he had a habit of attaching sense to them, he could ever bring himself to so prodigal and wholesale an expenditure of them?

To a short-sighted person, colours run together and intermix, outlines disappear, blues and reds and yellows become russets or browns, the lamps or candles of an illumination spread into an unmeaning glare, or dissolve into a milky way. He takes up an eye-glass, and the mist clears up; every image stands out distinct, and the rays of light fall back upon their centres. It is this haziness of intellectual vision which is the malady of all classes of men by nature, of those who read and write and compose, quite as well as of those who cannot,—of all who have not had a really good education. Those who cannot either read or write may, nevertheless, be in the number of those who have remedied and got rid of it; those who can, are too often still under its power. It is an acquisition quite separate from miscellaneous information, or knowledge of books. This is a large subject, which might be pursued at great length, and of which here I shall but attempt one or two illustrations.

§ 1. Grammar

1.

One of the subjects especially interesting to all persons who, from any point of view, as officials or as students, are regarding a University course, is that of the Entrance Examination. Now a principal subject introduced into this examination will be "the elements of Latin and Greek Grammar." "Grammar" in the middle ages was often used as almost synonymous with "literature," and a Grammarian was a "Professor literarum." This is the sense of the word in which a youth of an inaccurate mind delights. He rejoices to profess all the classics, and to learn none of them. On the other hand, by "Grammar" is now more commonly meant, as Johnson defines it, "the art of using *words* properly," and it "comprises four parts—Orthography, Etymology, Syntax, and Prosody." Grammar, in this sense, is the scientific analysis of language, and to be conversant with it, as regards a particular language, is to be able to understand the meaning and force of that language when thrown into sentences and paragraphs.

Thus the word is used when the "elements of Latin and Greek Grammar" are spoken of as subjects of our Entrance Examination; not, that is, the elements of Latin and Greek literature, as if a youth were intended to have a smattering of the classical writers in general, and were to be able to give an opinion about the eloquence of Demosthenes and Cicero, the value of Livy, or the existence of Homer; or need have read half a dozen Greek and Latin authors, and portions of a dozen others:—though of course it would be much to his credit if he had done so; only, such proficiency is not to be expected, and cannot be required, of him:—but we mean the structure and characteristics of the Latin and Greek languages, or an examination of his scholarship. That is, an examination in order to ascertain whether he knows Etymology and Syntax, the two principal departments of the science of language,—whether he understands how the separate portions of a sentence hang together, how they form a whole, how each has its own place in the government of it, what are the peculiarities of construction or the idiomatic expressions in it proper to the language in which it is written, what is the precise meaning of its terms, and what the history of their formation.

All this will be best arrived at by trying how far he can frame a possible, or analyze a given sentence. To translate an English sentence into Latin is to *frame* a sentence, and is the best test whether or not a student knows the difference of Latin from English construction; to construe and parse is to *analyze* a sentence, and is an evidence of the easier attainment of knowing what Latin construction is in itself. And this is the sense of the word "Grammar" which our inaccurate student detests, and this is the sense of the word which every sensible tutor will maintain. His maxim is, "a little, but well;" that is, really know what you say you know: know what you know and what you do not know; get one thing well before you go on to a second; try to ascertain what your words mean; when you read a sentence, picture it before your mind as a whole, take in the truth or information contained in it, express it in your own words, and, if it be important, commit it to the faithful memory. Again, compare one idea with another; adjust truths and facts; form them into one whole, or notice the obstacles which occur in doing so. This is the way to make progress; this is the way to arrive at results; not to swallow knowledge, but (according to the figure sometimes used) to masticate and digest it.

2.

To illustrate what I mean, I proceed to take an instance. I will draw the sketch of a candidate for entrance, deficient to a great extent. I shall put him below *par*, and not such as it is likely that a respectable school would turn out, with a view of clearly bringing before the reader, by the contrast, what a student ought *not* to be, or what is meant by *inaccuracy*. And, in order to simplify the case to the utmost, I shall take, as he will perceive as I proceed, one *single word* as a sort of text, and show how that one word, even by itself, affords matter for a sufficient examination of a youth in grammar, history, and geography. I set off thus:—

TUTOR. Mr. Brown, I believe? sit down. CANDIDATE. Yes.

T. What are the Latin and Greek books you propose to be examined in? C. Homer, Lucian, Demosthenes, Xenophon, Virgil, Horace, Statius, Juvenal, Cicero, Analecta, and Matthiæ.

T. No; I mean what are the books I am to examine you in? C. *is silent.*

T. The two books, one Latin and one Greek: don't flurry yourself. C. Oh, ... Xenophon and Virgil.

T. Xenophon and Virgil. Very well; what part of Xenophon? C. *is silent.*

T. What work of Xenophon? C. Xenophon.

T. Xenophon wrote many works. Do you know the names of any of them? C. I ... Xenophon ... Xenophon.

T. Is it the *Anabasis* you take up? C. (*with surprise*) O yes; the Anabasis.

T. Well, Xenophon's Anabasis; now what is the meaning of the word *anabasis*? C. *is silent.*

T. You know very well; take your time, and don't be alarmed. Anabasis means ... C. An ascent.

T. Very right; it means an ascent. Now how comes it to mean an ascent? What is it derived from? C. It comes from ... (*a pause*). *Anabasis* ... it *is* the nominative.

T. Quite right: but what part of speech is it? C. A noun,—a noun substantive.

T. Very well; a noun substantive, now what is the verb that *anabasis* is derived from? C. *is silent.*

T. From the verb ἀναβαίνω isn't it? from ἀναβαίνω. C. Yes.

T. Just so. Now, what does ἀναβαίνω mean? C. To go up, to ascend.

T. Very well; and which part of the word means *to go*, and which part *up*? C. ἀνά is *up*, and βαίνω is *go*.

T. βαίνω to go, yes; now βάσις? What does βάσις mean? C. A going.

T. That is right; and ἀνά-βάσις? C. A going up.

T. Now what is a going *down*? C. *is silent.*

T. What is down? ... Κατά ... don't you recollect? κατά. C. Κατά.

T. Well, then, what is a going *down*? Cat ... cat ... C. Cat ...

T. Cata ... C. Cata ...

T. Catabasis. C. Oh, of course, catabasis.

T. Now tell me what is the future of βαίνω? C. (*thinks*) βανω.

T. No, no; think again; you know better than that. C. (*objects*) Φαίνω, φανω?

T. Certainly, φανω is the future of φαίνω; but βαίνω is, you know, an irregular verb. C. Oh, I recollect, βήσω.

T. Well, that is much better; but you are not quite right yet; βήσομαι. C. Oh, of course, βήσομαι.

T. βήσομαι. Now do you mean to say that βήσομαι comes from βαίνω? C. *is silent.*

T. For instance: τύψω comes from τύπτω by a change of letters; does βήσομαι in any similar way come from βαίνω? C. It is an irregular verb.

T. What do you mean by an irregular verb? does it form tenses anyhow and by caprice? C. It does not go according to the paradigm.

T. Yes, but how do you account for this? C. *is silent.*

T. Are its tenses formed from several roots? C. *is silent.* T. *is silent; then he changes the subject.*

T. Well, now you say *Anabasis* means an *ascent*. *Who* ascended? C. The Greeks, Xenophon.

T. Very well: Xenophon and the Greeks; the Greeks ascended. To what did they ascend? C. Against the Persian king: they ascended to fight the Persian king.

T. That is right ... an ascent; but I thought we called it a *de*scent when a foreign army carried war into a country? C. *is silent.*

T. Don't we talk of a descent of barbarians? C. Yes.

T. Why then are the Greeks said to go *up*? C. They went up to fight the Persian king.

T. Yes; but why *up* … why not *down*? C. They came down afterwards, when they retreated back to Greece.

T. Perfectly right; they did … but could you give no reason why they are said to go *up* to Persia, not *down*? C. They went *up* to Persia.

T. Why do you not say they went *down*? C. *pauses, then,* … They went *down* to Persia.

T. You have misunderstood me.

A silence.

T. *Why* do you not say *down*? C. I do … *down*.

T. You have got confused; you know very well. C. I understood you to ask why I did not say "they went *down*".

A silence on both sides.

T. Have you come up to Dublin or down? C. I came up.

T. Why do you call it coming *up*? C. *thinks, then smiles, then* … We *always* call it coming up to Dublin.

T. Well, but you always have a *reason* for what you do … what is your reason here? C. *is silent.*

T. Come, come, Mr. Brown, I won't believe you don't know; I am sure you have a very good reason for saying you go up to Dublin, not *down*. C. *thinks, then* … It is the capital.

T. Very well; now was Persia the capital? C. Yes.

T. Well … no … not exactly … explain yourself; was Persia a city? C. A country.

T. That is right; well, but did you ever hear of Susa? *Now*, why did they speak of going *up* to Persia? C. *is silent.*

T. Because it was the seat of government; that was one reason. Persia was the seat of government; they went up because it was the seat of government. C. Because it was the seat of government.

T. Now where did they go up from? C. From Greece.

T. But where did this army assemble? whence did it set out? C. *is silent.*

T. It is mentioned in the first book; where did the troops *rendezvous*? C. *is silent*.

T. Open your book; now turn to Book I., chapter ii.; now tell me. C. Oh, at Sardis.

T. Very right: at Sardis; now where was Sardis? C. In Asia Minor? … no … it's an island … *a pause, then* … Sardinia.

T. In Asia Minor; the army set out from Asia Minor, and went on towards Persia; and therefore it is said to go *up*—because … C. *is silent*.

T. Because … Persia … C. Because Persia.

T. Of course; because Persia held a sovereignty over Asia Minor. C. Yes.

T. Now do you know how and when Persia came to conquer and gain possession of Asia Minor? C. *is silent*.

T. Was Persia in possession of many countries? C. *is silent*.

T. Was Persia at the head of an empire? C. *is silent*.

T. Who was Xerxes? C. Oh, Xerxes … yes … Xerxes; he invaded Greece; he flogged the sea.

T. Right; he flogged the sea: what sea? C. *is silent*.

T. Have you read any history of Persia? … what history? C. Grote, and Mitford.

T. Well, now, Mr. Brown, you can name some other reason why the Greeks spoke of going up to Persia? Do we talk of going *up* or *down* from the sea-coast? C. Up.

T. That is right; well, going from Asia Minor, would you go from the sea, or towards it? C. From.

T. What countries would you pass, going from the coast of Asia Minor to Persia? … mention any of them. C. *is silent*.

T. What do you mean by Asia *Minor*? … why called Minor? … how does it lie? C. *is silent*.

Etc., etc.

3.

I have drawn out this specimen at the risk of wearying the reader; but I have wished to bring out clearly what it really is which an Entrance Examination should aim at and require in its students.

This young man had read the Anabasis, and had some general idea what the word meant; but he had no accurate knowledge how the word came to have its meaning, or of the history and geography implied in it. This being the case, it was useless, or rather hurtful, for a boy like him to amuse himself with running through Grote's many volumes, or to cast his eye over Matthiæ's minute criticisms. Indeed, this seems to have been Mr. Brown's stumbling-block; he began by saying that he had read Demosthenes, Virgil, Juvenal, and I do not know how many other authors. Nothing is more common in an age like this, when books abound, than to fancy that the gratification of a love of reading is real study. Of course there are youths who shrink even from story books, and cannot be coaxed into getting through a tale of romance. Such Mr. Brown was not; but there are others, and I suppose he was in their number, who certainly have a taste for reading, but in whom it is little more than the result of mental restlessness and curiosity. Such minds cannot fix their gaze on one object for two seconds together; the very impulse which leads them to read at all, leads them to read on, and never to stay or hang over any one idea. The pleasurable excitement of reading what is new is their motive principle; and the imagination that they are doing something, and the boyish vanity which accompanies it, are their reward. Such youths often profess to like poetry, or to like history or biography; they are fond of lectures on certain of the physical sciences; or they may possibly have a real and true taste for natural history or other cognate subjects;—and so far they may be regarded with satisfaction; but on the other hand they profess that they do not like logic, they do not like algebra, they have no taste for mathematics; which only means that they do not like application, they do not like attention, they shrink from the effort and labour of thinking, and the process of true intellectual gymnastics. The consequence will be that, when they grow up, they may, if it so happen, be agreeable in conversation, they may be well informed in this or that department of knowledge, they may be what is called literary; but they will have no consistency, steadiness, or perseverance; they will not be able to make a telling speech, or to write a good letter, or to fling in debate a smart antagonist, unless so far as, now and then, mother-wit supplies a sudden capacity, which cannot be ordinarily counted on. They cannot state an argument or a question, or take a clear survey of a whole transaction, or give sensible and appropriate advice under difficulties, or do any of those things which inspire confidence and gain influence, which raise a man in life, and make him useful to his religion or his country.

And now, having instanced what I mean by the *want* of accuracy, and stated the results in which I think it issues, I proceed to sketch, by way of contrast, an examination which displays a student, who, whatever may be his proficiency, at least knows what he is about, and has tried to master what he has read. I am far from saying that every candidate for admission must come up to its standard:—

T. I think you have named Cicero's *Letters ad Familiares*, Mr. Black? Open, if you please, at Book xi., Epistle 29, and begin reading.

C. *reads*. Cicero Appio salutem. Dubitanti mihi (quod scit Atticus noster), de hoc toto consilio profectionis, quod in utramque partem in mentem multa veniebant, magnum pondus accessit ad tollendam dubitationem, judicium et consilium tuum. Nam et scripsisti aperte, quid tibi videretur; et Atticus ad me sermonem tuum pertulit. Semper judicavi, in te, et in capiendo consilio prudentiam summam esse, et in dando fidem; maximeque sum expertus, cum, initio civilis belli, per literas te consuluissem quid mihi faciendum esse censeres; eundumne ad Pompeium an manendum in Italiâ.

T. Very well, stop there; Now construe. C. Cicero Appio salutem ... *Cicero greets Appius.*

T. "*Greets Appius.*" True; but it sounds stiff in English, doesn't it? What is the real English of it? C. "My *dear* Appius?" ...

T. That will do; go on. C. Dubitanti mihi, quod scit Atticus noster, *While I was hesitating, as our friend Atticus knows...*

T. That is right. C. De hoc toto consilio profectionis, *about the whole plan ... entire project ...* de hoc toto consilio profectionis

... on the subject of my proposed journey ... on my proposed journey altogether.

T. Never mind; go on; any of them will do. C. Quod in utramque partem in mentem multa veniebant, *inasmuch as many considerations both for and against it came into my mind,* magnum pondus accessit ad tollendam dubitationem, *it came with great force to remove my hesitation.*

T. What do you mean by "accessit"? C. It means *it contributed to turn the scale;* accessit, *it was an addition to one side.*

T. Well, it may mean so, but the words run, ad tollendam dubitationem. C. *It was a great ... it was a powerful help toward removing my hesitation ... no ... this was a powerful help, viz., your judgment and advice.*

T. Well, what is the construction of "pondus" and "judicium"? C. *Your advice came as a great weight.*

T. Very well, go on. C. Nam et scripsisti aperte quid tibi videretur; *for you distinctly wrote your opinion.*

T. Now, what is the force of "nam"? C. *pauses; then,* It refers to "accessit" ... it is an explanation of the fact, that Appius's opinion was a help.

T. "Et"; you omitted "et" ... "et scripsisti." C. It is one of two "ets"; et scripsisti, et Atticus.

T. Well, but why don't you construe it? C. Et scripsisti, *you both distinctly ...*

T. No; tell me, *why* did you leave it out? had you a reason? C. I thought it was only the Latin style, to dress the sentence, to make it antithetical; and was not English.

T. Very good, still, you can express it; try. C. *Also,* with the second clause?

T. That is right, go on. C. Nam et, *for you distinctly stated in writing your opinion,* et Atticus ad me sermonem tuum pertulit, *and Atticus too sent me word of what you said ... of what you said to him in conversation.*

T. "Pertulit." C. It means that Atticus conveyed on to Cicero the conversation he had with Appius.

T. *Who* was Atticus? C. *is silent.*

T. *Who* was Atticus? C. I didn't think it came into the examination …

T. Well, I didn't say it did: but still you can tell me who Atticus was. C. A great friend of Cicero's.

T. Did he take much part in politics? C. No.

T. What were his opinions? C. He was an Epicurean.

T. What was an Epicurean? C. *is silent, then,* Epicureans lived for themselves.

T. You are answering very well, sir; proceed. C. Semper judicavi, *I have ever considered*; in te, et in capiendo consilio prudentiam summam esse, et in dando fidem; *that your wisdom was of the highest order … that you had the greatest wisdom … that nothing could exceed the wisdom of your resolves, or the honesty of your advice.*

T. "Fidem." C. It means *faithfulness to the person asking …* maximeque sum expertus, *and I had a great proof of it….*

T. *Great*; why don't you say *greatest*? "maxime" is superlative. C. The Latins use the superlative, when they only mean the positive.

T. You mean, when English uses the positive; can you give me an instance of what you mean? C. Cicero always speaks of others as amplissimi, optimi, doctissimi, clarissimi.

T. Do they ever use the comparative for the positive? C. *thinks, then,* Certior factus sum.

T. Well, perhaps; however, here, "maxime" may mean special, may it not? C. *And I had a special proof of it,* cum, initio civilis belli, per literas te consuluissem, *when, on the commencement of the civil war, I had written to ask your advice,* quid mihi faciendum esse censeres, *what you thought I ought to do,* eundumne ad Pompeium, an manendum in Italiâ, *to go to Pompey, or to remain in Italy.*

T. Very well, now stop. Dubitanti mihi, quod scit Atticus noster. You construed quod, *as.* C. I meant the relative *as.*

T. Is *as* a relative? C. *As* is used in English for the relative, as when we say *such as* for *those who.*

T. Well, but why do you use it here? What is the antecedent to "quod"? C. The sentence Dubitanti mihi, etc.

T. Still, construe "quod" literally. C. *A thing which.*

T. Where is *a thing*? C. It is understood.

T. Well, but put it in. C. Illud quod.

T. Is that right? what is the common phrase? C. *is silent.*

T. Did you ever see "illud quod" in that position? is it the phrase? C. *is silent.*

T. It is commonly "id quod," isn't it? id quod. C. Oh, I recollect, id quod.

T. Well, which is more common, "quod," or "id quod," when the sentence is the antecedent? C. I think "id quod."

T. At least it is far more distinct; yes, I think it is more common. What could you put instead of it? C. Quod quidem.

T. Now, dubitanti mihi; what is "mihi" governed by? C. Accessit.

T. No; hardly. C. *is silent.*

T. Does "accessit" govern the dative? C. I thought it did.

T. Well, it may; but would Cicero use the dative after it? what is the more common practice with words of motion? Do you say, Venit mihi, *he came to me*? C. No, Venit ad me;—I recollect.

T. That is right; venit ad me. Now, for instance, "incumbo:" what case does "incumbo" govern? C. Incumbite remis?

T. Where is that? in Cicero? C. No, in Virgil. Cicero uses "in"; I recollect, incumbere in opus ... ad opus.

T. Well, then, *is* this "mihi" governed by "accessit"? *what* comes after accessit? C. I see; it is, accessit ad tollendam dubitationem.

T. That is right; but then, what after all do you do with "mihi"? how is it governed? C. *is silent.*

T. How is "mihi" governed, if it does not come after "accessit"? C. *pauses, then,* "Mihi" ... "mihi" is often used so; and "tibi" and "sibi": I mean "suo sibi gladio hunc jugulo"; ... "venit mihi in mentem"; that is, *it came into my mind*; and so, "accessit mihi ad tollendam," etc.

T. That is very right. C. I recollect somewhere in Horace, vellunt tibi barbam.

Etc., etc.

4.

And now, my patient reader, I suspect you have had enough of me on this subject; and the best I can expect from you is, that you will say: "His first pages had some amusement in them, but he is dullish towards the end." Perhaps so; but then you must kindly bear in mind that the latter part is about a steady careful youth, and the earlier part is not; and that goodness, exactness, and diligence, and the correct and the unexceptionable, though vastly more desirable than their contraries in fact, are not near so entertaining in fiction.

§ 2. Composition

1.

I am able to present the reader by anticipation with the correspondence which will pass between Mr. Brown's father and Mr. White, the tutor, on the subject of Mr. Brown's examination for entrance at the University. And, in doing so, let me state the reason why I dwell on what many will think an extreme case, or even a caricature. I do so, because what may be called exaggeration is often the best means of bringing out certain faults of the mind which do indeed exist commonly, if not in that degree. If a master in carriage and deportment wishes to carry home to one of his boys that he slouches, he will caricature the boy himself by way of impressing on the boy's intellect a sort of abstract and typical representation of the ungraceful habit which he wishes corrected. When we once have the simple and perfect ideas of things in our minds, we refer the particular and partial manifestations of them to these types; we recognize what they are, good or bad, as we never did before, and we have a guide set up within us to direct our course by. So it is with principles of taste, good breeding, or of conventional fashion; so it is in the fine arts, in painting, or in music. We cannot even understand the criticism passed on these subjects until we have set up for ourselves the ideal standard of what is admirable and what is absurd.

So is it with the cultivation and discipline of the mind, as it should be conducted at College and University, and as it manifests itself afterwards in life. Clearness of head, accuracy, scholarlike precision, method, and the like, are ideas obvious to point out, and easy to grasp; yet they do not suggest themselves to youths at once, and have to be urged and inflicted upon them. And this is done best by a caricature of their opposites.

And, as I am now going to continue the caricature by bringing in Mr. Brown's father as well as himself, I have to make a fresh explanation, lest I should seem to imply there are fathers altogether such as he will prove to be. I do not mean to say there are; yet it may easily happen that many excellent fathers, many even able and thoughtful men, may be found, who in a certain measure are under the bias of that error of which Mr. Brown senior is the typical instance, and who may be led possibly to reconsider some of their views, and in a measure to modify them, if they are confronted with an exhibition of them in their full dimensions;— and that, in consequence of their being forced to master the typical representation, though the error is never found thus pure and complete in fact, but only in degrees and portions, so that, when represented pure, it is called, and may fairly be called, a caricature. With this explanation of my meaning, and this apology in anticipation, I hope to be able without misconstruction to put before the reader the correspondence of which I have spoken.

2.

Mr. Brown, jun., to his father.

"My Dear Father,

"It seems odd I never was in Dublin before, though we have been now some time in Ireland. Well, I find it a handsomer place than I thought for—really a respectable town. But it is sadly behind the world in many things. Think of its having no Social Science, not even a National Gallery or British Museum! nor have they any high art here: some good public buildings, but very pagan. The bay is a fine thing.

"I called with your letter on Mr. Black, who introduced me to the professors, some of whom, judging by their skulls, are clever men.

"There is a lot here for examination, and an Exhibition is to be given to the best. I should like to get it. Young Black,—you saw him once,—is one of them; I knew him at school; he is a large fellow now, though younger than I am. If he be the best of them, I shall not be much afraid.

"Well—in I went yesterday, and was examined. It was such a queer concern. One of the junior Tutors had me up, and he must be a new hand, he was so uneasy. He gave me the slowest examination! I don't know to this minute what he was at. He first said a word or two, and then was silent. He then asked me why we came up to Dublin, and did not go down; and put some absurd little questions about Βαίνω. I was tolerably satisfied with myself, but he gave me no opportunity to show off. He asked me literally nothing; he did not even give me a passage to construe for a long time, and then gave me nothing more than two or three easy sentences. And he kept playing with his paper knife, and saying: 'How are you now, Mr. Brown? don't be alarmed, Mr. Brown; take your time, Mr. Brown; you know very well, Mr. Brown;' so that I could hardly help laughing. I never was less afraid in my life. It would be wonderful if such an examination *could* put me out of countenance.

"There's a lot of things which I know very well, which the Examiner said not a word about. Indeed, I think I have been getting up a great many things for nothing;—provoking enough. I had read a good deal of Grote; but though I told him so, he did not ask me one question in it; and there's Whewell, Macaulay, and Schlegel, all thrown away.

"He has not said a word yet where I am to be lodged. He looked quite confused when I asked him. He is, I suspect, a *character*.

"Your dutiful son, etc.,

"ROBERT."

Mr. White to Mr. Brown, sen.

"My Dear Sir,

"I have to acknowledge the kind letter you sent me by your son, and I am much pleased to find the confidence you express in us. Your son seems an amiable young man, of studious habits, and there is every hope, when he joins us, of his passing his academical career with respectability, and his examination with credit. This is what I should have expected from his telling me that he had been educated at home under your own paternal eye; indeed, if I do not mistake, you have undertaken the interesting office of instructor yourself.

"I hardly know what best to recommend to him at the moment: his reading has been *desultory*; he knows *something* about a great many things, of which youths of his age commonly know nothing. Of course we could take him into residence now, if you urge it; but my advice is that he should first direct his efforts to distinct preparation for our examination, and to study its particular character. Our rule is to recommend youths to do a *little well*, instead of throwing themselves upon a large field of study. I conceive it to be your son's fault of mind not to see exactly the *point* of things, nor to be so well *grounded* as he might be. Young men are indeed always wanting in *accuracy*; this kind of deficiency is not peculiar to him, and he will doubtless soon overcome it when he sets about it.

"On the whole, then, if you will kindly send him up six months hence he will be more able to profit by our lectures. I will tell him what to read in the meanwhile. Did it depend on me, I should send him for that time to a good school or college, or I could find you a private Tutor for him.

"I am, etc."

Mr. Brown, sen., to Mr. White.

"Sir,

"Your letter, which I have received by this morning's post, is gratifying to a parent's feelings, so far as it bears witness to the impression which my son's amiableness and steadiness have made on you. He is indeed a most exemplary lad: fathers are partial, and their word about their children is commonly not to be taken; but I flatter myself that the present case is an exception to the rule; for, if ever there was a well-conducted youth, it is my dear son. He is certainly very clever; and a closer student, and, for his age, of more extensive reading and sounder judgment, does not exist.

"With this conviction, you will excuse me if I say that there were portions of your letter which I could not reconcile with that part of it to which I have been alluding. You say he is 'a young man of *studious habits*,' having '*every hope* of passing his academical career with respectability, and *his examination with credit*;' you allow that 'he knows something about a *great many things*, of which youths of his age commonly *know nothing*:' no common commendation, I consider; yet, in spite of this, you recommend, though you do not exact, as a complete disarrangement of my plans (for I do not know how long my duties will keep me in Ireland), a postponement of his coming into residence for six months.

"Will you allow me to suggest an explanation of this inconsistency? It is found in your confession that the examination is of a 'particular character.' Of course it is very right in the governors of a great Institution to be 'particular,' and it is not for me to argue with them. Nevertheless, I cannot help saying, that at this day nothing is so much wanted in education as *general* knowledge. This alone will fit a youth *for the world*. In a less stirring time, it may be well enough to delay in particularities, and to trifle over minutiæ; but the world will not stand still for us, and, unless we are up to its requisitions, we shall find ourselves thrown out of the contest. A man must have *something in him* now, to make his way; and the sooner we understand this, the better.

"It mortified me, I confess, to hear from my son, that you did not try him in a greater number of subjects, in handling which he would probably have changed your opinion of him. He has a good memory, and a great talent for history, ancient and modern, especially constitutional and parliamentary; another favourite study with him is the philosophy of history. He has read Pritchard's Physical History, Cardinal Wiseman's Lectures on Science, Bacon's Advancement of Learning, Macaulay, and Hallam: I never met with a faster reader. I have let him attend, in England, some of the most talented lecturers in chemistry, geology, and comparative anatomy, and he sees the Quarterly Reviews and the best Magazines, as a matter of course. Yet on these matters not a word of examination!

"I have forgotten to mention, he has a very pretty idea of poetical composition: I enclose a fragment which I have found on his table, as well as one of his prose Essays.

"Allow me, as a warm friend of your undertaking, to suggest, that the *substance* of knowledge is far more valuable than its *technicalities*; and that the vigour of the youthful mind is but *wasted* on *barren* learning, and its ardour is *quenched* in *dry* disquisition.

"I have the honour to be, etc."

On the receipt of this letter, Mr. White will find, to his dissatisfaction, that he has not advanced one hair's breadth in bringing home to Mr. Brown's father the real state of the case, and has done no more than present himself as a mark for certain commonplaces, very true, but very inappropriate to the matter in hand. Filled with this disappointing thought, for a while he will not inspect the enclosures of Mr. Brown's letter, being his son's attempts at composition. At length he opens them, and reads as follows:

Mr. Brown's poetry.

THE TAKING OF SEBASTOPOL[1]

Oh, might I flee to Araby the blest,
The world forgetting, but its gifts possessed,
Where fair-eyed peace holds sway from shore to shore,
And war's shrill clarion frights the air no more.

---

1 This was written in June, 1854, before the siege began.

Heard ye the cloud-compelling blast[2] awake
The slumbers of the inhospitable lake?[3]
Saw ye the banner in its pride unfold
The blush of crimson and the blaze of gold?

Raglan and St. Arnaud, in high command,
Have steamed from old Byzantium's hoary strand;
The famed Cyanean rocks presaged their fight,
Twin giants, with the astonished Muscovite.

So the loved maid, in Syria's balmy noon,
Forebodes the coming of the hot simoon,
And sighs ......
And longs ......
And dimly traces ......

Mr. Brown's prose.

"FORTES FORTUNA ADJUVAT."

"Of all the uncertain and capricious powers which rule our earthly destiny, fortune is the chief. Who has not heard of the poor being raised up, and the rich being laid low? Alexander the Great said he envied Diogenes in his tub, because Diogenes could have nothing less. We need not go far for an instance of fortune. Who was so great as Nicholas, the Czar of all the Russias, a year ago, and now he is "fallen, fallen from his high estate, without a friend to grace his obsequies."[4] The Turks are the finest specimen of the human race, yet they, too, have experienced the vicissitudes of fortune. Horace says that we should wrap ourselves in our virtue, when fortune changes. Napoleon, too, shows us how little we can rely on fortune; but his faults, great as they were, are being redeemed by his nephew, Louis Napoleon, who

2 Bombarding
3 The Black Sea
4 Here again Mr. Brown prophesies. He wrote in June, 1854.

has shown himself very different from what we expected, though he has never explained how he came to swear to the Constitution, and then mounted the imperial throne.

"From all this it appears, that we should rely on fortune only while it remains,—recollecting the words of the thesis, 'Fortes fortuna adjuvat;' and that, above all, we should ever cultivate those virtues which will never fail us, and which are a sure basis of respectability, and will profit us here and hereafter."

On reading these compositions over, Mr. White will take to musing; then he will reflect that he may as well spare himself the trouble of arguing with a correspondent, whose principle and standard of judgment is so different from his own; and so he will write a civil letter back to Mr. Brown, enclosing the two papers.

3.

Mr. Brown, however, has not the resignation of Mr. White; and, on his Dublin friend, Mr. Black, paying him a visit, he will open his mind to him; and I am going to tell the reader all that will pass between the two.

Mr. Black is a man of education and of judgment. He knows the difference between show and substance; he is penetrated with the conviction that Rome was not built in a day, that buildings will not stand without foundations, and that, if boys are to be taught well, they must be taught slowly, and step by step. Moreover, he thinks in his secret heart that his own son Harry, whose acquaintance we have already formed, is worth a dozen young Browns. To him, then, not quite an impartial judge, Mr. Brown unbosoms his dissatisfaction, presenting to him his son's Theme as an *experimentum crucis* between him and Mr. White. Mr. Black reads it through once, and then a second time; and then he observes—

"Well, it is only the sort of thing which any boy would write, neither better nor worse. I speak candidly."

On Mr. Brown expressing disappointment, inasmuch as the said Theme is *not* the sort of thing which any boy could write, Mr. Black continues—

"There's not one word of it upon the thesis; but all boys write in this way."

Mr. Brown directs his friend's attention to the knowledge of ancient history which the composition displays, of Alexander and Diogenes; of the history of Napoleon; to the evident interest which the young author takes in contemporary history, and his prompt application of passing events to his purpose; moreover, to the apposite quotation from Dryden, and the reference to Horace;—all proofs of a sharp wit and a literary mind.

But Mr. Black is more relentlessly critical than the occasion needs, and more pertinacious than any father can comfortably bear. He proceeds to break the butterfly on the wheel in the following oration:—

"Now look here," he says, "the subject is 'Fortes fortuna adjuvat'; now this is a *proposition*; it states a certain general principle, and this is just what an ordinary boy would be sure to miss, and Robert does miss it. He goes off at once on the word 'fortuna.' 'Fortuna' was not his subject; the thesis was intended to *guide* him, for his own good; he refuses to be put into leading-strings; he breaks loose, and runs off in his own fashion on the broad field and in wild chase of 'fortune,' instead of closing with a subject, which, as being definite, would have supported him.

"It would have been very cruel to have told a boy to write on 'fortune'; it would have been like asking him his opinion 'of things in general.' Fortune is 'good,' 'bad,' 'capricious,' 'unexpected,' ten thousand things all at once (you see them all in the Gradus), and one of them as much as the other. Ten thousand things may be said of it: give me *one* of them, and I will write upon it; I cannot write on more than one; Robert prefers to write upon all.

"'Fortune favours the bold;' here is a very definite subject: take hold of it, and it will steady and lead you on: you will know in what direction to look. Not one boy in a hundred does avail himself of this assistance; your boy is not solitary in his inaccuracy; all boys are more or less inaccurate, *because* they are boys; boyishness of mind means inaccuracy. Boys cannot deliver a message, or execute an order, or relate an occurrence, without a blunder. They do not rouse up their attention and reflect: they do not like the trouble of it: they cannot look at anything steadily; and, when they attempt to write, off they go in a rigmarole of words, which does them no good, and never would, though they scribbled themes till they wrote their fingers off.

"A really clever youth, especially as his mind opens, is impatient of this defect of mind, even though, as being a youth, he be partially under its influence. He shrinks from a vague subject, as spontaneously as a slovenly mind takes to it; and he will often show at disadvantage, and seem ignorant and stupid, from seeing more and knowing more, and having a clearer perception of things than another has. I recollect once hearing such a young man, in the course of an examination, asked very absurdly what 'his opinion' was of Lord Chatham. Well, this was like asking him his view of 'things in general.' The poor youth stuck, and looked like a fool, though it was not *he*. The examiner, blind to his own absurdity, went on to ask him 'what were the characteristics of English history.' Another silence, and the poor fellow seemed to lookers-on to be done for, when his only fault was that he had better sense than his interrogator.

"When I hear such questions put, I admire the tact of the worthy Milnwood in *Old Mortality*, when in a similar predicament. Sergeant Bothwell broke into his house and dining-room in the king's name, and asked him what he thought of the murder of the Archbishop of St. Andrew's; the old man was far too prudent to hazard any opinion of his own, even on a precept of the Decalogue, when a trooper called for it; so he glanced his eye down the Royal Proclamation in the Sergeant's hand, and appropriated its sentiments as an answer to the question before him. Thereby he was enabled to pronounce the said assassination to be 'savage,' 'treacherous,' 'diabolical,' and 'contrary to the king's peace and the security of the subject;' to the edification of all present, and the satisfaction of the military inquisitor. It was in some such way my young friend got off. His guardian angel reminded him in a whisper that Mr. Grey, his examiner, had himself written a book on Lord Chatham and his times. This set him up at once; he drew boldly on his knowledge of his man for the political views advanced in it; was at no loss for definite propositions to suit his purpose; recovered his ground, and came off triumphantly."

Here Mr. Black stops; and Mr. Brown takes advantage of the pause to insinuate that Mr. Black is not himself a disciple of his own philosophy, having travelled some way from his subject;—his friend stands corrected, and retraces his steps.

"The thesis," he begins again, "is 'Fortune favours the brave;' Robert has gone off with the nominative without waiting for verb and accusative. He might as easily have gone off upon 'brave,' or upon 'favour,' except that 'fortune' comes first. He does not merely ramble from his subject, but he starts from a false point. Nothing could go right after this beginning, for having never gone *off* his subject (as I did off mine), he never could come back to it. However, at least he might have kept to some subject or other; he might have shown some exactness or consecutiveness in detail; but just the contrary;—observe. He begins by calling fortune 'a power'; let that pass. Next, it is one of the powers 'which rule our earthly destiny,' that is, *fortune* rules *destiny*. Why, where there is fortune, there is no destiny; where there is destiny, there is no fortune. Next, after stating generally that fortune raises or depresses, he proceeds to exemplify: there's Alexander, for instance, and Diogenes,—instances, that is, of what fortune did *not* do, for they died, as they lived, in their respective states of life. Then comes the Emperor Nicholas *hic et nunc*; with the Turks on the other hand, place and time and case not stated. Then examples are dropped, and we are turned over to poetry, and what we ought to do, according to Horace, when fortune changes. Next, we are brought back to our examples, in order to commence a series of rambles, beginning with Napoleon the First. *Apropos* of Napoleon the First comes in Napoleon the Third; this leads us to observe that the latter has acted 'very differently from what we expected;' and this again to the further remark, that no explanation has yet been given of his getting rid of the Constitution. He then ends by boldly quoting the thesis, in proof that we may rely on fortune, when we cannot help it; and by giving us advice, sound, but unexpected, to cultivate virtue."

"O! Black, it is quite ludicrous" … breaks in Mr. Brown;—this Mr. Brown must be a very good-tempered man, or he would not bear so much:—this is my remark, not Mr. Black's, who will not be interrupted, but only raises his voice: "Now, I know how this Theme was written," he says, "first one sentence, and then your boy sat thinking, and devouring the end of his pen; presently down went the second, and so on. The rule is, first think, and then write: don't write when you have nothing to say; or, if you do, you will make a mess of it. A thoughtful youth may deliver himself clumsily, he may set down little; but depend upon it, his half sentences will be worth more than the folio sheet of another boy, and an experienced examiner will see it.

"Now, I will prophesy one thing of Robert, unless this fault is knocked out of him," continues merciless Mr. Black. "When he grows up, and has to make a speech, or write a letter for the papers, he will look out for flowers, full-blown flowers, figures, smart expressions, trite quotations, hackneyed beginnings and endings, pompous circumlocutions, and so on: but the meaning, the sense, the solid sense, the foundation, you may hunt the slipper long enough before you catch it."

"Well," says Mr. Brown, a little chafed, "you are a great deal worse than Mr. White; you have missed your vocation: you ought to have been a schoolmaster." Yet he goes home somewhat struck by what his friend has said, and turns it in his mind for some time to come, when he gets there. He is a sensible man at bottom, as well as good-tempered, this Mr. Brown.

§ 3. Latin Writing

1.

Mr. White, the Tutor, is more and more pleased with young Mr. Black; and, when the latter asks him for some hints for writing Latin, Mr. White takes him into his confidence and lends him a number of his own papers. Among others he puts the following into Mr. Black's hands.

Mr. White's view of Latin translation.

"There are four requisites of good Composition,—correctness of vocabulary, or diction, syntax, idiom, and elegance. Of these, the two first need no explanation, and are likely to be displayed by every candidate. The last is desirable indeed, but not essential. The point which requires especial attention is *idiomatic propriety*.

"By *idiom* is meant that *use* of words which is peculiar to a particular language. Two nations may have corresponding words for the same ideas, yet differ altogether in their *mode of using* those words. For instance, 'et' means 'and,' yet it does not always admit of being used in Latin, where 'and' is used in English. 'Faire' may be French for 'do'; yet in a particular phrase, for 'How do you *do*?' 'faire' is not *used*, but 'se porter,' *viz.*, 'Comment vous portez-vous?' An Englishman or a Frenchman would be almost unintelligible and altogether ridiculous to each other, who used the French or English *words*, with the idioms or *peculiar uses* of his own language. Hence, the most complete and exact acquaintance with dictionary and grammar will utterly fail to teach a student to write or compose. Something more is wanted, *viz.*, the knowledge of the *use* of words and constructions, or the knowledge of *idiom*.

"Take the following English of a modern writer:

"'This is a serious consideration:—Among men, as among wild beasts, the taste of blood creates the appetite for it, and the appetite for it is strengthened by indulgence.'

"Translate it word for word literally into Latin, thus:—

"'Hæc est seria consideratio. Inter homines, ut inter feras, gustus sanguinis creat ejus appetitum, et ejus appetitus indulgentiâ roboratur.'

"Purer Latin, as far as *diction* is concerned, more correct, as far as *syntax*, cannot be desired. Every word is classical, every construction grammatical: yet Latinity it simply has none. From beginning to end it follows the English *mode* of speaking, or English idiom, not the Latin.

"In proportion, then, as a candidate advances from this Anglicism into Latinity, so far does he write good Latin.

"We might make the following remarks upon the above literal version.

"1. 'Consideratio' is not '*a* consideration;' the Latins, having no article, are driven to expedients to supply its place, *e.g.*, *quidam* is sometimes used for *a*.

"2. 'Consideratio' is not 'a consideration,' *i.e.*, a *thing* considered, or a subject; but the *act* of considering.

"3. It must never be forgotten, that such words as 'consideratio' are generally metaphorical, and therefore cannot be used *simply*, and without limitation or explanation, in the English sense, according to which the *mental* act is primarily conveyed by the word. 'Consideratio,' it is true, can be used absolutely, with greater propriety than most words of the kind; but if we take a parallel case, for instance, 'agitatio,' we could not use it at once in the mental sense for 'agitation,' but we should be obliged to say 'agitatio *mentis, animi*,' etc., though even then it would not answer to 'agitation.'

"4. 'Inter homines, gustus,' etc. Here the English, as is not uncommon, throws two ideas together. It means, first, that something *occurs* among men, and *occurs* among wild beasts, and that it is the same thing which occurs among both; and secondly that this something is, that the taste of blood has a certain particular effect. In other words, it means, (1) '*this* occurs among beasts and men,' (2) *viz.*, that the 'taste of blood,' etc. Therefore, 'inter homines, etc., gustus creat, etc.,' does not express the English *meaning*, it only translates its *expression*.

"5. 'Inter homines' is not the Latin phrase for 'among.' 'Inter' generally involves some sense of *division*, *viz.*, interruption, contrast, rivalry, etc. Thus, with a singular noun, 'inter cœnam hoc accidit,' *i.e.*, this *interrupted* the supper. And so with two nouns, 'inter me et Brundusium Cæsar est.' And so with a plural noun, 'hoc *inter homines* ambigitur,' *i.e.*, man with man. 'Micat *inter omnes* Julium sidus,' *i.e.*, in the rivalry of star against star. 'Inter tot annos unus (vir) inventus est,' *i.e.*, though all those years, one by one, put in their claim, yet only one of them can produce a man, etc. 'Inter se diligunt,' they love each other. On the contrary, the Latin word for 'among,' simply understood, is 'in.'

"6. As a general rule, indicatives active followed by accusatives, are foreign to the main structure of a Latin sentence.

"7. 'Et;' here two clauses are *connected*; having *different* subjects or nominatives; in the former 'appetitus' is in the nominative, and in the latter in the accusative. It is usual in Latin to carry on the *same* subject, in *connected* clauses.

"8. 'Et' here connects two *distinct* clauses. 'Autem' is more common.

"These being some of the faults of the literal version, I transcribe the translations sent in to me by six of my pupils respectively, who, however deficient in elegance of composition, and though more or less deficient in hitting the Latin idiom, yet evidently know what idiom is.

"The first wrote:—Videte rem graviorem; quod feris, id hominibus quoque accidit,—sanguinis sitim semel gustantibus intus concipi, plenè potantibus maturari.

"The second wrote:—Res seria agitur; nam quod in feris, illud in hominibus quoque cernitur, sanguinis appetitionem et suscitari lambendo et epulando inflammari.

"The third:—Ecce res summâ consideratione digna; et in feris et in hominibus, sanguinis semel delibati sitis est, sæpius hausti libido.

"The fourth:—Sollicitè animadvertendum est, cum in feris tum in hominibus fieri, ut guttæ pariant appetitum sanguinis, frequentiores potus ingluviem.

"And the fifth:—Perpende sedulo, gustum sanguinis tam in hominibus quam in feris primò appetitionem sui tandem cupidinem inferre.

"And the sixth:—Hoc grave est, quod hominibus cum feris videmus commune, gustasse est appetere sanguinem, hausisse in deliciis habere."

Mr. Black, junr., studies this paper, and considers that he has gained something from it. Accordingly, when he sees his father, he mentions to him Mr. White, his kindness, his papers, and especially the above, of which he has taken a copy. His father begs to see it; and, being a bit of a critic, forthwith delivers his judgment on it, and condescends to praise it; but he says that it fails in this, *viz.*, in overlooking the subject of *structure*. He maintains that the turning-point of good or bad Latinity is, not idiom, as Mr. White says, but structure. Then Mr. Black, the father, is led on to speak of himself, and of his youthful studies; and he ends by giving Harry a history of his own search after the knack of writing Latin. I do not see quite how this is to the point of Mr. White's paper, which cannot be said to contradict Mr. Black's narrative; but for this very reason, I may consistently quote it, for from a different point of view it may throw light on the subject treated in common by both these literary authorities.

2.

Old Mr. Black's Confession of his search after a Latin style.

"The attempts and the failures and the successes of those who have gone before, my dear son, are the direction-posts of those who come after; and, as I am only speaking to you, it strikes me that I may, without egotism or ostentation, suggest views or cautions, which might indeed be useful to the University Student generally, by a relation of some of my own endeavours to improve my own mind, and to increase my own knowledge in my early life. I am no great admirer of self-taught geniuses; to be self-taught is a misfortune, except in the case of those extraordinary minds, to whom the title of genius justly belongs; for in most cases, to be self-taught is to be badly grounded, to be slovenly finished, and to be preposterously conceited. Nor, again, was that misfortune I speak of really mine; but I have been left at times just so much to myself, as to make it possible for young students to gain hints from the history of my mind, which will be useful to themselves. And now for my subject.

"At school I was reckoned a sharp boy; I ran through its classes rapidly; and by the time I was fifteen, my masters had nothing more to teach me, and did not know what to do with me. I might have gone to a public school, or to a private tutor for three or four years; but there were reasons against either plan, and at the unusual age I speak of, with some inexact acquaintance with Homer, Sophocles, Herodotus, and Xenophon, Horace, Virgil, and Cicero, I was matriculated at the University. I had from a child been very fond of composition, verse and prose, English and Latin, and took especial interest in the subject of style; and one of the wishes nearest my heart was to write Latin well. I had some idea of the style of Addison, Hume, and Johnson, in English; but I had no idea what was meant by good Latin style. I had read Cicero without learning what it was; the books said, 'This is neat Ciceronian language,' 'this is pure and elegant Latinity,' but they did not tell me why. Some persons told me to go by my ear; to get Cicero by heart; and then I should know how to turn my thoughts and marshal my words, nay, more, where to put subjunctive moods and where to put indicative. In consequence I had a vague, unsatisfied feeling on the subject, and kept grasping shadows, and had upon me something of the unpleasant sensation of a bad dream.

"When I was sixteen, I fell upon an article in the *Quarterly*, which reviewed a Latin history of (I think) the Rebellion of 1715; perhaps by Dr. Whitaker. Years afterwards I learned that the critique was the writing of a celebrated Oxford scholar; but at the time, it was the subject itself, not the writer, that took hold of me. I read it carefully, and made extracts which, I believe, I have to this day. Had I known more of Latin writing, it would have been of real use to me; but as it was concerned of necessity in verbal criticisms, it did but lead me deeper into the mistake to which I had already been introduced,—that Latinity consisted in using good phrases. Accordingly I began noting down, and using in my exercises, idiomatic or peculiar expressions: such as 'oleum perdidi,' 'haud scio an non,' 'cogitanti mihi,' 'verum enimvero,' 'equidem,' 'dixerim,' and the like; and I made a great point of putting the verb at the end of the sentence. What took me in the

same direction was Dumesnil's *Synonymes*, a good book, but
one which does not even profess to teach Latin writing. I was
aiming to be an architect by learning to make bricks.

"Then I fell in with the *Germania* and *Agricola* of Tacitus,
and was very much taken by his style. Its peculiarities were much
easier to understand, and to copy, than Cicero's; 'decipit exemplar vitiis imitabile;' and thus, without any advance whatever in
understanding the genius of the language, or the construction
of a Latin sentence, I added to my fine words and cut-and-dried
idioms, phrases smacking of Tacitus. The Dialogues of Erasmus,
which I studied, carried me in the same direction; for dialogues,
from the nature of the case, consist of words and clauses, and
smart, pregnant, or colloquial expressions, rather than of sentences with an adequate structure."

Mr. Black takes breath, and then continues:

"The labour, then, of years came to nothing, and when I was
twenty I knew no more of Latin composition than I had known
at fifteen. It was then that circumstances turned my attention to
a volume of Latin Lectures, which had been published by the
accomplished scholar of whose critique in the *Quarterly Review* I
have already spoken. The Lectures in question had been delivered
terminally while he held the Professorship of Poetry, and were
afterwards collected into a volume; and various circumstances
combined to give them a peculiar character. Delivered one by
one at intervals, to a large, cultivated, and critical audience, they
both demanded and admitted of special elaboration of the style.
As coming from a person of his high reputation for Latinity, they
were displays of art; and, as addressed to persons who had to follow
ex tempore the course of a discussion delivered in a foreign tongue,
they needed a style as neat, pointed, lucid, and perspicuous as
it was ornamental. Moreover, as expressing modern ideas in an
ancient language, they involved a new development and application of its powers. The result of these united conditions was a style
less simple, less natural and fresh, than Cicero's; more studied,
more ambitious, more sparkling; heaping together in a page the
flowers which Cicero scatters over a treatise; but still on that very

account more fitted for the purpose of inflicting upon the inquiring student what Latinity was. Any how, such was its effect upon me; it was like the 'Open Sesame' of the tale; and I quickly found that I had a new sense, as regards composition, that I understood beyond mistake what a Latin sentence should be, and saw how an English sentence must be fused and remoulded in order to make it Latin. Henceforth Cicero, as an artist, had a meaning, when I read him, which he never had had to me before; the bad dream of seeking and never finding was over; and, whether I ever wrote Latin or not, at least I knew what good Latin was.

"I had now learned that good Latinity lies in structure; that every word of a sentence may be Latin, yet the whole sentence remain English; and that dictionaries do not teach composition. Exulting in my discovery, I next proceeded to analyze and to throw into the shape of science that idea of Latinity to which I had attained. Rules and remarks, such as are contained in works on composition, had not led me to master the idea; and now that I really had gained it, it led me to form from it rules and remarks for myself. I could now turn Cicero to account, and I proceeded to make his writings the materials of an induction, from which I drew out and threw into form what I have called a science of Latinity,—with its principles and peculiarities, their connection and their consequences,—or at least considerable specimens of such a science, the like of which I have not happened to see in print. Considering, however, how much has been done for scholarship since the time I speak of, and especially how many German books have been translated, I doubt not I should now find my own poor investigations and discoveries anticipated and superseded by works which are in the hands of every schoolboy. At the same time, I am quite sure that I gained a very great deal in the way of precision of thought, delicacy of judgment, and refinement of taste, by the processes of induction to which I am referring. I kept blank books, in which every peculiarity in every sentence of Cicero was minutely noted down, as I went on reading. The force of words, their combination into phrases, their collocation—the carrying on of one subject or nominative through a sentence, the breaking up of a sentence into clauses, the evasion of its categorical form, the resolution of abstract nouns into verbs and participles;— what is possible in Latin composition and what is not, how to compensate for want of brevity by elegance, and to secure perspicuity by the use of figures, these, and a hundred similar points of art, I illustrated with a diligence which even bordered on subtlety. Cicero became a mere magazine of instances, and the main use of the river was to feed the canal. I am unable to say whether these elaborate inductions would profit any one else, but I have a vivid recollection of the great utility they were at that time to my own mind.

"The general subject of Latin composition, my dear son, has ever interested me much, and you see only one point in it has made me speak for a quarter of an hour; but now that I have had my say about it, what is its upshot? The great moral I would impress upon you is this, that in learning to write Latin, as in all learning, you must not trust to books, but only make use of them; not hang like a dead weight upon your teacher, but catch some of his life; handle what is given you, not as a formula, but as a pattern to copy and as a capital to improve; throw your heart and mind into what you are about, and thus unite the separate advantages of being tutored and of being self-taught,—self-taught, yet without oddities, and tutorized, yet without conventionalities."

"Why, my dear father," says young Mr. Black, "you speak like a book. You must let me ask you to write down for me what you have been giving out in conversation."

I have had the advantage of the written copy.

§ 4. General Religious Knowledge

1.

It has been the custom in the English Universities to introduce religious instruction into the School of Arts; and a very right custom it is, which every University may well imitate. I have certainly felt it ought to have a place in that School; yet the subject is not without its difficulty, and I intend to say a few words upon it here. That place, if it has one, should of course be determined on some intelligible principle, which, while it justifies the introduction of Religion into a secular Faculty, will preserve it from becoming an intrusion, by fixing the conditions under which it is to be admitted. There are many who would make over the subject of Religion to the theologian exclusively; there are others who allow it almost unlimited extension in the province of Letters. The latter of these two classes, if not large, at least is serious and earnest; it seems to consider that the Classics should be superseded by the Scriptures and the Fathers, and that Theology proper should be taught to the youthful aspirant for University honours. I am not here concerned with opinions of this character, which I respect, but cannot follow. Nor am I concerned with that large class, on the other hand, who, in their exclusion of Religion from the lecture-rooms of Philosophy and Letters (or of Arts, as it used to be called), are actuated by scepticism or indifference; but there are other persons, much to be consulted, who arrive at the same practical conclusion as the sceptic and unbeliever, from real reverence and pure zeal for the interests of Theology, which they consider sure to suffer from the superficial treatment of lay-professors, and the superficial reception of young minds, as soon as, and in whatever degree, it is associated with classical, philosophical, and historical studies;—and as very many persons of great consideration seem to be of this opinion, I will set down the reasons why I follow the English tradition instead, and in what sense I follow it.

I might appeal, I conceive, to authority in my favour, but I pass it over, because mere authority, however sufficient for my own guidance, is not sufficient for the definite direction of those who have to carry out the matter of it in practice.

2.

In the first place, then, it is congruous certainly that youths who are prepared in a Catholic University for the general duties of a secular life, or for the secular professions, should not leave it without some knowledge of their religion; and, on the other hand, it does, in matter of fact, act to the disadvantage of a Christian place of education, in the world and in the judgment of men of the world, and is a reproach to its conductors, and even a scandal, if it sends out its pupils accomplished in all knowledge except Christian knowledge; and hence, even though it were impossible to rest the introduction of religious teaching into the secular lecture-room upon any logical principle, the imperative necessity of its introduction would remain, and the only question would be, what matter was to be introduced, and how much.

And next, considering that, as the mind is enlarged and cultivated generally, it is capable, or rather is desirous and has need, of fuller religious information, it is difficult to maintain that that knowledge of Christianity which is sufficient for entrance at the University is all that is incumbent on students who have been submitted to the academical course. So that we are unavoidably led on to the further question, viz., shall we sharpen and refine the youthful intellect, and then leave it to exercise its new powers upon the most sacred of subjects, as it will, and with the chance of its exercising them wrongly; or shall we proceed to feed it with divine truth, as it gains an appetite for knowledge?

Religious teaching, then, is urged upon us in the case of University students, first, by its evident propriety; secondly, by the force of public opinion; thirdly, from the great inconveniences of neglecting it. And, if the subject of Religion is to have a real place in their course of study, it must enter into the examinations in which that course results; for nothing will be found to impress and occupy their minds but such matters as they have to present to their Examiners.

Such, then, are the considerations which actually oblige us to introduce the subject of Religion into our secular schools, whether it be logical or not to do so; but next, I think that we can do so without any sacrifice of principle or of consistency; and this, I trust, will appear, if I proceed to explain the mode which I should propose to adopt for the purpose:—

I would treat the subject of Religion in the School of Philosophy and Letters simply as a branch of knowledge. If the University student is bound to have a knowledge of History generally, he is bound to have inclusively a knowledge of sacred history as well as profane; if he ought to be well instructed in Ancient Literature, Biblical Literature comes under that general description as well as Classical; if he knows the Philosophy of men, he will not be extravagating from his general subject, if he cultivate also that Philosophy which is divine. And as a student is not necessarily superficial, though he has not studied all the classical poets, or all Aristotle's philosophy, so he need not be dangerously superficial, if he has but a parallel knowledge of Religion.

3.

However, it may be said that the risk of theological error is so serious, and the effects of theological conceit are so mischievous, that it is better for a youth to know nothing of the sacred subject, than to have a slender knowledge which he can use freely and recklessly, for the very reason that it is slender. And here we have the maxim in corroboration: "A little learning is a dangerous thing."

This objection is of too anxious a character to be disregarded. I should answer it thus:—In the first place it is obvious to remark, that one great portion of the knowledge here advocated is, as I have just said, historical knowledge, which has little or nothing to do with doctrine. If a Catholic youth mixes with educated Protestants of his own age, he will find them conversant with the outlines and the characteristics of sacred and ecclesiastical history as well as profane: it is desirable that he should be on a par with them, and able to keep up a conversation with them. It is desirable, if he has left our University with honours or prizes, that he should know as well as they about the great primitive divisions of Christianity, its polity, its luminaries, its acts, and its fortunes; its great eras, and its course down to this day. He should have some idea of its propagation, and of the order in which the nations, which have submitted to it, entered its pale; and of the list of its

Fathers, and of its writers generally, and of the subjects of their works. He should know who St. Justin Martyr was, and when he lived; what language St. Ephraim wrote in; on what St. Chrysostom's literary fame is founded; who was Celsus, or Ammonius, or Porphyry, or Ulphilas, or Symmachus, or Theodoric. Who were the Nestorians; what was the religion of the barbarian nations who took possession of the Roman Empire: who was Eutyches, or Berengarius, who the Albigenses. He should know something about the Benedictines, Dominicans, or Franciscans, about the Crusades, and the chief movers in them. He should be able to say what the Holy See has done for learning and science; the place which these islands hold in the literary history of the dark age; what part the Church had, and how her highest interests fared, in the revival of letters; who Bessarion was, or Ximenes, or William of Wykeham, or Cardinal Allen. I do not say that we can insure all this knowledge in every accomplished student who goes from us, but at least we can admit such knowledge, we can encourage it, in our lecture-rooms and examination-halls.

And so in like manner, as regards Biblical knowledge, it is desirable that, while our students are encouraged to pursue the history of classical literature, they should also be invited to acquaint themselves with some general facts about the canon of Holy Scripture, its history, the Jewish canon, St. Jerome, the Protestant Bible; again, about the languages of Scripture, the contents of its separate books, their authors, and their versions. In all such knowledge I conceive no great harm can lie in being superficial.

But now as to Theology itself. To meet the apprehended danger, I would exclude the teaching *in extenso* of pure dogma from the secular schools, and content myself with enforcing such a broad knowledge of doctrinal subjects as is contained in the catechisms of the Church, or the actual writings of her laity. I would have students apply their minds to such religious topics as laymen actually do treat, and are thought praiseworthy in treating. Certainly I admit that, when a lawyer or physician, or statesman, or merchant, or soldier sets about discussing theological points, he is likely to succeed as ill as an ecclesiastic who meddles with law, or medicine, or the exchange. But I am professing to contemplate Christian knowledge in what may be called its secular aspect, as it is practically useful in the intercourse of life and in general conversation; and I would encourage it so far as it bears upon the history, the literature, and the philosophy of Christianity.

It is to be considered that our students are to go out into the world, and a world not of professed Catholics, but of inveterate, often bitter, commonly contemptuous, Protestants; nay, of Protestants who, so far as they come from Protestant Universities and public schools, do know their own system, do know, in proportion to their general attainments, the doctrines and arguments of Protestantism. I should desire, then, to encourage in our students an intelligent apprehension of the relations, as I may call them, between the Church and Society at large; for instance, the difference between the Church and a religious sect; the respective prerogatives of the Church and the civil power; what the Church claims of necessity, what it cannot dispense with, what it can; what it can grant, what it cannot. A Catholic hears the celibacy of the clergy discussed in general society; is that usage a matter of faith, or is it not of faith? He hears the Pope accused of interfering with the prerogatives of her Majesty, because he appoints an hierarchy. What is he to answer? What principle is to guide him in the remarks which he cannot escape from the necessity of making? He fills a station of importance, and he is addressed by some friend who has political reasons for wishing to know what is the difference between Canon and Civil Law, whether the Council of Trent has been received in France, whether a Priest cannot in certain cases absolve prospectively, what is meant by his *intention*, what by the *opus operatum*; whether, and in what sense, we consider Protestants to be heretics; whether any one can be saved without sacramental confession; whether we deny the reality of natural virtue, or what worth we assign to it?

Questions may be multiplied without limit, which occur in conversation between friends, in social intercourse, or in the business of life, when no argument is needed, no subtle and delicate disquisition, but a few direct words stating the fact, and when perhaps a few words may even hinder most serious inconveniences to the Catholic body. Half the controversies which go on in the world arise from ignorance of the facts of the case; half the prejudices against Catholicity lie in the misinformation of the prejudiced parties. Candid persons are set right, and enemies silenced, by the mere statement of what it is that we believe. It will not answer the purpose for a Catholic to say, "I leave it to theologians," "I will ask my priest;" but it will commonly give him a triumph, as easy as it is complete, if he can then and there lay down the law. I say "lay down the law;" for remarkable it is that even those who speak against Catholicism like to hear about it, and will excuse its advocate from alleging arguments if he can gratify their curiosity by giving them information. Generally speaking, however, as I have said, what is given as information will really be an argument as well as information. I recollect, some twenty-five years ago, three friends of my own, as they then were, clergymen of the Establishment, making a tour through Ireland. In the West or South they had occasion to become pedestrians for the day; and they took a boy of thirteen to be their guide. They amused themselves with putting questions to him on the subject of his religion; and one of them confessed to me on his return that that poor child put them all to silence. How? Not, of course, by any train of arguments, or refined theological disquisition, but merely by knowing and understanding the answers in his catechism.

4.

Nor will argument itself be out of place in the hands of laymen mixing with the world. As secular power, influence, or resources are never more suitably placed than when they are in the hands of Catholics, so secular knowledge and secular gifts are then best employed when they minister to Divine Revelation. Theologians inculcate the matter, and determine the details of that Revelation; they view it from within; philosophers view it from without, and this external view may be called the Philosophy of Religion, and the office of delineating it externally is most gracefully performed by laymen. In the first age laymen were most commonly the Apologists. Such were Justin, Tatian, Athenagoras, Aristides, Hermias, Minucius Felix, Arnobius, and Lactantius. In like manner in this age some of the most prominent defences of the Church are from laymen: as De Maistre, Chateaubriand, Nicolas, Montalembert, and others. If laymen may write, lay students may read; they surely may read what their fathers may have written. They might surely study other works too, ancient and modern, written whether by ecclesiastics or laymen, which, although they do contain theology, nevertheless, in their structure and drift, are polemical. Such is Origen's great work against Celsus; and Tertullian's Apology; such some of the controversial treatises of Eusebius and Theodoret; or St. Augustine's City of God; or the tract of Vincentius Lirinensis. And I confess that I should not even object to portions of Bellarmine's Controversies, or to the work of Suarez on laws, or to Melchior Canus's treatises on the Loci Theologici. On these questions in detail, however,—which are, I readily acknowledge, very delicate,—opinions may differ, even where the general principle is admitted; but, even if we confine ourselves strictly to the Philosophy, that is, the external contemplation, of Religion, we shall have a range of reading sufficiently wide, and as valuable in its practical application as it is liberal in its character. In it will be included what are commonly called the Evidences; and what is a subject of special interest at this day, the Notes of the Church.

But I have said enough in general illustration of the rule which I am recommending. One more remark I make, though it is implied in what I have been saying:—Whatever students read in the province of Religion, they read, and would read from the very nature of the case, under the superintendence, and with the explanations, of those who are older and more experienced than themselves.

V

A FORM OF INFIDELITY OF THE DAY

§ 1. Its Sentiments

1.

Though it cannot be denied that at the present day, in consequence of the close juxtaposition and intercourse of men of all religions, there is a considerable danger of the subtle, silent, unconscious perversion and corruption of Catholic intellects, who as yet profess, and sincerely profess, their submission to the authority of Revelation, still that danger is far inferior to what it was in one portion of the middle ages. Nay, contrasting the two periods together, we may even say, that in this very point they differ, that, in the medieval, since Catholicism was then the sole religion recognized in Christendom, unbelief necessarily made its advances under the language and the guise of faith; whereas in the present, when universal toleration prevails, and it is open to assail revealed truth (whether Scripture or Tradition, the Fathers or the "Sense of the faithful"), unbelief in consequence throws off the mask, and takes up a position over against us in citadels of its own, and confronts us in the broad light and with a direct assault. And I have no hesitation in saying (apart of course from moral and ecclesiastical considerations, and under correction of the command and policy of the Church), that I prefer to live in an age when the fight is in the day, not in the twilight; and think it a gain to be speared by a foe, rather than to be stabbed by a friend.

I do not, then, repine at all at the open development of unbelief in Germany, supposing unbelief is to be, or at its growing audacity in England; not as if I were satisfied with the state of things, considered positively, but because, in the unavoidable alternative of avowed unbelief and secret, my own personal leaning is in favour of the former. I hold that unbelief is in some shape unavoidable in an age of intellect and in a world like this, considering that faith requires an act of the will, and presupposes the due exercise of religious advantages. You may persist in calling Europe Catholic, though it is not; you may enforce an outward acceptance of Catholic dogma, and an outward obedience to Catholic precept; and your enactments may be, so far, not only pious in themselves, but even merciful towards the teachers of false doctrine, as well as just towards their victims; but this is all that you can do; you cannot bespeak conclusions which, in spite of yourselves, you are leaving free to the human will. There will be, I say, in spite of you, unbelief and immorality to the end of the world, and you must be prepared for immorality more odious, and unbelief more astute, more subtle, more bitter, and more resentful, in proportion as it is obliged to dissemble.

It is one great advantage of an age in which unbelief speaks out, that Faith can speak out too; that, if falsehood assails Truth, Truth can assail falsehood. In such an age it is possible to found a University more emphatically Catholic than could be set up in the middle age, because Truth can entrench itself carefully, and define its own profession severely, and display its colours unequivocally, by occasion of that very unbelief which so shamelessly vaunts itself. And a kindred advantage to this is the confidence which, in such an age, we can place in all who are around us, so that we need look for no foes but those who are in the enemy's camp.

2.

The medieval schools were the *arena* of as critical a struggle between truth and error as Christianity has ever endured; and the philosophy which bears their name carried its supremacy by means of a succession of victories in the cause of the Church. Scarcely had Universities risen into popularity, when they were found to be infected with the most subtle and fatal forms of unbelief; and the heresies of the East germinated in the West of Europe and in Catholic lecture-rooms, with a mysterious vigour upon which history throws little light. The questions agitated were as deep as any in theology; the being and essence of the Almighty were the main subjects of the disputation, and Aristotle was introduced to the ecclesiastical youth as a teacher of Pantheism. Saracenic expositions of the great philosopher were in vogue; and, when a fresh treatise was imported from Constantinople, the curious and impatient student threw himself upon it, regardless of the Church's warnings, and reckless of the effect upon his own mind. The acutest intellects became sceptics and misbelievers; and the head of the Holy Roman Empire, the Cæsar Frederick the Second, to say nothing of our miserable king John, had the reputation of meditating a profession of Mahometanism. It is said that, in the community at large, men had a vague suspicion and mistrust of each other's belief in Revelation. A secret society was discovered in the Universities of Lombardy, Tuscany, and France, organized for the propagation of infidel opinions; it was bound together by oaths, and sent its missionaries among the people in the disguise of pedlars and vagrants.

The success of such efforts was attested in the south of France by the great extension of the Albigenses, and the prevalence of Manichean doctrine. The University of Paris was obliged to limit the number of its doctors in theology to as few as eight, from misgivings about the orthodoxy of its divines generally. The narrative of Simon of Tournay, struck dead for crying out after lecture, "Ah! good Jesus, I could disprove Thee, did I please, as easily as I have proved," whatever be its authenticity, at least may be taken as a representation of the frightful peril to which Christianity was exposed. Amaury of Chartres was the author of a school of Pantheism, and has given his name to a sect; Abelard, Roscelin, Gilbert, and David de Dinant, Tanquelin, and Eon, and others who might be named, show the extraordinary influence of anti-Catholic doctrines on high and low. Ten ecclesiastics and several of the populace of Paris were condemned for maintaining that our Lord's reign was past, that the Holy Ghost was to be incarnate, or for parallel heresies.

Frederick the Second established a University at Naples with a view to the propagation of the infidelity which was so dear to him. It gave birth to the great St. Thomas, the champion of revealed truth. So intimate was the intermixture, so close the grapple, between faith and unbelief. It was the conspiracy of traitors, it was a civil strife, of which the medieval seats of learning were the scene.

In this day, on the contrary, Truth and Error lie over against each other with a valley between them, and David goes forward in the sight of all men, and from his own camp, to engage with the Philistine. Such is the providential overruling of that principle of toleration, which was conceived in the spirit of unbelief, in order to the destruction of Catholicity. The sway of the Church is contracted; but she gains in intensity what she loses in extent. She has now a direct command and a reliable influence over her own institutions, which was wanting in the middle ages. A University is her possession in these times, as well as her creation: nor has she the need, which once was so urgent, to expel heresies from her pale, which have now their own centres of attraction elsewhere, and spontaneously take their departure. Secular advantages no longer present an inducement to hypocrisy, and her members in consequence have the consolation of being able to be sure of each other. How much better is it, for us at least, whatever it may be for themselves (to take a case before our eyes in Ireland), that those persons, who have left the Church to become ministers in the Protestant Establishment, should be in their proper place, as they are, than that they should have perforce continued in her communion! I repeat it, I would rather fight with unbelief as we find it in the nineteenth century, than as it existed in the twelfth and thirteenth.

3.

I look out, then, into the enemy's camp, and I try to trace the outlines of the hostile movements and the preparations for assault which are there in agitation against us. The arming and the manœuvring, the earth-works and the mines, go on incessantly; and one cannot of course tell, without the gift of prophecy, which of his projects will be carried into effect and attain its purpose, and which will eventually fail or be abandoned. Threatening demonstrations may come to nothing; and those who are to be our most formidable foes, may before the attack elude our observation. All these uncertainties, we know, are the lot of the soldier in the field: and they are parallel to those which befall the warriors of the Temple. Fully feeling the force of such considerations, and under their correction, nevertheless I make my anticipations according to the signs of the times; and such must be my *proviso*, when I proceed to describe some characteristics of one particular form of infidelity, which is coming into existence and activity over against us, in the intellectual citadels of England.

It must not be supposed that I attribute, what I am going to speak of as a form of infidelity of the day, to any given individual or individuals; nor is it necessary to my purpose to suppose that any one man as yet consciously holds, or sees the drift, of that portion of the theory to which he has given assent. I am to describe a set of opinions which may be considered as the true explanation of many floating views, and the converging point of a multitude of separate and independent minds; and, as of old Arius or Nestorius not only was spoken of in his own person, but was viewed as the abstract and typical teacher of the heresy which he introduced, and thus his name denoted a heretic more complete and explicit, even though not more formal, than the heresiarch himself, so here too, in like manner, I may be describing a school of thought in its fully developed proportions, which at present every one, to whom membership with it is imputed, will at once begin to disown, and I may be pointing to teachers whom no one will be able to descry. Still, it is not less true that I may be speaking of tendencies and elements which exist; and he may come in person at last, who comes at first to us merely in his spirit and in his power.

The teacher, then, whom I speak of, will discourse thus in his secret heart:—He will begin, as many so far have done before him, by laying it down as if a position which approves itself to the reason, immediately that it is fairly examined, which is of so axiomatic a character as to have a claim to be treated as a first principle, and is firm and steady enough to bear a large super-structure upon it,—that Religion is not the subject-matter of a science. "You may have opinions in religion, you may have theo-ries, you may have arguments, you may have probabilities; you may have anything but demonstration, and therefore you can-not have science. In mechanics you advance from sure premises to sure conclusions; in optics you form your undeniable facts into system, arrive at general principles, and then again infallibly apply them: here you have Science. On the other hand, there is at present no real science of the weather, because you cannot get hold of facts and truths on which it depends; there is no science of the coming and going of epidemics; no science of the breaking out and the cessation of wars; no science of popular likings and dislikings, or of the fashions. It is not that these subject-matters are themselves incapable of science, but that, under existing cir-cumstances, we are incapable of subjecting them to it. And so, in like manner," says the philosopher in question, "without deny-ing that in the matter of religion some things are true and some things false, still we certainly are not in a position to determine the one or the other. And, as it would be absurd to dogmatize about the weather, and say that 1860 will be a wet season or a dry season, a time of peace or war, so it is absurd for men in our pres-ent state to teach anything positively about the next world, that there is a heaven, or a hell, or a last judgment, or that the soul is immortal, or that there is a God. It is not that you have not a right to your own opinion, as you have a right to place implicit trust in your own banker, or in your own physician; but undeni-ably such persuasions are not knowledge, they are not scientific, they cannot become public property, they are consistent with your allowing your friend to entertain the opposite opinion; and, if you are tempted to be violent in the defence of your own view of the case in this matter of religion, then it is well to lay seriously to heart whether sensitiveness on the subject of your banker or your doctor, when he is handled sceptically by another, would not be taken to argue a secret misgiving in your mind about him, in spite of your confident profession, an absence of clear, unruffled certainty in his honesty or in his skill."

Such is our philosopher's primary position. He does not prove it; he does but distinctly state it; but he thinks it self-evident when it is distinctly stated. And there he leaves it.

4.

Taking his primary position henceforth for granted, he will proceed as follows:—"Well, then, if Religion is just one of those subjects about which we can know nothing, what can be so absurd as to spend time upon it? what so absurd as to quarrel with others about it? Let us all keep to our own religious opinions respectively, and be content; but so far from it, upon no subject whatever has the intellect of man been fastened so intensely as upon Religion. And the misery is, that, if once we allow it to engage our attention, we are in a circle from which we never shall be able to extricate ourselves. Our mistake reproduces and corroborates itself. A small insect, a wasp or a fly, is unable to make his way through the pane of glass; and his very failure is the occasion of greater violence in his struggle than before. He is as heroically obstinate in his resolution to succeed as the assailant or defender of some critical battlefield; he is unflagging and fierce in an effort which cannot lead to anything beyond itself. When, then, in like manner, you have once resolved that certain religious doctrines shall be indisputably true, and that all men ought to perceive their truth, you have engaged in an undertaking which, though continued on to eternity, will never reach its aim; and, since you are convinced it ought to do so, the more you have failed hitherto, the more violent and pertinacious will be your attempt in time to come. And further still, since you are not the only man in the world who is in this error, but one of ten thousand, all holding the general principle that Religion is scientific, and yet all differing as to the truths and facts and conclusions of this science, it follows that the misery of social disputation and disunion is added to the misery of a hopeless investigation, and life is not only wasted in fruitless speculation, but embittered by bigotted sectarianism.

"Such is the state in which the world has lain," it will be said, "ever since the introduction of Christianity. Christianity has been the bane of true knowledge, for it has turned the intellect away from what it can know, and occupied it in what it cannot. Differences of opinion crop up and multiply themselves, in proportion to the difficulty of deciding them; and the unfruitfulness of Theology has been, in matter of fact, the very reason, not for seeking better food, but for feeding on nothing else. Truth has been sought in the wrong direction, and the attainable has been put aside for the visionary."

Now, there is no call on me here to refute these arguments, but merely to state them. I need not refute what has not yet been proved. It is sufficient for me to repeat what I have already said, that they are founded upon a mere assumption. *Supposing*, indeed, religious truth cannot be ascertained, *then*, of course, it is not only idle, but mischievous, to attempt to do so; *then*, of course, argument does but increase the mistake of attempting it. But surely both Catholics and Protestants have written solid defences of Revelation, of Christianity, and of dogma, as such, and these are not simply to be put aside without saying why. It has not yet been shown by our philosophers to be self-evident that religious truth is really incapable of attainment; on the other hand, it has at least been powerfully argued by a number of profound minds that it *can* be attained; and the *onus probandi* plainly lies with those who are introducing into the world what the whole world feels to be a paradox.

5.

However, where men really are persuaded of all this, however unreasonable, what will follow? A feeling, not merely of contempt, but of absolute hatred, towards the Catholic theologian and the dogmatic teacher. The patriot abhors and loathes the partizans who have degraded and injured his country; and the citizen of the world, the advocate of the human race, feels bitter indignation at those whom he holds to have been its mis-leaders and tyrants for two thousand years. "The world has lost two thousand years. It is pretty much where it was in the days of Augustus. This is what has come of priests." There are those who are actuated by a benevolent liberalism, and condescend to say that Catholics are not worse than other maintainers of dogmatic theology. There are those, again, who are good enough to grant that the Catholic Church fostered knowledge and sci-ence up to the days of Galileo, and that she has only retrograded for the last several centuries. But the new teacher, whom I am contemplating in the light of that nebula out of which he will be concentrated, echoes the words of the early persecutor of Chris-tians, that they are the "enemies of the human race." "But for Athanasius, but for Augustine, but for Aquinas, the world would have had its Bacons and its Newtons, its Lavoisiers, its Cuviers, its Watts, and its Adam Smiths, centuries upon centuries ago. And now, when at length the true philosophy has struggled into existence, and is making its way, what is left for its champion but to make an eager desperate attack upon Christian theology, the scabbard flung away, and no quarter given? and what will be the issue but the triumph of the stronger,—the overthrow of an old error and an odious tyranny, and a reign of the beautiful Truth?" Thus he thinks, and he sits dreaming over the inspiring thought, and longs for that approaching, that inevitable day.

There let us leave him for the present, dreaming and longing in his impotent hatred of a Power which Julian and Frederic, Shaftesbury and Voltaire, and a thousand other great sovereigns and subtle thinkers, have assailed in vain.

§ 2. Its Policy

1.

IT is a miserable time when a man's Catholic profession is no voucher for his orthodoxy, and when a teacher of religion may be within the Church's pale, yet external to her faith. Such has been for a season the trial of her children at various eras of her history.

It was the state of things during the dreadful Arian ascendancy, when the flock had to keep aloof from the shepherd, and the unsuspicious Fathers of the Western Councils trusted and followed some consecrated sophist from Greece or Syria. It was the case in those passages of medieval history when simony resisted the Supreme Pontiff, or when heresy lurked in Universities. It was a longer and more tedious trial, while the controversies lasted with the Monophysites of old, and with the Jansenists in modern times. A great scandal it is and a perplexity to the little ones of Christ, to have to choose between rival claimants upon their allegiance, or to find a condemnation at length pronounced upon one whom in their simplicity they have admired. We, too, in this age have our scandals, for scandals must be; but they are not what they were once; and if it be the just complaint of pious men now, that never was infidelity so rampant, it is their boast and consolation, on the other hand, that never was the Church less troubled with false teachers, never more united.

False teachers do not remain within her pale now, because they can easily leave it, and because there are seats of error external to her to which they are attracted. "They went out from us," says the Apostle, "but they were not of us; for if they had been of us, they would no doubt have continued with us: but that they might be made manifest that they are not all of us." It is a great gain when error becomes manifest, for it then ceases to deceive the simple. With these thoughts I began to describe by anticipation the formation of a school of unbelief external to the Church, which perhaps as yet only exists, as I then expressed it, in a nebula. In the middle ages it might have managed, by means of subterfuges, to maintain itself for a while within the sacred limits,—now of course it is outside of it; yet still, from the intermixture of Catholics with the world, and the present immature condition of the false doctrine, it may at first exert an influence even upon those who would shrink from it if they recognized it as it really is and as it will ultimately show itself. Moreover, it is natural, and not unprofitable, for persons under our circumstances to speculate on the forms of error with which a University of this age will have to contend, as the medieval Universities had their own special antagonists. And for both reasons I am hazarding some remarks on a set of opinions and a line of action which seems to be at present, at least in its rudiments, in the seats of English intellect, whether the danger dies away of itself or not.

I have already said that its fundamental dogma is, that nothing can be known for certain about the unseen world. This being taken for granted as a self-evident point, undeniable as soon as stated, it goes on, or will go on, to argue that, in consequence, the immense outlay which has been made of time, anxiety, and toil, of health, bodily and mental, upon theological researches, has been simply thrown away; nay, has been, not useless merely, but even mischievous, inasmuch as it has indirectly thwarted the cultivation of studies of far greater promise and of an evident utility. This is the main position of the School I am contemplating; and the result, in the minds of its members, is a deep hatred and a bitter resentment against the Power which has managed, as they consider, to stunt the world's knowledge and the intellect of man for so many hundred years. Thus much I have already said, and now I am going to state the line of policy which these people will adopt, and the course of thought which that policy of theirs will make necessary to them or natural.

2.

Supposing, then, it is the main tenet of the School in question, that the study of Religion as a science has been the bane of philosophy and knowledge, what remedy will its masters apply for the evils they deplore? Should they profess themselves the antagonists of theology, and engage in argumentative exercises with theologians? This evidently would be to increase, to perpetuate the calamity. Nothing, they will say to themselves, do religious men desire so ardently, nothing would so surely advance the cause of Religion, as Controversy. The very policy of religious men, they will argue, is to get the world to fix its attention steadily upon the subject of Religion, and Controversy is the most effectual means of doing this. And their own game, they will consider, is, on the contrary, to be elaborately silent about it. Should they not then go on to shut up the theological schools, and exclude Religion from the subjects scientifically treated in philosophical education? This indeed has been, and is, a favourite mode of proceeding with very many of the enemies of Theology; but still it cannot be said to have been justified by any greater success than the policy of Controversy. The establishment of the London University only gave immediate occasion to the establishment of King's College, founded on the dogmatic principle; and the liberalism of the Dutch government led to the restoration of the University of Louvain. It is a well-known story how the very absence of the statues of Brutus and Cassius brought them more vividly into the recollection of the Roman people. When, then, in a comprehensive scheme of education, Religion alone is excluded, that exclusion pleads in its behalf. Whatever be the real value of Religion, say these philosophers to themselves, it has a name in the world, and must not be ill-treated, lest men should rally round it from a feeling of generosity. They will decide, in consequence, that the exclusive method, though it has met with favour in this generation, is quite as much a mistake as the controversial.

Turning, then, to the Universities of England, they will pronounce that the true policy to be observed there would be simply to let the schools of Theology alone. Most unfortunate it is that they have been roused from the state of decadence and torpor in which they lay some twenty or thirty years ago. Up to that time, a routine lecture, delivered once to successive batches of young men destined for the Protestant Ministry, not during their residence, but when they were leaving or had already left the University,—and not about dogmatics, history, ecclesiastical law, or casuistry, but about the list of authors to be selected and works to be read by those who had neither curiosity to read them nor money to purchase;—and again a periodical advertisement of a lecture on the Thirty-nine Articles, which was never delivered because it was never attended,—these two demonstrations, one undertaken by one theological Professor, the other by another, comprised the theological teaching of a seat of learning which had been the home of Duns Scotus and Alexander Hales. What envious mischance put an end to those halcyon days, and revived the *odium theologicum* in the years which followed? Let us do justice to the authoritative rulers of the University; they have their failings; but not to them is the revolution to be ascribed. It was nobody's fault among all the guardians of education and trustees of the intellect in that celebrated place. However, the mischief has been done; and now the wisest course for the interests of infidelity is to leave it to itself, and let the fever gradually subside; treatment would but irritate it. Not to interfere with Theology, not to raise a little finger against it, is the only means of superseding it. The more bitter is the hatred which such men bear it, the less they must show it.

3.

What, then, is the line of action which they must pursue? They think, and rightly think, that, in all contests, the wisest and largest policy is to conduct a positive, not a negative opposition, not to prevent but to anticipate, to obstruct by constructing, and to exterminate by supplanting. To cast any slight upon Theology, whether in its Protestant or its Catholic schools, would be to elicit an inexhaustible stream of polemics, and a phalanx of dogmatic doctors and confessors.

"Let alone Camarina, for 'tis best let alone."

The proper procedure, then, is, not to oppose Theology, but to rival it. Leave its teachers to themselves; merely aim at the introduction of other studies, which, while they have the accidental charm of novelty, possess a surpassing interest, richness, and practical value of their own. Get possession of these studies, and appropriate them, and monopolize the use of them, to the exclusion of the votaries of Religion. Take it for granted, and protest, for the future, that Religion has nothing to do with the studies to which I am alluding, nor those studies with Religion. Exclaim and cry out, if the Catholic Church presumes herself to handle what you mean to use as a weapon against her. The range of the Experimental Sciences, viz., psychology, and politics, and political economy, and the many departments of physics, various both in their subject-matter and their method of research; the great Sciences which are the characteristics of this era, and which become the more marvellous, the more thoroughly they are understood,—astronomy, magnetism, chemistry, geology, comparative anatomy, natural history, ethnology, languages, political geography, antiquities,—these be your indirect but effectual means of overturning Religion! They do but need to be seen in order to be pursued; you will put an end, in the Schools of learning, to the long reign of the unseen shadowy world, by the mere exhibition of the visible. This was impossible heretofore, for the visible world was so little known itself; but now, thanks to the New Philosophy, sight is able to contest the field with faith. The medieval philosopher had no weapon against Revelation but Metaphysics; Physical Science has a better temper, if not a keener edge, for the purpose.

Now here I interrupt the course of thought I am tracing, to introduce a *caveat*, lest I should be thought to cherish any secret disrespect towards the sciences I have enumerated, or apprehension of their legitimate tendencies; whereas my very object is to protest against a monopoly of them by others. And it is not surely a heavy imputation on them to say that they, as other divine gifts, may be used to wrong purposes, with which they have no natural connection, and for which they were never intended; and that, as in Greece the element of beauty, with which the universe is flooded, and the poetical faculty, which is its truest interpreter, were made to minister to sensuality; as, in the middle ages, abstract speculation, another great instrument of truth, was often frittered away in sophistical exercises; so now, too, the department of fact, and the method of research and experiment which is proper to it, may for the moment eclipse the light of faith in the imagination of the student, and be degraded into the accidental tool, *hic et nunc*, of infidelity. I am as little hostile to physical science as I am to poetry or metaphysics; but I wish for studies of every kind a legitimate application: nor do I grudge them to anti-Catholics, so that anti-Catholics will not claim to monopolize them, cry out when we profess them, or direct them against Revelation.

I wish, indeed, I could think that these studies were not intended by a certain school of philosophers to bear directly against its authority. There are those who hope, there are those who are sure, that in the incessant investigation of facts, physical, political, and moral, something or other, or many things, will sooner or later turn up, and stubborn facts too, simply contradictory of revealed declarations. A vision comes before them of some physical or historical proof that mankind is not descended from a common origin, or that the hopes of the world were never consigned to a wooden ark floating on the waters, or that the manifestations on Mount Sinai were the work of man or nature, or that the Hebrew patriarchs or the judges of Israel are mythical personages, or that St. Peter had no connection with Rome, or that the doctrine of the Holy Trinity or of the Real Presence was foreign to primitive belief. An anticipation possesses them that the ultimate truths embodied in mesmerism will certainly solve all the Gospel miracles; or that to Niebuhrize the Gospels or the Fathers is a simple expedient for stultifying the whole Catholic system. They imagine that the eternal, immutable word of God is to quail and come to nought before the penetrating intellect of man. And, where this feeling exists, there will be a still stronger motive for letting Theology alone. That party, with whom success is but a matter of time, can afford to wait patiently; and if an inevitable train is laid for blowing up the fortress, why need we be anxious that the catastrophe should take place today, rather than tomorrow?

4.

But, without making too much of their own anticipations on this point, which may or may not be in part fulfilled, these men have secure grounds for knowing that the sciences, as they would pursue them, will at least be prejudicial to the religious sentiment. Any one study, of whatever kind, exclusively pursued, deadens in the mind the interest, nay, the perception of any other. Thus, Cicero says that Plato and Demosthenes, Aristotle and Isocrates, might have respectively excelled in each other's province, but that each was absorbed in his own; his words are emphatic; "quorum uterque, suo studio delectatus, *contemsit* alterum." Specimens of this peculiarity occur every day. You can hardly persuade some men to talk about any thing but their own pursuit; they refer the whole world to their own centre, and measure all matters by their own rule, like the fisherman in the drama, whose eulogy on his deceased lord was, that "he was so fond of fish." The saints illustrate this on the other hand; St. Bernard had no eye for architecture; St. Basil had no nose for flowers; St. Aloysius had no palate for meat and drink; St. Paula or St. Jane Frances could spurn or could step over her own child;—not that natural faculties were wanting to those great servants of God, but that a higher gift outshone and obscured every lower attribute of man, as human features may remain in heaven, yet the beauty of them be killed by the surpassing light of glory. And in like manner it is clear that the tendency of science is to make men indifferentists or sceptics, merely by being exclusively pursued. The party, then, of whom I speak, understanding this well, would suffer disputations in the theological schools every day in the year, provided they can manage to keep the students of science at a distance from them.

Nor is this all; they trust to the influence of the modern sciences on what may be called the Imagination. When any thing, which comes before us, is very unlike what we commonly experience, we consider it on that account untrue; not because it really shocks our reason as improbable, but because it startles our imagination as strange. Now, Revelation presents to us a perfectly different aspect of the universe from that presented by the Sciences. The two informations are like the distinct subjects represented by the lines of the same drawing, which, accordingly as they are read on their concave or convex side, exhibit to us now a group of trees with branches and leaves, and now human faces hid amid the leaves, or some majestic figures standing out from the branches. Thus is faith opposed to sight: it is parallel to the contrast afforded by plane astronomy and physical; plane, in accordance with our senses, discourses of the sun's rising and setting, while physical, in accordance with our reason, asserts, on the contrary, that the sun is all but stationary, and that it is the earth that moves. This is what is meant by saying that truth lies in a well; phenomena are no measure of fact; *primâ facie* representations, which we receive from without, do not reach to the real state of things, or put them before us simply as they are.

While, then, Reason and Revelation are consistent in fact, they often are inconsistent in appearance; and this seeming discordance acts most keenly and alarmingly on the Imagination, and may suddenly expose a man to the temptation, and even hurry him on to the commission, of definite acts of unbelief, in which reason itself really does not come into exercise at all. I mean, let a person devote himself to the studies of the day; let him be taught by the astronomer that our sun is but one of a million central luminaries, and our earth but one of ten million globes moving in space; let him learn from the geologist that on that globe of ours enormous revolutions have been in progress through innumerable ages; let him be told by the comparative anatomist, of the minutely arranged system of organized nature; by the chemist and physicist, of the peremptory yet intricate laws to which nature, organized and inorganic, is subjected; by the ethnologist, of the originals, and ramifications, and varieties, and fortunes of nations; by the antiquarian, of old cities disinterred, and primitive countries laid bare, with the specific forms of human society once existing; by the linguist, of the slow formation and development of languages; by the psychologist, the physiologist, and the economist, of the subtle, complicated structure of the breathing, energetic, restless world of men; I say, let him take in and master the vastness of the view thus afforded him of Nature, its infinite complexity, its awful comprehensiveness, and its diversified yet harmonious colouring; and then, when he has for years drank in and fed upon this vision, let him turn round to peruse the inspired records, or listen to the authoritative teaching of Revelation, the book of Genesis, or the warnings and prophecies of the Gospels, or the Symbolum *Quicumque* or the Life of St. Antony or St. Hilarion, and he may certainly experience a most distressing revulsion of feeling,[1]—not that his reason really deduces any thing from his much loved studies contrary to the faith, but that his imagination is bewildered, and swims with the sense of the ineffable distance of that faith from the view of things which is familiar to him, with its strangeness, and then again its rude simplicity, as he considers it, and its apparent poverty contrasted with the exuberant life and reality of his own world. All this, the school I am speaking of understands well; it comprehends that, if it can but exclude the professors of Religion from the lecture-halls of science, it may safely allow them full play in their own; for it will be able to rear up infidels, without speaking a word, merely by the terrible influence of that faculty against which both Bacon and Butler so solemnly warn us.

I say, it leaves the theologian the full and free possession of his own schools, for it thinks he will have no chance of arresting the opposite teaching or of rivalling the fascination of modern science. Knowing little, and caring less for the depth and largeness of that heavenly Wisdom, on which the Apostle delights to expatiate, or the variety of those sciences, dogmatic or ethical, mystical or hagiological, historical or exegetical, which Revelation has created, these philosophers know perfectly well that, in matter of fact, to beings, constituted as we are, sciences which concern this world and this state of existence are worth far more, are more arresting and attractive, than those which relate to a system of things which they do not see and cannot master by their natural powers. Sciences which deal with tangible facts, practical results, evergrowing discoveries, and perpetual novelties, which feed curiosity, sustain attention, and stimulate expectation, require, they consider, but a fair stage and no favour to distance that Ancient Truth, which never changes and

---

1 *Vid*. University Sermons, vii., 14.

but cautiously advances, in the race for popularity and power. And therefore they look out for the day when they shall have put down Religion, not by shutting its schools, but by emptying them; not by disputing its tenets, but by the superior worth and persuasiveness of their own.

5.

Such is the tactic which a new school of philosophers adopt against Christian Theology. They have this characteristic, compared with former schools of infidelity, viz., the union of intense hatred with a large toleration of Theology. They are professedly civil to it, and run a race with it. They rely, not on any logical disproof of it, but on three considerations; first, on the effects of studies of whatever kind to indispose the mind towards other studies; next, on the special effect of modern sciences upon the imagination, prejudicial to revealed truth; and lastly, on the absorbing interest attached to those sciences from their marvellous results. This line of action will be forced upon these persons by the peculiar character and position of Religion in England.

And here I have arrived at the limits of my paper before I have finished the discussion upon which I have entered; and I must be content with having made some suggestions which, if worth anything, others may use.

VI.

UNIVERSITY PREACHING

1.

When I obtained from various distinguished persons the acceptable promise that they would give me the advantage of their countenance and assistance by appearing from time to time in the pulpit of our new University, some of them accompanied that promise with the natural request that I, who had asked for it, should offer them my own views of the mode and form in which the duty would be most satisfactorily accomplished. On the other hand, it was quite as natural that I on my part should be disinclined to take on myself an office which belongs to a higher station and authority in the Church than my own; and the more so, because, on the definite subject about which the inquiry is made, I should have far less direct aid from the writings of holy men and great divines than I could desire. Were it indeed my sole business to put into shape the scattered precepts which saints and doctors have delivered upon it, I might have ventured on such a task with comparatively little misgiving. Under the shadow of the great teachers of the pastoral office I might have been content to speak, without looking out for any living authority to prompt me. But this unfortunately is not the case; such venerable guidance does not extend beyond the general principles and rules of preaching, and these require both expansion and adaptation when they are to be made to bear on compositions addressed in the name of a University to University men. They define the essence of Christian preaching, which is one and the same in all cases; but not the subject-matter or the method, which vary according to circumstances. Still, after all, the points to which they do reach are more, and more important, than those which they fall short of. I therefore, though with a good deal of anxiety, have attempted to perform a task which seemed naturally to fall to me; and I am thankful to say that, though I must in some measure go beyond the range of the simple direction to which I have referred, the greater part of my remarks will lie within it.

2.

1. So far is clear at once, that the preacher's object is the spiritual good of his hearers. "Finis prædicanti sit," says St. Francis de Sales; "ut *vitam* (justitiæ) *habeant homines*, et abundantius habeant." And St. Charles: "Considerandum, ad Dei omnipotentis gloriam, ad animarumque salutem, referri omnem concionandi vim ac rationem." Moreover, "Prædicatorem esse ministrum Dei, per quem verbum Dei à spiritûs fonte ducitur ad fidelium animas irrigandas." As a marksman aims at the target and its bull's-eye, and at nothing else, so the preacher must have a definite point before him, which he has to hit. So much is contained for his direction in this simple maxim, that duly to enter into it and use it is half the battle; and if he mastered nothing else, still if he really mastered as much as this, he would know all that was imperative for the due discharge of his office.

For what is the conduct of men who have one object definitely before them, and one only? Why, that, whatever be their skill, whatever their resources, greater or less, to its attainment all their efforts are simply, spontaneously, visibly, directed. This cuts off a number of questions sometimes asked about preaching, and extinguishes a number of anxieties. "Sollicita es, et turbaris," says our Lord to St. Martha; "erga plurima; porro unum est necessarium." We ask questions perhaps about diction, elocution, rhetorical power; but does the commander of a besieging force dream of holiday displays, reviews, mock engagements, feats of strength, or trials of skill, such as would be graceful and suitable on a parade ground when a foreigner of rank was to be received and *fêted*; or does he aim at one and one thing only, viz., to take the strong place? Display dissipates the energy, which for the object in view needs to be concentrated and condensed. We have no reason to suppose that the Divine blessing follows the lead of human accomplishments. Indeed, St. Paul, writing to the Corinthians, who made much of such advantages of nature, contrasts the persuasive words of human wisdom "with the showing of the Spirit," and tells us that "the kingdom of God is not in speech, but in power."

But, not to go to the consideration of divine influences, which is beyond my subject, the very presence of simple earnestness is even in itself a powerful natural instrument to effect that toward which it is directed. Earnestness creates earnestness in others by sympathy; and the more a preacher loses and is lost to himself, the more does he gain his brethren. Nor is it without some logical force also; for what is powerful enough to absorb and possess a preacher has at least a *primâ facie* claim of attention on the part of his hearers. On the other hand, any thing which interferes with this earnestness, or which argues its absence, is still more certain to blunt the force of the most cogent argument conveyed in the most eloquent language. Hence it is that the great philosopher of antiquity, in speaking, in his Treatise on Rhetoric, of the various kinds of persuasives, which are available in the Art, considers the most authoritative of these to be that which is drawn from personal traits of an ethical nature evident in the orator; for such matters are cognizable by all men, and the common sense of the world decides that it is safer, where it is possible, to commit oneself to the judgment of men of character than to any considerations addressed merely to the feelings or to the reason.

On these grounds I would go on to lay down a precept, which I trust is not extravagant, when allowance is made for the preciseness and the point which are unavoidable in all categorical statements upon matters of conduct. It is, that preachers should neglect everything whatever besides devotion to their one object, and earnestness in pursuing it, till they in some good measure attain to these requisites. Talent, logic, learning, words, manner, voice, action, all are required for the perfection of a preacher; but "one thing is necessary,"—an intense perception and appreciation of the end for which he preaches, and that is, to be the minister of some definite spiritual good to those who hear him. Who could wish to be more eloquent, more powerful, more successful than the Teacher of the Nations? yet who more earnest, who more natural, who more unstudied, who more self-forgetting than he?

3.

(1.) And here, in order to prevent misconception, two remarks must be made, which will lead us further into the subject we are engaged upon. The first is, that, in what I have been saying, I do not mean that a preacher must aim at *earnestness*, but that he must aim at his *object*, which is to do some spiritual good to his hearers, and which will at once *make* him earnest. It is said that, when a man has to cross an abyss by a narrow plank thrown over it, it is his wisdom, not to look at the plank, along which lies his path, but to fix his eyes steadily on the point in the opposite precipice at which the plank ends. It is by gazing at the object which he must reach, and ruling himself by it, that he secures to himself the power of walking to it straight and steadily. The case is the same in moral matters; no one will become really earnest by aiming directly at earnestness; any one may become earnest by meditating on the motives, and by drinking at the sources, of earnestness. We may of course work ourselves up into a pretence, nay, into a paroxysm, of earnestness; as we may chafe our cold hands till they are warm. But when we cease chafing, we lose the warmth again; on the contrary, let the sun come out and strike us with his beams, and we need no artificial chafing to be warm. The hot words, then, and energetic gestures of a preacher, taken by themselves, are just as much signs of earnestness as rubbing the hands or flapping the arms together are signs of warmth; though they are natural where earnestness already exists, and pleasing as being its spontaneous concomitants. To sit down to compose for the pulpit with a resolution to be eloquent is one impediment to persuasion; but to be determined to be earnest is absolutely fatal to it.

He who has before his mental eye the Four Last Things will have the true earnestness, the horror or the rapture, of one who witnesses a conflagration, or discerns some rich and sublime prospect of natural scenery. His countenance, his manner, his voice, speak for him, in proportion as his view has been vivid and minute. The great English poet has described this sort of eloquence when a calamity had befallen:—

> Yea, this man's brow, like to a title page,
> Foretells the nature of a tragic volume.
> Thou tremblest, and the whiteness in thy cheek
> Is apter than thy tongue to tell thy errand.

It is this earnestness, in the supernatural order, which is the eloquence of saints; and not of saints only, but of all Christian preachers, according to the measure of their faith and love. As the case would be with one who has actually seen what he relates, the herald of tidings of the invisible world also will be, from the nature of the case, whether vehement or calm, sad or exulting, always simple, grave, emphatic, and peremptory; and all this, not because he has proposed to himself to be so, but because certain intellectual convictions involve certain external manifestations. St. Francis de Sales is full and clear upon this point. It is necessary, he says, "ut ipsemet penitus hauseris, ut persuasissimam tibi habeas, doctrinam quam aliis persuasam cupis. Artificium summum erit, nullum habere artificium. Inflammata sint verba, non clamoribus gesticulationibusve immodicis, sed interiore affectione. De corde plus quàm de ore proficiscantur. Quantumvis ore dixerimus, sanè cor cordi loquitur, lingua non nisi aures pulsat." St. Augustine had said to the same purpose long before: "Sonus verborum nostrorum aures percutit; magister intus est."

(2.) My second remark is, that it is the preacher's duty to aim at imparting to others, not any fortuitous, unpremeditated benefit, but some *definite* spiritual good. It is here that design and study find their place; the more exact and precise is the subject which he treats, the more impressive and practical will he be; whereas no one will carry off much from a discourse which is on the general subject of virtue, or vaguely and feebly entertains the question of the desirableness of attaining Heaven, or the rashness of incurring eternal ruin. As a distinct image before the mind makes the preacher earnest, so it will give him something which it is worth while to communicate to others. Mere sympathy, it is true, is able, as I have said, to transfer an emotion or sentiment from mind to mind, but it is not able to fix it there. He must aim at imprinting on the heart what will never leave it, and this he cannot do unless he employ himself on some definite subject, which he has to handle and weigh, and then, as it were, to hand over from himself to others.

Hence it is that the Saints insist so expressly on the necessity of his addressing himself to the intellect of men, and of convincing as well as persuading. "Necesse est ut *doceat* et moveat," says St. Francis; and St. Antoninus still more distinctly: "Debet prædicator clare loqui, *ut instruat intellectum* auditoris, et doceat." Hence, moreover, in St. Ignatius's Exercises, the act of the intellect precedes that of the affections. Father Lohner seems to me to be giving an instance in point when he tells us of a court-preacher, who delivered what would be commonly considered eloquent sermons, and attracted no one; and next took to simple explanations of the Mass and similar subjects, and then found the church thronged. So necessary is it to have something to say, if we desire any one to listen.

Nay, I would go the length of recommending a preacher to place a distinct categorical proposition before him, such as he can write down in a form of words, and to guide and limit his preparation by it, and to aim in all he says to bring it out, and nothing else. This seems to be implied or suggested in St. Charles's direction: "Id omnino studebit, ut quod in concione dicturus est antea *bene cognitum* habeat." Nay, is it not expressly conveyed in the Scripture phrase of "preaching the *word*"? for what is meant by "the word" but a proposition addressed to the intellect? nor will a preacher's earnestness show itself in anything more unequivocally than in his rejecting, whatever be the temptation to admit it, every remark, however original, every period, however eloquent, which does not in some way or other tend to bring out this one distinct proposition which he has chosen. Nothing is so fatal to the effect of a sermon as the habit of preaching on three or four subjects at once. I acknowledge I am advancing a step beyond the practice of great Catholic preachers when I add that, even though we preach on only one at a time, finishing and dismissing the first before we go to the second, and the second before we go to the third, still, after all, a practice like this, though not open to the inconvenience which the confusing of one subject with another involves, is in matter of fact nothing short of the delivery of three sermons in succession without break between them.

Summing up, then, what I have been saying, I observe that, if I have understood the doctrine of St. Charles, St. Francis, and other saints aright, *definiteness of object* is in various ways the one virtue of the preacher;—and this means that he should set out with the intention of conveying to others some spiritual benefit; that, with a view to this, and as the only ordinary way to it, he should select some distinct fact or scene, some passage in history, some truth, simple or profound, some doctrine, some principle, or some sentiment, and should study it well and thoroughly, and first make it his own, or else have already dwelt on it and mastered it, so as to be able to use it for the occasion from an habitual understanding of it; and that then he should employ himself, as the one business of his discourse, to bring home to others, and to leave deep within them, what he has, before he began to speak to them, brought home to himself. What he feels himself, and feels deeply, he has to make others feel deeply; and in proportion as he comprehends this, he will rise above the temptation of introducing collateral matters, and will have no taste, no heart for going aside after flowers of oratory, fine figures, tuneful periods, which are worth nothing, unless they come to him spontaneously, and are spoken "out of the abundance of the heart." Our Lord said on one occasion: "I am come to send fire on the earth, and what will I but that it be kindled?" He had one work, and He accomplished it. "The words," He says, "which Thou gavest Me, I have *given* to them, and they have *received* them, … *and now* I come to Thee." And the Apostles, again, as they had received, so were they to give. "That which *we* have seen and have heard," says one of them, "we declare unto *you*, that you may have *fellowship* with us." If, then, a preacher's subject only be some portion of the Divine message, however elementary it may be, however trite, it will have a dignity such as to possess him, and a virtue to kindle him, and an influence to subdue and convert those to whom it goes forth from him, according to the words of the promise, "My word, which shall go forth from My mouth, shall not return to Me void, but it shall do whatsoever I please, and shall prosper in the things for which I sent it."

4.

2. And now having got as far as this, we shall see without difficulty what a University Sermon ought to be just so far as it is distinct from other sermons; for, if all preaching is directed towards a hearer, such as is the hearer will be the preaching, and, as a University auditory differs from other auditories, so will a sermon addressed to it differ from other sermons. This, indeed, is a broad maxim which holy men lay down on the subject of preaching. Thus, St. Gregory Theologus, as quoted by the Pope his namesake, says: "The self-same exhortation is not suitable for all hearers; for all have not the same disposition of mind, and what profits these is hurtful to those." The holy Pope himself throws the maxim into another form, still more precise: "Debet prædicator," he says, "perspicere, ne plus prædicet, quàm ab audiente capi possit." And St. Charles expounds it, referring to Pope St. Gregory: "Pro audientium genere locos doctrinarum, ex quibus concionem conficiat, non modo distinctos, sed optimè explicatos habebit. Atque in hoc quidem multiplici genere concionator videbit, ne quæcumque, ut S. Gregorius scitè monet, legerit, aut scientiâ comprehenderit, oninia enunciet atque effundat; sed delectum habebit, ita ut documenta alia exponat, alia tacitè relinquat, prout locus, ordo, conditioque auditorum deposcat." And, by way of obviating the chance of such a rule being considered a human artifice inconsistent with the simplicity of the Gospel, he had said shortly before: "Ad Dei gloriam, ad cœlestis regni propagationem, et ad animarum salutem, pluri-

mum interest, non solum quales sint prædicatores, sed quâ viâ, quâ ratione prædicent."

It is true, this is also one of the elementary principles of the Art of Rhetoric; but it is no scandal that a saintly Bishop should in this matter borrow a maxim from secular, nay, from pagan schools. For divine grace does not overpower nor supersede the action of the human mind according to its proper nature; and if heathen writers have analyzed that nature well, so far let them be used to the greater glory of the Author and Source of all Truth. Aristotle, then, in his celebrated treatise on Rhetoric, makes the very essence of the Art lie in the precise recognition of a hearer. It is a relative art, and in that respect differs from Logic, which simply teaches the right use of reason, whereas Rhetoric is the art of persuasion, which implies a person who is to be persuaded. As, then, the Christian Preacher aims at the Divine Glory, not in any vague and general way, but definitely by the enunciation of some article or passage of the Revealed Word, so further, he enunciates it, not for the instruction of the whole world, but directly for the sake of those very persons who are before him. He is, when in the pulpit, instructing, enlightening, informing, advancing, sanctifying, not all nations, nor all classes, nor all callings, but those particular ranks, professions, states, ages, characters, which have gathered around him. Proof indeed is the same all over the earth; but he has not only to prove, but to persuade;—*Whom?* A hearer, then, is included in the very idea of preaching; and we cannot determine how in detail we ought to preach, till we know whom we are to address.

In all the most important respects, indeed, all hearers are the same, and what is suitable for one audience is suitable for another. All hearers are children of Adam, all, too, are children of the Christian adoption and of the Catholic Church. The great topics which suit the multitude, which attract the poor, which sway the unlearned, which warn, arrest, recall, the wayward and wandering, are in place within the precincts of a University as elsewhere. A *Studium Generale* is not a cloister, or noviciate, or seminary, or boarding-school; it is an assemblage of the young, the inexperienced, the lay and the secular; and not even the simplest of religious truths, or the most elementary article of the Christian faith, can be unseasonable from its pulpit. A sermon on the Divine Omnipresence, on the future judgment, on the satisfaction of Christ, on the intercession of saints, will be not less, perhaps more, suitable there than if it were addressed to a parish congregation. Let no one suppose that any thing recondite is essential to the idea of a University sermon. The most obvious truths are often the most profitable. Seldom does an opportunity occur for a subject there which might not under circumstances be treated before any other auditory whatever. Nay, further; an academical auditory might be well content if it never heard any subject treated at all but what would be suitable to any general congregation.

However, after all, a University has a character of its own; it has some traits of human nature more prominently developed than others, and its members are brought together under circumstances which impart to the auditory a peculiar colour and expression, even where it does not substantially differ from another. It is composed of men, not women; of the young rather than the old; and of persons either highly educated or under education. These are the points which the preacher will bear in mind, and which will direct him both in his choice of subject, and in his mode of treating it.

5.

(1.) And first as to his *matter* or subject. Here I would remark upon the circumstance, that courses of sermons upon theological points, polemical discussions, treatises *in extenso*, and the like, are often included in the idea of a University Sermon, and are considered to be legitimately entitled to occupy the attention of a University audience; the object of such compositions being, not directly and mainly the edification of the hearers, but the defence or advantage of Catholicism at large, and the gradual formation of a volume suitable for publication. Without absolutely discountenancing such important works, it is not necessary to say more of them than that they rather belong to the divinity school, and fall under the idea of Lectures, than have a claim to be viewed as University Sermons. Anyhow, I do not feel called upon to speak of such discourses here. And I say the same of panegyrical orations, discourses on special occasions, funeral sermons, and the like. Putting such exceptional compositions aside, I will confine myself to the consideration of what may be called Sermons proper. And here, I repeat, any general subject will be seasonable in the University pulpit which would be seasonable elsewhere; but, if we look for subjects especially suitable, they will be of two kinds. The temptations which ordinarily assail the young and the intellectual are two: those which are directed against their virtue, and those which are directed against their faith. All divine gifts are exposed to misuse and perversion; youth and intellect are both of them goods, and involve in them certain duties respectively, and can be used to the glory of the Giver; but, as youth becomes the occasion of excess and sensuality, so does intellect give accidental opportunity to religious error, rash speculation, doubt, and infidelity. That these are in fact the peculiar evils to which large Academical Bodies are liable is shown from the history of Universities; and if a preacher would have a subject which has especial significancy in such a place, he must select one which bears upon one or other of these two classes of sin. I mean, he would be treating on some such subject with the same sort of appositeness as he would discourse upon almsgiving when addressing the rich, or on patience, resignation, and industry, when he was addressing the poor, or on forgiveness of injuries when he was addressing the oppressed or persecuted.

To this suggestion I append two cautions. First, I need hardly say, that a preacher should be quite sure that he understands the persons he is addressing before he ventures to aim at what he considers to be their ethical condition; for, if he mistakes, he will probably be doing harm rather than good. I have known consequences to occur very far from edifying, when strangers have fancied they knew an auditory when they did not, and have by implication imputed to them habits or motives which were not theirs. Better far would it be for a preacher to select one of those more general subjects which are safe than risk what is evidently ambitious, if it is not successful.

My other caution is this:—that, even when he addresses himself to some special danger or probable deficiency or need of his hearers, he should do so covertly, not showing on the surface of his discourse what he is aiming at. I see no advantage in a preacher professing to treat of infidelity, orthodoxy, or virtue, or the pride of reason, or riot, or sensual indulgence. To say nothing else, common-places are but blunt weapons; whereas it is particular topics that penetrate and reach their mark. Such subjects rather are, for instance, the improvement of time, avoiding the occasions of sin, frequenting the Sacraments, divine warnings, the inspirations of grace, the mysteries of the Rosary, natural virtue, beauty of the rites of the Church, consistency of the Catholic faith, relation of Scripture to the Church, the philosophy of tradition, and any others, which may touch the heart and conscience, or may suggest trains of thought to the intellect, without proclaiming the main reason why they have been chosen.

(2.) Next, as to the *mode of treating* its subject, which a University discourse requires. It is this respect, after all, I think, in which it especially differs from other kinds of preaching. As translations differ from each other, as expressing the same ideas in different languages, so in the case of sermons, each may undertake the same subject, yet treat it in its own way, as contemplating its own hearers. This is well exemplified in the speeches of St. Paul, as recorded in the book of Acts. To the Jews he quotes the Old Testament; on the Areopagus, addressing the philosophers of Athens, he insists,—not indeed upon any recondite doctrine, contrariwise, upon the most elementary, the being and unity of God;—but he treats it with a learning and depth of thought, which the presence of that celebrated city naturally suggested. And in like manner, while the most simple subjects are apposite in a University pulpit, they certainly would there require a treatment more exact than is necessary in merely popular exhortations. It is not asking much to demand for academical discourses a more careful study beforehand, a more accurate conception of the idea which they are to enforce, a more cautious use of words, a more anxious consultation of writers of authority, and somewhat more of philosophical and theological knowledge.

But here again, as before, I would insist on the necessity of such compositions being unpretending. It is not necessary for a preacher to quote the Holy Fathers, or to show erudition, or to construct an original argument, or to be ambitious in style and profuse of ornament, on the ground that the audience is a University: it is only necessary so to keep the character and necessities of his hearers before him as to avoid what may offend them, or mislead, or disappoint, or fail to profit.

6.

(3.) But here a distinct question opens upon us, on which I must say a few words in conclusion, viz., whether or not the preacher should preach without book.

This is a delicate question to enter upon, considering that the Irish practice of preaching without book, which is in accordance with that of foreign countries, and, as it would appear, with the tradition of the Church from the first, is not universally adopted in England, nor, as I believe, in Scotland; and it might seem unreasonable or presumptuous to abridge a liberty at present granted to the preacher. I will simply set down what occurs to me to say on each side of the question.

First of all, looking at the matter on the side of usage, I have always understood that it was the rule in Catholic countries, as I have just said, both in this and in former times, to preach without book; and, if the rule be really so, it carries extreme weight with it. I do not speak as if I had consulted a library, and made my ground sure; but at first sight it would appear impossible, even from the number of homilies and commentaries which are assigned to certain Fathers, as to St. Augustine or to St. Chrysostom, that they could have delivered them from formally-written compositions. On the other hand, St. Leo's sermons certainly are, in the strict sense of the word, compositions; nay, passages of them are carefully dogmatic; nay, further still, they have sometimes the character of a symbol, and, in consequence, are found repeated in other parts of his works; and again, though I do not profess to be well read in the works of St. Chrysostom, there is generally in such portions of them as are known to those of us who are in Holy Orders, a peculiarity, an identity of style, which enables one to recognize the author at a glance, even in the Latin version of the Breviary, and which would seem to be quite beyond the mere fidelity of reporters. It would seem, then, he must after all have written them; and if he did write at all, it is more likely that he wrote with the stimulus of preaching before him, than that he had time and inducement to correct and enlarge them afterwards from notes, for what is now called "publication," which at that time could hardly be said to exist at all. To this consideration we must add the remarkable fact (which, though in classical history, throws light upon our inquiry) that, not to produce other instances, the greater part of Cicero's powerful and brilliant orations against Verres were never delivered at all. Nor must it be forgotten that Cicero specifies memory in his enumeration of the distinct talents necessary for a great orator. And then we have in corroboration the French practice of writing sermons and learning them by heart.

These remarks, as far as they go, lead us to lay great stress on the *preparation* of a sermon, as amounting in fact to composition, even in writing, and *in extenso*. Now consider St. Carlo's direction, as quoted above: "Id omnino studebit, ut quod in concione dicturus est, antea bene cognitum habeat." Now a parish priest has neither time nor occasion for any but elementary and ordinary topics; and any such subject he has habitually made his own, "cognitum habet," already; but when the matter is of a more select and occasional character, as in the case of a University Sermon, then the preacher has to study it well and thoroughly, and master it beforehand. Study and meditation being imperative, can it be denied that one of the most effectual means by which we are able to ascertain our understanding of a subject, to bring out our thoughts upon it, to clear our meaning, to enlarge our views of its relations to other subjects, and to develop it generally, is to write down carefully all we have to say about it? People indeed differ in matters of this kind, but I think that writing is a stimulus to the mental faculties, to the logical talent, to originality, to the power of illustration, to the arrangement of topics, second to none. Till a man begins to put down his thoughts about a subject on paper he will not ascertain what he knows and what he does not know; and still less will he be able to express what he does know. Such a formal preparation of course cannot be required of a parish priest, burdened, as he may be, with other duties, and preaching on elementary subjects, and supported by the systematic order and the suggestions of the Catechism; but in occasional sermons the case is otherwise. In these it is both possible and generally necessary; and the fuller the sketch, and the more clear and continuous the thread of the discourse, the more the preacher will find himself at home when the time of delivery arrives. I have said "generally necessary," for of course there will be exceptional cases, in which such a mode of preparation does not answer, whether from some mistake in carrying it out, or from some special gift superseding it.

To many preachers there will be another advantage besides;—such a practice will secure them against venturing upon really *extempore* matter. The more ardent a man is, and the greater power he has of affecting his hearers, so much the more will he need self-control and sustained recollection, and feel the advantage of committing himself, as it were, to the custody of his previous intentions, instead of yielding to any chance current of thought which rushes upon him in the midst of his preaching. His very gifts may need the counterpoise of more ordinary and homely accessories, such as the drudgery of composition.

It must be borne in mind too, that, since a University Sermon will commonly have more pains than ordinary bestowed on it, it will be considered in the number of those which the author would especially wish to preserve. Some record of it then will be natural, or even is involved in its composition; and, while the least elaborate will be as much as a sketch or abstract, even the most minute, exact, and copious assemblage of notes will not be found too long hereafter, supposing, as time goes on, any reason occurs for wishing to commit it to the press.

Here are various reasons, which are likely to lead, or to oblige, a preacher to have recourse to his pen in preparation for his special office. A further reason might be suggested, which would be more intimate than any we have given, going indeed so far as to justify the introduction of a manuscript into the pulpit itself, if the case supposed fell for certain under the idea of a University Sermon. It may be urged with great cogency that a process of argument, or a logical analysis and investigation, cannot at all be conducted with suitable accuracy of wording, completeness of statement, or succession of ideas, if the composition is to be prompted at the moment, and breathed out, as it were, from the intellect together with the very words which are its vehicle. There are indeed a few persons in a generation, such as Pitt, who are able to converse like a book, and to speak a pamphlet; but others must be content to write and to read their writing. This is true; but I have already found reason to question whether such delicate and complicated organizations of thought have a right to the name of Sermons at all. In truth, a discourse, which, from its fineness and precision of ideas, is too difficult for a preacher to deliver without such extraneous assistance, is too difficult for a hearer to follow; and, if a book be imperative for teaching, it is imperative for learning. Both parties ought to read, if they are to be on equal terms;—and this remark furnishes me with a principle which has an application wider than the particular case which has suggested it.

While, then, a preacher will find it becoming and advisable to put into writing any important discourse beforehand, he will find it equally a point of propriety and expedience not to read it in the pulpit. I am not of course denying his right to use a manuscript, if he wishes; but he will do well to conceal it, as far as he can, unless, which is the most effectual concealment, whatever be its counterbalancing disadvantages, he prefers, mainly not verbally, to get it by heart. To conceal it, indeed, in one way or other, will be his natural impulse; and this very circumstance seems to show us that to read a sermon needs an apology. For, why should he commit it to memory, or conceal his use of it, unless he felt that it was more natural, more decorous, to do without it? And so again, if he employs a manuscript, the more he appears to dispense with it, the more he looks off from it, and directly addresses his audience, the more will he be considered to preach; and, on the other hand, the more will he be judged to come short of preaching the more sedulous he is in following his manuscript line after line, and by the tone of his voice makes it clear that he has got it safely before him. What is this but a popular testimony to the fact that preaching is not reading, and reading is not preaching?

There is, as I have said, a principle involved in this decision. It is a common answer made by the Protestant poor to their clergy or other superiors, when asked why they do not go to church, that "they can read their book at home quite as well." It is quite true, they can read their book at home, and it is difficult what to rejoin, and it is a problem, which has employed before now the more thoughtful of their communion, to make out what is got by going to public service. The prayers are from a printed book, the sermon is from a manuscript. The printed prayers they have already; and, as to the manuscript sermon, why should it be in any respects better than the volume of sermons which they have at home? Why should not an approved author be as good as one who has not yet submitted himself to criticism? And again, if it is to be read in the church, why may not one person read it quite as well as another? Good advice is good advice, all the world over. There is something more, then, than composition in a sermon; there is something personal in preaching; people are drawn and moved, not simply by what is said, but by how it is said, and who says it. The same things said by one man are not the same as when said by another. The same things when read are not the same as when they are preached.

7.

In this respect the preacher differs from the minister of the sacraments, that he comes to his hearers, in some sense or other, with antecedents. Clad in his sacerdotal vestments, he sinks what is individual in himself altogether, and is but the representative of Him from whom he derives his commission. His words, his tones, his actions, his presence, lose their personality; one bishop, one priest, is like another; they all chant the same notes, and observe the same genuflexions, as they give one peace and one blessing, as they offer one and the same sacrifice. The Mass must not be said without a Missal under the priest's eye; nor in any language but that in which it has come down to us from the early hierarchs of the Western Church. But, when it is over, and the celebrant has resigned the vestments proper to it, then he resumes himself, and comes to us in the gifts and associations which attach to his person. He knows his sheep, and they know him; and it is this direct bearing of the teacher on the taught, of his mind upon their minds, and the mutual sympathy which exists between them, which is his strength and influence when he addresses them. They hang upon his lips as they cannot hang upon the pages of his book. Definiteness is the life of preaching. A definite hearer, not the whole world; a definite topic, not the whole evangelical tradition; and, in like manner, a definite speaker. Nothing that is anonymous will preach; nothing that is dead and gone; nothing even which is of yesterday, however religious in itself and useful. Thought and word are one in the Eternal Logos, and must not be separate in those who are His shadows on earth. They must issue fresh and fresh, as from the preacher's mouth, so from his breast, if they are to be "spirit and life" to the hearts of his hearers. And what is true of a parish priest applies, *mutatis mutandis*, to a University preacher; who, even more, perhaps, than the ordinary *parochus*, comes to his audience with a name and a history, and excites a personal interest, and persuades by what he is, as well as by what he delivers.

I am far from forgetting that every one has his own talent, and that one has not what another has. Eloquence is a divine gift, which to a certain point supersedes rules, and is to be used, like other gifts, to the glory of the Giver, and then only to be discountenanced when it forgets its place, when it throws into the shade and embarrasses the essential functions of the Christian preacher, and claims to be cultivated for its own sake instead of being made subordinate and subservient to a higher work and to sacred objects. And how to make eloquence subservient to the evangelical office is not more difficult than how to use learning or intellect for a supernatural end; but it does not come into consideration here.

In the case of particular preachers, circumstances may constantly arise which render the use of a manuscript the more advisable course; but I have been considering how the case stands in itself, and attempting to set down what is to be aimed at as best. If religious men once ascertain what is abstractedly desirable, and acquiesce in it with their hearts, they will be in the way to get over many difficulties which otherwise will be insurmountable. For myself, I think it no extravagance to say that a very inferior sermon, delivered without book, answers the purposes for which all sermons are delivered more perfectly than one of great merit, if it be written and read. Of course, all men will not speak without book equally well, just as their voices are not equally clear and loud, or their manner equally impressive. Eloquence, I repeat, is a gift; but most men, unless they have passed the age for learning, may with practice attain such fluency in expressing their thoughts as will enable them to convey and manifest to their audience that earnestness and devotion to their object, which is the life of preaching,—which both covers, in the preacher's own consciousness, the sense of his own deficiencies, and makes up for them over and over again in the judgment of his hearers.

VII.

CHRISTIANITY AND PHYSICAL SCIENCE

A LECTURE IN THE SCHOOL OF MEDICINE

1.

Now that we have just commenced our second Academical Year, it is natural, Gentlemen, that, as in November last, when we were entering upon our great undertaking, I offered to you some remarks suggested by the occasion, so now again I should not suffer the first weeks of the Session to pass away without addressing to you a few words on one of those subjects which are at the moment especially interesting to us. And when I apply myself to think what topic I shall in consequence submit to your consideration, I seem to be directed what to select by the principle of selection which I followed on that former occasion to which I have been referring. Then[1] we were opening the Schools of Philosophy and Letters, as now we are opening those of Medicine; and, as I then attempted some brief investigation of the mutual bearings of Revelation and Literature, so at the present time I shall not, I trust, be unprofitably engaging your attention, if I make one or two parallel reflections on the relations existing between Revelation and Physical Science.

This subject, indeed, viewed in its just dimensions, is far too large for an occasion such as this; still I may be able to select some one point out of the many which it offers for discussion, and, while elucidating it, to throw light even on others which at the moment I do not formally undertake. I propose, then, to discuss the antagonism which is popularly supposed to exist between Physics and Theology; and to show, first, that such antagonism does not really exist, and,

---

1 *Vid.* Article 1.

next, to account for the circumstance that so groundless an imagination should have got abroad.

I think I am not mistaken in the fact that there exists, both in the educated and half-educated portions of the community, something of a surmise or misgiving, that there really is at bottom a certain contrariety between the declarations of religion and the results of physical inquiry; a suspicion such, that, while it encourages those persons who are not over-religious to anticipate a coming day, when at length the difference will break out into open conflict, to the disadvantage of Revelation, it leads religious minds, on the other hand, who have not had the opportunity of considering accurately the state of the case, to be jealous of the researches, and prejudiced against the discoveries, of Science. The consequence is, on the one side, a certain contempt of Theology; on the other, a disposition to undervalue, to deny, to ridicule, to discourage, and almost to denounce, the labours of the physiological, astronomical, or geological investigator.

I do not suppose that any of those gentlemen who are now honouring me with their presence are exposed to the temptation either of the religious or of the scientific prejudice; but that is no reason why some notice of it may not have its use even in this place. It may lead us to consider the subject itself more carefully and exactly; it may assist us in attaining clearer ideas than before how Physics and Theology stand relatively to each other.

2.

Let us begin with a first approximation to the real state of the case, or a broad view, which, though it may require corrections, will serve at once to illustrate and to start the subject. We may divide knowledge, then, into natural and supernatural. Some knowledge, of course, is both at once; for the moment let us put this circumstance aside, and view these two fields of knowledge in themselves, and as distinct from each other in idea. By nature is meant, I suppose, that vast system of things, taken as a whole, of which we are cognizant by means of our natural powers. By the supernatural world is meant that still more marvellous and awful universe, of which the Creator Himself is the fulness, and which becomes known to us, not through our natural faculties, but by superadded and direct communication from Him. These two great circles of knowledge, as I have said, intersect; first, as far as supernatural knowledge includes truths and facts of the natural world, and secondly, as far as truths and facts of the natural world are on the other hand data for inferences about the supernatural. Still, following this interference to the full, it will be found, on the whole, that the two worlds and the two kinds of knowledge respectively are separated off from each other; and that, therefore, as being separate, they cannot on the whole contradict each other. That is, in other words, a person who has the fullest knowledge of one of these worlds, may be nevertheless, on the whole, as ignorant as the rest of mankind, as unequal to form a judgment, of the facts and truths of the other. He who knows all that can possibly be known about physics, about politics, about geography, ethnology, and ethics, will have made no approximation whatever to decide the question whether or not there are angels, and how many are their orders; and on the other hand, the most learned of dogmatic and mystical divines,—St. Augustine, St. Thomas,—will not on that score know more than a peasant about the laws of motion, or the wealth of nations. I do not mean that there may not be speculations and guesses on this side and that, but I speak of any conclusion which merits to be called, I will not say knowledge, but even opinion. If, then, Theology be the philosophy of the supernatural world, and Science the philosophy of the natural, Theology and Science, whether in their respective ideas, or again in their own actual fields, on the whole, are incommunicable, incapable of collision, and needing, at most to be connected, never to be reconciled.

Now this broad general view of our subject is found to be so far true in fact, in spite of such deductions from it that have to be made in detail, that the recent French editors of one of the works of St. Thomas are able to give it as one of their reasons why that great theologian made an alliance, not with Plato, but with Aristotle, because Aristotle (they say), unlike Plato, confined himself to human science, and therefore was secured from coming into collision with divine.

"Not without reason," they say, "did St. Thomas acknowledge Aristotle as if the Master of human philosophy; for, inasmuch as Aristotle was not a Theologian, he had only treated of logical, physical, psychological, and metaphysical theses, to the exclusion of those which are concerned about the supernatural relations of man to God, that is, religion; which, on the other hand, had been the source of the worst errors of other philosophers, and especially of Plato."

3.

But if there be so substantial a truth even in this very broad statement concerning the independence of the fields of Theology and general Science severally, and the consequent impossibility of collision between them, how much more true is that statement, from the very nature of the case, when we contrast Theology, not with Science generally, but definitely with Physics! In Physics is comprised that family of sciences which is concerned with the sensible world, with the phenomena which we see, hear, and handle, or, in other words, with matter. It is the philosophy of matter. Its basis of operations, what it starts from, what it falls back upon, is the phenomena which meet the senses. Those phenomena it ascertains, catalogues, compares, combines, arranges, and then uses for determining something beyond themselves, viz., the order to which they are subservient, or what we commonly call the laws of nature. It never travels beyond the examination of cause and effect. Its object is to resolve the complexity of phenomena into simple elements and principles; but when it has reached those first elements, principles, and laws, its mission is at an end; it keeps within that material system with which it began, and never ventures beyond the "flammantia mœnia mundi." It may, indeed, if it chooses, feel a doubt of the completeness of its analysis hitherto, and for that reason endeavour to arrive at more simple laws and fewer principles. It may be dissatisfied with its own combinations, hypotheses, systems; and leave Ptolemy for Newton, the alchemists for Lavoisier and Davy;—that is, it may decide that it has not yet touched the bottom of its own subject; but still its aim will be to get to the bottom, and nothing more. With matter it began, with matter it will end; it will never trespass into the province of mind. The Hindoo notion is said to be that the earth stands upon a tortoise; but the physicist, as such, will never ask himself by what influence, external to the universe, the universe is sustained; simply because he is a physicist.

If indeed he be a religious man, he will of course have a very definite view of the subject; but that view of his is private, not professional,—the view, not of a physicist, but of a religious man; and this, not because physical science says any thing different, but simply because it says nothing at all on the subject, nor can do so by the very undertaking with which it set out. The question is simply *extra artem*. The physical philosopher has nothing whatever to do with final causes, and will get into inextricable confusion, if he introduces them into his investigations. He has to look in one definite direction, not in any other. It is said that in some countries, when a stranger asks his way, he is at once questioned in turn what place he came from: something like this would be the unseasonableness of a physicist, who inquired how the phenomena and laws of the material world primarily came to be, when his simple task is that of ascertaining what they are. Within the limits of those phenomena he may speculate and prove; he may trace the operation of the laws of matter through periods of time; he may penetrate into the past, and anticipate the future; he may recount the changes which they have effected upon matter, and the rise, growth, and decay of phenomena; and so in a certain sense may write the history of the material world, as far as he can; still he will always advance from phenomena, and conclude upon the internal evidence which they supply. He will not come near the questions, what that ultimate element is, which we call matter, how it came to be, whether it can cease to be, whether it ever was not, whether it will ever come to nought, in what its laws really consist, whether they can cease to be, whether they can be suspended, what causation is, what time is, what the relations of time to cause and effect, and a hundred other questions of a similar character.

Such is Physical Science, and Theology, as is obvious, is just what such Science is not. Theology begins, as its name denotes, not with any sensible facts, phenomena, or results, not with nature at all, but with the Author of nature,—with the one invisible, unapproachable Cause and Source of all things. It begins at the other end of knowledge, and is occupied, not with the finite, but the Infinite. It unfolds and systematizes what He Himself has told us of Himself; of His nature, His attributes, His will, and His acts. As far as it approaches towards Physics, it takes just the counterpart of the questions which occupy the Physical Philosopher. He contemplates facts before him; the Theologian gives the reasons of those facts. The Physicist treats of efficient causes; the Theologian of final. The Physicist tells us of laws; the Theologian of the Author, Maintainer, and Controller of them; of their scope, of their suspension, if so be; of their beginning and their end. This is how the two schools stand related to each other, at that point where they approach the nearest; but for the most part they are absolutely divergent. What Physical Science is engaged in I have already said; as to Theology, it contemplates the world, not of matter, but of mind; the Supreme Intelligence; souls and their destiny; conscience and duty; the past, present, and future dealings of the Creator with the creature.

4.

So far, then, as these remarks have gone, Theology and Physics cannot touch each other, have no intercommunion, have no ground of difference or agreement, of jealousy or of sympathy. As well may musical truths be said to interfere with the doctrines of architectural science; as well may there be a collision between the mechanist and the geologist, the engineer and the grammarian; as well might the British Parliament or the French nation be jealous of some possible belligerent power upon the surface of the moon, as Physics pick a quarrel with Theology. And it may be well,—before I proceed to fill up in detail this outline, and to explain what has to be explained in this statement,—to corroborate it, as it stands, by the remarkable words upon the subject of a writer of the day:[2]—

"We often hear it said," he observes, writing as a Protestant (and here let me assure you, Gentlemen, that though his words have a controversial tone with them, I do not quote them in that aspect, or as wishing here to urge any thing against Protestants, but merely in pursuance of my own point, that Revelation and Physical Science cannot really come into collision), "we often hear it said that the world is constantly becoming more and more enlightened, and that this enlightenment must be favourable to Protestantism, and unfavourable to Catholicism. We wish that we could think so. But we see great reason to doubt whether this is a well-founded expectation. We see that during the last two hundred and fifty years the human mind has been in the highest degree active; that it has made great advances in every branch of natural philosophy; that it has produced innumerable inventions tending to promote the convenience of life; that medicine, surgery, chemistry, engineering, have been very greatly improved, that government, police, and law have been improved, though not to so great an extent as the physical sciences. Yet we see that, during these two hundred and fifty years, Protestantism has made no conquests worth speaking of. Nay, we believe that, as far as there has been change, that change has, on the whole, been in favour of the Church of Rome. We cannot, therefore, feel confident that the progress of knowledge will necessarily be fatal to a system which has, to say the least, stood its ground in spite of the immense progress made by the human race in knowledge since the days of Queen Elizabeth.

"Indeed, the argument which we are considering seems to us to be founded on an entire mistake. There are branches of knowledge with respect to which the law of the human mind is prog-

---

2 Macaulay's Essays.

ress. In mathematics, when once a proposition has been demonstrated, it is never afterwards contested. Every fresh storey is as solid a basis for a new superstructure as the original foundation was. Here, therefore, there is a constant addition to the stock of truth. In the inductive sciences, again, the law is progress …

"But with theology the case is very different. As respects natural religion (Revelation being for the present altogether left out of the question), it is not easy to see that a philosopher of the present day is more favourably situated than Thales or Simonides. He has before him just the same evidences of design in the structure of the universe which the early Greeks had … As to the other great question, the question what becomes of man after death, we do not see that a highly educated European, left to his unassisted reason, is more likely to be in the right than a Blackfoot Indian. Not a single one of the many sciences, in which we surpass the Blackfoot Indians, throws the smallest light on the state of the soul after the animal life is extinct …

"Natural Theology, then, is not a progressive science. That knowledge of our origin and of our destiny which we derive from Revelation is indeed of very different clearness, and of very different importance. But neither is Revealed Religion of the nature of a progressive science … In divinity there cannot be a progress analogous to that which is constantly taking place in pharmacy, geology, and navigation. A Christian of the fifth century with a Bible is neither better nor worse situated than a Christian of the nineteenth century with a Bible, candour and natural acuteness being of course supposed equal. It matters not at all that the compass, printing, gunpowder, steam, gas, vaccination, and a thousand other discoveries and inventions, which were unknown in the fifth century, are familiar to the nineteenth. None of these discoveries and inventions has the smallest bearing on the question whether man is justified by faith alone, or whether the invocation of saints is an orthodox practice … We are confident that the world will never go back to the solar system of Ptolemy; nor is our confidence in the least shaken by the circumstance that so great a man as Bacon rejected the theory of Galileo with scorn; for Bacon had not all the means of arriving at a sound conclusion ... But when we reflect that Sir Thomas More was ready to die for the doctrine of Transubstantiation, we cannot but feel some doubt whether the doctrine of Transubstantiation may not triumph over all opposition. More was a man of eminent talents. He had all the information on the subject that we have, or *that, while the world lasts, any human being will have* ... *No progress that science has made, or will make*, can add to what seems to us the overwhelming force of the argument against the Real Presence. We are therefore unable to understand why what Sir Thomas More believed respecting Transubstantiation may not be believed to the end of time by men equal in abilities and honesty to Sir Thomas More. But Sir Thomas More is one of the choice specimens of human wisdom and virtue; and the doctrine of Transubstantiation is a kind of proof charge. The faith which stands that test will stand any test ...

"The history of Catholicism strikingly illustrates these observations. During the last seven centuries the public mind of Europe has made constant progress in every department of secular knowledge; but in religion we can trace no constant progress ... Four times since the authority of the Church of Rome was established in Western Christendom has the human intellect risen up against her yoke. Twice that Church remained completely victorious. Twice she came forth from the conflict bearing the marks of cruel wounds, but with the principle of life still strong within her. When we reflect on the tremendous assaults she has survived, we find it difficult to conceive in what way she is to perish."

You see, Gentlemen, if you trust the judgment of a sagacious mind, deeply read in history, Catholic Theology has nothing to fear from the progress of Physical Science, even independently of the divinity of its doctrines. It speaks of things supernatural; and these, by the very force of the words, research into nature cannot touch.

5.

It is true that the author in question, while saying all this, and much more to the same purpose, also makes mention of one exception to his general statement, though he mentions it in order to put it aside. I, too, have to notice the same exception here; and you will see at once, Gentlemen, as soon as it is named, how little it interferes really with the broad view which I have been drawing out. It is true, then, that Revelation has in one or two instances advanced beyond its chosen territory, which is the invisible world, in order to throw light upon the history of the material universe. Holy Scripture, it is perfectly true, does declare a few momentous facts, so few that they may be counted, of a physical character. It speaks of a process of formation out of chaos which occupied six days; it speaks of the firmament; of the sun and moon being created for the sake of the earth; of the earth being immovable; of a great deluge; and of several other similar facts and events. It is true; nor is there any reason why we should anticipate any difficulty in accepting these statements as they stand, whenever their meaning and drift are authoritatively determined; for, it must be recollected, their meaning has not yet engaged the formal attention of the Church, or received any interpretation which, as Catholics, we are bound to accept, and in the absence of such definite interpretation, there is perhaps some presumption in saying that it means this, and does not mean that. And this being the case, it is not at all probable that any discoveries ever should be made by physical inquiries incompatible at the same time with one and all of those senses which the letter admits, and which are still open. As to certain popular interpretations of the texts in question, I shall have something to say of them presently; here I am only concerned with the letter of the Holy Scriptures itself, as far as it bears upon the history of the heavens and the earth; and I say that we may wait in peace and tranquillity till there is some real collision between Scripture authoritatively interpreted, and results of science clearly ascertained, before we consider how we are to deal with a difficulty which we have reasonable grounds for thinking will never really occur.

And, after noticing this exception, I really have made the utmost admission that has to be made about the existence of any common ground upon which Theology and Physical Science may fight a battle. On the whole, the two studies do most surely occupy distinct fields, in which each may teach without expecting any interposition from the other. It might indeed have pleased the Almighty to have superseded physical inquiry by revealing the truths which are its object, though He has not done so: but whether it had pleased Him to do so or not, anyhow Theology and Physics would be distinct sciences; and nothing which the one says of the material world ever can contradict what the other says of the immaterial. Here, then, is the end of the question; and here I might come to an end also, were it not incumbent on me to explain how it is that, though Theology and Physics cannot quarrel, nevertheless, Physical Philosophers and Theologians have quarrelled in fact, and quarrel still. To the solution of this difficulty I shall devote the remainder of my Lecture.

6.

I observe, then, that the elementary methods of reasoning and inquiring used in Theology and Physics are contrary the one to the other; each of them has a method of its own; and in this, I think, has lain the point of controversy between the two schools, viz., that neither of them has been quite content to remain on its own homestead, but that, whereas each has its own method, which is the best for its own science, each has considered it the best for all purposes whatever, and has at different times thought to impose it upon the other science, to the disparagement or rejection of that opposite method which legitimately belongs to it.

The argumentative method of Theology is that of a strict science, such as Geometry, or deductive; the method of Physics, at least on starting, is that of an empirical pursuit, or inductive. This peculiarity on either side arises from the nature of the case. In Physics a vast and omnigenous mass of information lies before the inquirer, all in a confused litter, and needing arrangement and analysis. In Theology such varied phenomena are wanting, and Revelation presents itself instead. What is known in Christianity is just that which is revealed, and nothing more; certain truths, communicated directly from above, are committed to the keeping of the faithful, and to the very last nothing can really be added to those truths. From the time of the Apostles to the end of the world no strictly new truth can be added to the theological information which the Apostles were inspired to deliver. It is possible of course to make numberless deductions from the original doctrines; but, as the conclusion is ever in its premises, such deductions are not, strictly speaking, an addition; and, though experience may variously guide and modify those deductions, still, on the whole, Theology retains the severe character of a science, advancing syllogistically from premises to conclusion.

The method of Physics is just the reverse of this: it has hardly any principles or truths to start with, externally delivered and already ascertained. It has to commence with sight and touch; it has to handle, weigh, and measure its own exuberant *sylva* of phenomena, and from these to advance to new truths,—truths, that is, which are beyond and distinct from the phenomena from which they originate. Thus Physical Science is experimental, Theology traditional; Physical Science is the richer, Theology the more exact; Physics the bolder, Theology the surer; Physics progressive, Theology, in comparison, stationary; Theology is loyal to the past, Physics has visions of the future. Such they are, I repeat, and such their respective methods of inquiry, from the nature of the case.

But minds habituated to either of these two methods can hardly help extending it beyond its due limits, unless they are put upon their guard, and have great command of themselves. It cannot be denied that divines have from time to time been much inclined to give a traditional, logical shape to sciences which do not admit of any such treatment. Nor can it be denied, on the other hand, that men of science often show a special irritation at theologians for going by antiquity, precedent, authority, and logic, and for declining to introduce Bacon or Niebuhr into their own school, or to apply some new experimental and critical process for the improvement of that which has been given once for all from above. Hence the mutual jealousy of the two parties; and I shall now attempt to give instances of it.

7.

First, then, let me refer to those interpretations of Scripture, popular and of long standing, though not authoritative, to which I have already had occasion to allude. Scripture, we know, is to be interpreted according to the unanimous consent of the Fathers; but, besides this consent, which is of authority, carrying with it the evidence of its truth, there have ever been in Christendom a number of floating opinions, more or less appended to the divine tradition; opinions which have a certain probability of being more than human, or of having a basis or admixture of truth, but which admit of no test, whence they came, or how far they are true, besides the course of events, and which meanwhile are to be received at least with attention and deference. Sometimes they are comments on Scripture prophecy, sometimes on other obscurities or mysteries. It was once an opinion, for instance, drawn from the sacred text, that the Christian Dispensation was to last a thousand years, and no more; the event disproved it. A still more exact and plausible tradition, derived from Scripture, was that which asserted that, when the Roman Empire should fall to pieces, Antichrist should appear, who should be followed at once by the Second Coming. Various Fathers thus interpret St. Paul, and Bellarmine receives the interpretation as late as the sixteenth century. The event alone can decide if, under any aspect of Christian history, it is true; but at present we are at least able to say that it is not true in that broad plain sense in which it was once received.

Passing from comments on prophetical passages of Scripture to those on cosmological, it was, I suppose, the common belief of ages, sustained by received interpretations of the sacred text, that the earth was immovable. Hence, I suppose, it was that the Irish Bishop who asserted the existence of the Antipodes alarmed his contemporaries; though it is well to observe that, even in the dark age in which he lived, the Holy See, to which reference was made, did not commit itself to any condemnation of the unusual opinion. The same alarm again occupied the public mind when the Copernican System was first advocated: nor were the received traditions, which were the ground of that alarm, hastily to be rejected; yet rejected they ultimately have been. If in any quarter these human traditions were enforced, and, as it were, enacted, to the prejudice and detriment of scientific investigations (and this was never done by the Church herself), this was a case of undue interference on the part of the Theological schools in the province of Physics.

So much may be said as regards interpretations of Scripture; but it is easy to see that other received opinions, not resting on the sacred volume, might with less claim and greater inconvenience be put forward to harass the physical inquirer, to challenge his submission, and to preclude that process of examination which is proper to his own peculiar pursuit. Such are the dictatorial formula against which Bacon inveighs, and the effect of which was to change Physics into a deductive science, and to oblige the student to assume implicitly, as first principles, enunciations and maxims, which were venerable, only because no one could tell whence they came, and authoritative, only because no one could say what arguments there were in their favour. In proportion as these encroachments were made upon his own field of inquiry would be the indignation of the physical philosopher; and he would exercise a scepticism which relieved his feelings, while it approved itself to his reason, if he was called on ever to keep in mind that light bodies went up, and heavy bodies fell down, and other similar maxims, which had no pretensions to a divine origin, or to be considered self-evident principles, or intuitive truths.

And in like manner, if a philosopher with a true genius for physical research found the Physical Schools of his day occupied with the discussion of final causes, and solving difficulties in material nature by means of them; if he found it decided, for instance, that the roots of trees make for the river, *because* they need moisture, or that the axis of the earth lies at a certain angle to the plane of its motion by *reason* of certain advantages thence accruing to its inhabitants, I should not wonder at his exerting himself for a great reform in the process of inquiry, preaching the method of Induction, and, if he fancied that theologians were indirectly or in any respect the occasion of the blunder, getting provoked for a time, however unreasonably, with Theology itself.

I wish the experimental school of Philosophers had gone no further in its opposition to Theology than indulging in some indignation at it for the fault of its disciples; but it must be confessed that it has run into excesses on its own side for which the school of high Deductive Science has afforded no precedent; and that, if it once for a time suffered from the tyranny of the logical method of inquiry, it has encouraged, by way of reprisals, encroachments and usurpations on the province of Theology far more serious than that unintentional and long obsolete interference with its own province, on the part of Theologians, which has been its excuse. And to these unjustifiable and mischievous intrusions made by the Experimentalists into the department of Theology I have now, Gentlemen, to call your attention.

8.

You will let me repeat, then, what I have already said, that, taking things as they are, the very idea of Revelation is that of a direct interference from above, for the introduction of truths otherwise unknown; moreover, as such a communication implies recipients, an authoritative depositary of the things revealed will be found practically to be involved in that idea. Knowledge, then, of these revealed truths, is gained, not by any research into facts, but simply by appealing to the authoritative keepers of them, as every Catholic knows, by learning what is a matter of teaching, and by dwelling upon, and drawing out into detail, the doctrines which are delivered; according to the text, "Faith cometh by hearing." I do not prove what, after all, does not need proof, because I speak to Catholics; I am stating what we Catholics know, and ever will maintain to be the method proper to Theology, as it has ever been recognized. Such, I say, is the theological method, deductive; however, the history of the last three centuries is only one long course of attempts, on the part of the partisans of the

Baconian Philosophy, to get rid of the method proper to Theology and to make it an experimental science.

But, I say, for an experimental science, we must have a large collection of phenomena or facts: where, then, are those which are to be adopted as a basis for an inductive theology? Three principal stores have been used, Gentlemen: the first, the text of Holy Scripture; the second, the events and transactions of ecclesiastical history; the third, the phenomena of the visible world. This triple subject-matter,—Scripture, Antiquity, Nature,—has been taken as a foundation, on which the inductive method may be exercised for the investigation and ascertainment of that theological truth, which to a Catholic is a matter of teaching, transmission, and deduction.

Now let us pause for a moment and make a reflection before going into any detail. Truth cannot be contrary to truth; if these three subject-matters were able, under the pressure of the inductive method, to yield respectively theological conclusions in unison and in concord with each other, and also contrary to the doctrines of Theology as a deductive science, then that Theology would not indeed at once be overthrown (for still the question would remain for discussion, which of the two doctrinal systems was the truth, and which the apparent truth), but certainly the received deductive theological science would be in an anxious position, and would be on its trial.

Again, truth cannot be contrary to truth;—if then, on the other hand, these three subject-matters,—Scripture, Antiquity, and Nature,—worked through three centuries by men of great abilities, with the method or instrument of Bacon in their hands, have respectively issued in conclusions contradictory of each other, nay, have even issued, this or that taken by itself, Scripture or Antiquity, in various systems of doctrine, so that on the whole, instead of all three resulting in one set of conclusions, they have yielded a good score of them; then and in that case—it does not at once follow that no one of this score of conclusions may happen to be the true one, and all the rest false; but at least such a catastrophe will throw a very grave shade of doubt upon them all, and bears out the antecedent declaration, or rather prophecy, of theologians, before these experimentalists started, that it was nothing more than a huge mistake to introduce the method of research and of induction into the study of Theology at all.

Now I think you will allow me to say, Gentlemen, as a matter of historical fact, that the latter supposition has been actually fulfilled, and that the former has not. I mean that, so far from a scientific proof of some one system of doctrine, and that antagonistic to the old Theology, having been constructed by the experimental party, by a triple convergence, from the several bases of Scripture, Antiquity, and Nature, on the contrary, that empirical method, which has done such wonderful things in physics and other human sciences, has sustained a most emphatic and eloquent reverse in its usurped territory,— has come to no one conclusion,—has illuminated no definite view,—has brought its glasses to no focus,—has shown not even a tendency towards prospective success; nay, further still, has already confessed its own absolute failure, and has closed the inquiry itself, not indeed by giving place to the legitimate method which it dispossessed, but by announcing that nothing can be known on the subject at all,—that religion is not a science, and that in religion scepticism is the only true philosophy; or again, by a still more remarkable avowal, that the decision lies between the old Theology and none at all, and that, certain though it be that religious truth is nowhere, yet that, if anywhere it is, it undoubtedly is not in the new empirical schools, but in that old teaching, founded on the deductive method, which was in honour and in possession at the time when Experiment and Induction commenced their brilliant career. What a singular break-down of a noble instrument, when used for the arrogant and tyrannical invasion of a sacred territory! What can be more sacred than Theology? What can be more noble than the Baconian method? But the two do not correspond; they are mismatched. The age has mistaken lock and key. It has broken the key in a lock which does not belong to it; it has ruined the wards by a key which never will fit into then. Let us hope that its present disgust and despair at the result are the preliminaries of a generous and great repentance.

I have thought, Gentlemen, that you would allow me to draw this moral in the first place; and now I will say a few words on one specimen of this error in detail.

9.

It seems, then, that instead of having recourse to the tradition and teaching of the Catholic Church, it has been the philosophy of the modern school to attempt to determine the doctrines of Theology by means of Holy Scripture, or of ecclesiastical antiquity, or of physical phenomena. And the question may arise, *why*, after all, should not such informations, scriptural, historical, or physical, be used? and if used, why should they not lead to true results? Various answers may be given to this question: I shall confine myself to one; and again, for the sake of brevity, I shall apply it mainly to one out of the three expedients, to which the opponents to Theology have had recourse. Passing over, then, what might be said respecting what is called Scriptural Religion, and Historical Religion, I propose to direct your attention, in conclusion, to the real character of Physical Religion, or Natural Theology, as being more closely connected with the main subject of this Lecture.

The school of Physics, from its very drift and method of reasoning, has, as I have said, nothing to do with Religion. However, there is a science which avails itself of the phenomena and laws of the material universe, as exhibited by that school, as a means of establishing the existence of Design in their construction, and thereby the fact of a Creator and Preserver. This science has, in these modern times, at least in England, taken the name of Natural Theology;[3] and, though absolutely distinct from Physics, yet Physical Philosophers, having furnished its most curious and interesting data, are apt to claim it as their own, and to pride themselves upon it accordingly.

---

3 I use the word, not in the sense of "Naturalis Theologia," but in the sense in which Paley uses it in the work which he has so entitled.

I have no wish to speak lightly of the merits of this so-called Natural or, more properly, Physical Theology. There are a great many minds so constituted that, when they turn their thoughts to the question of the existence of a Supreme Being, they feel a comfort in resting the proof mainly or solely on the Argument of Design which the Universe furnishes. To them this science of Physical Theology is of high importance. Again, this science exhibits, in great prominence and distinctness, three of the more elementary notions which the human reason attaches to the idea of a Supreme Being, that is, three of His simplest attributes, Power, Wisdom, and Goodness.

These are great services rendered to faith by Physical Theology, and I acknowledge them as such. Whether, however, Faith on that account owes any great deal to Physics or Physicists, is another matter. The Argument from Design is really in no sense due to the philosophy of Bacon. The author I quoted just now has a striking passage on this point, of which I have already read to you a part. "As respects Natural Religion," he says, "it is not easy to see that the philosopher of the present day is more favourably situated than Thales or Simonides. He has before him just the same evidences of design in the structure of the universe which the early Greeks had. We say, just the same; for the discoveries of modern astronomers and anatomists *have really added nothing* to the force of that argument which a reflecting mind finds in every beast, bird, insect, fish, leaf, flower, and shell. The reasoning by which Socrates, in Xenophon's hearing, confuted the little atheist, Aristodemus, is exactly the reasoning of Paley's Natural Theology. Socrates makes precisely the same use of the statues of Polycletus and the pictures of Zeuxis, which Paley makes of the watch."

Physical Theology, then, is pretty much what it was two thousand years ago, and has not received much help from modern science: but now, on the contrary, I think it has received from it a positive disadvantage,—I mean, it has been taken out of its place, has been put too prominently forward, and thereby has almost been used as an instrument against Christianity,—as I will attempt in a few words to explain.

10.

I observe, then, that there are many investigations in every subject-matter which only lead us a certain way towards truth, and not the whole way: either leading us, for instance, to a strong probability, not to a certainty, or again, proving only some things out of the whole number which are true. And it is plain that if such investigations as these are taken as the measure of the whole truth, and are erected into substantive sciences, instead of being understood to be, what they really are, inchoate and subordinate processes, they will, accidentally indeed, but seriously, mislead us.

1. Let us recur for a moment, in illustration, to the instances which I have put aside. Consider what is called Scriptural Religion, or the Religion of the Bible. The fault which the theologian, over and above the question of private judgment, will find with a religion logically drawn from Scripture only, is, not that it is not true, as far as it goes, but that it is not the whole truth; that it consists of only some out of the whole circle of theological doctrines, and that, even in the case of those which it includes, it does not always invest them with certainty, but only with probability. If, indeed, the Religion of the Bible is made subservient to Theology, it is but a specimen of useful induction; but if it is set up, as something complete in itself against Theology, it is turned into a mischievous paralogism. And if such a paralogism has taken place, and that in consequence of the influence of the Baconian philosophy, it shows us what comes of the intrusion of that philosophy into a province with which it had no concern.

2. And so, again, as to Historical Religion, or what is often called Antiquity. A research into the records of the early Church no Catholic can view with jealousy: truth cannot be contrary to truth; we are confident that what is there found will, when maturely weighed, be nothing else than an illustration and confirmation of our own Theology. But it is another thing altogether whether the results will go to the full lengths of our Theology; they will indeed concur with it, but only as far as they go. There is no reason why the data for investigation supplied by the extant documents of Antiquity should be sufficient for all that

was included in the Divine Revelation delivered by the Apostles; and to expect that they will is like expecting that one witness in a trial is to prove the whole case, and that his testimony actually contradicts it, unless it does. While, then, this research into ecclesiastical history and the writings of the Fathers keeps its proper place, as subordinate to the magisterial sovereignty of the Theological Tradition and the voice of the Church, it deserves the acknowledgments of theologians; but when it (so to say) sets up for itself, when it professes to fulfil an office for which it was never intended, when it claims to issue in a true and full teaching, derived by a scientific process of induction, then it is but another instance of the encroachment of the Baconian empirical method in a department not its own.

3. And now we come to the case of Physical Theology, which is directly before us. I confess, in spite of whatever may be said in its favour, I have ever viewed it with the greatest suspicion. As one class of thinkers has substituted what is called a Scriptural Religion, and another a Patristical or Primitive Religion, for the theological teaching of Catholicism, so a Physical Religion or Theology is the very gospel of many persons of the Physical School, and therefore, true as it may be in itself, still under the circumstances is a false gospel. Half of the truth is a falsehood:— consider, Gentlemen, what this so-called Theology teaches, and then say whether what I have asserted is extravagant.

Any one divine attribute of course virtually includes all; still if a preacher always insisted on the Divine Justice, he would practically be obscuring the Divine Mercy, and if he insisted only on the incommunicableness and distance from the creature of the Uncreated Essence, he would tend to throw into the shade the doctrine of a Particular Providence. Observe, then, Gentlemen, that Physical Theology teaches three Divine Attributes, I may say, exclusively; and of these, most of Power, and least of Goodness.

And in the next place, what, on the contrary, are those special Attributes, which are the immediate correlatives of religious sentiment? Sanctity, omniscience, justice, mercy, faithfulness. What does Physical Theology, what does the Argument from

Design, what do fine disquisitions about final causes, teach us, except very indirectly, faintly, enigmatically, of these transcendently important, these essential portions of the idea of Religion? Religion is more than Theology; it is something relative to us; and it includes our relation towards the Object of it. What does Physical Theology tell us of duty and conscience? of a particular providence? and, coming at length to Christianity, what does it teach us even of the four last things, death, judgment, heaven, and hell, the mere elements of Christianity? It cannot tell us anything of Christianity at all.

Gentlemen, let me press this point upon your earnest attention. I say Physical Theology cannot, from the nature of the case, tell us one word about Christianity proper; it cannot be Christian, in any true sense, at all:—and from this plain reason, because it is derived from informations which existed just as they are now, before man was created, and Adam fell. How can that be a real substantive Theology, though it takes the name, which is but an abstraction, a particular aspect of the whole truth, and is dumb almost as regards the moral attributes of the Creator, and utterly so as regards the evangelical?

Nay, more than this; I do not hesitate to say that, taking men as they are, this so-called science tends, if it occupies the mind, to dispose it against Christianity. And for this plain reason, because it speaks only of laws; and cannot contemplate their suspension, that is, miracles, which are of the essence of the idea of a Revelation. Thus, the God of Physical Theology may very easily become a mere idol; for He comes to the inductive mind in the medium of fixed appointments, so excellent, so skilful, so beneficent, that, when it has for a long time gazed upon them, it will think them too beautiful to be broken, and will at length so contract its notion of Him as to conclude that He never could have the heart (if I may dare use such a term) to undo or mar His own work; and this conclusion will be the first step towards its degrading its idea of God a second time, and identifying Him with His works. Indeed, a Being of Power, Wisdom, and Goodness, and nothing else, is not very different from the God of the Pantheist.

In thus speaking of the Theology of the modern Physical School, I have said but a few words on a large subject; yet, though few words, I trust they are clear enough not to hazard the risk of being taken in a sense which I do not intend. Graft the science, if it is so to be called, on Theology proper, and it will be in its right place, and will be a religious science. Then it will illustrate the awful, incomprehensible, adorable Fertility of the Divine Omnipotence; it will serve to prove the real miraculousness of the Revelation in its various parts, by impressing on the mind vividly what are the laws of nature, and how immutable they are in their own order; and it will in other ways subserve theological truth. Separate it from the supernatural teaching, and make it stand on its own base, and (though of course it is better for the individual philosopher himself), yet, as regards his influence on the world and the interests of Religion, I really doubt whether I should not prefer that he should be an Atheist at once than such a naturalistic, pantheistic religionist. His profession of Theology deceives others, perhaps deceives himself.

Do not for an instant suppose, Gentlemen, that I would identify the great mind of Bacon with so serious a delusion: he has expressly warned us against it; but I cannot deny that many of his school have from time to time in this way turned physical research against Christianity.

But I have detained you far longer than I had intended; and now I can only thank you for the patience which has enabled you to sustain a discussion which cannot be complete, upon a subject which, however momentous, cannot be popular.

VIII.

CHRISTIANITY AND SCIENTIFIC INVESTIGATION

A LECTURE WRITTEN FOR THE SCHOOL OF SCIENCE

1.

This is a time, Gentlemen, when not only the Classics, but much more the Sciences, in the largest sense of the word, are looked upon with anxiety, not altogether ungrounded, by religious men; and, whereas a University such as ours professes to embrace all departments and exercises of the intellect, and since I for my part wish to stand on good terms with all kinds of knowledge, and have no intention of quarrelling with any, and would open my heart, if not my intellect (for that is beyond me), to the whole circle of truth, and would tender at least a recognition and hospitality even to those studies which are strangers to me, and would speed them on their way,—therefore, as I have already been making overtures of reconciliation, first between Polite Literature and Religion, and next between Physics and Theology, so I would now say a word by way of deprecating and protesting against the needless antagonism, which sometimes exists in fact, between divines and the cultivators of the Sciences generally.

2.

Here I am led at once to expatiate on the grandeur of an Institution which is comprehensive enough to admit the discussion of a subject such as this. Among the objects of human enterprise,—I may say it surely without extravagance, Gentlemen,—none higher or nobler can be named than that which is contemplated in the erection of a University. To set on foot and to maintain in life and vigour a real University, is confessedly, as soon as the word "University" is understood, one of those greatest works, great in their difficulty and their importance, on which are deservedly expended the rarest intellects and the most varied endowments. For, first of all, it professes to teach whatever has to be taught in any whatever department of human knowledge, and it embraces in its scope the loftiest subjects of human thought, and the richest fields of human inquiry. Nothing is too vast, nothing too subtle, nothing too distant, nothing too minute, nothing too discursive, nothing too exact, to engage its attention.

This, however, is not the reason why I claim for it so sovereign a position; for, to bring schools of all knowledge under one name, and call them a University, may be fairly said to be a mere generalization; and to proclaim that the prosecution of all kinds of knowledge to their utmost limits demands the fullest reach and range of our intellectual faculties is but a truism. My reason for speaking of a University in the terms on which I have ventured is, not that it occupies the whole territory of knowledge merely, but that it is the very realm; that it professes much more than to take in and to lodge as in a caravanserai all art and science, all history and philosophy. In truth, it professes to assign to each study, which it receives, its own proper place and its just boundaries; to define the rights, to establish the mutual relations, and to effect the intercommunion of one and all; to keep in check the ambitious and encroaching, and to succour and maintain those which from time to time are succumbing under the more popular or the more fortunately circumstanced; to keep the peace between them all, and to convert their mutual differences and contrarieties into the common good. This, Gentlemen, is why I say that to erect a University is at once so arduous and beneficial an undertaking, viz., because it is pledged to admit, without fear, without prejudice, without compromise, all comers, if they come in the name of Truth; to adjust views, and experiences, and habits of mind the most independent and dissimilar; and to give full play to thought and erudition in their most original forms, and their most intense expressions, and in their most ample circuit. Thus to draw many things into one, is its special function; and it learns to do it, not by rules reducible to writing, but by sagacity, wisdom, and forbearance, acting upon a profound insight into the subject-matter of knowledge, and by a vigilant repression of aggression or bigotry in any quarter.

We count it a great thing, and justly so, to plan and carry out a wide political organization. To bring under one yoke, after the manner of old Rome, a hundred discordant peoples; to maintain each of them in its own privileges within its legitimate range of action; to allow them severally the indulgence of national feelings, and the stimulus of rival interests; and yet withal to blend them into one great social establishment, and to pledge them to the perpetuity of the one imperial power;—this is an achievement which carries with it the unequivocal token of genius in the race which effects it.

"Tu regere imperio populos, Romane, memento."

This was the special boast, as the poet considered it, of the Roman; a boast as high in its own line as that other boast, proper to the Greek nation, of literary pre-eminence, of exuberance of thought, and of skill and refinement in expressing it.

What an empire is in political history, such is a University in the sphere of philosophy and research. It is, as I have said, the high protecting power of all knowledge and science, of fact and principle, of inquiry and discovery, of experiment and speculation; it maps out the territory of the intellect, and sees that the boundaries of each province are religiously respected, and that there is neither encroachment nor surrender on any side. It acts as umpire between truth and truth, and, taking into account the nature and importance of each, assigns to all their due order of precedence. It maintains no one department of thought exclusively, however ample and noble; and it sacrifices none. It is deferential and loyal, according to their respective weight, to the claims of literature, of physical research, of history, of metaphysics, of theological science. It is impartial towards them all, and promotes each in its own place and for its own object. It is ancillary certainly, and of necessity, to the Catholic Church; but in the same way that one of the Queen's judges is an officer of the Queen's, and nevertheless determines certain legal proceedings between the Queen and her subjects. It is ministrative to the Catholic Church, first, because truth of any kind can but minister to truth; and next, still more, because Nature ever will pay homage to Grace, and Reason cannot but illustrate and defend Revelation; and thirdly, because the Church has a sovereign authority, and, when she speaks *ex cathedra*, must be obeyed. But this is the remote end of a University; its immediate end (with which alone we have here to do) is to secure the due disposition, according to one sovereign order, and the cultivation in that order, of all the provinces and methods of thought which the human intellect has created.

In this point of view, its several professors are like the ministers of various political powers at one court or conference. They represent their respective sciences, and attend to the private interests of those sciences respectively; and, should dispute arise between those sciences, they are the persons to talk over and arrange it, without risk of extravagant pretensions on any side, of angry collision, or of popular commotion. A liberal philosophy becomes the habit of minds thus exercised; a breadth and spaciousness of thought, in which lines, seemingly parallel, may converge at leisure, and principles, recognized as incommensurable, may be safely antagonistic.

3.

And here, Gentlemen, we recognize the special character of the Philosophy I am speaking of, if Philosophy it is to be called, in contrast with the method of a strict science or system. Its teaching is not founded on one idea, or reducible to certain formulæ. Newton might discover the great law of motion in the physical world, and the key to ten thousand phenomena; and a similar resolution of complex facts into simple principles may be possible in other departments of nature; but the great Universe itself, moral and material, sensible and supernatural, cannot be gauged and meted by even the greatest of human intellects, and its constituent parts admit indeed of comparison and adjustment, but not of fusion. This is the point which bears directly on the subject which I set before me when I began, and towards which I am moving in all I have said or shall be saying.

I observe, then, and ask you, Gentlemen, to bear in mind, that the philosophy of an imperial intellect, for such I am considering a University to be, is based, not so much on simplification as on discrimination. Its true representative defines, rather than analyses. He aims at no complete catalogue, or interpretation of the subjects of knowledge, but a following out, as far as man can, what in its fulness is mysterious and unfathomable. Taking into his charge all sciences, methods, collections of facts, principles, doctrines, truths, which are the reflexions of the universe upon the human intellect, he admits them all, he disregards none, and, as disregarding none, he allows none to exceed or encroach. His watchword is, Live and let live. He takes things as they are; he submits to them all, as far as they go; he recognizes the insuperable lines of demarcation which run between subject and subject; he observes how separate truths lie relatively to each other, where they concur, where they part company, and where, being carried too far, they cease to be truths at all. It is his office to determine how much can be known in each province of thought; when we must be contented not to know; in what direction inquiry is hopeless, or on the other hand full of promise; where it gathers into coils insoluble by reason, where it is absorbed in mysteries, or runs into the abyss. It will be his care to be familiar with the signs of real and apparent difficulties, with the methods proper to particular subject-matters, what in each particular case are the limits of a rational scepticism, and what the claims of a peremptory faith. If he has one cardinal maxim in his philosophy, it is, that truth cannot be contrary to truth; if he has a second, it is, that truth often *seems* contrary to truth; and, if a third, it is the practical conclusion, that we must be patient with such appearances, and not be hasty to pronounce them to be really of a more formidable character.

It is the very immensity of the system of things, the human record of which he has in charge, which is the reason of this patience and caution; for that immensity suggests to him that the contrarieties and mysteries, which meet him in the various sciences, may be simply the consequences of our necessarily defective comprehension. There is but one thought greater than that of the universe, and that is the thought of its Maker. If, Gentlemen, for one single instant, leaving my proper train of thought, I allude to our knowledge of the Supreme Being, it is in order to deduce from it an illustration bearing upon my subject. He, though One, is a sort of world of worlds in Himself, giving birth in our minds to an indefinite number of distinct truths, each ineffably more mysterious than any thing that is found in this universe of space and time. Any one of His attributes, considered by itself, is the object of an inexhaustible science: and the attempt to reconcile any two or three of them together,—love, power, justice, sanctity, truth, wisdom,—affords matter for an everlasting controversy. We are able to apprehend and receive each divine attribute in its elementary form, but still we are not able to accept them in their infinity, either in themselves or in union with each other. Yet we do not deny the first because it cannot be perfectly reconciled with the second, nor the second because it is in apparent contrariety with the first and the third. The case is the same in its degree with His creation material and moral. It is the highest wisdom to accept truth of whatever kind, wherever it is clearly ascertained to be such, though there be difficulty in adjusting it with other known truth.

Instances are easily producible of that extreme contrariety of ideas, one with another, which the contemplation of the Universe forces upon our acceptance, making it clear to us that there is nothing irrational in submitting to undeniable incompatibilities, which we call apparent, only because, if they were not apparent but real, they could not co-exist. Such, for instance, is the contemplation of Space; the existence of which we cannot deny, though its idea is capable, in no sort of posture, of seating itself (if I may so speak) in our minds;—for we find it impossible to say that it comes to a limit anywhere; and it is incomprehensible to say that it runs out infinitely; and it seems to be unmeaning if we say that it does not exist till bodies come into it, and thus is enlarged according to an accident.

And so again in the instance of Time. We cannot place a beginning to it without asking ourselves what was before that beginning; yet that there should be no beginning at all, put it as far back as we will, is simply incomprehensible. Here again, as in the case of Space, we never dream of denying the existence of what we have no means of understanding.

And, passing from this high region of thought (which, high as it may be, is the subject even of a child's contemplations), when we come to consider the mutual action of soul and body, we are specially perplexed by incompatibilities which we can neither reject nor explain. How it is that the will can act on the muscles, is a question of which even a child may feel the force, but which no experimentalist can answer.

Further, when we contrast the physical with the social laws under which man finds himself here below, we must grant that Physiology and Social Science are in collision. Man is both a physical and a social being; yet he cannot at once pursue to the full his physical end and his social end, his physical duties (if I may so speak) and his social duties, but is forced to sacrifice in part one or the other. If we were wild enough to fancy that there were two creators, one of whom was the author of our animal frames, the other of society, then indeed we might understand how it comes to pass that labour of mind and body, the useful arts, the duties of a statesman, government, and the like, which are required by the social system, are so destructive of health, enjoyment, and life. That is, in other words, we cannot adequately account for existing and undeniable truths except on the hypothesis of what we feel to be an absurdity.

And so in Mathematical Science, as has been often insisted on, the philosopher has patiently to endure the presence of truths, which are not the less true for being irreconcileable with each other. He is told of the existence of an infinite number of curves, which are able to divide a space, into which no straight line, though it be length without breadth, can even enter. He is told, too, of certain lines, which approach to each other continually, with a finite distance between them, yet never meet; and these apparent contrarieties he must bear as he best can, without attempting to deny the existence of the truths which constitute them in the Science in question.

4.

Now, let me call your attention, Gentlemen, to what I would infer from these familiar facts. It is, to urge you with an argument *à fortiori:* viz., that, as you exercise so much exemplary patience in the case of the inexplicable truths which surround so many departments of knowledge, human and divine, viewed in themselves; as you are not at once indignant, censorious, suspicious, difficult of belief, on finding that in the secular sciences one truth is incompatible (according to our human intellect) with another or inconsistent with itself; so you should not think it very hard to be told that there exists, here and there, not an inextricable difficulty, not an astounding contrariety, not (much less) a contradiction as to clear facts, between Revelation and Nature; but a hitch, an obscurity, a divergence of tendency, a temporary antagonism, a difference of tone, between the two,—that is, between Catholic opinion on the one hand, and astronomy, or geology, or physiology, or ethnology, or political economy, or history, or antiquities, on the other. I say that, as we admit, because we are Catholics, that the Divine Unity contains in it attributes, which, to our finite minds, appear in partial contrariety with each other; as we admit that, in His revealed Nature are things, which, though not opposed to Reason, are infinitely strange to the Imagination; as in His works we can neither reject nor admit the ideas of space, and of time, and the necessary properties of lines, without intellectual distress, or even torture; really, Gentlemen, I am making no outrageous request, when, in the name of a University, I ask religious writers, jurists, economists, physiologists, chemists, geologists, and historians, to go on quietly, and in a neighbourly way, in their own respective lines of speculation, research, and experiment, with full faith in the consistency of that multiform truth, which they share between them, in a generous confidence that they will be ultimately consistent, one and all, in their combined results, though there may be momentary collisions, awkward appearances, and many forebodings and prophecies of contrariety, and at all times things hard to the Imagination, though not, I repeat, to the Reason. It surely is not asking them a great deal to beg of them,—since they are forced to admit mysteries in the truths of Revelation, taken by themselves, and in the truths of Reason, taken by themselves,— to beg of them, I say, to keep the peace, to live in good will, and to exercise equanimity, if, when Nature and Revelation are compared with each other, there be, as I have said, discrepancies,—not in the issue, but in the reasonings, the circumstances, the associations, the anticipations, the accidents, proper to their respective teachings.

It is most necessary to insist seriously and energetically on this point, for the sake of Protestants, for they have very strange notions about us. In spite of the testimony of history the other way, they think that the Church has no other method of putting down error than the arm of force, or the prohibition of inquiry. They defy us to set up and carry on a School of Science. For their sake, then, I am led to enlarge upon the subject here. I say, then, he who believes Revelation with that absolute faith which is the prerogative of a Catholic, is not the nervous creature who startles at every sudden sound, and is fluttered by every strange or novel appearance which meets his eyes. He has no sort of apprehension, he laughs at the idea, that any thing can be discovered by any other scientific method, which can contradict any one of the dogmas of his religion. He knows full well there is no science whatever, but, in the course of its extension, runs the risk of infringing, without any meaning of offence on its own part, the path of other sciences: and he knows also that, if there be any one science which, from its sovereign and unassailable position can calmly bear such unintentional collisions on the part of the children of earth, it is Theology. He is sure, and nothing shall make him doubt, that, if anything seems to be proved by astronomer, or geologist, or chronologist, or antiquarian, or ethnologist, in contradiction to the dogmas of faith, that point will eventually turn out, first, *not* to be proved, or, secondly, not *contradictory*, or thirdly, not contradictory to any thing *really revealed*, but to something which has been confused with revelation. And if, at the moment, it appears to be contradictory, then he is content to wait, knowing that error is like other delinquents; give it rope enough, and it will be found to have a strong suicidal propensity. I do not mean to say he will not take his part in encouraging, in helping forward the prospective suicide; he will not only give the error rope enough, but show it how to handle and adjust the rope;—he will commit the matter to reason, reflection, sober judgment, common sense; to Time, the great interpreter of so many secrets. Instead of being irritated at the momentary triumph of the foes of Revelation, if such a feeling of triumph there be, and of hurrying on a forcible solution of the difficulty, which may in the event only reduce the inquiry to an inextricable tangle, he will recollect that, in the order of Providence, our seeming dangers are often our greatest gains; that in the words of the Protestant poet,

> The clouds you so much dread
> Are big with mercy, and shall break
> In blessings on your head.

5.

To one notorious instance indeed it is obvious to allude here. When the Copernican system first made progress, what religious man would not have been tempted to uneasiness, or at least fear of scandal, from the seeming contradiction which it involved to some authoritative tradition of the Church and the declaration of Scripture? It was generally received, as if the Apostles had expressly delivered it both orally and in writing, as a truth of Revelation, that the earth was stationary, and that the sun, fixed in a solid firmament, whirled round the earth. After a little time, however, and on full consideration, it was found that the Church had decided next to nothing on questions such as these, and that Physical Science might range in this sphere of thought almost at will, without fear of encountering the decisions of ecclesiastical authority. Now, besides the relief which it afforded to Catholics to find that they were to be spared this addition, on the side of Cosmology, to their many controversies already existing, there is something of an argument in this very circumstance in behalf of the divinity of their Religion. For it surely is a very remarkable fact, considering how widely and how long one certain interpretation of these physical statements in Scripture had been received by Catholics, that the Church should not have formally acknowledged it. Looking at the matter in a human point of view, it was inevitable that she should have made that opinion her own. But now we find, on ascertaining where we stand, in the face of the new sciences of these latter times, that in spite of the bountiful comments which from the first she has ever been making on the sacred text, as it is her duty and her right to do, nevertheless, she has never been led formally to explain the texts in question, or to give them an authoritative sense which modern science may question.

Nor was this escape a mere accident, but rather the result of a providential superintendence; as would appear from a passage of history in the dark age itself. When the glorious St. Boniface, Apostle of Germany, great in sanctity, though not in secular knowledge, complained to the Holy See that St. Virgilius taught the existence of the Antipodes, the Holy See was guided what to do; it did not indeed side with the Irish philosopher, which would have been going out of its place, but it passed over, in a matter not revealed, a philosophical opinion.

Time went on; a new state of things, intellectual and social, came in; the Church was girt with temporal power; the preachers of St. Dominic were in the ascendant: now at length we may ask with curious interest, did the Church alter her ancient rule of action, and proscribe intellectual activity? Just the contrary; this is the very age of Universities; it is the classical period of the schoolmen; it is the splendid and palmary instance of the wise policy and large liberality of the Church, as regards philosophical inquiry. If there ever was a time when the intellect went wild, and had a licentious revel, it was at the date I speak of. When was there ever a more curious, more meddling, bolder, keener, more penetrating, more rationalistic exercise of the reason than at that time? What class of questions did that subtle, metaphysical spirit not scrutinize? What premiss was allowed without examination? What principle was not traced to its first origin, and exhibited in its most naked shape? What whole was not analyzed? What complex idea was not elaborately traced out, and, as it were, finely painted for the contemplation of the mind, till it was spread out in all its minutest portions as perfectly and delicately as a frog's foot shows under the intense scrutiny of the microscope? Well, I repeat, here was something which came somewhat nearer to Theology than physical research comes; Aristotle was a somewhat more serious foe then, beyond all mistake, than Bacon has been since. Did the Church take a high hand with philosophy then? No, not though that philosophy was metaphysical. It was a time when she had temporal power, and could have exterminated the spirit of inquiry with fire and sword; but she determined to put it down by *argument*, she said: "Two can play at that, and my argument is the better." She sent her controversialists into the philosophical arena. It was the Dominican and Franciscan doctors, the greatest of them being St. Thomas, who in those medieval Universities fought the battle of Revelation with the weapons of heathenism. It was no matter whose the weapon was; truth was truth all the world over. With the jawbone of an ass, with the skeleton philosophy of pagan Greece, did the Samson of the schools put to flight his thousand Philistines.

Here, Gentlemen, observe the contrast exhibited between the Church herself who has the gift of wisdom, and even the ablest, or wisest, or holiest of her children. As St. Boniface had been jealous of physical speculations, so had the early Fathers shown an extreme aversion to the great heathen philosopher whom I just now named, Aristotle. I do not know who of them could endure him; and when there arose those in the middle age who would take his part, especially since their intentions were of a suspicious character, a strenuous effort was made to banish him out of Christendom. The Church the while had kept silence; she had as little denounced heathen philosophy in the mass as she had pronounced upon the meaning of certain texts of Scripture of a cosmological character. From Tertullian and Caius to the two Gregories of Cappadocia, from them to Anastasius Sinaita, from him to the school of Paris, Aristotle was a word of offence; at length St. Thomas made him a hewer of wood and drawer of water to the Church. A strong slave he is; and the Church herself has given her sanction to the use in Theology of the ideas and terms of his philosophy.

6.

Now, while this free discussion is, to say the least, so safe for Religion, or rather so expedient, it is on the other hand simply necessary for progress in Science; and I shall now go on to insist on this side of the subject. I say, then, that it is a matter of primary importance in the cultivation of those sciences, in which truth is discoverable by the human intellect, that the investigator should be free, independent, unshackled in his movements; that he should be allowed and enabled, without impediment, to fix his mind intently, nay, exclusively, on his special object, without the risk of being distracted every other minute in the process and progress of his inquiry, by charges of temerariousness, or by warnings against extravagance or scandal. But in thus speaking, I must premise several explanations, lest I be misunderstood.

First, then, Gentlemen, as to the fundamental principles of religion and morals, and again as to the fundamental principles of Christianity, or what are called the *dogmas* of faith,—as to this double creed, natural and revealed,—we, none of us, should say that it is any shackle at all upon the intellect to maintain these inviolate. Indeed, a Catholic cannot put off his thought of them; and they as little impede the movements of his intellect as the laws of physics impede his bodily movements. The habitual apprehension of them has become a second nature with him, as the laws of optics, hydrostatics, dynamics, are latent conditions which he takes for granted in the use of his corporeal organs. I am not supposing any collision with dogma, I am but speaking of opinions of divines, or of the multitude, parallel to those in former times of the sun going round the earth, or of the last day being close at hand, or of St. Dionysius the Areopagite being the author of the works which bear his name.

Nor, secondly, even as regards such opinions, am I supposing any direct intrusion into the province of religion, or of a teacher of Science actually laying down the law *in a matter of Religion*; but of such unintentional collisions as are incidental to a discussion pursued on some subject of his own. It would be a great mistake in such a one to propose his philosophical or historical conclusions as the formal interpretation of the sacred text, as Galileo is said to have done, instead of being content to hold his doctrine of the motion of the earth as a scientific conclusion, and leaving it to those whom it really concerned to compare it with Scripture. And, it must be confessed, Gentlemen, not a few instances occur of this mistake at the present day, on the part, not indeed of men of science, but of religious men, who, from a nervous impatience lest Scripture should for one moment seem inconsistent with the results of some speculation of the hour, are ever proposing geological or ethnological comments upon it, which they have to alter or obliterate before the ink is well dry, from changes in the progressive science, which they have so officiously brought to its aid.

And thirdly, I observe that, when I advocate the independence of philosophical thought, I am not speaking of any *formal teaching* at all, but of investigations, speculations, and discussions. I am far indeed from allowing, in any matter which even borders on Religion, what an eminent Protestant divine has advocated on the most sacred subjects,—I mean "the liberty of Prophesying." I have no wish to degrade the professors of Science, who ought to be Prophets of the Truth, into mere advertisers of crude fancies or notorious absurdities. I am not pleading that they should at random shower down upon their hearers ingenuities and novelties; or that they should teach even what has a basis of truth in it, in a brilliant, off-hand way, to a collection of youths, who may not perhaps hear them for six consecutive lectures, and who will carry away with them into the country a misty idea of the half-created theories of some ambitious intellect.

Once more, as the last sentence suggests, there must be great care taken to avoid scandal, or shocking the popular mind, or unsettling the weak; the association between truth and error being so strong in particular minds that it is impossible to weed them of the error without rooting up the wheat with it. If, then, there is the chance of any current religious opinion being in any way compromised in the course of a scientific investigation, this would be a reason for conducting it, not in light ephemeral publications, which come into the hands of the careless or ignorant, but in works of a grave and business-like character, answering to the medieval schools of philosophical disputation, which, removed as they were from the region of popular thought and feeling, have, by their vigorous restlessness of inquiry, in spite of their extravagances, done so much for theological precision.

7.

I am not, then, supposing the scientific investigator (1) to be *coming into collision with dogma*; nor (2) venturing, by means of his investigations, upon any interpretation of *Scripture*, or upon other conclusion *in the matter of religion*; nor (3) of his *teaching*, even in his own science, religious parodoxes, when he should be investigating and proposing; nor (4) of his recklessly *scandalizing the weak*; but, these explanations being made, I still say that a scientific speculator or inquirer is not bound, in conducting his researches, to be every moment adjusting his course by the maxims of the schools or by popular traditions, or by those of any other science distinct from his own, or to be ever narrowly watching what those external sciences have to say to him, or to be determined to be edifying, or to be ever answering heretics and unbelievers; being confident, from the impulse of a generous faith, that, however his line of investigation may swerve now and then, and vary to and fro in its course, or threaten momentary collision or embarrassment with any other department of knowledge, theological or not, yet, if he lets it alone, it will be sure to come home, because truth never can really be contrary to truth, and because often what at first sight is an "exceptio," in the event most emphatically "probat regulam."

This is a point of serious importance to him. Unless he is at liberty to investigate on the basis, and according to the peculiarities, of his science, he cannot investigate at all. It is the very law of the human mind in its inquiry after and acquisition of truth to make its advances by a process which consists of many stages, and is circuitous. There are no short cuts to knowledge; nor does the road to it always lie in the direction in which it terminates, nor are we able to see the end on starting. It may often seem to be diverging from a goal into which it will soon run without effort, if we are but patient and resolute in following it out; and, as we are told in Ethics to gain the mean merely by receding from both extremes, so in scientific researches error may be said, without a paradox, to be in some instances the way to truth, and the only way. Moreover, it is not often the fortune of any one man to live through an investigation; the process is one of not only many stages, but of many minds. What one begins another finishes; and a true conclusion is at length worked out by the co-operation of independent schools and the perseverance of successive generations. This being the case, we are obliged, under circumstances, to bear for a while with what we feel to be error, in consideration of the truth in which it is eventually to issue.

The analogy of locomotion is most pertinent here. No one can go straight up a mountain; no sailing vessel makes for its port without tacking. And so, applying the illustration, we can indeed, if we will, refuse to allow of investigation or research altogether; but, if we invite reason to take its place in our schools, we must let reason have fair and full play. If we reason, we must submit to the conditions of reason. We cannot use it by halves; we must use it as proceeding from Him who has also given us Revelation; and to be ever interrupting its processes, and diverting its attention by objections brought from a higher knowledge, is parallel to a lands-man's dismay at the changes in the course of a vessel on which he has deliberately embarked, and argues surely some distrust either in the powers of Reason on the one hand, or the certainty of Revealed Truth on the other. The passenger should not have embarked at all, if he did not reckon on the chance of a rough sea, of currents, of wind and tide, of rocks and shoals; and we should act more wisely in discountenancing altogether the exercise of Reason than in being alarmed and impatient under the suspense, delay, and anxiety which, from the nature of the case, may be found to attach to it. Let us eschew secular history, and science, and philosophy for good and all, if we are not allowed to be sure that Revelation is so true that the altercations and perplexities of human opinion cannot really or eventually injure its authority. That is no intellectual triumph of any truth of Religion, which has not been preceded by a full statement of what can be said against it; it is but the ego vapulando, ille verberando, of the Comedy.

Great minds need elbow-room, not indeed in the domain of faith, but of thought. And so indeed do lesser minds, and all minds. There are many persons in the world who are called, and with a great deal of truth, geniuses. They had been gifted by nature with some particular faculty or capacity; and, while vehemently excited and imperiously ruled by it, they are blind to everything else. They are enthusiasts in their own line, and are simply dead to the beauty of any line except their own. Accordingly, they think their own line the only line in the whole world worth pursuing, and they feel a sort of contempt for such studies as move upon any other line. Now, these men may be, and often are, very good Catholics, and have not a dream of any thing but affection and deference towards Catholicity, nay, perhaps are zealous in its interests. Yet, if you insist that in their speculations, researches, or conclusions in their particular science, it is not enough that they should submit to the Church generally, and acknowledge its dogmas, but that they must get up all that divines have said or the multitude believed upon religious matters, you simply crush and stamp out the flame within them, and they can do nothing at all.

This is the case of men of genius: now one word on the contrary in behalf of master minds, gifted with a broad philosophical view of things, and a creative power, and a versatility capable of accommodating itself to various provinces of thought. These persons perhaps, like those I have already spoken of, take up some idea and are intent upon it;—some deep, prolific, eventful idea, which grows upon them, till they develop it into a great system. Now, if any such thinker starts from radically unsound principles, or aims at directly false conclusions, if he be a Hobbes, or a Shaftesbury, or a Hume, or a Bentham, then, of course, there is an end of the whole matter. He is an opponent of Revealed Truth, and he means to be so;—nothing more need be said. But perhaps it is not so; perhaps his errors are those which are inseparable accidents of his system or of his mind, and are spontaneously evolved, not pertinaciously defended. Every human system, every human writer, is open to just criticism. Make him shut up his portfolio; good! and then perhaps you lose what, on the whole and in spite of incidental mistakes, would have been one of the ablest defences of Revealed Truth (directly or indirectly, according to his subject) ever given to the world.

This is how I should account for a circumstance, which has sometimes caused surprise, that so many great Catholic thinkers have in some points or other incurred the criticism or animadversion of theologians or of ecclesiastical authority. It must be so in the nature of things; there is indeed an animadversion which implies a condemnation of the author; but there is another which means not much more than the "piè legendum" written against passages in the Fathers. The author may not be to blame; yet the ecclesiastical authority would be to blame, if it did not give notice of his imperfections. I do not know what Catholic would not hold the name of Malebranche in veneration;[1] but he may have accidentally come into collision with theologians,

---

1   Cardinal Gerdil speaks of his "Metaphysique," as "brillante à la verité, mais non moins solide" (p. 9.), and that "la liaison qui enchaine toutes les parties du système philosophique du Père Malebranche, ... pourra servir d'apologie à la noble assurance, avec laquelle il propose ses sentiments." (p. 12, Œuvres, t. iv.)

or made temerarious assertions, notwithstanding. The practical question is, whether he had not much better have written as he has written, than not have written at all. And so fully is the Holy See accustomed to enter into this view of the matter, that it has allowed of its application, not only to philosophical, but even to theological and ecclesiastical authors, who do not come within the range of these remarks. I believe I am right in saying that, in the case of three great names, in various departments of learning, Cardinal Noris, Bossuet, and Muratori,[2] while not concealing its sense of their having propounded each what might have been said better, nevertheless it has considered, that their services to Religion were on the whole far too important to allow of their being molested by critical observation in detail.

8.

And now, Gentlemen, I bring these remarks to a conclusion. What I would urge upon every one, whatever may be his particular line of research,—what I would urge upon men of Science in their thoughts of Theology,—what I would venture to recommend to theologians, when their attention is drawn to the

---

2 Muratori's work was not directly theological. I think it worth while in illustration to append the following passage from Grandorgæus's catalogue of Muratori's works.

"Sanctissimus D.N. Benedictus xiv. Pont. Max. Epistolam sapientiæ ac roboris plenam dederat ... ad Episcopum Terulensem Hispaniæ Inquisitionis Majorem Inquisitorem, quâ illum hortabatur, ut 'Historiam Pelagianam et dissertationem, etc.,' editas à claræ memoriæ Henrico Cardinali Norisio, in Indicem Expurgatorium Hispanum nuper ingestas, perinde ac si aliquid Baianismi aut Jansenismi redolerent, prout auctor 'Bibiothecæ Jansenisticæ' immerito autumavit, quamprimum expungendas curaret. Eoque nomine Sapientissimus Pontifex plura in medium attulit prudentis œconomiæ exempla, qua semper usum, supremum S. R. Congr. Indicis Tribunal, à proscribendis virorum doctissimorum operibus aliquando temperavit.

"Quum autem summus Pontifex, ea inter nomina illustria Tillemontii, Bollandistarum, Bosoueti Ep. Meld., et illud recensuerit L. A. Muratorii, his ad Auctorem nostrum delatis, quam maximè indoluit, veritus ne in tantâ operum copiâ ab se editorum, aliquid Fidei aut Religioni minùs consonum sibi excidisset ...

"Verùm clementissimus Pontifex ne animum desponderet doctus et humilis filius, pernumaniter ad ipsum rescripsit ... eumque paternè consolatus, inter alia hæc habet: 'Quanto si era detto nella nostra Lettera all' Inquisitore di Spagna in ordine alle di Lei Opere, non aveva che fare con la materia delle Feste, nè con verun dogma o disciplina. Il contenuto delle Opere chi qui non è piaciuto (nè che Ella poteva mai lusingarsi che fosse per piacere), riguarda la Giurisdizione Temporale del Romano Pontifice nè suoi stati,'" etc. (pp. lx., lxi).

subject of scientific investigations,—is a great and firm belief in the sovereignty of Truth. Error may flourish for a time, but Truth will prevail in the end. The only effect of error ultimately is to promote Truth. Theories, speculations, hypotheses, are started; perhaps they are to die, still not before they have suggested ideas better than themselves. These better ideas are taken up in turn by other men, and, if they do not yet lead to truth, nevertheless they lead to what is still nearer to truth than themselves; and thus knowledge on the whole makes progress. The errors of some minds in scientific investigation are more fruitful than the truths of others. A Science seems making no progress, but to abound in failures, yet imperceptibly all the time it is advancing, and it is of course a gain to truth even to have learned what is not true, if nothing more.

On the other hand, it must be of course remembered, Gentlemen, that I am supposing all along good faith, honest intentions, a loyal Catholic spirit, and a deep sense of responsibility. I am supposing, in the scientific inquirer, a due fear of giving scandal, of seeming to countenance views which he does not really countenance, and of siding with parties from whom he heartily differs. I am supposing that he is fully alive to the existence and the power of the infidelity of the age; that he keeps in mind the moral weakness and the intellectual confusion of the majority of men; and that he has no wish at all that any one soul should get harm from certain speculations today, though he may have the satisfaction of being sure that those speculations will, as far as they are erroneous or misunderstood, be corrected in the course of the next half-century.

IX.

DISCIPLINE OF MIND

AN ADDRESS TO THE EVENING CLASSES

1.

When I found that it was in my power to be present here at the commencement of the new Session, one of the first thoughts, Gentlemen, which thereupon occurred to me, was this, that I should in consequence have the great satisfaction of meeting you, of whom I had thought and heard so much, and the opportunity of addressing you, as Rector of the University. I can truly say that I thought of you before you thought of the University; perhaps I may say, long before;—for it was previously to our commencing that great work, which is now so fully before the public, it was when I first came over here to make preparations for it, that I had to encounter the serious objection of wise and good men, who said to me, "There is no class of persons in Ireland who *need* a University;" and again, "Whom will you get to belong to it? who will fill its lecture-rooms?" This was said to me, and then, without denying their knowledge of the state of Ireland, or their sagacity, I made answer, "We will give lectures in the evening, we will fill our classes with the young men of Dublin."

And some persons here may recollect that the very first thing I did, when we opened the School of Philosophy and Letters, this time four years, was to institute a system of Evening Lectures, which were suspended after a while, only because the singularly inclement season which ensued, and the want of publicity and interest incident to a new undertaking, made them premature. And it is a satisfaction to me to reflect that the Statute, under which you will be able to pass examinations and take degrees, is one to which I specially obtained the consent of the Academical Senate, nearly two years ago, in addition to our original Regulations, and that you will be the first persons to avail yourselves of it.

Having thus prepared, as it were, the University for you, it was with great pleasure that I received from a number of you, Gentlemen, last May year, a spontaneous request which showed that my original anticipations were not visionary. You suggested then what we have since acted upon,—acted upon, not so quickly as both you might hope and we might wish, because all important commencements have to be maturely considered—still acted on at length according to those anticipations of mine, to which I have referred; and, while I recur to them as an introduction to what I have to say, I might also dwell upon them as a sure presage that other and broader anticipations, too bold as they may seem now, will, if we are but patient, have their fulfilment in their season.

2.

For I should not be honest, Gentlemen, if I did not confess that, much as I desire that this University should be of service to the young men of Dublin, I do not desire this benefit to you, simply for your own sakes. For your own sakes certainly I wish it, but not on your account only. Man is not born for himself alone, as the classical moralist tells us. *You* are born for Ireland; and, in your advancement, Ireland is advanced;—in your advancement in what is good and what is true, in knowledge, in learning, in cultivation of mind, in enlightened attachment to your religion, in good name and respectability and social influence, I am contemplating the honour and renown, the literary and scientific aggrandisement, the increase of political power, of the Island of the Saints.

I go further still. If I do homage to the many virtues and gifts of the Irish people, and am zealous for their full development, it is not simply for the sake of themselves, but because the name of Ireland ever has been, and, I believe, ever will be, associated with the Catholic Faith, and because, in doing any service, however poor it may be, to Ireland, a man is ministering, in his own place and measure, to the cause of the Holy Roman Apostolic Church.

Gentlemen, I should consider it an impertinence in me thus to be speaking to you of myself, were it not that, in recounting to you the feelings with which I have witnessed the establishment of these Evening Classes, I am in fact addressing to you at the same time words of encouragement and advice, such words as it becomes a Rector to use in speaking to those who are submitted to his care.

I say, then, that, had I been younger than I was when the high office which I at present hold was first offered to me, had I not had prior duties upon me of affection and devotion to the Oratory of St. Philip, and to my own dear country, no position whatever, in the whole range of administrations which are open to the ambition of those who wish to serve God in their generation, and to do some great work before they die, would have had more attractions for me than that of being at the head of a University like this. When I became a Catholic, one of my first questions was, "Why have not our Catholics a University?" and Ireland, and the metropolis of Ireland, was obviously the proper seat of such an institution.

Ireland is the proper seat of a Catholic University, on account of its ancient hereditary Catholicity, and again of the future which is in store for it. It is impossible, Gentlemen, to doubt that a future is in store for Ireland, for more reasons than can here be enumerated. First, there is the circumstance, so highly suggestive, even if there was nothing else to be said, viz., that the Irish have been so miserably ill-treated and misused hitherto; for, in the times now opening upon us, nationalities are waking into life, and the remotest people can make themselves heard into all the quarters of the earth. The lately invented methods of travel and of intelligence have destroyed geographical obstacles; and the wrongs of the oppressed, in spite of oceans or of mountains, are brought under the public opinion of Europe,—not before kings and governments alone, but before the tribunal of the European populations, who are becoming ever more powerful in the determination of political questions. And thus retribution is demanded and exacted for past crimes in proportion to their heinousness and their duration.

And in the next place, it is plain that, according as intercommunion grows between Europe and America, it is Ireland that must grow with it in social and political importance. For Ireland is the high road by which that intercourse is carried on; and the traffic between hemispheres must be to her a source of material as well as social benefit,—as of old time, though on the minute geographical scale of Greece, Corinth, as being the thoroughfare of commerce by sea and land, became and was called "the rich."

And then, again, we must consider the material resources of Ireland, so insufficiently explored, so poorly developed,—of which it belongs to them rather to speak, who by profession and attainments are masters of the subject.

That this momentous future, thus foreshadowed, will be as glorious for Catholicity as for Ireland we cannot doubt from the experience of the past; but, as Providence works by means of human agencies, that natural anticipation has no tendency to diminish the anxiety and earnestness of all zealous Catholics to do their part in securing its fulfilment. And the wise and diligent cultivation of the intellect is one principal means, under the Divine blessing, of the desired result.

3.

Gentlemen, the seat of this intellectual progress must necessarily be the great towns of Ireland; and those great towns have a remarkable and happy characteristic, as contrasted with the cities of Catholic Europe. Abroad, even in Catholic countries, if there be in any part of their territory scepticism and insubordination in religion, cities are the seat of the mischief. Even Rome itself has its insubordinate population, and its concealed free-thinkers; even Belgium, that nobly Catholic country, cannot boast of the religious loyalty of its great towns. Such a calamity is unknown to the Catholicism of Dublin, Cork, Belfast, and the other cities of Ireland; for, to say nothing of higher and more religious causes of the difference, the very presence of a rival religion is a perpetual incentive to faith and devotion in men who, from the circumstances of the case, would be in danger of becoming worse than lax Catholics, unless they resolved on being zealous ones.

Here, then, is one remarkable ground of promise in the future of Ireland, that that large and important class, members of which I am now addressing,—that the middle classes in its cities, which will be the depositaries of its increasing political power, and which elsewhere are opposed in their hearts to the Catholicism which they profess,—are here so sound in faith, and so exemplary in devotional exercises, and in works of piety.

And next I would observe, that, while thus distinguished for religious earnestness, the Catholic population is in no respect degenerate from the ancient fame of Ireland as regards its intellectual endowments. It too often happens that the religiously disposed are in the same degree intellectually deficient; but the Irish ever have been, as their worst enemies must grant, not only a Catholic people, but a people of great natural abilities, keen-witted, original, and subtle. This has been the characteristic of the nation from the very early times, and was especially prominent in the middle ages. As Rome was the centre of authority, so, I may say, Ireland was the native home of speculation. In this respect they were as remarkably contrasted to the English as they are now, though, in those ages, England was as devoted to the Holy See as it is now hostile. The Englishman was hard-working, plodding, bold, determined, persevering, practical, obedient to law and precedent, and, if he cultivated his mind, he was literary and classical rather than scientific, for Literature involves in it the idea of authority and prescription. On the other hand, in Ireland, the intellect seems rather to have taken the line of Science, and we have various instances to show how fully this was recognized in those times, and with what success it was carried out. "Philosopher," is in those times almost the name for an Irish monk. Both in Paris and Oxford, the two great schools of medieval thought, we find the boldest and most subtle of their disputants an Irishman,—the monk John Scotus Erigena, at Paris, and Duns Scotus, the Franciscan friar, at Oxford.

Now, it is my belief, Gentlemen, that this character of mind remains in you still. I think I rightly recognize in the Irishman now, as formerly, the curious, inquisitive observer, the acute reasoner, the subtle speculator. I recognize in you talents which are fearfully mischievous, when used on the side of error, but which, when wielded by Catholic devotion, such as I am sure will ever be the characteristic of the Irish disputant, are of the highest importance to Catholic interests, and especially at this day, when a subtle logic is used against the Church, and demands a logic still more subtle on the part of her defenders to expose it.

Gentlemen, I do not expect those who, like you, are employed in your secular callings, who are not monks or friars, not priests, not theologians, not philosophers, to come forward as champions of the faith; but I think that incalculable benefit may ensue to the Catholic cause, greater almost than that which even singularly gifted theologians or controversialists could effect, if a body of men in your station of life shall be found in the great towns of Ireland, not disputatious, contentious, loquacious, presumptuous (of course I am not advocating inquiry for mere argument's sake), but gravely and solidly educated in Catholic knowledge, intelligent, acute, versed in their religion, sensitive of its beauty and majesty, alive to the arguments in its behalf and aware both of its difficulties and of the mode of treating them. And the first step in attaining this desirable end is that you should submit yourselves to a curriculum of studies, such as that which brings you with such praiseworthy diligence within these walls evening after evening; and, though you may not be giving attention to them with this view, but from the laudable love of knowledge, or for the advantages which will accrue to you personally from its pursuit, yet my own reason for rejoicing in the establishment of your classes is the same as that which led me to take part in the establishment of the University itself, viz., the wish, by increasing the intellectual force of Ireland, to strengthen the defences, in a day of great danger, of the Christian religion.

4.

Gentlemen, within the last thirty years, there has been, as you know, a great movement in behalf of the extension of knowledge among those classes in society whom you represent. This movement has issued in the establishment of what have been called Mechanics' Institutes through the United Kingdom; and a new species of literature has been brought into existence, with a view, among its objects, of furnishing the members of these institutions with interesting and instructive reading. I never will deny to that literature its due praise. It has been the production of men of the highest ability and the most distinguished station, who have not grudged, moreover, the trouble, and, I may say in a certain sense, the condescension, of presenting themselves before the classes for whose intellectual advancement they were showing so laudable a zeal; who have not grudged, in the cause of Literature, History, or Science, to make a display, in the lecture room or the public hall, of that eloquence, which was, strictly speaking, the property, as I may call it, of Parliament, or of the august tribunals of the Law. Nor will I deny to the speaking and writing, to which I am referring, the merit of success, as well as that of talent and good intention, so far as this,—that it has provided a fund of innocent amusement and information for the leisure hours of those who might otherwise have been exposed to the temptation of corrupt reading or bad company.

So much may be granted,—and must be granted in candour: but, when I go on to ask myself the question, what *permanent* advantage the mind gets by such desultory reading and hearing, as this literary movement encourages, then I find myself altogether in a new field of thought, and am obliged to return an answer less favourable than I could wish to those who are the advocates of it. We must carefully distinguish, Gentlemen, between the mere diversion of the mind and its real education. Supposing, for instance, I am tempted to go into some society which will do me harm, and supposing, instead, I fall asleep in my chair, and so let the time pass by, in that case certainly I escape the danger, but it is as if by accident, and my going to sleep has not had any real effect upon me, or made me more able to resist the temptation on some future occasion. I wake, and I am what I was before. The opportune sleep has but removed the temptation for this once. It has not made me better; for I have not been shielded from temptation by any act of my own, but I was passive under an accident, for such I may call sleep. And so in like manner, if I hear a lecture indolently and passively, I cannot indeed be elsewhere *while* I am here hearing it,—but it produces no positive effect on my mind,—it does not tend to create any power in my breast capable of resisting temptation by its own vigour, should temptation come a second time.

Now this is no fault, Gentlemen, of the books or the lectures of the Mechanics' Institute. They could not do more than they do, from their very nature. They do their part, but their part is not enough. A man may hear a thousand lectures, and read a thousand volumes, and be at the end of the process very much where he was, as regards knowledge. Something more than merely *admitting* it in a negative way into the mind is necessary, if it is to remain there. It must not be passively received, but actually and actively entered into, embraced, mastered. The mind must go half-way to meet what comes to it from without.

This, then, is the point in which the institutions I am speaking of fail; here, on the contrary, is the advantage of such lectures as you are attending, Gentlemen, in our University. You have come, not merely to be taught, but to learn. You have come to exert your minds. You have come to make what you hear your own, by putting out your hand, as it were, to grasp it and appropriate it. You do not come merely to hear a lecture, or to read a book, but you come for that catechetical instruction, which consists in a sort of conversation between your lecturer and you. He tells you a thing, and he asks you to repeat it after him. He questions you, he examines you, he will not let you go till he has proof, not only that you have heard, but that you know.

5.

Gentlemen, I am induced to quote here some remarks of my own, which I put into print on occasion of those Evening Lectures, already referred to, with which we introduced the first terms of the University. The attendance upon them was not large, and in consequence we discontinued them for a time, but I attempted to explain in print what the object of them had been; and while what I then said is pertinent to the subject I am now pursuing, it will be an evidence too, in addition to my opening remarks, of the hold which the idea of these Evening Lectures has had upon me.

"I will venture to give you my thoughts," I then said, writing to a friend,[1] "on the *object* of the Evening Public Lectures lately delivered in the University House, which, I think, has been misunderstood.

"I can bear witness, not only to their remarkable merit as lectures, but also to the fact that they were very satisfactorily attended. Many, however, attach a vague or unreasonable idea to the word 'satisfactory,' and maintain that no lectures can be called satisfactory which do not make a great deal of noise in the place, and they are disappointed otherwise. This is what I mean by misconceiving their object; for such an expectation, and consequent regret, arise from confusing the ordinary with the extraordinary object of a lecture,—upon which point we ought to have clear and definite ideas.

"The *ordinary* object of lectures is *to teach*; but there *is* an object, sometimes demanding attention, and not incongruous, which, nevertheless, cannot be said properly to belong to them, or to be more than occasional. As there are kinds of eloquence which do not aim at any thing beyond their own exhibition, and are content with being eloquent, and with the sensation which eloquence creates; so in Schools and Universities there are seasons, festive or solemn, anyhow extraordinary, when academical acts are not directed towards their proper ends, so much as intended to amuse, to astonish, and to attract, and thus to have

---

1   University Gazette, No. 42, p. 420.

an effect upon public opinion. Such are the exhibition days of Colleges; such the annual Commemoration of Benefactors at one of the English Universities, when Doctors put on their gayest gowns, and Public Orators make Latin Speeches. Such, too, are the Terminal Lectures, at which divines of the greatest reputation for intellect and learning have before now poured forth sentences of burning eloquence into the ears of an audience brought together for the very sake of the display. The object of all such Lectures and Orations is to excite or to keep up an interest and reverence in the public mind for the Institutions from which the exhibition proceeds:"—I might have added, such are the lectures delivered by celebrated persons in Mechanics' Institutes.

I continue: "Such we have suitably had in the new University;—such were the Inaugural Lectures. Displays of strength and skill of this kind, in order to succeed, *should* attract attention, and if they do not attract attention, they have failed. They do not invite an audience, but an attendance; and perhaps it is hardly too much to say that they are intended for seeing rather than for hearing.

"Such celebrations, however, from the nature of the case, must be rare. It is the novelty which brings, it is the excitement which recompenses, the assemblage. The academical body which attempts to make such extraordinary acts the normal condition of its proceedings, is putting itself and its Professors in a false position.

"It is, then, a simple misconception to suppose that those to whom the government of our University is confided have aimed at an object, which could not be contemplated at all without a confusion or inadvertence, such as no considerate person will impute to them. Public lectures, delivered with such an object, could not be successful; and, in consequence, our late lectures have, I cannot doubt (for it could not be otherwise), ended unsatisfactorily in the judgment of any zealous person who has assumed for them an office with which their projectors never invested them.

"What their object really was the very meaning of academical institutions suggests to us. It is, as I said when I began, *to teach*.

Lectures are, properly speaking, not exhibitions or exercises of art, but matters of business; they profess to impart something definite to those who attend them, and those who attend them profess on their part to receive what the lecturer has to offer. It is a case of contract:—'I will speak, if you will listen:'—'I will come here to learn, if you have any thing worth teaching me.' In an oratorical display, all the effort is on one side; in a lecture, it is shared between two parties, who co-operate towards a common end.

"There should be ever something, on the face of the arrangements, to act as a memento that those who come, come to gain something, and not from mere curiosity. And in matter of fact, such were the persons who did attend, in the course of last term, and such as those, and no others, will attend. Those came who wished to gain information on a subject new to them, from informants whom they held in consideration, and regarded as authorities. It was impossible to survey the audience which occupied the lecture-room without seeing that they came on what may be called business. And this is why I said, when I began, that the attendance was satisfactory. That attendance is satisfactory,—not which is numerous, but—which is steady and persevering. But it is plain, that to a mere bystander, who came merely from general interest or good will to see how things were going on, and who did not catch the object of advertising the Lectures, it would not occur to look into the faces of the audience; he would think it enough to be counting their heads; he would do little more than observe whether the staircase and landing were full of loungers, and whether there was such a noise and bustle that it was impossible to hear a word; and if he could get in and out of the room without an effort, if he could sit at his ease, and actually hear the lecturer, he would think he had sufficient grounds for considering the attendance unsatisfactory.

"The stimulating system may easily be overdone, and does not answer on the long run. A blaze among the stubble, and then all is dark. I have seen in my time various instances of the way in which Lectures really gain upon the public; and I must express my opinion that, even were it the sole object of our great undertaking to make a general impression upon public opinion, instead of that of doing definite good to definite persons, I should reject that method, which the University indeed itself has *not* taken, but which young and ardent minds may have thought the more promising. Even did I wish merely to get the intellect of all Dublin into our rooms, I should not dream of doing it all at once, but at length. I should not rely on sudden, startling effects, but on the slow, silent, penetrating, overpowering effects of patience, steadiness, routine, and perseverance. I have known individuals set themselves down in a neighbourhood where they had no advantages, and in a place which had no pretensions, and upon a work which had little or nothing of authoritative sanction; and they have gone on steadily lecturing week after week, with little encouragement, but much resolution. For months they were ill attended, and overlooked in the bustle of the world around them. But there was a secret, gradual movement going on, and a specific force of attraction, and a drifting and accumulation of hearers, which at length made itself felt, and could not be mistaken. In this stage of things, a friend said in conversation to me, when at the moment I knew nothing of the parties: 'By-the-bye, if you are interested in such and such a subject, go by all means, and hear such a one. So and so does, and says there is no one like him. I looked in myself the other night, and was very much struck. Do go, you can't mistake; he lectures every Tuesday night, or Wednesday, or Thursday,' as it might be. An influence thus gradually acquired endures; sudden popularity dies away as suddenly."

As regards ourselves, the time is passed now, Gentlemen, for such modesty of expectation, and such caution in encouragement, as these last sentences exhibit. The few, but diligent, attendants upon the Professors' lectures, with whom we began, have grown into the diligent and zealous many; and the speedy fulfilment of anticipations, which then seemed to be hazardous, surely is a call on us to cherish bolder hopes and to form more extended plans for the years which are to follow.

6.

You will ask me, perhaps, after these general remarks, to suggest to you the particular intellectual benefit which I conceive
students have a right to require of us, and which we engage by
means of our evening classes to provide for them. And, in order
to this, you must allow me to make use of an illustration, which
I have heretofore employed,[2] and which I repeat here, because
it is the best that I can find to convey what I wish to impress
upon you. It is an illustration which includes in its application
all of us, teachers as well as taught, though it applies of course to
some more than to others, and to those especially who come for
instruction.

I consider, then, that the position of our minds, as far as
they are uncultivated, towards intellectual objects,—I mean of
our minds, before they have been disciplined and formed by
the action of our reason upon them,—is analogous to that of a
blind man towards the objects of vision, at the moment when
eyes are for the first time given to him by the skill of the opera-
tor. Then the multitude of things, which present themselves
to the sight under a multiplicity of shapes and hues, pour in
upon him from the external world all at once, and are at first
nothing else but lines and colours, without mutual connection,
dependence, or contrast, without order or principle, without
drift or meaning, and like the wrong side of a piece of tapestry
or carpet. By degrees, by the sense of touch, by reaching out the
hands, by walking into this maze of colours, by turning round
in it, by accepting the principle of perspective, by the various
slow teaching of experience, the first information of the sight is
corrected, and what was an unintelligible wilderness becomes a
landscape or a scene, and is understood to consist of space, and
of bodies variously located in space, with such consequences as
thence necessarily follow. The knowledge is at length gained of
things or objects, and of their relation to each other; and it is a
kind of knowledge, as is plain, which is forced upon us all from

---

2 *Vid.* supr. p. 231.

infancy, as to the blind on their first seeing, by the testimony of our other senses, and by the very necessity of supporting life; so that even the brute animals have been gifted with the faculty of acquiring it.

Such is the case as regards material objects; and it is much the same as regards intellectual. I mean that there is a vast host of matters of all kinds, which address themselves, not to the eye, but to our mental sense; viz., all those matters of thought which, in the course of life and the intercourse of society, are brought before us, which we hear of in conversation, which we read of in books; matters political, social, ecclesiastical, literary, domestic; persons, and their doings or their writings; events, and works, and undertakings, and laws, and institutions. These make up a much more subtle and intricate world than that visible universe of which I was just now speaking. It is much more difficult in this world than in the material to separate things off from each other, and to find out how they stand related to each other, and to learn how to class them, and where to locate them respectively. Still, it is not less true that, as the various figures and forms in a landscape have each its own place, and stand in this or that direction towards each other, so all the various objects which address the intellect have severally a substance of their own, and have fixed relations each of them with everything else,—relations which our minds have no power of creating, but which we are obliged to ascertain before we have a right to boast that we really know any thing about them. Yet, when the mind looks out for the first time into this manifold spiritual world, it is just as much confused and dazzled and distracted as are the eyes of the blind when they first begin to see; and it is by a long process, and with much effort and anxiety, that we begin hardly and partially to apprehend its various contents and to put each in its proper place.

We grow up from boyhood; our minds open; we go into the world; we hear what men say, or read what they put in print; and thus a profusion of matters of all kinds is discharged upon us. Some sort of an idea we have of most of them, from hearing what others say; but it is a very vague idea, probably a very mistaken idea. Young people, especially, because they are young, colour the assemblage of persons and things which they encounter with the freshness and grace of their own springtide, look for all good from the reflection of their own hopefulness, and worship what they have created. Men of ambition, again, look upon the world as a theatre for fame and glory, and make it that magnificent scene of high enterprise and august recompence which Pindar or Cicero has delineated. Poets, too, after their wont, put their ideal interpretation upon all things, material as well as moral, and substitute the noble for the true. Here are various obvious instances, suggestive of the discipline which is imperative, if the mind is to grasp things as they are, and to discriminate substances from shadows. For I am not concerned merely with youth, ambition, or poetry, but with our mental condition generally. It is the fault of all of us, till we have duly practised our minds, to be unreal in our sentiments and crude in our judgments, and to be carried off by fancies, instead of being at the trouble of acquiring sound knowledge.

In consequence, when we hear opinions put forth on any new subject, we have no principle to guide us in balancing them; we do not know what to make of them; we turn them to and fro, and over, and back again, as if to pronounce upon them, if we could, but with no means of pronouncing. It is the same when we attempt to speak upon them: we make some random venture; or we take up the opinion of some one else, which strikes our fancy; or perhaps, with the vaguest enunciation possible of any opinion at all, we are satisfied with ourselves if we are merely able to throw off some rounded sentences, to make some pointed remarks on some other subject, or to introduce some figure of speech, or flowers of rhetoric, which, instead of being the vehicle, are the mere substitute of meaning. We wish to take a part in politics, and then nothing is open to us but to follow some person, or some party, and to learn the commonplaces and the watchwords which belong to it. We hear about landed interests, and mercantile interests, and trade, and higher and lower classes, and their rights, duties, and prerogatives; and we attempt to transmit what we have received; and soon our minds become loaded and perplexed by the incumbrance of ideas which we have not mastered and cannot use. We have some vague idea, for instance, that constitutional government and slavery are inconsistent with each other; that there is a connection between private judgment and democracy, between Christianity and civilization; we attempt to find arguments in proof, and our arguments are the most plain demonstration that we simply do not understand the things themselves of which we are professedly treating.

7.

Reflect, Gentlemen, how many disputes you must have listened to, which were interminable, because neither party understood either his opponent or himself. Consider the fortunes of an argument in a debating society, and the need there so frequently is, not simply of some clear thinker to disentangle the perplexities of thought, but of capacity in the combatants to do justice to the clearest explanations which are set before them,—so much so, that the luminous arbitration only gives rise, perhaps, to more hopeless altercation. "Is a constitutional government better for a population than an absolute rule?" What a number of points have to be clearly apprehended before we are in a position to say one word on such a question! What is meant by "constitution"? by "constitutional government"? by "better"? by "a population"? and by "absolutism"? The ideas represented by these various words ought, I do not say, to be as perfectly defined and located in the minds of the speakers as objects of sight in a landscape, but to be sufficiently, even though incompletely, apprehended, before they have a right to speak. "How is it that democracy can admit of slavery, as in ancient Greece?" "How can Catholicism flourish in a republic?" Now, a person who knows his ignorance will say, "These questions are beyond me;" and he tries to gain a clear notion and a firm hold of them; and, if he speaks, it is as investigating, not as deciding. On the other hand, let him never have tried to throw things together, or to discriminate between them, or to denote their peculiarities, in that case he has no hesitation in undertaking any subject, and perhaps has most to say upon those questions which are most new to him. This is why so many men are one-sided, narrow-minded, prejudiced, crotchety. This is why able men have to change their minds and their line of action in middle age, and to begin life again, because they have followed their party, instead of having secured that faculty of true perception as regards intellectual objects which has accrued to them, without their knowing how, as regards the objects of sight.

But this defect will never be corrected,—on the contrary, it will be aggravated,—by those popular institutions to which I referred just now. The displays of eloquence, or the interesting matter contained in their lectures, the variety of useful or entertaining knowledge contained in their libraries, though admirable in themselves, and advantageous to the student at a later stage of his course, never can serve as a substitute for methodical and laborious teaching. A young man of sharp and active intellect, who has had no other training, has little to show for it besides a litter of ideas heaped up into his mind anyhow. He can utter a number of truths or sophisms, as the case may be, and one is as good to him as another. He is up with a number of doctrines and a number of facts, but they are all loose, and straggling, for he has no principles set up in his mind round which to aggregate and locate them. He can say a word or two on half a dozen sciences, but not a dozen words on any one. He says one thing now, and another thing presently; and when he attempts to write down distinctly what he holds upon a point in dispute, or what he understands by its terms, he breaks down, and is surprised at his failure. He sees objections more clearly than truths, and can ask a thousand questions which the wisest of men cannot answer; and withal, he has a very good opinion of himself, and is well satisfied with his attainments, and he declares against others, as opposed to the spread of knowledge altogether, who do not happen to adopt his ways of furthering it, or the opinions in which he considers it to result.

This is that barren mockery of knowledge which comes of attending on great Lecturers, or of mere acquaintance with reviews, magazines, newspapers, and other literature of the day, which, however able and valuable in itself, is not the instrument of intellectual education. If this is all the training a man has, the chance is that, when a few years have passed over his head, and he has talked to the full, he wearies of talking, and of the subjects on which he talked. He gives up the pursuit of knowledge, and forgets what he knew, whatever it was; and, taking things at their best, his mind is in no very different condition from what it was when he first began to improve it, as he hoped, though perhaps he never thought of more than of amusing himself. I say, "at the best," for perhaps he will suffer from exhaustion and a distaste of the subjects which once pleased him; or perhaps he has suffered some real intellectual mischief; perhaps he has contracted some serious disorder, he has admitted some taint of scepticism, which he will never get rid of.

And here we see what is meant by the poet's maxim, "A little learning is a dangerous thing." Not that knowledge, little or much, if it be real knowledge, is dangerous; but that many a man considers a mere hazy view of many things to be real knowledge, whereas it does but mislead, just as a short-sighted man sees only so far as to be led by his uncertain sight over the precipice.

Such, then, being true cultivation of mind, and such the literary institutions which do not tend to it, I might proceed to show you, Gentlemen, did time admit, how, on the other hand, that kind of instruction of which our Evening Classes are a specimen, is especially suited to effect what they propose. Consider, for instance, what a discipline in accuracy of thought it is to have to construe a foreign language into your own; what a still severer and more improving exercise it is to translate from your own into a foreign language. Consider, again, what a lesson in memory and discrimination it is to get up, as it is called, any one chapter of history. Consider what a trial of acuteness, caution, and exactness, it is to master, and still more to prove, a number of definitions. Again, what an exercise in logic is classification, what an exercise in logical precision it is to understand and enunciate the proof of any of the more difficult propositions of Euclid, or to master any one of the great arguments for Christianity so thoroughly as to bear examination upon it; or, again, to analyze sufficiently, yet in as few words as possible, a speech, or to draw up a critique upon a poem. And so of any other science,— chemistry, or comparative anatomy, or natural history; it does not matter what it is, if it be really studied and mastered, as far as it is taken up. The result is a formation of mind,—that is, a habit of order and system, a habit of referring every accession of knowledge to what we already know, and of adjusting the one with the other; and, moreover, as such a habit implies, the actual acceptance and use of certain principles as centres of thought, around which our knowledge grows and is located. Where this critical faculty exists, history is no longer a mere story-book, or biography a romance; orators and publications of the day are no longer infallible authorities; eloquent diction is no longer a substitute for matter, nor bold statements, or lively descriptions, a substitute for proof. This is that faculty of perception in intellectual matters, which, as I have said so often, is analogous to the capacity we all have of mastering the multitude of lines and colours which pour in upon our eyes, and of deciding what every one of them is worth.

8.

But I should be transgressing the limits assigned to an address of this nature were I to proceed. I have not said any thing, Gentlemen, on the religious duties which become the members of a Catholic University, because we are directly concerned here with your studies only. It is my consolation to know that so many of you belong to a Society or Association, which the zeal of some excellent priests, one especially, has been so instrumental in establishing in your great towns. You do not come to us to have the foundation laid in your breasts of that knowledge which is highest of all: it has been laid already. You have begun your mental training with faith and devotion; and then you come to us to

404 THE IDEA OF A UNIVERSITY

add the education of the intellect to the education of the heart. Go on as you have begun, and you will be one of the proudest achievements of our great undertaking. We shall be able to point to you in proof that zeal for knowledge may thrive even under the pressure of secular callings; that mother-wit does not necessarily make a man idle, nor inquisitiveness of mind irreverent; that shrewdness and cleverness are not incompatible with firm faith in the mysteries of Revelation; that attainment in Literature and Science need not make men conceited, nor above their station, nor restless, nor self-willed. We shall be able to point to you in proof of the power of Catholicism to make out of the staple of great towns exemplary and enlightened Christians,—of those classes which, external to Ireland, are the problem and perplexity of patriotic statesmen, and the natural opponents of the teachers of every kind of religion.

As to myself, I wish I could by actual service and hard work of my own respond to your zeal, as so many of my dear and excellent friends, the Professors of the University, have done and do. They have a merit, they have a claim on you, Gentlemen, in which I have no part. If I admire the energy and bravery with which you have undertaken the work of self-improvement, be sure I do not forget their public spirit and noble free devotion to the University any more than you do. I know I should not satisfy you with any praise of this supplement of our academical arrangements which did not include those who give to it its life. It is a very pleasant and encouraging sight to see both parties, the teachers and the taught, co-operating with a pure *esprit-de-corps* thus voluntarily,—they as fully as you can do,— for a great object; and I offer up my earnest prayers to the Author of all good, that He will ever bestow on you all, on Professors and on Students, as I feel sure He will bestow, Rulers and Superiors, who, by their zeal and diligence in their own place, shall prove themselves worthy both of your cause and of yourselves.

X.

CHRISTIANITY AND MEDIAL SCIENCE

AN ADDRESS TO THE STUDENTS OF MEDICINE

1.

I have had so few opportunities, Gentlemen, of addressing you, and our present meeting is of so interesting and pleasing a character, by reason of the object which occasions it, that I am encouraged to speak freely to you, though I do not know you personally, on a subject which, as you may conceive, is often before my own mind: I mean, the exact relation in which your noble profession stands towards the Catholic University itself and towards Catholicism generally. Considering my own most responsible office as Rector, my vocation as an ecclesiastic, and then again my years, which increase my present claim, and diminish my future chances, of speaking to you, I need make no apology, I am sure, for a step, which will be recommended to you by my good intentions, even though it deserves no consideration on the score of the reflections and suggestions themselves which I shall bring before you. If indeed this University, and its Faculty of Medicine inclusively, were set up for the promotion of any merely secular object,—in the spirit of religious rivalry, as a measure of party politics, or as a commercial speculation, then indeed I should be out of place, not only in addressing you in the tone of advice, but in being here at all; for what reason could I in that case have had for having now given some of the most valuable years of my life to this University, for having placed it foremost in my thoughts and anxieties,—(I had well nigh said) to the prejudice of prior, dearer, and more sacred ties,—except that I felt that the highest and most special religious interests were bound up in its establishment and in its success? Suffer me, then, Gentlemen, if with these views and feelings I conform my observations to the sacred building in which we find ourselves, and if I speak to you for a few minutes as if I were rather addressing you authoritatively from the pulpit than in the Rector's chair.

Now I am going to set before you, in as few words as I can, what I conceive to be the principal duty of the Medical Profession towards Religion, and some of the difficulties which are found in the observance of that duty: and in speaking on the subject I am conscious how little qualified I am to handle it in such a way as will come home to your minds, from that want of acquaintance with you personally, to which I have alluded, and from my necessary ignorance of the influences of whatever kind which actually surround you, and the points of detail which are likely to be your religious embarrassments. I can but lay down principles and maxims, which you must apply for yourselves, and which in some respects or cases you may feel have no true application at all.

2.

All professions have their dangers, all general truths have their fallacies, all spheres of action have their limits, and are liable to improper extension or alteration. Every professional man has rightly a zeal for his profession, and he would not do his duty towards it without that zeal. And that zeal soon becomes exclusive or rather necessarily involves a sort of exclusiveness. A zealous professional man soon comes to think that his profession is all in all, and that the world would not go on without it. We have heard, for instance, a great deal lately in regard to the war in India, of *political* views suggesting one plan of campaign, and *military* views suggesting another. How hard it must be for the military man to forego his own strategical dispositions, not on the ground that they are not the best,—not that they are not acknowledged by those who nevertheless put them aside to *be* the best *for* the object of military success,—but because military success is not the highest of objects, and the end of ends,—because it is not the sovereign science, but must ever be subordinate to political considerations or maxims of government, which is a higher science with higher objects,—and that therefore his sure success on the field must be relinquished because the interests of the council and the cabinet require the sacrifice, that the war must yield to the statesman's craft, the commander-in-chief to the governor-general. Yet what the soldier feels is natural, and what the statesman does is just. This collision, this desire on the part of every profession to be supreme,—this necessary, though reluctant, subordination of the one to the other, is a process ever going on, ever acted out before our eyes. The civilian is in rivalry with the soldier, the soldier with the civilian. The diplomatist, the lawyer, the political economist, the merchant, each wishes to usurp the powers of the state, and to mould society upon the principles of his own pursuit.

Nor do they confine themselves to the mere province of secular matters. They intrude into the province of Religion. In England, in the reign of Queen Elizabeth, lawyers got hold of religion, and never have let it go. Abroad, bureaucracy keeps hold of Religion with a more or less firm grasp. The circles of literature and science have in like manner before now made Religion a mere province of their universal empire.

I remark, moreover, that these various usurpations are frequently made in perfectly good faith. There is no intention of encroachment on the part of the encroachers. The commander recommends what with all his heart and soul he thinks best for his country when he presses on Government a certain plan of campaign. The political economist has the most honest intentions of improving the Christian system of social duty by his reforms. The statesman may have the best and most loyal dispositions towards the Holy See, at the time that he is urging changes in ecclesiastical discipline which would be seriously detrimental to the Church.

And now I will say how this applies to the Medical Profession, and what is its special danger, viewed in relation to Catholicity.

3.

Its province is the physical nature of man, and its object is the preservation of that physical nature in its proper state, and its restoration when it has lost it. It limits itself, by its very profession, to the health of the body; it ascertains the conditions of that health; it analyzes the causes of its interruption or failure; it seeks about for the means of cure. But, after all, bodily health is not the only end of man, and the medical science is not the highest science of which he is the subject. Man has a moral and a religious nature, as well as a physical. He has a mind and a soul; and the mind and soul have a legitimate sovereignty over the body, and the sciences relating to them have in consequence the precedence of those sciences which relate to the body. And as the soldier must yield to the statesman, when they come into collision with each other, so must the medical man to the priest; not that the medical man may not be enunciating what is absolutely certain, in a medical point of view, as the commander may be perfectly right in what he enunciates strategically, but that his action is suspended in the given case by the interests and duty of a superior science, and he retires not confuted but superseded.

Now this general principle thus stated, all will admit: who will deny that health must give way to duty? So far there is no perplexity: supposing a fever to break out in a certain place, and the medical practitioner said to a Sister of Charity who was visiting the sick there, "You will die to a certainty if you remain there," and her ecclesiastical superiors on the contrary said, "You have devoted your life to such services, and there you must stay;" and supposing she stayed and was taken off; the medical adviser would be right, but who would say that the Religious Sister was wrong? She did not doubt his word, but she denied the importance of that word, compared with the word of her religious superiors. The medical man was right, yet he could not gain his point. He was right in what he said, he said what was true, yet he had to give way.

Here we are approaching what I conceive to be the especial temptation and danger to which the medical profession is exposed: it is a certain sophism of the intellect, founded on this maxim, implied, but not spoken or even recognized—"What is true is lawful." Not so. Observe, here is the fallacy,—What is true in one science is dictated to us indeed according to that science, but not according to another science, or in another department. What is certain in the military art has force in the military art, but not in statesmanship; and if statesmanship be a higher department of action than war, and enjoins the contrary, it has no claim on our reception and obedience at all. And so what is true in medical science might in all cases be carried out, *were* man a mere animal or brute without a soul; but since he is a rational, responsible being, a thing may be ever so true in medicine, yet may be unlawful in fact, in consequence of the higher law of morals and religion having come to some different conclusion. Now I must be allowed some few words to express, or rather to suggest, more fully what I mean.

The whole universe comes from the good God. It is His creation; *it* is good; it is all good, as being the work of the Good, though good only in its degree, and not after His Infinite Perfection. The physical nature of man is good; nor can there be any thing sinful in itself in acting according to that nature. Every natural appetite or function is lawful, speaking abstractedly. No natural feeling or act is in itself sinful. There can be no doubt of all this; and there can be no doubt that science can determine what is natural, what tends to the preservation of a healthy state of nature, and what on the contrary is injurious to nature. Thus the medical student has a vast field of knowledge spread out before him, true, because knowledge, and innocent, because true.

So much in the abstract—but when we come to *fact*, it may easily happen that what is in itself innocent may not be innocent to this or that person, or in this or that mode or degree. Again, it may easily happen that the impressions made on a man's mind by his own science may be indefinitely more vivid and operative than the enunciations of truths belonging to some other branch of knowledge, which strike indeed his ear, but do not come home to him, are not fixed in his memory, are not imprinted on his imagination. And in the profession before us, a medical student may realize far more powerfully and habitually that certain acts are *advisable in themselves* according to the law of physical nature, than the fact that they are forbidden according to the law of some higher science, as theology; or again, that they are accidentally wrong, as being, though lawful in themselves, wrong in this or that individual, or under the circumstances of the case.

Now to recur to the instance I have already given: it is supposable that that Sister of Charity, who, for the sake of her soul, would not obey the law of self-preservation as regards her body, might cause her medical adviser great irritation and disgust. His own particular profession might have so engrossed his mind, and the truth of its maxims have so penetrated it, that he could not understand or admit any other or any higher system. He might in process of time have become simply dead to all religions truths, because such truths were not present to him, and those of his own science were ever present. And observe, his fault would be, not that of taking error for truth, for what he relied on *was* truth—but in not understanding that there were other truths, and those higher than his own.

Take another case, in which there will often in particular circumstances be considerable differences of opinion among really religious men, but which does not cease on that account to illustrate the point I am insisting on. A patient is dying: the priest wishes to be introduced, lest he should die without due preparation: the medical man says that the thought of religion will disturb his mind and imperil his recovery. Now in the particular case, the one party or the other may be right in urging his own view of what ought to be done. I am merely directing attention to the *principle* involved in it. Here are the representatives of two great sciences, Religion and Medicine. Each says what is true in his own science, each will think he has a right to insist on seeing that the truth which he himself is maintaining is carried out in action; whereas, one of the two sciences is above the other, and the end of Religion is indefinitely higher than the end of Medicine. And, however the decision ought to go, in the particular case, as to introducing the subject of religion or not, I think the priest ought to have that decision; just as a Governor-General, not a Commander-in-Chief, would have the ultimate decision, were politics and strategics to come into collision.

You will easily understand, Gentlemen, that I dare not pursue my subject into those details, which are of the greater importance for the very reason that they cannot be spoken of. A medical philosopher, who has so simply fixed his intellect on his own science as to have forgotten the existence of any other, will view man, who is the subject of his contemplation, as a being who has little more to do than to be born, to grow, to eat, to drink, to walk, to reproduce his kind, and to die. He sees him born as other animals are born; he sees life leave him, with all those phenomena of annihilation which accompany the death of a brute. He compares his structure, his organs, his functions, with those of other animals, and his own range of science leads to the discovery of no facts which are sufficient to convince him that there is any difference in kind between the human animal and them. His practice, then, is according to his facts and his theory. Such a person will think himself free to give advice, and to insist upon rules, which are quite insufferable to any religious mind, and simply antagonistic to faith and morals. It is not, I repeat, that he says what is untrue, supposing that man *were* an animal and nothing else: but he thinks that whatever is true in his own science is at once lawful in practice—as if there were not a number of rival sciences in the great circle of philosophy, as if there were not a number of conflicting views and objects in human nature to be taken into account and reconciled, or as if it were his duty to forget all but his own; whereas

> There are more things in heaven and earth, Horatio,
> Than are dreamt of in your philosophy.

I have known in England the most detestable advice given to young persons by eminent physicians, in consequence of this contracted view of man and his destinies. God forbid that I should measure the professional habits of Catholics by the rules of practice of those who were not! but it is plain that what is actually carried out where religion is not known, exists as a temptation and a danger in the Science of Medicine itself, where religion is known ever so well.

4.

And now, having suggested, as far as I dare, what I consider the consequences of that radical sophism to which the medical profession is exposed, let me go on to say in what way it is corrected by the action of Catholicism upon it.

You will observe, then, Gentlemen, that those higher sciences of which I have spoken, Morals and Religion, are not represented to the intelligence of the world by intimations and notices strong and obvious, such as those which are the foundation of Physical Science. The physical nature lies before us, patent to the sight, ready to the touch, appealing to the senses in so unequivocal a way that the science which is founded upon it is as real to us as the fact of our personal existence. But the phenomena, which are the basis of morals and Religion, have nothing of this luminous evidence. Instead of being obtruded upon our notice, so that we cannot possibly overlook them, they are the dictates either of Conscience or of Faith. They are faint shadows and tracings, certain indeed, but delicate, fragile, and almost evanescent, which the mind recognizes at one time, not at another,—discerns when it is calm, loses when it is in agitation. The reflection of sky and mountains in the lake is a proof that sky and mountains are around it, but the twilight, or the mist, or the sudden storm hurries away the beautiful image, which leaves behind it no memorial of what it was. Something like this are the Moral Law and the informations of Faith, as they present themselves to individual minds. Who can deny the existence of Conscience? who does not feel the force of its injunctions? but how dim is the illumination in which it is invested, and how feeble its influence, compared with that evidence of sight and touch which is the foundation of Physical Science! How easily can we be talked out of our clearest views of duty! how does this or that moral precept crumble into nothing when we rudely handle it! how does the fear of sin pass off from us, as quickly as the glow of modesty dies away from the countenance! and then we say, "It is all superstition." However, after a time we look round, and then to our surprise we see, as before, the same law of duty, the same moral precepts, the same protests against sin, appearing over against us, in their old places, as if they never had been brushed away, like the divine handwriting upon the wall at the banquet. Then perhaps we approach them rudely, and inspect them irreverently, and accost them sceptically, and away they go again, like so many spectres,—shining in their cold beauty, but not presenting themselves bodily to us, for our inspection, so to say, of their hands and their feet. And thus these awful, supernatural, bright, majestic, delicate apparitions, much as we may in our hearts acknowledge their sovereignty, are no match as a foundation of Science for the hard, palpable, material facts which make up the province of Physics. Recurring to my original illustration, it is as if the India Commander-in-Chief, instead of being under the control of a local seat of government at Calcutta, were governed simply from London, or from the moon. In that case, he would be under a strong temptation to neglect the home government, which nevertheless in theory he acknowledged. Such, I say, is the natural condition of mankind:—we depend upon a seat of government which is in another world; we are directed and governed by intimations from above; we need a local government on earth.

That great institution, then, the Catholic Church, has been set up by Divine Mercy, as a present, visible antagonist, and the only possible antagonist, to sight and sense. Conscience, reason, good feeling, the instincts of our moral nature, the traditions of Faith, the conclusions and deductions of philosophical Religion, are no match at all for the stubborn facts (for they *are* facts, though there are other facts besides them), for the facts, which are the foundation of physical, and in particular of medical, science. Gentlemen, if you feel, as you must feel, the whisper of a law of moral truth within you, and the impulse to believe, be sure there is nothing whatever on earth which can be the sufficient champion of these sovereign authorities of your soul, which can vindicate and preserve them to you, and make you loyal to them, but the Catholic Church. You fear they will go, you see with dismay that they are going, under the continual impression created on your mind by the details of the material science to which you have devoted your lives. It is so—I do not deny it; except under rare and happy circumstances, go they will, unless you have Catholicism to back you up in keeping faithful to them. The world is a rough antagonist of spiritual truth: sometimes with mailed hand, sometimes with pertinacious logic, sometimes with a storm of irresistible facts, it presses on against you. What it says is true perhaps as far as it goes, but it is not the whole truth, or the most important truth. These more important truths, which the natural heart admits in their substance, though it cannot maintain,—the being of a God, the certainty of future retribution, the claims of the moral law, the reality of sin, the hope of supernatural help,—of these the Church is in matter of fact the undaunted and the only defender.

Even those who do not look on her as divine must grant as much as this. I do not ask you for more here than to contemplate and recognize her as a fact,—as other things are facts. She has been eighteen hundred years in the world, and all that time she has been doing battle in the boldest, most obstinate way in the cause of the human race, in maintenance of the undeniable but comparatively obscure truths of Religion. She is always alive, always on the alert, when any enemy whatever attacks them. She has brought them through a thousand perils. Sometimes preaching, sometimes pleading, sometimes arguing,—sometimes exposing her ministers to death, and sometimes though rarely, inflicting blows herself,—by peremptory deeds, by patient concessions,—she has fought on and fulfilled her trust. No wonder so many speak against her, for she deserves it; she has earned the hatred and obloquy of her opponents by her success in opposing them. Those even who speak against her in this day, own that she was of use in a former day. The historians in fashion with us just now, much as they may disown her in their own country, where she is an actual, present, unpleasant, inconvenient monitor, acknowledge that, in the middle ages which are gone, in her were lodged, by her were saved, the fortunes and the hopes of the human race. The very characteristics of her discipline, the very maxims of her policy, which they reprobate now, they perceive to have been of service then. They understand, and candidly avow, that once she was the patron of the arts, the home and sanctuary of letters, the basis of law, the principle of order and government, and the saviour of Christianity itself. They judge clearly enough in the case of others, though they are slow to see the fact in their own age and country; and, while they do not like to be regulated by her, and kept in order by her, themselves, they are very well satisfied that the populations of those former centuries should have been so ruled, and tamed, and taught by her resolute and wise teaching. And be sure of this, that as the generation now alive admits these benefits to have arisen from her presence in a state of society now gone by, so in turn, when the interests and passions of this day are passed away, will future generations ascribe to her a like special beneficial action upon this nineteenth century in which we live. For she is ever the same,—ever young and vigorous, and ever overcoming new errors with the old weapons.

And now I have explained, Gentlemen, why it has been so highly expedient and desirable in a country like this to bring the Faculty of Medicine under the shadow of the Catholic Church. I say "in a country like this;" for, if there be any country which deserves that Science should not run wild, like a planet broken loose from its celestial system, it is a country which can boast of such hereditary faith, of such a persevering confessorship, of such an accumulation of good works, of such a glorious name, as Ireland. Far be it from this country, far be it from the counsels of Divine Mercy, that it should grow in knowledge and not grow in religion! and Catholicism is the strength of Religion, as Science and System are the strength of Knowledge.

Aspirations such as these are met, Gentlemen, I am well aware, by a responsive feeling in your own hearts; but by my putting them into words, thoughts which already exist within you are brought into livelier exercise, and sentiments which exist in many breasts hold inter-communion with each other. Gentlemen, it will be your high office to be the links in your generation between Religion and Science. Return thanks to the Author of all good that He has chosen you for this work. Trust the Church of God implicitly, even when your natural judgment would take a different course from hers, and would induce you to question her prudence or her correctness. Recollect what a hard task she has; how she is sure to be criticized and spoken against, whatever she does;—recollect how much she needs your loyal and tender devotion. Recollect, too, how long is the experience gained in eighteen hundred years, and what a right she has to claim your assent to principles which have had so extended and so triumphant a trial. Thank her that she has kept the faith safe for so many generations, and do your part in helping her to transmit it to generations after you.

For me, if it has been given me to have any share in so great a work, I shall rejoice with a joy, not such indeed as I should feel were I myself a native of this generous land, but with a joy of my own, not the less pure, because I have exerted myself for that which concerns others more nearly than myself. I have had no other motive, as far as I know myself, than to attempt, according to my strength, some service to the cause of Religion, and to be the servant of those to whom as a nation the whole of Christendom is so deeply indebted; and though this University, and the Faculty of Medicine which belongs to it, are as yet only in the commencement of their long career of usefulness, yet while I live, and (I trust) after life, it will ever be a theme of thankfulness for my heart and my lips, that I have been allowed to do even a little, and to witness so much, of the arduous, pleasant, and hopeful toil which has attended on their establishment.